PRAYING BY THE BOOK

SOCIETY OF BIBLICAL LITERATURE

EARLY JUDAISM AND ITS LITERATURE

Number 14

PRAYING BY THE BOOK
The Scripturalization of Prayer in
Second Temple Judaism

by
Judith H. Newman

PRAYING BY THE BOOK
The Scripturalization of Prayer in Second Temple Judaism

by
Judith H. Newman

Scholars Press
Atlanta, Georgia

PRAYING BY THE BOOK
The Scripturalization of Prayer in Second Temple Judaism

by
Judith H. Newman

Library of Congress Cataloging-in-Publication Data

Newman, Judith H. (Judith Hood), 1961–
    Praying by the book : the scripturalization of prayer in Second
Temple Judaism / by Judith H. Newman.
        p.   cm. — (Early Judaism and its literature ; no. 14)
    Includes bibliographical references and index.
    ISBN 0-7885-0564-5 (cloth : alk. paper)
    1. Bible. O.T.—Prayers—History and criticism.   2. Worship in
the Bible.   3. Bible. O.T. Nehemiah IX—Criticism, interpretation,
etc.   4. Bible. O.T. Apocrypha. Judith IX—Criticism, interpretation,
etc.   5. Third Book of Maccabees II—Criticism, interpretation, etc.
6. Judaism—History—Post-exilic period, 586 B.C.–210 A.D.   I. Title.
II. Series.
BS1199.P68N48   1999
296.4'9—dc21   99-28361
                                                              CIP

Printed in the United States of America
on acid-free paper

For my parents

Janice and Murray Newman

Table of Contents

Acknowledgments ix

Introduction 1
    The Need for the Present Study 3
    Defining Prayer 5
    The Corpus of Prayers 7
    Determining "Scripturalization" 11

Chapter 1
    A Quest for Origins:
    Pre-exilic Prayers and the Beginnings of Scripturalization 19
    The Earliest Prayers 21
    The Evolution of Pre-Exilic Prayers 28
    Exilic Prayers 38
    Conclusion 52

Chapter 2
    Scripturalization in the Telling of History: Nehemiah 9 55
    Nehemiah 9:5–37 56
    Scripturalization in Nehemiah 9 63
    Creation 65
    Abraham and the Divine Promise 70
    Exodus 76
    Sinai 82
    Wilderness Wanderings 86
    Conquest/Bequest of Land and Settlement 92
    Israel in the Land 95
    Life in the Land after Exile 100
    The Use of Scripture in Nehemiah 9 102
    Related Prayers Containing Historical Reviews 108
    Conclusion 114

Chapter 3
    The Past as Blueprint for Present:
    Salvation by Typology in Judith 9 117
    Judith 9 and Genesis 34 123
    Judith 9 and Isaiah 138

Judith 9 and the Prayer of Hezekiah..............................139
Judith 9 and Thematic Connections to Isaiah.............................145
Judith 9 and Exodus 15 146
Salvation by Typology 148
Typology in Contemporaneous Prayers..150
Conclusion 154

Chapter 4
Biblical Exempla:
The Arrogance of Power in 3 Maccabees 2 155
3 Maccabees 2:2–20..157
The Use of Examples..159
The Use of Scripture in Exempla..171
Giants Connected with Punishment by Flood............................172
Sodomites Notorious for their Vices...180
Pharaoh as Arrogant and Audacious 186
Zion/Temple Chosen at Time of Creation 187
Other Significant Citations and Allusions in 3 Macc 2..........193
Prayer and the Temple in 1 Kings 8..193
LXX Psalm 78:8..196
Conclusion 197

Chapter 5
From Prayers to Liturgy 201
Scripturalization in Prayers...201
The Changing Role of Prayer...205
Implications of Scripturalization for
the Study of Jewish and Christian Liturgy.............................210
Continuities with Jewish Liturgy...210
Continuities in Christian Liturgies..214
In Summary..218

Appendix
A Selective History of Scholarship on Prayer and Liturgy...........221
Jewish Liturgy..231

Index of Ancient Citations 243

Index of Modern Authors 261

Bibliography..265

Acknowledgments

This book represents a revised version of my doctoral dissertation accepted by the Department of Near Eastern Languages and Civilizations at Harvard University in November 1996. Many individuals have buoyed me as I planned, wrote, and revised the manuscript.

I owe my deepest debt to James Kugel, my *Doktorvater*. Without overstatement, his teaching and writing have transformed the way I think about the Bible both in its ancient and modern contexts. I thank him for his continual encouragement and his well-timed guidance of my work. I am also very grateful to have studied with Jon Levenson, who has had a similar impact on me. Both his written work and his conversation never fail to stimulate my own thinking.

I thank Gary Anderson for his willingness to join my dissertation committee at a late date and for his helpful comments about the project. Paul Hanson, Ted Hiebert, and Peter Machinist were involved at its inception and I thank them for their valuable advice in shaping the project in its early stages.

Outside the nest of my graduate school formation, I would like to single out Eileen Schuller for her early and continued interest in my dissertation project. She offered invaluable assistance at different stages as the project slowly evolved. My thanks are due especially for her careful reading of the manuscript and her insightful suggestions about revising the work for publication. In reference to all those mentioned above, I must also add the well-worn caveat that I accept full responsibility for the contents of this book, which means, in part, for good advice not taken!

My thanks are also owed to John Reeves, editor of the Early Judaism and Its Literature series, whose extraordinarily thorough reading of my manuscript improved the product immeasurably.

I wish also to express my gratitude to two institutions. Generous funding from the Episcopal Church Foundation over several years provided the support necessary to complete my graduate work and ample time to devote to researching and writing this volume. Sheffield Academic Press kindly granted permission to reproduce a large part of "Nehemiah 9 and the Scripturalization of Prayer in the Second Temple Period," *The Function of Scripture in Early Judaism and Christianity* (Craig A. Evans and James A. Sanders, eds; JSNT Sup. 154; SSEJC 6; Sheffield: Sheffield Academic Press, 1998) as part of what is now Chapter 2 of this book.

Although family is ever first in my thoughts, it is last in my preface. I thank my husband David whose devotion to me and to our children Madeleine and Sebastian makes my academic work possible. All three give me a joy-filled existence. I thank two pairs of parents: John and Marilyn Holt, whose manifold means of support helped sustain our family and me personally as I wrote, wrote, and then rewrote a few times; and finally, Murray and Janice Newman, to whom this book is dedicated, and who continue to teach me about the Bible and varied particularities of life. David Holt, Janice Newman, and Murray Newman also contributed in a very concrete way by helping to prepare the indexes. I also thank the Rev. Estelle Webb who provided invaluable help with the indexes and proofreading at the final stages of manuscript preparation.

Unless otherwise noted, all biblical translations are my own. For citations of ancient and modern sources, I have followed the "*Journal of Biblical Literature* Instructions for Contributors," available on the SBL website <http://www.sbl-site.org>.

Judith H. Newman
New York, NY

Introduction

The starting point for this book is my observation that the literature of the exilic and post-exilic period reflects a great interest in prayer. In contrast to pre-exilic literature, characters in Second Temple narratives are more frequently depicted as praying. There is also a proliferation of prayer texts in the books themselves. Chronicles, for instance, includes many more prayers than its source in Samuel-Kings. Long prayers appear in Ezra-Nehemiah, the books of Daniel, Judith, and Tobit, as well as pseudepigraphical works like *Jubilees* and Pseudo-Philo. Included with the wealth of writings found at Qumran are many and varied prayers, psalms, and hymns, which are both imbedded in narrative works and independent compositions. The prayers are longer and more elaborate than pre-exilic prayers. In short, the literary evidence indicates that prayer and praying became a central feature of religious life in the centuries following the return from the Babylonian Exile.

A prominent feature of the vast majority of Second Temple prayers is that they reflect the clear imprint of earlier scripture. This book examines and partially delineates a broad phenomenon that can most aptly be called the "scripturalization of prayer" during the Second Temple Period. "Scripturalization" is evident both in prayer forms and in their composition. The authors of prayers sometimes patterned their prayers after prayers found in biblical literature. The language of many late prayers also shows a reliance on, and increasingly intensive engagement with, scripture. Such scripturalization in prayers is itself a complex phenomenon. The content of prayers, specifically, how prayers were composed and the sources that they derive from, allows us to understand one important

1

dimension of prayer life. This study illustrates three paradigmatic ways in which scripture is appropriated in prayers of the post-exilic period: reviews of history, a typological reprise of one event from the biblical period, and the use of a list of biblical characters as archetypes of some good or bad behavior. As will become apparent, even within the broader parameters of these three categories, the degree of scripturalization is complex. Scripture appears in many ways: it appears as quotes, or as phrases woven into the warp and woof of the piece. Scripture is also interpreted, at times in proto-midrashic ways. Some of these interpretations are well-developed and are shared with other Second Temple texts.

Successive chapters demonstrate that the broad phenomenon of scripturalization has tentative beginnings in prayers of the First Temple Period and that the use of scripture in prayers comes to full flower in the later post-exilic period. What appear as brief references to the past and earlier traditions in a handful of pre-exilic prayers gradually becomes an unself-conscious use of scriptural words, phrases, and interpretations. By the late Second Temple Period, the use of scripture in prayers has become a convention that needs no justification. Thus tracing the origins and varieties of scripturalization in prayers illuminates the origins of a literary convention in liturgy. The types of scripturalization in Second Temple prayers sketched above exhibit important lines of continuity with the use of scripture in Jewish and Christian liturgies, as we shall discuss in more depth in the conclusion.

This picture of the development of prayers also sheds light on the mentality of Judaism in the Second Temple period. The orientation toward scripture implicit in its deployment in prayers, that it can be endlessly mined for quotes and endlessly interpreted, and that the characters depicted within it could serve as either positive or negative exempla, are part of a larger phenomenon of the Second Temple Period, the elevation of scripture, in which the biblical books have become living organisms from which new literature and liturgies are propagated. To extend this organic metaphor, old bits of scripture and interpretation are used as compost to fertilize the new soil and encourage new growth. It is in this milieu that Judaism and Christianity developed their distinctive shapes and their distinctive ways of praying that continue in large part to the present.

The Need for the Present Study

Very few scholars have devoted their attention to the study of prayer in extra-biblical Second Temple texts.[1] Until recently, the topic of biblical prayer has also been neglected, although not to the extent that prayer in extra-biblical literature has been overlooked. In part, the explanation for this neglect lies in the fact that scholarship on prayer has proceeded in separate spheres, biblical studies and liturgical studies. For those readers with a special interest in one or both spheres, I have included a more detailed discussion of scholarship on biblical prayer and Jewish liturgy in the Appendix. I here summarize the results in broad terms. In the field of biblical scholarship, study has focused on prayer in the Bible proper, especially the book of Psalms, but with scant attention devoted to extra-canonical writings. A search for the origins of prayer in Israelite worship has led biblical scholars to examine comparative material, particularly possible Mesopotamian antecedents that accompanied temple sacrifice. The search is thus one that tends to begin in the second millennium, but to end with the last books included in the Bible, the post-exilic works of the fifth, fourth, and third centuries B.C.E. On the other hand, scholars who have concentrated on the development of liturgy tend to launch their studies by examining existing liturgical texts and working back in time, making forays into early rabbinic texts or early patristic texts as necessary. More recent research has investigated liturgical compositions from Qumran, such as the *Thanksgiving Scroll*, or the *Songs of David* found in the Cairo Genizah, for the light they shed on Jewish prayers and liturgy, but for the most part writings that are not overtly liturgical but may nonetheless contain prayers, like the Qumran *War Scroll*, the books of Tobit, and *Jubilees*, have not all been included in the same pool of "data." Thus the efforts of scholars in both camps have left a gap of numerous centuries in late Second Temple Jewish literature that deserves closer scrutiny.

The virtue in choosing the Second Temple period, an historical span, in which to study the proliferation of prayers as opposed to limiting study to those books later accepted as canonical by Jews and Christians is that the entire spectrum of literature can be examined.

---

[1] Two scholars from different quarters have called attention to this neglect. See the essays of James H. Charlesworth, "The Jewish Background of the Hymns in the New Testament," *JJS* 33 (1982) 267–268 and David Flusser, "Psalms, Hymns and Prayers," *Jewish Writings of the Second Temple Period* (CRINT 2, II, M. Stone, ed.; Assen: Van Gorcum/Philadelphia: Fortress, 1984) 551–577.

It is clear that many of the works here termed non-canonical had a wide circulation throughout the period and influenced later writers and liturgists in the Rabbinic and early Christian era.[2] But even if their influence over centuries was negligible, they nonetheless provide a window into Second Temple thinking.

In addition to embracing a more inclusive "data set" by disregarding the canon line, the present study uses a methodological approach distinct from other recent scholarship on ancient Jewish prayer and liturgy. Scholars on both sides of the divide, biblical and liturgical, have focused on form-critical concerns, that is, the categorization of prayers by formal genre such as petition, thanksgiving, and so on, and the formal elements these genres of prayers contain. The overarching approach in this book is to trace the history of biblical interpretation, albeit within the confines of a particular type of composition: prayers.[3] The particular literary method used to reconstruct a segment of the history of biblical interpretation involves a close examination of the biblical wording and themes contained within selected prayers and other related texts. The results of this research are intended not to shed light specifically on the formal development of Jewish liturgy but on the relationship of prayer to biblical traditions. Exegetical and hermeneutical questions lie at the fore. The questions that lie behind this study are not "What forms of prayer populate Second Temple literature?" or "What are the origins of fixed liturgical prayer in Judaism?" Rather, the motivating questions are "Why did prayer become so important in the Second Temple period? Why was scripture used so extensively in the composition of prayers? In what ways was scripture used and interpreted? In what way is the interpretive use of scripture in prayers distinct from its interpretive use in other Second Temple compositions?" The foregoing questions have not been addressed

---

[2] For instance, Tobit 8:5–7, which is the prayer Tobias offers on his wedding night, includes a reference to Adam and Eve and quotes Gen 2:18, seems to have influenced later Jewish nuptial liturgy. On this point, see David Flusser, "Psalms, Hymns, and Prayers," *Jewish Writings*, 556.

[3] Biblical scholars increasingly look to the history of interpretation as an indispensable means for understanding biblical and post-biblical texts. Jon Levenson succeeds in integrating the insights of the history of interpretation of biblical texts into a historical-critical methodological framework, while at the same time deriving theological insights from the text. His approach to biblical texts can be seen implicitly in any of his recent books. See for example, *The Death and Resurrection of the Beloved Son: The Transformation of Child Sacrifice in Judaism and Christianity* (New Haven, CT: Yale University Press, 1993).

straightforwardly in a systematic or comprehensive way. While this book does not provide complete answers to all of the questions, they serve well to initiate our journey into the realm of Second Temple prayer.

Just as important as the history-of-interpretation questions is the contribution of this study to the history of liturgy. The composition of prayer did not come to an end with the beginning of obligatory daily prayer in Judaism. Even after elements in the basic liturgies were fixed, the scripturalization of prayer continued. Liturgies were in flux for an even longer period in Christianity. So we are also tracing the origins and development of a literary convention in the composition of Jewish and Christian liturgies. Though scripturalization began tentatively in prayers of the pre-exilic period, it eventually became an unquestioned convention. This book, then, is a study of the uses of scripture in Second Temple prayers. But before examining any prayers in depth, we must offer some working definitions of prayer and scripturalization, as well as a delineation of the exact corpus of prayers that is included in this study.

Defining Prayer

An essential preliminary measure for this study is to provide a definition of prayer. It is not easy, but consideration of the efforts of other scholars provides a helpful measuring stick. Some scholars have allowed their focus of inquiry to determine in large measure their definition of prayer. For instance, in a study of biblical prayer, Edwin Staudt outlines the following definition:

> Prayer is communication with God which is articulated. Prayer in the Deuteronomist is initiated by the people by means of petition for the purpose of receiving response from God. Prayer is motivated by a situation which is fraught with confusion, fear, and uncertainty. When prayer is spoken, it results in significant implications for the events of the historical moment to which it is addressed.[4]

Staudt begins with a general statement about prayer as communication with God. He then makes a narrow claim equating prayer with petition in the Deuteronomistic History, which excludes other compositions also directed to God in the Deuteronomistic History, such as laments, songs, hymns, and praise. The definition is also dependent on prayer in a narrative context, that the prayer must

---

[4] Edwin E. Staudt, "Prayer and the People in the Deuteronomist" (unpublished dissertation, Vanderbilt, 1980) 66.

be motivated by "confusion, fear, and uncertainty" and result in "significant implications for the events of the historical moment to which it is addressed." His definition thus overemphasizes contextual aspects of prayer.

Other definitions of prayer proposed by biblical scholars who have written on the subject seem too broad in certain ways. Esther Chazon defines prayer as "any form of human communication directed at God."[5] Moshe Greenberg's definition of prayer is more specific: "nonpsalmic speech to God—less often about God—expressing dependence, subjection, or obligation; it includes petition, confession, benediction, and curse (but excludes references to nothing more than oracle-seeking)."[6] Samuel Balentine has discussed the difficulty in stating a simple definition of prayer so he simply does not offer one. He rightly points to the problem in another scholar's definition that calls all communication addressed to God in the second person as "prayer" because this would include communication of a conversational nature, such as Adam's interaction with God in Eden.[7] He nonetheless considers such conversational speech as prayer in his study. For Balentine, intentionality is an important criterion in identifying prayers. He determines intentionality in one of two ways. He uses the presence of particular Hebrew vocabulary, like התפלל or קרא בשם as identifying markers. He also uses the less objective criterion of those texts "that lack specific prayer language or clear introductions but nevertheless . . . convey intentional and weighty address to God."[8] The second criterion would include divine-human conversations. From the perspective of this study, these definitions are inadequate because they would include all conversation or dialogue with God.

The working definition of prayer in this study includes three criteria.[9] Prayer is address to God that is initiated by humans; it is not

---

[5] Esther G. Chazon, "Prayers from Qumran and Their Historical Implications," *Dead Sea Discoveries* 1 (1994) 266.

[6] Moshe Greenberg, *Biblical Prose Prayer* (Berkeley: University of California Press, 1983) 7.

[7] Samuel E. Balentine, *Prayer in the Hebrew Bible: The Drama of Divine-Human Dialogue* (Overtures to Biblical Theology; Minneapolis: Augsburg Fortress, 1993) 30.

[8] Balentine, *Prayer in the Hebrew Bible*, 31.

[9] While the definition used in this study refers to verbal prayer, we must also recognize that the broadest definition of prayer must include non-verbal forms of prayer. For instance, the Christian tradition recognizes different types of prayer, such as contemplative prayer, which is characterized by silent meditation on God.

conversational in nature; and it includes address to God in the second person, although it can include third person description of God. This working definition excludes Cain's address to God in Gen 4:13–14: "My punishment is greater than I can bear. Today you have driven me away from the soil, and I will be hidden from your face; I will be a fugitive and a wanderer on the earth, and anyone who meets me will kill me." Cain's address to God is not properly prayer for two reasons. First, Cain did not initiate the exchange; God started the conversation by asking Cain a question. A preeminent characteristic of prayer, not sufficiently emphasized in previous studies, is that it is a reaching out to God by a human. In the Genesis passage, Cain is reacting to God's punishment of him which God has announced in the immediately preceding verses, Gen 4:10–12. Second, the address is conversational in nature. There is a continued exchange of words. By the same criteria, Abraham's dialogue with God over the fate of the Sodomites in Genesis 18:23–32 does not qualify as prayer. God initiates the exchange of views in Gen 18:20 and the bargaining session is conversational. According to our criteria, also excluded would be the response of Benaiah to King David's request that Solomon be anointed king: "Amen! Thus may the Lord, the God of my lord the king, so confirm. Just as the Lord has been with my lord the King, so shall he be with Solomon. May his throne prosper more than that of my lord, King David." (1 Kgs 1:36–37)

Although the formulaic introduction of many blessings addresses God in the second person, "Blessed are you O Lord God," and as such they could be considered prayers according to our definition, they are excluded from this study's primary focus because of their distinguishable form-critical structure. Moreover, many blessings occur solely in the third person. Gen 48:15–16, for instance, which Greenberg includes in his list of *ad hoc* prayers, is actually a third-person blessing by Jacob over Joseph. A limitation to second-person address to God would also exclude a third-person blessing such as the Aaronic benediction of Num 6:24–26. Having proposed a working definition of prayer, let us move on to other preliminary matters.

The Corpus of Prayers

I began by noting the proliferation of prayers in Second Temple literature. The sheer volume and variety of prayers in this body of literature makes many generalizations about them difficult. Prayers are found inside and outside the Bible. They are found imbedded in all genres of literature: wisdom, history, novella, apocalyptic vision accounts. They are found as independent compositions, either alone (e.g., the Prayer of Manasseh) or grouped as a cluster of prayers (e.g., the *Words of the Luminaries*). If, as I suggest, we think about prayers in terms of the degree to which they reuse scripture, this permits us to find a unifying characteristic that appears in the vast majority of prayers.

But what can we say in terms of other similarities or differences among the prayers to provide a sense of the contours of this large corpus? One might try to distinguish qualitatively between prayers found in narratives and independent prayers. Yet this is a problematic distinction. It is not at all clear that prayers found in narratives were originally composed as part of the contexts that now house them. For example, most scholars think that the prayer in Nehemiah 9 was combined with other materials to make up the Ezra-Nehemiah memoir. The prayer's narrative connection to its context is filament thin. On the reverse side of the ledger, there are now independent prayers that were conceived in relation to a larger narrative context. The Prayer of Manasseh is a prime example of this phenomenon. It is closely related to the book of Chronicles, in particular, 2 Chr 33:11–19, which mentions that Manasseh offered a prayer of repentance for his idolatry and was restored by God to Jerusalem on the basis of his pious act.[10] The Prayer of Manasseh is thus more of a "narrative prayer" than Nehemiah 9 because it can be linked verbally to a particular narrative context.

Some might think that such prayers bound by narrative would preclude reuse by other pray-ers.[11] Yet, to take the same example, the Prayer of Manasseh is written in the first person, but the "I" never identifies himself by name. In addition, the prayer, like the Psalms, contains many stereotyped phrases, so there is nothing that might prevent other penitents from using the prayer as their own. Thus we see that the distinction between a prayer imbedded in a narrative and an independent prayer is in many cases not so clear-cut as would appear at first glance. Moreover, the now independent prayers and the prayers imbedded in Second Temple narrative literature do not

---

[10] The prayer also seems to have been modeled to some degree after Psalm 51. See the discussion of James H. Charlesworth in his introduction to the *Prayer of Manasseh, OTP Vol. II* (Garden City, NY: Doubleday, 1985) esp. 628–630 on the prayer's relationship to 2 Chr 33:11–19 and Psalm 51.

[11] I use the term "pray-er" to indicate the person offering a prayer.

exhibit any other distinctive characteristics that would constitute them as two classes of prayers to be treated separately.

Might there be some difference between "poetic" prayers and "prose" prayers that could offer a helpful grouping? The distinction between prose and poetry is assumed in a number of studies. The title of Moshe Greenberg's study, *Biblical Prose Prayer*, betrays his assumption that such a distinction can be made.[12] Greenberg uses the designation "prose" primarily in order to bracket discussion of the Psalms and psalm-like compositions within biblical narratives. So, too, in the introduction to her book on Qumran prayer, Bilhah Nitzan discusses "prayer" and "religious poetry" as if they are categories that do not overlap. She assumes a difference, prayer for her seems to be a "prose" phenomenon, yet she nowhere provides an explicit definition of the two.[13] I would maintain that making a neat division between prose and poetic prayer is a problematic distinction. The main reason is that the precise characteristics of Hebrew poetry remain debated.[14] One can see degrees of rhetorical heightening, verses that contain a "seconding" clause, in prayers that have conventionally been considered prose.[15] It is thus more sound not to make a distinction. Prayer is a mode of special discourse to God and as such easily lends itself to such features of rhetorical heightening as parallel or "seconding" clauses, repetitions, hyperbolic language and elaborate divine epithets.

---

[12] Greenberg, *Biblical Prose Prayer*.

[13] Consider her comment: ". . it seems that the people of Qumran were not content to utilize poetry as an expression of their heartfelt feelings and of their ideology, but wrote extensive prayers and hymns to be recited at various ceremonies, in the daily fixed prayers and on festivals and holidays." Bilhah Nitzan, *Qumran Prayer and Religious Poetry* (Jonathan Chipman, trans.; STDJ 22; Leiden: Brill, 1994), 10.

[14] Once thought a settled issue in biblical scholarship, the existence of rhyme, meter, and the nature of parallelism are now much debated. A number of scholars have been influential in overturning a scholarly consensus. Based on a thorough analysis of the syntax of Hebrew poetry, Michael O'Connor has argued that the parallel clauses making up each line of Hebrew "poetry" exhibit a range of syntactic relationships; *Hebrew Verse Structure* (Winona Lake, IN: Eisenbraun's, 1980). James L. Kugel has argued that there was a range of rhetorical heightening used in classical Hebrew, and that such heightening could occur in "prose narrative" and in "poetry." See *The Idea of Biblical Poetry* (New Haven: Yale University Press, 1981).

[15] The notion of a "seconding" clause that reinforces or extends the sense of the first clause comes from James Kugel; see *The Idea of Biblical Poetry*, 51–57 and 95–100.

Another potential criterion for distinguishing prayers might relate to their use. It may have been the case that some prayers were used in communal worship as part of a liturgy, some in private, individual devotion, or some other form of worship. Recent work on the Qumran literature has made helpful strides in suggesting some liturgical practices in this era.[16] We must admit, however, that there is much to learn about which prayers were offered and on what occasions. A reconstruction of liturgical practices among various Jewish communities during the Second Temple period is highly desirable, but at this point remains out of reach, given the infrequent and incomplete references regarding the details and timing of prayer activity in the extant sources.

Given the ambiguities outlined above, I have chosen to make no hard-and-fast distinction between prose and poetic prayers, prayers in narrative and independent prayers, prayers that clearly betray the sectarian beliefs of the Qumran community and those that do not. Because of the wealth of prayers to study, for practical reasons, my treatment is necessarily selective. Because scripturalization is so pervasive a phenomenon, this study cannot treat the issue of the use of scripture and scriptural interpretation in prayers exhaustively. I isolate three discernible types of scripturalization that appear with some frequency in Second Temple prayers: historical retrospects, typological appropriation of one biblical episode, and the use of biblical characters as examples of a moral or immoral characteristic. Let me restate: the book does not contain a complete taxonomy. The choice of particular prayers follows in part from looking at the great variety of compositions and isolating the preceding three kinds of scripturalization. The prayers in chapters 2–4 were chosen because each represents a clear example of that particular type of scripturalization, but that criterion was not the sole consideration. Qumran prayers, whether clearly sectarian or not, manifest the same patterns of scripturalization found in Second Temple literature as a whole, but the prayers at Qumran have received more sustained

---

[16] The work of a number of scholars has shed light in particular on prayer practice at Qumran. See Moshe Weinfeld, "Prayer and Liturgical Practice in the Qumran Sect," *The Dead Sea Scrolls: Forty Years of Research* (Devorah Dimant and Uriel Rappaport, eds.; Leiden: Brill, 1992) 241–58; Lawrence Schiffman, "The Dead Sea Scrolls and the Early History of Jewish Liturgy," *The Synagogue in Late Antiquity* (Lee I. Levine, ed.; New York: Jewish Theological Seminary, 1987) 33–48; Esther Chazon on *4QDibHam* in "4Q DibHam: Liturgy or Literature?" *Revue de Qumran* 15 (1991) 447–456; and Bilhah Nitzan, *Qumran Prayer*.

attention from scholars in recent years.[17] I decided to focus, therefore, on the prayers that have been most neglected, namely those encased in the narratives of the Hebrew Bible, the Apocrypha and Pseudepigrapha. I could equally well have chosen examples from the Psalms or the Qumran *War Scroll* as my primary focus, but I suspect fewer people have read the book of 3 Maccabees. The prayers contained therein are fascinating from the perspective of how they reuse scripture, thus 3 Maccabees' prayers deserve a spotlight. Indeed, there is an embarrassment of riches in terms of the number of Second Temple prayers that might be studied from the perspective of scripturalization.

Determining "Scripturalization"

There is no circumventing the fact that the term "scripture," which is used throughout this study, is an anachronism. Although readers up to this point may have been nodding an intuitive assent to the assertion that post-exilic prayers use "scripture," even brief critical reflection on the use of the term in reference to the post-exilic period should cause unease. During the biblical period itself, no such word was used. "Scripture" is a designation for a body of literature regarded as sacred by a religious community and was only *post facto* applied to a collection of texts, as was another term later coined in Christianity, "canon." I nonetheless use the word scripture throughout this book, but the reader deserves to be apprised of the limitations in using the term. What I mean in part by "scripture" in this pre-canonical period is the collection of texts that would eventually become the Jewish and part of the Christian Bible. It is clear that the entire Tanakh was compiled over a period of centuries and that the notion of a fixed and normative "scripture" in the sense of the thirty-nine books of the Hebrew Bible is out of the question. But it is also clear that some of the biblical writings had obtained an authoritative status by the end of the exilic period. During the Persian period, the Pentateuch, first, and the prophetic literature, second, obtained a "scriptural," that is, a sacred and authoritative, status before the Writings. "Scripturalization" thus assumes the existence of a body of sacred writings, which we may loosely identify with most of the Pentateuch and some of the prophetic corpus in the early post-exilic period, but the content of "scripture" surely evolved in the centuries following the Exile. Even various communities of Jews likely held to different notions of "scripture" at the same time. It

---

[17] See the Appendix and the discussion of their work in the final chapter.

cannot be gainsaid that Second Temple scholarship is still in the process of determining when and how "scripture" came into being.

The Latin root of scripture refers, of course, to something written, but what I also occasionally mean by the term is the collection of oral "texts," that developed alongside the Bible. There is a great difficulty in separating these two notions of text—written and oral—entirely.[18] Throughout its history, Israel relied on oral transmission of tradition as well as written texts. Indeed, both the historical-critical concept underlying Gunkel's hypothesis of form-criticism and the traditional Jewish notion of oral Torah presuppose that there was oral transmission of "texts" or traditions.[19] Such oral "texts" contained at times interpretive elaboration of stories now contained in the canonical biblical texts. Evidence of such transmission can be seen in the Bible itself. For instance, Joshua's review of Israel's history in Josh 24:2–15 preserves certain distinctive traditions about Abraham's ancestors not found elsewhere in the biblical account.[20] One of these traditions is the notion that Terah, Abraham, and Nahor worshipped other gods in Aram Naharaim. This tradition ultimately shows up in later rabbinic sources in a much more elaborate form. So in other words, different interpretive memories of the ancestors, presumably transmitted orally, are preserved in this written text.

The definition of "scripturalization" in this project is the reuse of biblical texts or interpretive traditions to shape the composition of new

---

[18] I cannot do justice here to scholarship on the dynamics of oral culture vs. written culture and their interaction in antiquity. Suffice it to say that a more sophisticated and nuanced discussion of the oral transmission of texts and traditions would greatly benefit the field of Second Temple studies. Werner Kelber's fascinating study stimulated interesting work among New Testament scholars, but more needs to be said. Consider his comment: "Contrary to the assumptions of historical criticism, a text's substantial and multifaceted investment in tradition does not suggest intertextuality in the sense of scanning through multiple, physically accessible scrolls but, more likely, accessibility to a shared 'cultural memory.'" *The Oral and the Written Gospel: The Hermeneutics of Speaking and Writing in the Synoptic Tradition, Mark, Paul, and Q* (Philadelphia: Fortress, 1983; republished with a new introduction, Bloomington: Indiana University Press, 1997) xxiii.

[19] For a historical-critical discussion of the relation between oral and written transmission of Old Testament traditions, see Klaus Koch, *The Growth of the Biblical Tradition: The Form-Critical Method* (NY: Charles Scribner's Sons, 1969) 78–89.

[20] James L. Kugel made this point in a lecture for a Harvard undergraduate course, "The Bible and Its Interpreters" during the spring semester, 1993.

literature.[21] Some of this new literature itself became scripture, as we shall see in the second chapter is the case in Nehemiah. Scripturalization as used here is primarily the observable re-contextualization of identifiable scriptural language. Scripturalization differs from the process of "inner-biblical interpretation" used by such scholars as Michael Fishbane or Yair Zakovitch because the reuse of scripture does not necessarily entail the presumed author's *conscious* interpretation of scripture.[22] My use of the term "scripturalization" is broad enough to include at times clear references to biblical stories or incidents that may contain no biblical reference other than an identifiable personal or place name. It also includes instances in which the author seemed to be using biblical

---

[21] The term "scripturalization" was, to my knowledge, first coined by James L. Kugel in reference to the Psalms. In his usage, the scripturalization of the Psalms refers to the process by which the psalms came to be understood as "scripture," that is, the words of God to humans, as opposed to their original usage in the Temple for worship as human words to God. See his article, "Topics in the History of the Spirituality of the Psalms," in *Jewish Spirituality from the Bible through the Middle Ages* (NY: Crossroad, 1986) 113–144. Steven Weitzman has also employed the term to refer to the process by which biblical literature came gradually to have religious significance as sacred scripture. Weitzman argues that the rise of sacred scripture triggered certain imitative patterns on the part of Second Temple authors and editors including the insertion of songs into older biblical compositions which he terms "scripturalizing revisions." See especially chapter 4 of his book, *Song and Story in Biblical Narrative: The History of a Literary Convention in Ancient Israel* (Bloomington: Indiana University Press, 1997) 59–92.

My use of the term scripturalization also differs from the definition of Gary Anderson when he describes the "scripturalization of the cult." What he means in part by this term are post-biblical rabbinic and contemporary discussions of sacrifice in *haburoth* in which details of Temple sacrifice are recalled, indeed, made to come to life in the present, on the basis of textual exegesis. Anderson also points out that the biblical accounts of Temple sacrifice are already "scripturalized" in the sense of being secondary representations of the actual pre-exilic sacrificial system. For the entire discussion, see his article, "Sacrifice and Sacrificial Offerings (OT)," *ABD* V, 870–886.

[22] Many scholars have examined the Hebrew Bible with an eye to discerning the development of interpretive traditions within its books. To name but a few more recent works: Yair Zakovitch, *"And You Shall Tell Your Son...": The Concept of the Exodus in the Bible* (Jerusalem: Magnes, 1991); James L. Kugel and Rowan A. Greer, *Early Biblical Interpretation* (Philadelphia: Westminster, 1986); Michael Fishbane, *Biblical Interpretation in Ancient Israel* (New York: Oxford University Press, 1985); Daniel Patte, *Early Jewish Hermeneutic in Palestine* (SBLDS 22; Missoula, MT: Scholars Press, 1975).

wording without regard to its source, but simply to provide a biblical "ring" to the composition.

The variety of ways in which scripture shapes prayers precludes a thorough discussion of each type here, but a review of related discussions of biblical interpretation in Second Temple literature by some scholars will help situate the approach taken in this study. Svend Holm-Nielsen represents something of a pioneer in exploring the use of scripture in the Qumran *Hodayot*.[23] His commentary on the hymns identifies the sources of a great number of scriptural phrases and expressions used in the *Hodayot*. The hymns reveal the predominant influence of the psalms and the prophetic literature; however, he does not provide much analysis of the ways in which scripture was redeployed. His general characterization of the *Hodayot* as "mosaics of Old Testament quotations," with the nature of quotation left vague, was qualified in important ways by Bonnie Kittel in her own work on the Qumran hymns.[24] Kittel determines four categories of use of biblical language: quotation or allusion to a specific passage; imitation of biblical literary forms through the use of a standardized phrase; biblical imagery characteristic of certain types of literature or theological ideas; and thoughts expressed in a manner consistent with biblical language and terminology. Kittel's delineation of the use of scripture correlates in large measure to a number of the ways in which I think scripture is used.

Devorah Dimant has sought to make a comprehensive classification of the uses of scripture in the Apocrypha and Pseudepigrapha.[25] She posits a fundamental division between explicit and implicit biblical elements. She links the different types to their use in two particular genres of Second Temple literature, "rewritten

---

[23] *Hodayot: Psalms from Qumran* (Aarhus: Universitetsforlaget, 1960). Jean Carmignac lay some groundwork already in his article, "Les citations de l'Ancien Testament, et spécialement des Poèmes du Serviteur, dans les *Hymnes* de Qumrân," *Revue de Qumrân* 2 (1959–1960) 357–394. For another contemporaneous study on the use of the Hebrew Bible at Qumran, see, J.A. Fitzmyer, "The Use of Explicit Old Testament Quotations in Qumran Literature and in the New Testament," *NTS* 7 (1960–61) 297–333.

[24] *The Hymns of Qumran* (Chico, CA: Scholar's Press, 1981) 48–55.

[25] See her article, "Use and Interpretation of Mikra in the Apocrypha and Pseudepigrapha," *Mikra: Text, Translation, Reading and Interpretation of the Hebrew Bible in Ancient Judaism and Early Christianity* (CRINT, M.J. Mulder, ed.; Assen: Van Gorcum/Philadelphia: Fortress, 1990) 379–419.

Bible" and "free narrative."[26] Explicit usages of biblical elements encompass quotations and mention of biblical persons and events. Implicit use of scripture covers a wide range of what she terms "compositional" uses of scripture. She identifies implicit quotations, allusions, and motifs and models as implicit uses of scripture. She classifies two kinds of explicit uses of scripture. The first is citations of scripture signaled formally by a marker, such as "as it is written. . .." Her analysis of explicit quotations reveals a significant finding. Of the nineteen explicit quotes she finds, thirteen come from the Pentateuch. Of the remaining five, one each from Amos, Isaiah, Ezekiel; two from the Psalms, and one from Proverbs. The distribution of the sources indicates clearly that the Pentateuch held a special authority in Second Temple Jewish communities.

Dimant's division into explicit and implicit uses of scripture and the subcategories she establishes are very helpful and have influenced my own classification of the uses of scripture in prayer, but as she herself says, there is more to be said on the subject. She also points to one difficulty within her own work, that is, the lack of a clear definition between her category "implicit quotation" and allusion. A second, and more important, issue is that the reinterpretation of scripture cannot be understood simply by looking at a biblical source and its reuse in a particular text. Quite frequently, interpretive reuse of scripture makes reference to multiple texts, either earlier biblical texts or contemporaneous works.

My own approach to identifying and explaining the use of scripture in prayers builds on others' work. The most important fact to be stated is that the use of scripture ranges from the most overt use of biblical citations to highly nuanced allusions which militates against a single overly neat classification scheme. Biblical forms are also imitated, both on the level of genres—I contend that Judith 9 is modeled after Hezekiah's prayer for Jerusalem in Isa 37:16–20//2 Kgs 19:15–19—and in formulas which are short phrase "forms" that might distinguish a psalm of thanksgiving with its initial אודך from a petition with its frequent transitional ועתה. Explicit and implicit scriptural quotations are easy to identify for anyone steeped in the Bible. At the other end of the spectrum, allusions, as has been

---

[26] Her linkage to different genres is not completely convincing. She does not make a strong case for a distinct use of "implicit quotations" in "rewritten Bible" works as opposed to "free narratives" for instance. She also omits discussion of the use of scripture in apocalyptic literature and its two main genres, the historical apocalypse and otherworldly journeys.

often noted by those who study them, are notoriously difficult to define, and can be equally troublesome to find.[27] I track verbal parallels among likely sources in scripture, with a particular sensitivity to distinctive language and phrasing used. In some cases a single distinctive word can mark a biblical allusion. Just as the verb create, ברא, is used only with God as subject, so too, we shall see in chapter 3 that the use of בחר with God as the subject has a special significance in the prayer of Nehemiah 9. I am also careful to assess the nature of the biblical source; for instance, whether it is divine speech, or prophetic speech, or whether it is typical language used in the Deuteronomistic history.

Yet this study does not claim to trace all biblical allusions contained in the prayers I examine because the task is impossible. Allusions assume a shared intimate knowledge of the text alluded to within its larger context. The totality of this "context" is inaccessible in the current age. A biblical source, to be sure, has its immediate written context. The availability of the written context, both its immediate context and its larger biblical context, is unassailable; but my thesis also includes the notion of oral traditions of textual transmission and interpretation which are not available in their entirety to contemporary readers. There is as yet no scholarly hypothesis that reconstructs the Second Temple social contexts in which such oral texts were given shape and transmitted.[28] This qualification having been stated, I nonetheless do assume shared interpretive motifs, which are dependent on a common body of oral traditions of interpretation, and I try to identify them and elaborate on their significance. The interpretive motifs are constructed on the exegesis of one or more biblical texts and their inner-biblical and post-

---

[27]Among those who have tried, Richard Hays provides some helpful guidelines. He isolates seven criteria that guide his own identification of scriptural allusions and that work as a check on his own subjectivity in finding allusions. Among the criteria is the history of interpretation of the scriptural passage, to see if other commentators have used scripture in the same way as Paul. For the other criteria and a helpful discussion of Pauline hermeneutics in general, see chapter one of *Echoes of Scripture in the Letters of Paul* (New Haven, CT: Yale University Press, 1989) 1–33.

[28] Although cf. Howard Jacobson's brief treatment of the transmission of oral tradition in Hellenistic Egypt in relation to the author of the *Exagoge*'s knowledge of midrashic motifs; *The Exagoge of Ezekiel* (Cambridge: Cambridge University Press, 1983) 20–23.

biblical interpretation.[29] Such interpretive motifs themselves sometimes become the primary "texts" to which allusions are made.[30]

These preliminary matters of definition and method having been established, let us outline what follows. The first chapter discusses the origins of scripturalization by reviewing the evidence from pre-exilic and exilic prayers that show incipient stages of scripturalization. The long prayer at Solomon's dedication of the Temple in 1 Kings 8 marks an important transition bridging pre- and post-exilic prayer. One significant feature of a number of earlier biblical prayers is their reuse of divine promises as a means of inducing God to listen to the prayer and act on behalf of the supplicant. The prayer in Numbers 14, for example, is the earliest prayer to quote the divine self-disclosure that occurs in Exod 34:6–7. The second chapter focuses on the long historical retrospect in the prayer of the Levites in Neh 9:5–37. The penitential prayer in Nehemiah 9 is recited as a means of recalling God's former mercy to the people Israel and on that basis asking for help in the current situation of hardship. Written traditions become the means through which the past is recalled. The sequence of redemptive events as they appear in the Bible: creation, promise to the patriarchs, slavery, exodus, providence in the wilderness, and delivery into the land, becomes the norm and hope for future divine response. Chapter two is primarily an examination of the sources of Nehemiah 9, though it also evaluates briefly other examples of "historical prayers" from the Second Temple Period. A second way in which scripture appears in prayers is in recalling a single incident from the past with the expectation that God will behave analogously in the present: "You did x to y, now do x to z." The third chapter focuses on the prayer in Judith 9:2–14. Like the prayer in Nehemiah 9, this prayer also includes interpretive elements not found in the written scripture, but

---

[29] In a closely related issue, George J. Brooke has stressed the need to look at the reuse of a common combination of biblical passages, which might represent a distinct tradition of interpretation. See his "Shared Intertextual Interpretations in the Dead Sea Scrolls and the New Testament," *Biblical Perspectives: Early Use and Interpretation of the Bible in Light of the Dead Sea Scrolls*. Michael E. Stone and Esther G. Chazon, eds. (STDJ 28; Leiden: Brill, 1998) 35–57.

[30] In the art of identifying interpretive motifs and tracing their exegetical origins, I have been most influenced by the methods employed by James L. Kugel. Kugel's approach has been most explicitly articulated in the final chapter of *In Potiphar's House:The Interpretive Life of Biblical Texts* (San Francisco: HarperCollins, 1990) 247–270. See also his more recent *The Bible As It Was* (Cambridge, MA: Harvard University Press, 1997) especially 1–49.

that can be seen in other contemporaneous works. The use of scripture in this prayer also reflects an interpretive use that comes to predominate in early Christianity: typology. The chapter explores not only some other Second Temple prayers that recast a single biblical event, but also other texts that reflect typological interpretation in Second Temple literature. The fourth chapter explores another distinctive use of scripture, in which the Bible has become a source of moral, or in this case, immoral, exempla. In 3 Maccabees 2, the high priest Simon prays that the Temple be spared desecration by the arrogant Ptolemy Philopater. In the prayer, he recalls biblical exempla of arrogant and insolent individuals. Other Second Temple prayers that contain similar depictions of biblical characters are 3 Maccabees 6, *Jubilees* 22:11–23, and *Hellenistic Synagogal Prayer* 12 which recalls fifteen biblical "heroes," including "pious Lot," and Joshua "the soldier." The conclusion includes only a brief summary of the results of the study, that is, *how* scripture was used in these prayers, because this is summarized largely in the chapters themselves. The conclusion is rather an attempt to explain the status of prayer in the life of Second Temple Jews, in other words, *why* the scripturalization of prayer occurred against the backdrop of an increased emphasis on prayer in Second Temple texts. The conclusion also suggests some lines of continuity between the ways in which scripture was used in Second Temple prayers and the scripturalization of Jewish and Christian liturgical prayers.

Chapter 1

A Quest for Origins
Pre-exilic Prayers and the Beginnings of Scripturalization

In 1 Kings 17, Elijah the prophet and miracle worker is faced with a formidable test. A widow's son lies at the precipice of death, and the widow has blamed Elijah for bringing this curse on her household. In 1 Kings 17:22, we find out where the source of his miracle working ability abides. He prays to God in simple and direct terms: "O Lord, my God, let this child's life come into him again." The prayer is effective. Elijah, after invoking God's power, revives the widow's son. Her faith in God and, perhaps more important from the narrator's perspective, her faith in Elijah as a man of God, is solidified. There are other such powerful intercessions. In Numbers 12:13, Moses, hoping that God will spare Miriam from leprosy, offers a prayer that is even shorter than Elijah's petition: "God, please heal her." In Hebrew, this amounts to just five words: אל נא רפא נא לה. In the case of Moses, God also hears him and responds by restoring Miriam's health. These prayers contain no fillips, no flourishes, no elaborations of divine address. And for that matter, what more need be said? Prompted by the needs of the moment, an individual makes a pointed request; God promptly responds. These simple petitions are met with positive action from God. There are many such brief prayers in the pre-exilic literature.

A strong contrast lies in Solomon's prayer for the dedication of the Temple found in 1 Kings 8:23-53. The prayer is thirty-one verses long and contains seven situations or cases in which petitions offered in the direction of the Temple in Jerusalem might be answered by God. The purpose of that prayer is not only to thank God for fulfilling his promise to David that the Temple would be built during the days of his son's reign, but to ask God to hear the prayers of Israel should

19

they find themselves in various straits. The multi-layered prayer in 1 Kings 8 bespeaks a complex process of transmission and editing, but likely became a part of the text in final form during the exilic period. It contains references to the exodus and the promise of land to the ancestors, as well as the more recent promise to David narrated in the Deuteronomistic history. In short, Solomon's prayer of dedication is as different from the simple intercession of Moses in Numbers 12 as is the hilly city of Jerusalem from the desert terrain of the Sinai peninsula.

Is there something inherent in the prayer of a king that calls for long, elaborate liturgical oration? Does the difference rather have something to do with the era in which the prayer was composed? What accounts for these differences? This chapter will reveal that the answer to the first two questions is no. Kings offer short prayers as well as long prayers. The answer to the second question will become evident in this chapter: there is a historical trend toward longer prayers that make increasing reference to earlier traditions and scripture. The trend can be discerned by comparing the prayers found in the earliest literature in the Bible with those dating from the exilic period. The answer to the last question, the difficult question of why this development occurred, is complicated. The root causes seem to lie in part with changes in the culture of ancient Israel brought about by the exile. A discussion of the possible causes of this transformation is included in the final chapter. The aim of this chapter is more narrowly to illustrate that a general transition takes place in biblical prayers. There are hints of the phenomenon we term "scripturalization" even among some of the earliest prayers in the Bible but the trend becomes more pronounced in the later pre-exilic and exilic literature. These simple prayers predominate in the earliest phase of Israelite literature and, although simple, unadorned prayers continue to appear in exilic literature, they become outnumbered by "scripturalized" prayers, in which the past is remembered through the words of scriptural tradition.[1]

---

[1] Short prayers appear also in the post-exilic literature. Indeed, the last words of the book of Nehemiah constitute a four-word prayer: זכרה־לי אלהי לטובה, "Remember me, my God, for good." The point to be underscored is their relative frequency in the pre-exilic literature as opposed to the later literature.

The Earliest Prayers

Let us first focus on those brief prayers, petitions, intercessions, and thanks that we noted at the outset of the chapter. As defined in the Introduction, a prayer for the purposes of our study is address to God, initiated by an individual, which is in the second person. There are a number of prayers in the early literature but we will review only a representative sampling of them.[2] One important consideration in our discussion must be a relative dating of the sources in which these prayers are found. Historical criticism of the Bible, and one of its constituent components, source criticism, has come under considerable attack in the past twenty years.[3] Nevertheless, in order to make any conclusions about the historical development of biblical prayer, it is necessary to make some cautious source-critical assessments. Our working assumption lies with the consensus of historical-critical scholarship, that there was a "Jahwist" source and that it contains some of the oldest literary material in the Bible, most of it found in the narrative sections of Genesis, Exodus, and Numbers.[4] No hypothesis about its putative

---

[2] Greenberg includes a list of almost all of the prayers that appear in the Hebrew Bible outside the book of Psalms (*Biblical Prose Prayer*, 59, n.3). However, some are problematic from the standpoint of my working definition of prayer. Thus Jer 3:22–25 contains third person discussion *about* God (v. 23b) and only v.22b is second-person address to God. Greenberg also excludes some prayers that have no explicit introductory address and are therefore somewhat ambiguous. For instance, Hagar's prayer in Gen 21:16 "Do not let me look on the death of the child," which is not on Greenberg's list, is a request that elicits a positive response from God. Deut 21:7 and Judges 6:22 are two other omissions from his list.

[3] This has come along with a general shift in some parts of the academy from examining the historical context and origins of the biblical literature to looking at the final shape of the text and its interpretation, both inner-biblical and post-biblical in order to derive narrative or theological meaning. Like all such trends in scholarship, this is itself an overreaction to certain excessive tendencies of a previous generation, e.g. the tendency of some scholars to divide literature into fragments of verses and to ignore the larger meaning of the text as a whole in its final redacted integrity. Some critics of historical-critical scholarship have called into question source-criticism's utility in deriving theological or literary meaning from the text. For a thorough discussion of the possible contributions of "canonical criticism" to Christian biblical theology, see Brevard S. Childs, *Biblical Theology of the Old and New Testaments* (Minneapolis: Augsburg Fortress, 1992) 53–94.

[4] We must, of course, acknowledge the challenge to the documentary hypothesis and in particular a tenth-century dating of the Jahwist epic that has been mounted in the past two decades. The redating of the J source of the Pentateuch was given its initial impetus in the work of Thomas L. Thompson

pre-history and the setting of its composition (e.g., as part of Gerhard von Rad's "Solomonic Enlightenment") is here proposed, nor is it necessary for our purposes. It is only necessary to establish the relative dating of certain Pentateuchal passages as earlier than such clearly post-exilic works as Nehemiah in order to demonstrate a diachronic evolution in the composition of prayers. A defense of the classic view of J as a pre-exilic source cannot be contained in this chapter; suffice it to say that the alternative proposals for a late dating of the sources found in J by Thompson, Van Seters, Schmid, and others, are problematic and have not convinced this writer.

According to our working definition of prayer, there are relatively few prayers in those parts of the narrative that can be tentatively identified as J.[5] One of the first prayers that appears in the

---

who called into question the second-millennium setting for the ancestral stories in his book *The Historicity of the Patriarchal Narratives* (BZAW 133; Berlin: de Gruyter, 1974). See, too, Thompson's more recent work, *The Origin Tradition of Ancient Israel: The Literary Formation of Genesis and Exodus 1–23* (JSOTSup 55; Sheffield: JSOT Press, 1987). John Van Seters' work has also been influential in shaking the consensus about a Jahwist epic. Van Seters views J as a source written by an author in the exilic period; *Abraham in History and Tradition*. (New Haven: Yale University Press, 1975). Hans Heinrich Schmid produced *Der sogennante Jahwist: Beobachtungen und Fragen zur Pentateuchforschung* (Zurich: Theologischer Verlag, 1975) in which he argues for a close relationship between the "so-called J sources" and the Deuteronomist. See the helpful review of the documentary hypothesis and its critics in Joseph Blenkinsopp, *The Pentateuch: An Introduction to the First Five Books of the Bible* (ABRL; New York: Doubleday, 1992), especially chapter one.

The most extreme position with accompanying skepticism at recon-structing pre-exilic history on the basis of the Bible is contained in the imaginative work of Philip Davies. Davies views the entirety of the Hebrew Bible as a product of the post-exilic period. Many scholars have successfully argued against parts of his larger thesis and there is no need to include a refutation of Davies here. See Davies' book *In Search of Ancient Israel* (JSOT Sup 148; Sheffield: Sheffield Academic Press, 1992).

[5] There are two third-person exclamatory wishes mentioned in connection with the births of Judah and Joseph that have a prayer-like character because they mention God. Gen 29:35 "And she [Leah] conceived again and bore a son, and said, "This time I will praise the Lord;" therefore she called his name יהודה; then she ceased bearing." Another appears in Gen 30:24: And she called his name יוסף saying, "May the Lord add to me another son!" In the narrative, the naming has become part of the etiology of the clan and in these two cases, the prayers are a play on the Hebrew for Judah and Joseph. Another short prayer appears in the Joseph narrative. In Gen 43:14, Jacob is blessing his sons as they prepare to return to Egypt to retrieve their ransomed brother Benjamin, "May God Almighty grant you mercy before the man and

Bible and likely a very early one, is offered by Abram in Gen 15:2-3: "O Lord God, what will you give me, for I continue childless, and the heir of my house is Eliezer of Damascus? You have given me no offspring, and so an attendant born in my house is to be my heir."⁶ In Gen 15:5–21, God answers him by promising him heirs and land which is sealed by a covenant. Like Elijah's prayer in 1 Kings 17:22, this prayer is a simple petition, unadorned by extensive divine attributes. Another slightly longer prayer is Lot's request of the angels in Gen 19:18–20 after having been rescued from the conflagration in Sodom: "Please my Lords, your servant has found favor in your sight, and you have magnified your mercy by saving my life, but I am unable to flee to the hills, lest the disaster overtake me and I die. Look, that city is close enough to escape to, and it is a little one. Let me flee there—is it not a little one?—and my life will be saved." The form is simple, comprising an address, motivation, and request. The unit also involves a play on words. The wording reflects no special ornamentation yet because of the wordplay involved, one is left with the sense that an author deliberately shaped the composition. This request also serves as an etiology for the name of the town. There are other requests made of God in J that are not included in our discussion as prayers because they are conversational.⁷

---

send back with you your other brother Benjamin. As for me, if I am bereaved, I am bereaved."

⁶ According to traditional source-criticism, Gen 15:2 comes from the hand of J. Gen 15:3 is considered a doublet, and also early, part of the fragmentary E source. The first address to God is Cain's lament in Gen 4:13–14 that his punishment is too severe. As discussed in the introduction, this does not fit our strict definition of prayer because Cain did not initiate the discussion; he complains in response to God's edict in Gen 4:10–12. Gen 15:2,3 are two of the first actual prayer texts, although a sequentially earlier passage in Genesis mentions the act of praying. Also attributed to J, Genesis 4:26 states that after Enosh was born, that is the third generation of humans on the earth, people first began to "call on the name of the Lord." Abraham also "calls on the name of the Lord" in Gen 12:8.

Patrick D. Miller places Gen 15:2 in the form-critical category of complaint, in which the most obvious feature includes a question directed against God. Cf. also Exod 5:22, 17:4, 32:11, Num 10:11, 16:22; Josh 7:7–9, Judg 6:13, 15:18, 21:3; 1 Kgs 17:20; Jer 15:18; Jonah 4:2; *They Cried to the Lord: The Form and Theology of Biblical Prayer* (Minneapolis: Fortress, 1994) 70–71.

⁷ In Exod 4:13 Moses pleads to be excused from his leadership duties in leading the people out of Egypt in one such request: "Pardon me, O Lord, but please, send anyone else!" It contains a simple petition which has been form-critically analyzed by scholars as the objection of the prophet, a standard part

Let us also consider literature from a somewhat later date, those traditions that were given shape as part of the Deuteronomistic History (DtrH), which, according to one widely accepted theory, dates in its first editorial recension to the seventh century.[8] As a whole in the DtrH, the people who utter prayers are the prophetic leaders of the community and in particular those leaders who are portrayed in the most positive light by the author: Joshua, Gideon, Samson, David, Elijah, and Elisha.[9] Most of these prayers are short; only a handful are longer than three verses.[10] Of the forty-three prayers and blessings in the Deuteronomistic History, only four, three of which occur in 1 Kings 8 in connection with the Temple dedication, contain any reference to earlier traditions. 1 Kings 8, which we shall argue underwent at least two recensions, was given

---

of a call narrative. See the discussion of Exod 4: Brevard S. Childs, *Exodus* (OTL; Philadelphia: Westminster, 1974) 53–54.

Another prayer that is conversational, that is to say, God responds through direct speech and dialogue as opposed to actions, appears in Exodus 17. Moses prays to God after the exodus in the wilderness at Rephidim when the people are up in arms against Moses. Exod 17:4: "So Moses cried out to the Lord, 'What shall I do with this people? They are close to stoning me.'"

[8] The most prominent exponent of the two recension theory is F.M. Cross, who dates the first edition to the time of Josiah and argues that the compilation and editing of the historical sources was done as part of Josiah's reformation. See especially his discussion in *Canaanite Myth and Hebrew Epic* (Cambridge, MA: Harvard University Press, 1973) 274–290. Another treatment of this theory is Richard D. Nelson's *The Double Redaction of the Deuteronomistic History* (Sheffield: JSOT Press, 1981).

[9] Moshe Greenberg counts forty-three prayers in the Deuteronomistic History. Although he does not summarize who offers the prayers, the list is revealing: eight are prayed by David; four by Solomon (three of which are offered in 1 Kings 8 in connection with the Temple dedication); four by Elijah; three each by Joshua, Samson, Gideon, and Elisha; two by Samson and Hezekiah; and one by Deborah. One each is offered by Benaiah, Sheba, a nameless woman, Ahimaaz, the kings' servants, and Joab, but all of these are blessings; none is a petition. In addition, the Israelites or "the people" as a whole pray six times, five of which are confessions. The other instance in which the Israelites pray, in Judges 21:3, they ask God a question about why one tribe is lacking in Israel. The statistics above reflect a clear pattern regarding who should pray and for what purpose, according to the Deuteronomistic Historian. These findings also undermine Moshe Greenberg's argument that biblical prayer can be considered "popular" prayer. See *Biblical Prose Prayer*, 59-60.

[10] Greenberg's list of prayers in the DtrH includes thirty-seven prayers and blessings of one and two verses. There are six prayers longer than two verses: 2 Sam 7:18–29; 1 Kgs 3:6–9; 8:15–21, 22–53, 55–61, and 2 Kgs 19:15–19, offered by three kings, David, Solomon, and Hezekiah.

final shape during the time of the Babylonian exile. The other prayer is 2 Sam 7:18-29, a prayer that recalls the dynastic promise to David, which has a unique place in the Deuteronomistic theology as a whole. Like 1 Kings 8, 2 Samuel 7 was also probably redacted in the exile. These we will discuss in the latter part of the chapter.

Outside of the narrative sections of the Pentateuch in Genesis, Exodus, and Numbers, there are relatively few prayers. Indeed, there are no prayers at all in Leviticus, and Deuteronomy contains only four prayers (Deut 3:23-25; 9:25-29; 21:7-8; and 26:5-10.)[11] The first two are offered by Moses; the third and fourth are actually prescribed prayers and do not appear in the course of narrated events. Deut 21:7-8 is an absolution to be said by the clan elders in the case of an unsolved murder. Deut 26:5-10 is a thanksgiving enjoined of a farmer on the occasion of the offering of the first fruits of the harvest.

Like the prayers in the Pentateuch, most of the prayers in the Deuteronomistic History are short. They appear in the narrative as if uttered spontaneously, in situations that call for the immediate attention or intervention of God. For instance, in Judges 16:28, Samson, having been blinded by his Philistine captors, offers this prayer for justice: "Lord God, remember me and strengthen me only this once, O God, so that I may be avenged against the Philistines for one of my two eyes." God immediately fortifies Samson for this act of vengeance, and the Temple roof collapses, crushing scores of Philistines along with the now avenged Samson. After the call of Gideon in Judges 6:21, having looked upon a divine messenger, Gideon expresses the fear that he might die. In the following verse, he cries, "Help me, Lord God. For I have seen the angel of the Lord face to face." God answers him immediately and reassures him that he will not die.

The Deuteronomistic History ascribes many prayers to Elijah and Elisha as part of their status as commissioned prophets. Prophetic prayer thus seems to be particularly important in the Deuteronomistic literature.[12] Not coincidentally, there are a great

---

[11] Prayer is mentioned, however, in Lev 9:24; 16:21; 26:40 and in Deut 9:20. There is also a blessing in Deut 1:11, in which Moses recounts his blessing of the people at Horeb.

[12] Samuel Balentine states more broadly that "The general understanding of the prophet as especially skilled in the practice of prayer is frequently registered in Hebrew Bible studies. To cite one opinion, A. Johnson has argued in two influential publications that with respect to cultic duties, prophet and priest are distinguished by their different responsibilities. [A.

many prayers in Jeremiah, too, a book that is universally understood to be closely related in style and theology to the book of Deuteronomy and the Deuteronomistic literature.[13] As for other prophetic prayers in DtrH, one of Elijah's prayers was mentioned at the outset of this chapter. Elijah also offers a prayer in 1 Kings 19:4 when he is fleeing from Jezebel who was seeking to kill him. "It is enough; now, O Lord, take away my life, for I am no better than my ancestors."[14] Elisha offers three brief prayers in the context of the Aramean threat to Israel (2 Kgs 6:17, 18, 20). The last of these is "Strike this people, please, with blindness."

There are many short confessions in the DtrH as well, most of them offered by the Israelites repenting for the transgression of idolatry, the chief sin according to the Dtr Historian.[15] In Judg 10:6-9, the Israelites are being oppressed by the Philistines and the Ammonites as punishment for worshipping foreign gods. When the Israelites realize their mistake, they pray to God. Judg 10:10 records their confession: "So the Israelites cried to the Lord, saying, 'We have

---

Johnson, *The Cultic Prophet in Ancient Israel* (2d ed.; Cardiff: University of Wales, 1962) 58–60.] While the priest exercises sole prerogative in matters relating to sacrifice, the prophet functions as a specialist in prayer." Balentine, *Prayer in the Hebrew Bible*, 50. In his book, Balentine discusses in particular the example of Elijah. See also Balentine's article "The Prophet as Intercessor: A Reassessment," *JBL* 103 (1984) 161–73.

[13] Indeed, Jeremiah is the most prayerful of all the prophets, offering a total of thirteen. Balentine suggests that " . . . Moses, Samuel, and Jeremiah are three intercessors par excellence in the Hebrew Bible." *Prayer in the Hebrew Bible*, 51.

[14] Elijah's prayer is echoed in Jonah's words under the bush when he asks God to kill him because he is so angry that the Ninevites were not killed. Jonah 4:3 "And now, Lord, please take my life from me, for it is better for me to die than to live." The setting is also similar: they both pray in the wilderness at some distance from the city, and a tree/bush figures in both. The book of Jonah elsewhere contains quotes from scripture and other biblical references. Elijah's prayer is the only other instance in the Bible where someone asks God to kill him. The exilic author of Jonah was thus likely trying to allude to the Elijah story and in doing so, seeking to portray his protagonist in a certain light by contrasting Jonah's words with those of one of Israel's greatest prophets. In its new context, the prayer shows Jonah as an embittered and vengeful man. Balentine, making reference to Magonet's literary study of Jonah, offers the following comment on the connection of the Elijah and Jonah prayers: "Yet the irony is that whereas Elijah's wish to die (cf. 1 Kgs 19:10) comes after his apparent failure as a prophet, Jonah's is the response to a dramatic success." *Prayer in the Hebrew Bible*, 79.

[15] Cf. similar confessions in 1 Sam 12:10 (the Israelites); 2 Sam 12:13 (David), 2 Sam 24:10, 17 (David); 1 Kgs 8:47 (Israelites).

sinned against you, because we have abandoned our God and have worshipped the Baals.'"

A noteworthy fact relating to the Dtr Historian's depiction of character is that David is the only individual in the Deuteronomistic History who offers confessions. He does so three times: once for his adultery with Bathsheba (1 Sam 12:13), and twice for commissioning a census of the people (2 Sam 24:10, 17). David offers other prayers aside from confessions as well. When David learns that Absalom has added Ahitophel, David's former counselor, to the band of traitors, he makes the following petition as he walks up the Mount of Olives: "O Lord, turn the counsel of Ahitophel into foolishness." (2 Sam 15:31).

Short prayers predominate in the pre-exilic literature, but there is not a uniformly linear development from all short and simple petitions and intercessions to long and complex prayers. Short prayers continue to appear in exilic and post-exilic literature. In fact, many such short post-exilic prayers could be adduced to illustrate this point. Nehemiah prays briefly in Neh 5:19: "Remember for my good, O my God, all that I have done for this people." King Asa offers this prayer in 2 Chr 14:11: "Help us, O Lord our God." In Judith 13:4, right before the heroine lops off Holofernes' drunken head, she steels herself for the act with this short plea: "Give me strength today, O Lord God of Israel." That prayer uttered, she finishes him off with two deft strokes of the sword. There also seems to be an increased occurrence of short blessings in the late literature which are uttered "spontaneously" according to the narratives, by various people, leaders as well as "commoners." 3 Macc 7:23 "Blessed be the Deliverer of Israel through all times. Amen." The book of Tobit is especially full of blessings (3:11-15; 8:5-6; 8:15-17; 11:14-15; 12:17), as is the book of Judith; e.g., Jdt 13:17 "Blessed art thou, our God, who has brought into contempt this day the enemies of your people."

It is thus clear that short prayers continue to appear in the literature of the exilic and post-exilic period. The point to be underscored here is that the simple prayers *predominate* in the literature of the pre-exilic period and to remark the decided *absence* of highly scripturalized prayers in the early literature. There is a tendency in scholarship on biblical prayer to overstate a tidy trajectory in the development of prayer from highly spontaneous utterances to longer, more formal prayers such as those found in the late books of Ezra-Nehemiah.[16] Although a tendency toward longer

---

16 Claus Westermann has made this claim most forcefully in his delineation of three stages of biblical prayer; *Elements of Old Testament*

prayers is clear, the trajectory is not tidy because the roots of this development are found in a number of early prayers themselves. In a handful of these early pre-exilic prayers, two from J, two in the book of Deuteronomy, and one in the DtrH, we can see the tentative beginnings of this phenomenon of "scripturalization." Let us now consider them more closely to see how they recast earlier traditions and how they are therefore none too distant cousins of the scripturalized prayers that we will examine in subsequent chapters.

The Evolution of Pre-Exilic Prayers

"God, please heal her." Moses's simple intercession on behalf of his sister Miriam, found in Numbers 12:13, is markedly different from the long multi-part prayer in 1 Kings 8 offered by Solomon at the dedication of the Temple, which as we shall elaborate in this chapter already reflects a nuanced interpretative use of earlier traditions. To be sure, there is a certain continuity in the basic form of the two prayers, which includes an address to God and a petition, but the differences between the early prayers and the later exilic prayers are quite marked.[17] Aside from sharing essential formal elements, it

---

Theology (Atlanta: John Knox, 1982) 153-172. So too, J. Corvin has suggested a shift from anthropomorphic, conversational "prayers" that predominate in J narrative to formal prayers that may have little to do with their narrative context. Balentine summarizes his thesis: "Corvin proposes an evolution from conversational to formal prayers in keeping with a shift in theological perception from God's immanence to God's transcendence." I was unable to examine Corwin's unpublished study for this dissertation, and thus rely on Balentine's assessment of his thesis. See Balentine, *Prayer in the Hebrew Bible*, 18–21.

Patrick Miller offers an important corrective to Westermann's theory. Miller agrees that different groups of prayers are evident in the Bible, but he is more cautious about making claims about diachronic developmental stages: "This is less a sharp historical difference than it is a difference in function and setting. In that sense, one may connect with the distinction that Moshe Greenberg makes between the "unmediated, direct forms of popular piety" present in the prose prayers (Westermann's first stage) and the "mediated" and "refined" piety of the populace present in the Psalms (Westermann's second stage)." *They Cried to the Lord*, 86.

[17] Miller characterizes the basic form of the petitionary prayer in this way: "It consists of address to the deity, petition, and motivation clauses. Elements of lament about one's situation and expressions of confidence or trust are regularly enough present to be included in the basic form, especially for the psalm prayers. In the prose prayers, both lament and expressions of confidence are less frequent." *They Cried to the Lord*, 57. See also Appendix 1 of his book which provides a simple structural analysis of most of the prose

is possible to see another link between the earliest stage of prayer and the later stages. We shall now argue that there is an early-intermediate stage in the evolution of the scripturalization process that can be discerned in the earlier strata of the Pentateuch. This stage comprises six prayers—Gen 32:10–12; Exod 32:11–13; Num 14:13–19; and Deut 9:26–29; 21:7–8; and 26:5–10—all of which are still relatively short, but that show some development beyond the more frequent unadorned requests to God reviewed above. This early phase in the evolution of scripturalization is not characterized by a full-blown interpretive use of scripture as is true of the later prayers of the post-exilic period. The pre-exilic origins of scripturalization lie in the remembrance of past events in the book of Deuteronomy, and, for the Jahwist, especially in the remembrance of past divine promises.

The prayer in Gen 32:10–12 is generally agreed to be a product of the Jahwist.[18] The passage reads:

> 10. And Jacob said, "O God of my father Abraham, God of my father Isaac, O Lord who said to me, 'Return to your country and to your kindred and I will deal well with you,' 11. I am unworthy of the mercies and the faithfulness that you have shown your servant because with my staff I crossed this Jordan and now I have become two camps. 12. Deliver me, oh please, from the hand of my brother, from the hand of Esau because I fear him, lest he come and smite me, mother as well as children. For you promised: 'I will surely do good by you and I will make your descendants like the sand of the sea that cannot be counted from abundance.'"

This prayer is uttered by Jacob as he and his now large family are about to enter Esau's territory after his long sojourn abroad with Laban. He is anticipating Esau's revenge for having stolen Esau's blessing and so the prayer comes in the form of a request for God's help. Two interesting particulars of this prayer call for comment. One concerns Jacob's address to God. Jacob prays to the God of his father and the God of his grandfather, thereby associating himself with the God who will become the God of Jacob/Israel as well. This is the first use in a prayer of the "God of the fathers" formula that

---

prayers for help. Later prayers contain an elaboration of the form with longer lists of divine attributes and lengthy motivation clauses.

[18] One exception to the general consensus is Norman Gottwald who divides this prayer into J, 32:10–11, and E, 32:12; *The Hebrew Bible: A Socio-Literary Introduction* (Philadelphia: Fortress, 1985), 151–152.

becomes a routine way of invoking God in prayer.[19] In contrast to other early prayers that address God simply as "O Lord" or with no address at all, this marks the first elaboration of divine address. Jacob here addresses God in the same way that God has identified himself when announcing the divine promise of offspring and land to Jacob in Gen 28:13, "I am the Lord, the God of your father Abraham and the God of Isaac." The use of this appellation in the prayer thus calls on the personal, historical relationship of God to the pray-er, calling on God using the same words of the divine self-revelation.

A second feature of this prayer is the use of wording from earlier parts of the tradition. There are two quotes of divine speech in this prayer, both of which, to be precise, are divine *promises* made to Jacob. Here, then, is a piece of evidence for the origins of scripturalization: the author of Genesis has used earlier traditions of divine promises in composing this prayer. One quote appears as the second half of verse 10, the invocation that identifies the God of Israel as the one who said: "Return to your country and to your kindred and I will deal well with you." The second appears in the last verse of the prayer: "For you promised: 'I will surely do good by you and I will make your descendants like the sand of the sea that cannot be counted from abundance.'" Where do these two quotes come from? When did God make these promises?

As Nahum Sarna has noticed, verse 10 uses phrases from Gen 28:13–15 and 31:3, the divine declarations at Bethel and Haran, which mark the beginning and end of Jacob's twenty-year exile.[20] One quote derives from God's initial promise to Jacob, given during the Jacob's ladder theophany.

Gen 28:13 reads:

והנה יהוה נצב עליו ויאמר אני יהוה אלהי אברהם אביך
ואלהי יצחק הארץ אשר אתה שכב עליה לך אתננה ולזרעך

Gen 31:3 reads:

ויאמר יהוה אל־יעקב שוב אל־ארץ אבותיך ולמולדתך
ואהיה עמך

---

[19] Note also the fourfold occurrence of "God of my master Abraham" in the prayers of Abraham's servant in Gen 24:12, 27, 42, 48. This divine appellation for God does not recur in later prayers.

[20] Nahum Sarna, *Genesis* (Philadelphia: Jewish Publication Society, 1989) 225.

Compare these with Gen 32:10b.

וַיֹּאמֶר יַעֲקֹב אֱלֹהֵי אָבִי אַבְרָהָם וֵאלֹהֵי אָבִי יִצְחָק יהוה
הָאֹמֵר אֵלַי שׁוּב לְאַרְצְךָ וּלְמוֹלַדְתְּךָ וְאֵיטִיבָה עִמָּךְ

Gen 32:10 alters this command and its promise in a slightly more positive vein. There is no analogue in the other divine promises from Genesis to the wording found in verse 10, "I will deal well with you." The alteration seems instead to be an interpretive modification. Perhaps the author intentionally included this change so that the wording of the prayer would be in keeping with Jacob's tricky nature, reflecting his trademark tendency to grab the best deal or heel he could in any given situation, even from God.

An equally tricky question comes to mind. Was the author of this prayer using earlier written traditions or was he in fact the author of all the material quoted as well? Before attempting to answer that question, let us consider two prayers that appear in the pre-exilic literature, Exod 32:11–13 and Deut 9:26–29. These two prayers offer different versions of Moses' intercession for the Israelites after the episode with the molten calf. Here is Exod 32:11–13:

> 11. And Moses petitioned the Lord his God, saying: "Why, O Lord, does your anger burn at your people whom you brought forth out of the land of Egypt with <u>great power</u> and a strong arm? 12. Why should the Egyptians say '<u>With wicked purpose he brought them forth to slay them in the hills and to consume them from upon the face of the earth?</u>' Turn from your burning anger and repent from the wicked purpose for your people. 13. <u>Remember Abraham and Isaac and Israel, your servants</u> to whom you swore by yourself and said to them: 'I will multiply your descendants like the stars of the heavens and all this land of which I spoke I will give to your descendants and they will possess it forever.'"

According to Brevard Childs, Exodus 32 reflects one basic source, probably J, to which two expansions have been made.[21] One

---

[21] Childs thinks chs. 32–34 were edited in one of the last stages of the book. The other expansion lies in vv. 25–29, which he suggests was originally an independent unit. As support for his contention about the two expansions, Childs points out that the first intercession of Moses, which is successful, stands in tension with Moses' intercession in Exod 32:31–32, which God does not accept. He also argues, as have many others, that the parallel between Exod 32:8 and 1 Kgs 12:28, "These are your gods, O Israel, that brought you out of the land of Israel" indicates some editorial reshaping on the part of a DtrH editor in order underscore his condemnation of Jeroboam's rival cult sites in

expansion comprises vv.7–14, which Childs states are "saturated with Deuteronomic language" showing particular similarities with Deut 9:25–29.[22] He does not, however, list any specific parallels and there are actually more Deuteronomic parallels with the parts of Exodus 32 outside of vv.7–14.[23] His characterization of this passage thus leaves unresolved the exact relationship between this prayer and a similar report of Moses' prayer in Deut 9:25–29.

Like Gen 32:10–12, Exod 32:11–13 is a prayer that recalls the divine promise to the ancestors with a specific divine quote. Moses intercedes to God on behalf of the idolatrous Israelites, asking God to relent from his decision expressed in Exod 32:10 to destroy them. He calls on the merit of Israel's ancestors and quotes the divine promise that appears three times in Genesis. The first is simply the fact that it is a divine promise. Moses is not recalling third person history of the Exodus; in this prayer he recalls first person dialogue between God and the patriarchs. Whereas Gen 32:10 and 12 include the aspect of the divine promise related to the blessing of Jacob and multiplying of descendants, Exod 32:13 emphasizes not only numerous descendants but the promise of the land. Compare the following parallels:

Exod 32: 13   זכר לאברהם ליצחק ולישראל עבדיך אשר נשבעת
להם בך ותדבר אלהם ארבה את־זרעכם
ככוכבי השמים וכל־הארץ הזאת אשר אמרתי
אתן לזרעכם ונחלו לעלם

Gen 22:17   והרבה ארבה את־זרעך ככוכבי השמים וכחול
אשר על־שפת הים

---

the north; *The Book of Exodus* (OTL; Philadelphia: Westminster, 1974), 557–560.

[22] He has been influenced by Martin Noth's understanding of vv.9–14 as a Deuteronomistic addition; *Exodus* (OTL; Philadelphia: Westminster, 1962) 244.

[23] As listed in Appendix A of Moshe Weinfeld's book, *Deuteronomy and the Deuteronomic School* (Winona Lake, IN: Eisenbrauns, 1972), which offers a listing of Deuteronomic phraseology, the phrase בכח גדול וביד נטויה is a Deuteronomic phrase that appears in Deut 9:29, 2 Kgs 17:36, and Jer 32:17. Weinfeld notes, however, that the phrase in Exod 32:11 reads וביד חזקה בכח גדול, "strong hand" instead of "outstretched hand." It is possible that the phrase in Deut 9:29 is a later standardized form of this phrase and the prayer in Exodus 32 may not be a Deuteronomic addition, but a part of the fragmentary Elohist source on which the Deuteronomist drew. Weinfeld points out two parallels between Exod 32:7–10 and Deuteronomic sources, the phrases סור מן הדרך and the distinctive term שחת; and only one between Exod 32:11–14 and Deuteronomic sources: בכח גדול as mentioned above.

Gen 26:4 וְהִרְבֵּיתִי אֶת־זַרְעֲךָ כְּכוֹכְבֵי הַשָּׁמַיִם וְנָתַתִּי לְזַרְעֲךָ
אֵת כָּל־הָאֲרָצֹת הָאֵל

Deut 8:1 רָאֵה נָתַתִּי לִפְנֵיכֶם אֶת־הָאָרֶץ בֹּאוּ וּרְשׁוּ
אֶת־הָאָרֶץ אֲשֶׁר נִשְׁבַּע יהוה לַאֲבֹתֵיכֶם לְאַבְרָהָם
לְיִצְחָק וּלְיַעֲקֹב לָתֵת לָהֶם וּלְזַרְעָם אַחֲרֵיהֶם

Deut 11:9 וּלְמַעַן תַּאֲרִיכוּ יָמִים עַל־הָאֲדָמָה אֲשֶׁר נִשְׁבַּע יהוה
לַאֲבֹתֵיכֶם לָתֵת לָהֶם וּלְזַרְעָם אֶרֶץ זָבַת חָלָב וּדְבָשׁ

Deut 34:4 וַיֹּאמֶר יהוה אֵלָיו זֹאת הָאָרֶץ אֲשֶׁר נִשְׁבַּעְתִּי
לְאַבְרָהָם לְיִצְחָק וּלְיַעֲקֹב לֵאמֹר לְזַרְעֲךָ אֶתְּנֶנָּה
הֶרְאִיתִיךָ בְעֵינֶיךָ וְשָׁמָּה לֹא תַעֲבֹר

The question arises: how are we to understand the exact relationship between this quotation of the divine promise and the other occurrences of the divine promise to the ancestors as it appears in its various forms? One of three possibilities seems likely. The author who wrote this prayer also wrote the other narratives in which the promise to the patriarchs appears. A second possibility is that the author was using written traditions to compose his prayer, and the divine promise to the ancestors figured prominently in the Jahwistic account that he was using as a source. A third possibility is a traditio-historical one, that the author was simply using an oral formula, well-known in Israel, that he placed in the mouth of Moses in a verisimilar fashion. Although this question cannot be answered definitively because our knowledge of the composition of the Bible is largely conjectural, a tentative answer can illuminate the origins of this putative "scripturalization" because it can suggest how the author used traditions. Given the parallels found in the exilic frame of the book of Deuteronomy, the last answer seems to be the most plausible. As will become evident in later chapters, the answer to the question about the nature of the sources is not necessarily the same for post-exilic prayers, because later authors had a different relationship to tradition than did the first authors and editors of the Bible. Indeed, post-exilic tradents were undoubtedly using written traditions as much if not more than oral traditions.

The prayer that is related to Exod 32:11–13, Deut 9:26–29, appears in a passage in which Moses is recounting the experience of the Sinai covenant in the wilderness. It contains a prayer that recalls the intercessory prayer described in Exodus 32.

And I prayed to the Lord and I said, "O Lord God, do not destroy your people, your inheritance whom you redeemed according to your greatness, whom you brought up from Egypt with a strong hand. 27. Remember your servants, Abraham, Isaac, and Jacob. Pay no heed to the stubbornness of this people and to their wickedness and to their sin, 28. lest the land from which you brought us forth should say: 'Because the Lord is unable to have them enter the land which he promised them and because of his hatred for them, he brought them forth to kill them in the desert.' 29. But they are your people, your inheritance, whom you brought forth with your great power and your outstretched arm."

There are different emphases in the two prayers. The prayer in Exodus emphasizes the anger of God at the behavior of the people. Anger is mentioned twice. By contrast, the focus in the Deuteronomic prayer is on the sin of the people who are described as stubborn, wicked, and sinful. In spite of this decided emphasis on the weaknesses of Israel in the Deuteronomic prayer, Israel is referred to twice as God's נחלה or inheritance. Another difference lies in the wording used to describe the exodus. Deut 9:26 uses the phrase, "you redeemed," פדית, from Egypt, a distinctively Deuteronomic term for God's activity in the Exodus.[24] The prayer in Exodus uses the more general phrase "bring forth from Egypt."

Deut 9:26–29 also makes reference to past traditions. The strongest parallels between the two prayers are underlined. They both contain the same petition to remember the patriarchs, with slightly different syntax. The expression זכר ל- in reference to the patriarchs occurs only in these two verses. Both prayers contain a quote with the same motif: "what will the neighbors down in Egypt think?," though with different wording. Both prayers contain the same phrase, "great power" to describe God's work in the Exodus from Egypt. It is difficult to determine the exact historical relationship of these two prayers and their relative priority. Like the pentateuchal passages containing references to the patriarchal covenant, the similarities can be explained in a few ways. One prayer might be dependent on the other; the prayers might have been written by the same author; the prayers are two different accounts of a historical memory, passed down orally through the ages. Although the question is significant in terms of understanding the precise historical development of the literature, it is not essential to

---

[24] The use of פדה to refer to the Exodus from Egypt occurs in Deut 7:8, 9:26, 13:6, 15:15, 21:8, and also in Mic 6:4; Ps 78:42; 2 Sam 7:23; Neh 1:10, the last three of which are prayers.

determine the exact relationship between the two prayers to sustain the argument of this chapter that the use of past traditions originates in pre-exilic prayers.[25]

Let us now consider another early specimen of scripturalization, Num 14:13–19:

> 13. And Moses said to the Lord: "But the Egyptians will hear that you in your might brought this people up from among them. 14. And they will say to those who dwell in this land, 'They heard that you, O Lord, are in the midst of this people because you are seen eye to eye, O Lord, and your presence stands before them; in a pillar of cloud you go before them by day and in a column of fire by night. 15. Will you kill this people altogether? Then the nations who hear this report will talk, saying, 16. because you were unable, O Lord, to bring this people to the land that was sworn to them, you slew them in the desert. 17. And now, O Lord, magnify your power as you promised saying, 18. 'The Lord is patient and abundant in mercy, forgiving sin and transgression, but he will surely not acquit [the guilty], visiting the sins of the parents upon the children to the third and fourth generation.'[26] 19. Forgive, please, the sin of this people in the greatness of your mercy as you have pardoned this people from Egypt until now."
>
> 20. And the Lord said, "I will forgive, as you have asked."[27]

This prayer in Numbers 14, generally attributed to the Jahwist, is the second intercession Moses makes for the people.[28] There are

---

[25] Although the prayers are similar in theme, the differences in wording and emphasis suggest that they may have developed in parallel from an ancient oral tradition. The prayer in Deuteronomy seems to be the later prayer based on its slightly more regular form and its language. The prayer in Exod 32:11 begins with a question; Deut 9:26 starts with a standard invocation and petition to God. The use of the term נחלה in parallel with עם, or people, occurs primarily in prayers and psalms of a late pre-exilic or exilic date. Cf. 1 Kings 8:53; Ps 28:9; 78:62,71; 94:5,4; 106:40; Joel 2:17; 4:2.

[26] The Greek and a number of manuscripts from the Samaritan Pentateuch add "and truth" after merciful, and "and sin" after trespass, both of which occur in the divine attribute formula found in Exodus 34:6ff. This variant reading likely reflects an "interpretive insertion" on the part of the translators.

[27] On the use of נשא and סלח in this prayer and in other prayers for forgiveness such as Exod 34:9, 1 Kgs 8:30,35,36; Neh 9:17, Dan 9:19, see Balentine, *Prayer in the Hebrew Bible*, 133–134.

[28] Martin Noth attributes Num 14:13–19 to the Jahwist. He also attributes Exodus 34:6–7 to the same source, which he includes as part of the longer Jahwistic portion of the Sinai tradition in 32–34. *A History of Pentateuchal Traditions*, (Bernhard W. Anderson, transl.; Englewood Cliffs, NJ: Prentice-Hall, 1972) 273.

two features of scripturalization. One is the use of the formulaic "pillar of cloud/column of fire" wording that has come to be shorthand for the Israelites' experience of divine guidance in the wilderness.

The other more prominent one is the reuse of the divine attribute formula of Exod 34:6–7:

> And the Lord passed before him and the Lord called out: "The Lord God is compassionate and gracious, patient and abundant in mercy and truth, who preserves mercy to the thousandth generation, forgiving sin and transgression and iniquity. But he will surely not acquit the guilty, visiting the sin of the parents upon the children and the children's children to the third and fourth generation."

The consensus among those scholars who have closely studied this formula is that Exod 34:6–7 is its earliest formulation.[29] Like the prayers in Gen 32:10–12 and Exod 32:11–13, Num 14:13–19 also employs divine speech that appears elsewhere as part of a divine revelation. In this case, the divine revelation concerns God's self-revealed nature as opposed to a covenantal responsibility bound up with the promise to the patriarchs. Here again, the divine speech is turned around by the author of the prayer as a way of claiming certain expectations from God.

What are we to make of this interpretive appropriation of the divine attribute formula in Exod 34:6–7? As it appears in Numbers 14, only the first part of this formula is quoted, the part referring to

---

[29] See the form-critical work of J. Scharbert, "Formgeschichte und Exegese von Ex 34, 6f und seiner Parallelism," *Biblica* 38 (1957) 130–150 who asserts that Exod 34:6–7 is the oldest appearance of the divine attribute formulary. See also R.C Dentan, "The Literary Affinities of Exodus XXXIV 6f," *VT* 13 (1963) 34–51, and, more recently, the discussion of Michael Fishbane, *Biblical Interpretation in Ancient Israel* (New York: Oxford, 1985) 335–350, and T.B. Dozeman, "Inner-Biblical Interpretation of Yahweh's Gracious and Compassionate Character," *JBL* 108 (1989) 207–223.

Martin Noth characterizes the divine attribute formula, as "stereotyped," but he does not clarify the nature or origins of the formula. As we will discuss at greater length in the next chapter, what Noth perceives as the "stereotyped" and "customary" nature of the formula comes from its deployment and interpretation in later literature. It is much more likely that this formula, dealing as it does with the essential character of Israel's God, was an early part of the oral tradition relating to the theophany and law-giving at Sinai. Certainly this formula comes to have a special place in later tradition, and so its recurrence in other biblical literature gives Noth the impression that it is "stereotyped," but this suggests a misunderstanding of the relationship between Exod 34:6–7 and later passages.

divine mercy. In Num 14:13–19, a later tradent, wishing to emphasize only that merciful part of the divine character that would save the Israelites in the desert, used only part of the original formulation from Exodus. As Jacob Milgrom has discussed, the truncated form of this formula is basic to the penitential prayers of the Jewish liturgy.[30] The appearance of the shortened form in Num 14:18 thus makes clear that authors of liturgical prayers were not departing from tradition; there is ample biblical precedent for using only half the formula, in the prayer in Numbers 14 and elsewhere.

The examples of rudimentary "scripturalization" in the Deuteronomic prayers date from a later period than those from the Jahwist source. They do not rely on certain traditional wording of the divine promise to the patriarchs in the same way that the Jahwistic prayers do. The three Deuteronomic prayers are notable for their retrospective references to Israel's redemption from slavery in the exodus. The briefest such reference to the exodus is found in Deut 21:7–8, a prayer for absolution of the community from blood guilt when the murderer of a dead person is unknown. The elders of the town are instructed to wash their hands over a dead heifer and recite: "Our hands did not shed this blood, nor were we witnesses to it. Absolve, O Lord, your people Israel, whom you redeemed; do not let the guilt of innocent blood remain in the midst of your people Israel." This prayer contains a brief reference to the past, specifically the exodus from Egypt and the redemption of God's people from slavery. That remembrance serves to "remind" God of their relationship and with it their expectation of absolution of any possible ill consequences from the blood guilt. Such a remembrance of the past within a prayer, brief and allusive though it is, also marks an important step in the process of scripturalization. Deut 9:26–29, discussed above, refers to the exodus twice, once at the beginning of the prayer and once at the end. The third prayer from Deuteronomy, Deut 26:5–10, offers a historical retrospective stretching from the time of Abraham to the entry to the land, with the exodus mentioned in the middle. We will review its contents in greater detail in the next chapter in our discussion of historical reviews in prayers. It is sufficient to point out

---

[30] Jacob Milgrom, *Numbers* (Philadelphia: Jewish Publication Society, 1990) Excursus 32, 392–398. Other scholars have noted its liturgical use within the biblical literature itself. Walter Beyerlin has pointed out a connection between God's initial self-revelation and the use of the divine attribute formula in the regular liturgy. He observes that other appearances of this formula appear in cultic contexts, *Herkunft und Geschichte der ältesten Sinaitraditionen* (Tübingen, J.C.B. Mohr, 1961) 156.

that God's work in liberating Israel from slavery stands at the center of the covenantal relationship for the Deuteronomic writer.

Exilic Prayers

The turning point in the scripturalization of prayer lies in the exilic literature. We have seen some tentative steps in that direction in the pre-exilic literature, but in the exilic literature, prayers have turned a corner. The "corner" here is the difference between the Jahwist's use of the ancient wording of the divine promise in the composition of a literary strand of the Bible, which functions to provide narrative continuity, and the self-conscious use of past traditions and editorial melding of sources that we find in 1 Kings 8. A number of prayers dating from the late pre-exilic or exilic period could be cited to illustrate the point: 2 Sam 7:18–29, a prayer of David, 2 Kings 19:15–19, Hezekiah's prayer during the siege of Jerusalem by Sennacherib, and Jonah 4:2–3 offer other important examples of this phenomenon.[31] We will focus, however, on one premier example

---

[31] 2 Sam 7:18–29 relates to our concern in this chapter because like many of the prayers reviewed above and like 1 Kings 8:23–53, it refers to a divine promise, in this case, the promise to David of a house in 1 Samuel 7. 2 Kgs 19:15–19, paralleled in Isa 37:33–35, is discussed at greater length in chapter three in conjunction with the scripturalization of the prayer in Judith 9.

One other prayer from the exilic frame of Deuteronomy warrants mention. Deut. 3:24–25, a prayer of Moses, appears in Moses's historical recital in Deut 1:6–4:40. As a prayer presented in part of a longer historical retrospect, this is similar to the prayer in Deut 9:26–29, in which Moses recounts his prayer of Exodus 32. There are two features of this prayer relevant to our concept of scripturalization. The first is that Moses reports the words of a prayer he made to God in the wilderness at Pisgah, yet curiously neither the words of this prayer nor reference to such a prayer is mentioned in Numbers 27. In that sense the text of the prayer is an interpretive "filling of the gaps" presented by the traditions in Numbers. The authorial process by which this happened remains murky, but seemingly the author of this Deuteronomic framework reviewed the J traditions in Numbers associated with the transfer of leadership from Moses to Joshua, found them wanting, and in his own retelling, incorporated this prayer of Moses.

A second feature is that it contains some stock phrases that appear in other Deuteronomistic prayers. For instance, the phrase expressing the incomparability of God is likewise found in 2 Sam 7:22b–24, 1 Kgs 8:23, and 2 Kgs 19:15. So, too, the reference to God's work in the exodus is described with the phrases "your greatness and your mighty hand" as well as "your deeds and mighty acts," that recur not only throughout the Exodus account itself, but also in later prayers. We see here then the beginnings of more formal liturgical wording that suggest a learned reflection on earlier exodus traditions.

that sits on the cusp of the exilic period, 1 Kgs 8:23–53, Solomon's prayer at the Temple dedication.[32] A distinctly literary process has given final shape to this prayer in which there is clear evidence of reflection on and reworking of older material.[33]

The contents of 1 Kings 8 are as follows: Solomon assembles the Israelites (1–2); the priests transfer the ark, the tent of meeting, and the priestly utensils to the sanctum sanctorum of the Temple (3–11); he announces that he has built the Temple as a dwelling place for God (12–14); he gives a first blessing of all the assembly of Israel (15–21); he stands and pronounces a prayer at the altar of the Temple (22–53); he moves from kneeling at the altar and blesses the assembly a second time (54–61), Solomon and all Israel offer sacrifices (62–64); and Solomon and all Israel observe a festival for seven days and the people depart on the eighth day (65–66). As the contents indicate, there are not one but three liturgical pieces in 1 Kings 8, two of which occur in the form of a blessing (1 Kings 8:15–21 and 56–61).

The prayer reads:

> 23. And he said, "O Lord God of Israel, there is no God like you in the heavens above or upon the earth below who keeps covenant and shows mercy to your servants who walk before you in all their heart.[34] 24. The covenant that you kept with your servant David, my father, which you spoke to him and you promised with your mouth and with your hands you have fulfilled it this day. 25. And now O

---

[32] H.W. Wolff, who dated the DtrH to the exile like his predecessors Martin Noth and Gerhard von Rad, pointed to the special significance of this prayer in his understanding of the purpose of the DtrH editor, especially its use of the term for repentance, שׁוּב, in vv.46–53. See his "The Kerygma of the Deuteronomic Historical Work," *The Vitality of Old Testament Traditions*, (W. Brueggemann and H.W. Wolff, eds.; Atlanta: John Knox, 1975) 90–93. This essay is a translation of the original German, "Das Kerygma des deuteronomischen Geschichtswerk," *ZAW* 73 (1961) 171–186.

[33] Consider the comment of Hans-Peter Mathys, who refers to the prayer in 1 Kings 8:23–53 as "Das" alttestamentliche Gebet: "Die älteste Darstellung der Tempelweihung hat wie ein Magnet allerlei grössere und kleinere Ergänzungen verschiedenen Inhalts an sich gezogen, darin etwa der Sinaiperikope zu vergleichen." *Dichter und Beter. Theologen aus spätalttestamentlicher Zeit.* (Orbis Biblicus Orientalis 132; Göttingen: Vandenhoeck & Ruprecht, 1994) 65.

[34] The Greek has the singular "servant" here, which would indicate merely a self-referential mention of Solomon as servant. As clarified in the next verse, the covenant mentioned is the Davidic covenant. The MT contains a broader construal of the parties to the covenant, the plural "servants" presumably indicating Solomon's progeny as inheritors of the divine promise.

Lord God of Israel, keep for your servant David, my father, what you have promised him saying, **"No successor of yours will be cut off from before me as one who sits on the throne of Israel, but only if your children watch their ways and walk before me as you have walked before me."**[35] 26. And now O God of Israel, please confirm the promise that you have spoken to your servant David, my father. 27. For will God in fact dwell upon the earth? Behold, the heavens and the highest heavens cannot contain you; how then can this house that I have built? 28. Turn your face to your servant's prayer and his petition O Lord my God, to listen to the cry and the prayer that your servant prays before you today, 29. that your eyes may be open toward this house night and day, to the place about which you said **"My name will be there."** 30. Hear the supplication of your servant and of your people Israel who pray to[ward] this place, and you, hearken from the place of your dwelling, the heavens, hear and forgive.

(1) 31. If someone sins against a neighbor and is given an oath to swear, and comes and swears before your altar in this house, 32. then hear in heaven, and act, and judge your servants, condemning the guilty by bringing their conduct on their own head, and vindicating the righteous by rewarding them according to their righteousness.

(2) 33. When your people Israel, having sinned against you, is defeated before an enemy but turns again to you, confesses your name, prays and pleads with you in this house, 34. then hear in heaven, forgive the sin of your people Israel, and bring them again to the land that you gave to their ancestors.

(3) 35. When heaven is shut up and there is no rain because they have sinned against you, and then they pray toward this place, confess your name, and turn from their sin, because you answer it, 36. then hear in heaven, and forgive the sin of your servants, your people Israel, when you teach them the good way in which they should go; and send rain on your land, which you have given to your people as an inheritance.

(4) 37. If there is a famine in the land, if there is pestilence, blight, mildew, locust, or caterpillar; if their enemy besieges them in the land; whatever pestilence, whatever sickness there is, 38. whatever prayer, whatever plea there is from any individual or from all your people Israel, all knowing the afflictions of their own hearts so that they stretch out their hands toward this house; 39. then, you, hear in heaven your dwelling place, forgive, act, and render to each whose hearts you know—according to his ways, for only you know what is in every human heart—40. so that they may live all the days of their lives upon the land that you gave to their ancestors.

(5) 41. Moreover if there is a foreigner who is not from your people Israel who comes from a distant land on account of your name 42.

---

[35] The parallel to this verse in 2 Chr 6:16 reads, "only if your children watch their ways to walk before my Torah as you have walked." In the post-exilic period, Torah has become the embodiment of the divine commandments.

because they hear of your great name and your mighty hand and your outstretched arm and so comes to pray in this house, 43. you, hear in heaven the place of your dwelling and do all that the foreigner calls to you so that all the peoples of the earth may know your name to fear you like your people Israel and to know that your name is invoked upon this house that I built.

(6) 44. When your people go forth to war against its enemy on the path that you send them and they pray to the Lord[36] on the way to the city that you have chosen and the house that I have built for your name, 45. hear in heaven their prayer and their supplication and render them justice.

(7) 46. When they sin against you because there is no person who does not sin and you are angry with them and you have given them up to the enemy and they are carried away captive to the land of the enemy, far distant or near, 47. and they turn their hearts to the land to which they were taken captive and repent and make supplication to you in the land where they are captive, saying, "**we have sinned; we have done wrong; and we are wicked,**" 48. and they turn to you with all their heart and all their soul in the land of their enemies who have captured them, and they pray to you on the way to their land that you gave to their ancestors, the city that you chose and the house that I built for your name, 49. then hear their prayer and their supplication in heaven, the place of your dwelling and render them justice. 50. and forgive your people who sinned against you and their transgressions that they committed against you and grant them compassion before their captors that they might have compassion on them. 51. Because they are your people and your inheritance whom you brought out of Egypt from the midst of the iron-smelter. 52. Let your eyes be open to the supplication of your servant and to the supplication of your people Israel to hear whenever they call to you 53. because **you have separated them from all the people of the earth for yourself as an inheritance as you promised by the hand of Moses your servant when you O Lord God brought our ancestors out of Egypt.**

Before discussing how the prayer uses earlier sources, it is necessary to establish the nature of the prayer's composition. Is the second prayer in 1 Kgs 8:23–53 a unified piece by one author or does it have an augmented core with indications of editing? At stake in the answer to this question is the degree of scripturalization that can be ascribed to this prayer. If 23–53 represent the work of one author, then the next question is how the author used earlier sources. But if the prayer itself is composite, with an earlier section and later sections that were written consciously to comment on and expand the earlier section, as some scholars have argued, this reflects a more

---

[36] The MT of 2 Chr contains the second person singular, אֵלֶיךָ, as does the Vulgate; the Greek has pray "in the name of" the Lord ἐν ὀνόματι = בְּשֵׁם.

42 *Praying By the Book*

subtle melding of earlier and later traditions by one or more skillful authors/editors and care must be taken to disentangle its compositional threads.

In pointing out the difficulty of describing the literary history of Nathan's oracle to David in 2 Samuel 7, P. Kyle McCarter writes:

> We must rely as much on identifiable thematic inconsistencies as on more strictly literary criteria. Indeed, the chief indication of the presence of diverse materials in the oracle is its fundamental conceptual inconsistency.[37]

The same can be affirmed in reconstructing the literary history of 1 Kings 8. Major thematic inconsistencies signal different authorial hands at work. Scholars disagree about the date of this chapter and its composition, though no one would date its final form any earlier than the late pre-exilic period.

Gary Knoppers represents the minority view that the chapter in its entirety dates from the late pre-exilic period, specifically from the time of Josiah.[38] According to Knoppers, the author's purpose in writing this piece was to serve the propagandistic end of bolstering Josiah's attempts at centralization of the cult.[39] Knoppers argues for the essential unity of the entire chapter, 1 Kings 8, on the basis of its symmetrical literary structure, though he admits the existence of "scattered later additions."[40] He correctly discerns a certain heptadic

---

[37] *II Samuel* (AB 9; Garden City, NY: Doubleday) 221. On this basis McCarter reconstructs the literary history of the oracle in 2 Sam 7:1–17 in three phases, each of which expresses a different view of temple and dynasty.

[38] Another scholar who has accepts this view is Baruch Halpern, *The First Historians: The Hebrew Bible and History*, (San Francisco: Harper & Row, 1988) 168–71. Moreover, he asserts the existence of eight petitions by dividing 46–51 into two separate cases.

[39] Gary Knoppers, "Prayer and Propaganda: Solomon's Dedication of the Temple and the Deuteronomist's Program," *CBQ* 57 (1995) 252.

[40] Knoppers, "Dedication," 232. His argument about the chapter's essential literary structure is compelling; however he does not admit the possibility that this literary unity could be the result of post-exilic additions and editing, perhaps because of his conclusion about the propagandistic nature of the dedication ceremony itself. Knoppers states that "The deuteronomistic emphasis on popular prayer is best understood as a part of a preexilic program that links king, city, temple, and people." The link among these four, however, is not always evident. The dedicatory prayer itself outlines cases in which people might petition God for help, in Knoppers' words "popular prayer." According to Knoppers, it is significant that neither king nor priest is mentioned as necessary mediator in order for prayers to be heard by God. There is no hint of royal theology akin to the Davidic royal theology. In

structure within the chapter; however, he minimizes the asymmetrical effects of one block of text (vv.6–13, which describe the placing of the ark into the sanctuary) on this arrangement. In the case of Solomon's prayer, and especially the seven petitions found within it, he also presses the evidence for symmetry too far. He asserts a basic six-part structure for each petition, while at the same time recognizing that the first petition contains only five parts and the fifth, sixth, and seventh petitions contain seven parts.[41] Less convincing still is his assertion that the last petition "concerning exile need not be exilic," but instead could have been written by someone pondering the possible fate of the Judahites in light of other ancient Near Eastern deportations.[42] Furthermore, the inference he draws from this perceived literary symmetry that the chapter is almost entirely from the hand of one author is flawed. It is one thing to argue that there is a rhetorical unity based on its structural pattern; it is another to suggest on the basis of this pattern that this is owing to authorial unity. In other words, an exilic author could well have arranged older units of text and tradition into such a pattern by adding some material himself. Knoppers's argument would be easier to sustain if he did not date the major redaction of this chapter to the

---

contrast, the location and direction in which the prayer is offered—either in or toward the Temple—is mentioned in each of the seven cases, which suggests the Temple's utmost importance. Some scholars have argued that the mention of the Temple also supports a pre-exilic dating of 23–53, but this assumption is problematic because it relies on an overly materialistic/literalistic view of the Temple as actual building as opposed to building site. Today, Jews pray toward the Temple as the holiest site on the earth with hope for its eschatological restoration, yet this does not involve affirmation of a "king, city, temple, people program" as Knoppers suggests was the case in the pre-exilic period. As Jon D. Levenson has stated in reference to this prayer, "1 Kgs 8:23–53 (61) is thus a pivotal text in the transition from Israelite faith to Judaism and Christianity. It is a great paradox that both these communities are descended from a Temple-centered faith, yet have no Temple in them. Their understanding of the Temple must be explored very carefully if we are to comprehend them in a profound way." "From Temple to Synagogue: 1 Kings 8," *Traditions in Transformation: Turning Points in Biblical Faith* (B. Halpern, J. Levenson, eds.; Winona Lake, IN: Eisenbrauns, 1981), 164.

[41] Knoppers, "Dedication," 237.

[42] Knoppers considers that there may have been some exilic "retouching" in the last petition, but sees "no reason on the basis of location to deny the existence of a preexilic substratum of this final petition; Knoppers, 237, n. 31. On the reference to the exile, see Knoppers, "Dedication," 248. This perspective is not Knoppers's alone; but is similar to John Gray's view that this refers to the eighth century exile of the Northerners by Assyria, *I and II Kings* (OTL; 2d ed.; Philadelphia: Westminster, 1970).

Josianic era, but he dismisses too quickly arguments supporting its exilic origins.[43] Tryggve Mettinger has mounted a strong argument for the post-597 or exilic provenance of the transcendent view of God found in the exilic Deuteronomistic "name theology," yet Knoppers does not tackle the arguments of Mettinger or others in detail.[44] He denies that 1 Kings 8:41–43 derives from the exilic period, dismissing arguments for its exilic origins in a single footnote.[45]

More compelling are the arguments of Jon Levenson about the compositional history of the chapter. Levenson accepts Frank Cross's theory of the dual edition of the Deuteronomistic History, with the first edition finished in the pre-exilic period at the time of Josiah and the second in the exilic period, perhaps mid-5th century B.C.E.[46] He argues that 1 Kings 8 took its final form during the exilic period. In keeping with the scholarly consensus that 1 Kgs 8:12–13 are a pre-Dtr source, he understands these two poetic verses as the oldest part of the chapter which betray no signs of later redaction. Their distinctive view of God as immanent in the Temple reflects a pre-exilic theology. He views 1 Kgs 8:15–21 as Dtr1 because of its citation of 2 Sam 7:8–16, Nathan's oracle of divine promise to David.[47] Other

---

[43] Consider the following comment of William Schniedewind in his review of Knoppers' book, *Two Nations under God: The Deuteronomistic History of Solomon and the Dual Monarchies, Vol. 1, The Reign of Solomon and the Rise of Jeroboam* (HSM 52; Atlanta: Scholars Press, 1993), in which Knoppers first put forth his theory. "For the most part, Knoppers assigns the prayer's composition to his Josianic redactor. In doing so, however, he should account not only for the composition of this passage, but also that of related texts such as 2 Sam 7:1–6 and especially Deuteronomy 28. Since 1 Kgs 8:14–21 explicitly reworks the Dynastic Oracle, we must ask why it was in need of reworking." "The Problem with Kings: Recent Study of the Deuteronomistic History," *RelStRev* 22 (1996) 24–25.

[44] See Mettinger's monograph, *The Dethronement of Sabaoth: Studies in the Shem and Kabod Theologies* (ConBOT 18; Lund: CWK Gleerup, 1982).

[45] Knoppers cites the commentaries of C. Westermann on Second Isaiah, E. Würthwein and Jones on Kings, and Balentine's work on prayer, but does not discuss their arguments in detail; "Dedication," 247, n.68.

[46] Levenson also provides a succinct review of modern historical-critical scholarship on the compositional question of 1 Kings 8, "From Temple to Synagogue," 152–153. Cross's position on the material in this chapter is that verses 12–21 are attributable to Dtr1 (though quoting older liturgical material in v.12); verses 44–53 are exilic, Dtr; and much of the material in 22–44 is debatable. Cross, *Canaanite Myth and Hebrew Epic* (Cambridge: Harvard University Press, 1973) 252, n.141.

[47] According to Levenson, " . . . 1 Kgs 8:15–21 does not dwell upon 2 Sam 7:8–16 so much as it recreates it, or most of it, without deviation or innovation. Nothing in these verses adds to what we find in Nathan's original prophecy."

parts of the chapter betray a later hand at work because they accord with the changed perspective on the divine promise to David in light of the Exile.

Levenson's more disputable argument is that 1 Kgs 8:23–53 is a unity that comes from the hand of the second Deuteronomistic editor. The principal scholar whose arguments he counters is Alfred Jepsen.[48] Jepsen asserts that 23–43 are pre-exilic and 44–53 are exilic on the basis of five verbal discrepancies between these two pericopes. Levenson successfully calls two of these cases into question, but the other points that Jepsen makes tip the scales in his favor.[49]

"From Temple to Synagogue," 154. Yet Marc Brettler points out two discrepancies between these versions of the Davidic covenant, changes that do literally add to the dimensions of God's promise to David. Brettler bases his assessment on a close comparison of 1 Kgs 8:14–21 and 2 Samuel 7. Brettler argues that the author of these verses was writing with two equally authoritative texts or traditions in front of him; one was Deut 12:11, which concerned centralization in which God chose (בחר) a specific location and that God would put his name there; the other was 2 Samuel 7, concerning the dynastic promise, which refers to God as dwelling (ישב) in the Temple but does not contain the verb בחר. According to Brettler, the author wanted to suggest that the choosing of David and Jerusalem were two events that happened at the same time. Brettler does not propose a specific date for 1 Kgs 8:14–21, but suggests that 2 Samuel 7 comes from a different level of Dtr redaction than do Deut 12:11 and 1 Kgs 8:15–21, thus positing a more complex development for the Dtr History than does Levenson. See his argument in "Interpretation and Prayer: Notes on the Composition of 1 Kings 8:15–53," *Biblical and Other Studies Presented to Nahum M. Sarna in Honour of his 70th Birthday* (Marc Brettler and Michael Fishbane, eds.; Sheffield: JSOT, 1993) 19–22.

48 He also dismisses J. Montgomery's position [(*1 Kings* (Edinburgh: T&T Clark, 1951)] that the different postures of Solomon at the beginning (standing in v. 22) and ending of the prayer (kneeling in v. 54) point to multiple authorship as "the hypercritical eye of a literary critic." Levenson, 156.

49 Jepsen argues that the different referents to נחלה "inheritance," or, as Levenson translates, "special possession," within the prayer point to two authors. In v. 36 נחלה refers to the land of Israel. In 51–53 נחלה refers to the people Israel. Levenson rightly argues that this dual referent to land and people is not unusual and that in fact Deut 4:1–40 refers to God's "special possession" as both land and people. He might also have pointed out the two-fold reference to Israel as God's possession in the core of Deuteronomy, Deut 9:26 and 29. The evidence, in other words, is inconclusive one way or the other. A second point that Levenson attacks is Jepsen's contention that the initial use of the particle כי in 44 and 46 separates them from the other petitions. Levenson argues that the appearance of this particle in vv. 37–40, the fourth petition, negates Jepsen's argument. My own view is that the particle appears in the fourth petition because this was the conclusion of the original prayer. The particle occurs not once, but four times in the fourth petition, a rare

The strongest evidence lies in the two different locations toward which to direct prayer. Levenson suggests that "the meaning is substantially the same, but the diction is not."[50]

Here are the pertinent clauses:

31 ובא אלה לפני מזבחך בבית הזה
33 והתפללו והתחננו אליך בבית הזה
35 והתפללו אל־המקום הזה
38 ופרש כפיו אל־הבית הזה

44 והתפללו אל־יהוה דרך העיר אשר בחרת בה
48 והתפללו אליך דרך ארצם אשר נתתה לאבותם
העיר אשר בחרת

Two features of the last two petitions suggest a different hand and an exilic date. The expression דרך העיר/דרך ארצם is a late expression, a way of expressing "toward" that is absent from the pre-exilic literature. דרך in this sense appears elsewhere only in exilic literature: 2 Chr 18:43, Job 24:18 and (primarily) in Ezekiel (Ezek 8:5, 21:2, 40:6, 10, 20, 22, 41:12, 42:7, 43:1, 2, and 44:3). A second feature of the last two petitions is that they both mention praying on the way to/toward the city *that you have chosen*/to the land that you gave their ancestors, *the city that you have chosen*. The divine election of the city of Jerusalem, as opposed to the more general "place of sacrifice" or to Mount Zion, is a specifically late theological

---

repetition that according to the Massorah parvah occurs in a single verse in only two other instances. We should note that the particle כי is notoriously problematic because of its use not only as a clausal adverb but also as a conjunction introducing various types of subordinate clauses. See B.K. Waltke-M. O'Connor's comments in *An Introduction to Biblical Hebrew Syntax* (Winona Lake, Ind: Eisenbrauns, 1990) 39.3.4e, 665. The fourth petition is the most general, something of a catch-all case, that would have been fitting at the end of the prayer. It also ends with the clause in v. 40 "so that they may live in the land that you gave to our ancestors." This emphasis on the blessing of the land is a common pre-exilic, Dtr 1 theme as Brettler points out, "Interpretation and Prayer," 29. The fourth petition reflects no knowledge of the loss of the land; indeed, it presupposes that an enemy might besiege them in the land. Levenson avoids this complication to his argument by reading with the LXX "if their enemy besiege them in any of their cities" for the MT, "if their enemy besieges them in their land of their settlements." His rationale for accepting some LXX readings and rejecting others (e.g., the omission of the phrase "in all your people Israel" in the next verse) is not made explicit.

[50] Levenson, "From Temple to Synagogue," 154.

motif that argues strongly for a late provenance for these verses.[51] Its absence from the first five petitions does not prove that they are pre-exilic, but it weakens any argument for its unity. The last two petitions thus depart from the first five in their verbal expression as well as their specific theology.

Jepsen notes two other important discrepancies. One is the observation that in 49–50, "hear them in heaven, the place of your dwelling" is separated from "forgive," whereas the two appear next to each other in vv. 34, 36, 39. Another argument for distinguishing more than one author is the difference in grammatical form between ושמעת in vv.45 and 49 vs. אתה שמע in vv.32, 34, 36, 38, and 43. Levenson dismisses both of these differences as inconsequential, but weighed with other evidence pointing to multiple authorship, they are significant.

Levenson's positive arguments for the exilic provenance of the prayer hinge on two sorts of evidence, verbal links to passages that he has argued elsewhere come from Dtr2, and putatively exilic themes in 1 Kgs 8:23–53. Levenson convincingly establishes that there are seven verbal parallels between material in the Dtr2 "frame" of the book of Deuteronomy and parts of Solomon's prayer. He points out that the parallels derive not only from verses 44–53 which most scholars would agree are exilic, but from the core of the prayer as well. He sees an especially strong connection between the speech in Deut 4:1–40 and 1 Kgs 8:23–53.[52] Levenson is correct in saying that the parallels extend beyond the part most scholars would indubitably call exilic. Yet full five of them do come from the last section of the prayer, the seventh case and the conclusion in vv.46–53. One of the other parallels appears in the invocation (1 Kgs 8:23//Deut 4:39), and one appears in the fifth petition in 8:41 (1 Kgs 8:41//Deut 29:21), which concerns foreigners, another case many scholars have viewed as possibly exilic. He does not draw any parallels between the first four petitions and the exilic material from Deuteronomy. Thus the argument Levenson uses for the exilic unity of the prayer is not watertight.

---

[51] On this point, see J.Z. Smith, "Jerusalem: The City as Place," in *Civitas: Religious Interpretation of the City* (P.S. Hawkins, ed; Atlanta: Scholars, 1986) 25–38; *op cit*, Brettler, "Interpretation and Prayer," 29, n.2.

[52] The verbal parallels Levenson locates are 1 Kgs 8:23//Deut 4:39; 1 Kgs 8:41//Deut 29:21; 1 Kgs 8:47//Deut 4:39, 30:1; 1 Kgs 8:48//Deut 30:10; 1 Kgs 8:51//Deut 4:20; 1 Kgs 8:52//Deut 4:7; "From Temple to Synagogue," 160–162. Some of these connections are also noted by H.W. Wolff who also draws parallels from Jeremiah, "Kerygma," 93–95.

Let us consider arguments that the prayer reflects a more complex written history. Marc Brettler refers to the writing and editing of this chapter as "the work of a learned author, who copied and revised other biblical compositions."[53] Close scrutiny supports his view. He argues on literary and grammatical grounds that an original prayer concluded at the end of case four in verse 40 and that the final three cases are a set of separate additions to the original four cases.[54]

Brettler offers evidence of two kinds of "scripturalization" in this prayer. 1 Kings 8:22–53 make references to earlier texts and traditions, and it also shows signs of intratextual interpretation, in other words, that an original core of the prayer was carefully augmented by a later author/editor. Brettler suggests that the last three cases in Solomon's prayer were conscious attempts to interpret and comment upon not only earlier biblical passages, but the first four cases of the prayer. Our own examination of the prayer bears out Brettler's findings that the prayer has a complicated textual history and that the question of dating an original core and subsequent additions and redactions remains open. It seems likely that there was more than one exilic redaction of the prayer.

One level of redaction can be seen in the reuse of Deuteronomy 28 in the prayer. Brettler points out a number of close connections between the first four cases and the curses list of Deuteronomy 28. Similar phraseology can be found, for example, in the following correspondences:

Deut 28:25 יִתֶּנְךָ יְהוָה נִגָּף לִפְנֵי אֹיְבֶיךָ
1 Kgs 8:33 בְּהִנָּגֵף עַמְּךָ יִשְׂרָאֵל לִפְנֵי אוֹיֵב

Deut 28:52 וְהֵצַר לְךָ בְּכָל־שְׁעָרֶיךָ
1 Kgs 8:37 כִּי יָצַר־לוֹ אֹיְבוֹ בְּאֶרֶץ שְׁעָרָיו

---

[53] Brettler, "Interpretation and Prayer," 17.

[54] In what follows, I rely heavily on his observations. See the detailed discussion in his article, cited in note 47 above. He makes five points to support his contention that v. 40 concluded the four cases listed in the original prayer. In my opinion the strongest arguments are 1) the repetition in v. 39 of the phrase found in v. 30, "you will hear and forgive," which acts as an inclusio around the four original cases; 2) the fact that v.40 ends with a motive clause that is a common ending for a Dtr speech: "so that they may live in the land that you gave to their ancestors; and 3) the fact that case 5, v. 41, begins with וְגַם, which is elsewhere used to introduce supplementary material (e.g., Deut 7:20). I would disagree with Brettler's argument for three separate authors for each of the last three cases described in the prayer. I do not think there is sufficient evidence to suggest three distinct authorial hands at work.

He underscores the fact that the correspondences do not extend beyond the first four cases of the prayer in vv. 31–40. What is important from our perspective is that the author of the prayer in 1 Kings 8 is consciously reusing these traditions in a new context.

Another significant feature of the prayer in terms of its use of earlier traditions is its citation of divine promises. In this way it shares an aspect of "scripturalization" that we saw in pre-exilic prayers that contain references or citations of the promise to the patriarchs. There are three promises/assurances cited, in verses 25, 29, and 51–53. Two of these, verses 25 and 29, contain quotations in first-person speech.

1 Kgs 8:25 reads:

> And now O Lord God of Israel, keep (שׁמר) the promise you made to your servant David, my father, saying, "No man will be cut off from before me as one who sits on the throne of Israel, but only if your children watch (שׁמר) their ways to walk before me as you have walked before me."

As Jon Levenson points out, the promise stated in v. 25 is not a verbatim promise as expressed in 2 Sam 7:14–16 and Psalm 89:31–38, but a reinterpreted version of the promise. The promise of dynastic succession to David's descendants as stated in 1 Kings 8:24–25 now stands conditional to the observance of the commandments.[55] There are also signs of other verbal reworking. William Schniedewind has argued that the repetition in verse 25 results from the exegetical and midrashic play on the word "to keep" (שׁמר): "The importance of this technique (*Wiederaufnahme*) here is to underscore the exegetical and even midrashic nature of the textual transformations."[56] Schniedewind observes an important feature of this verse. The divine promise to David is quoted but it also contains some conscious wordplay.

---

[55] In Levenson's words: "The subordination of the Davidic covenant to the Sinaitic in 1 Kgs 8:25, therefore, must be seen as a reinterpretation of the pristine Davidic covenantal material, a reinterpretation that reflects the growing canonical status of the Sinaitic traditions that will become the Pentateuch. 1 Kgs 8:25 is the vengeance of Moses upon David, of the "kingdom of priests" upon the hubris of the political state, for it resolves the clash between the two covenants in favor of the Mosaic one. . .The ultimate implication of the alteration of the promise to David in 1 Kgs 8:25 becomes manifest in the work of the Chronicler, who changes "walking before me" to "walking in my Torah" (2 Chr 6:16)." *Sinai and Zion: An Entry Into the Jewish Bible* (New York: Harper & Row, 1985) 211.

[56] William Schniedewind, "The Problem with Kings," 25.

The second promise quoted in this prayer, which appears in 1 Kgs 8:28–29, concerns the divine promise to David:

> 28. Turn your face to your servant's prayer and his petition, O Lord my God, to listen to the cry and the prayer that your servant prays before you today. 29. that your eyes may be open toward this house night and day, to the place about which you said, "My name will be there."

Like 1 Kgs 8:25, this quote also makes reference to 2 Samuel 7, the Davidic covenant. This quote calls upon the second part of the divine covenant made with David, that the Jerusalem Temple will serve as the dwelling place for the divine name. It is important to note that the words "My name will be there" do not appear in 2 Samuel 7. 2 Sam 7:13 reads: "He will build a house for my name and I will establish the throne of his kingdom forever." The author of the prayer has thus adapted the words of the promise to this new context.

The final two verses of the prayer in 1 Kgs 8:52–53 contain mention of a third divine promise:

> 52. Let your eyes be open to the supplication of your servant and to the supplication of your people Israel to hear whenever they call to you 53. because you have separated them from all the people of the earth for yourself as an inheritance as you promised by the hand of Moses your servant when you, O Lord God, brought our ancestors out of Egypt.

Not only does this verse contain a divine promise, but it also contains an arranged marriage of biblical terminology from two tradition streams. The wording of this statement reflects a combination of priestly (to separate) and Deuteronomistic (special possession) expressions. Solomon states that God's promise was to "separate" Israel from the rest of the nations. The verb used is the Hifil of בדל. Elsewhere, the same construction, with God as subject and Israel as the object, appears only in priestly passages (Lev 20:24, Lev 20:26).[57] Deuteronomic uses of this verb appear only in reference to the separation of the three cities of refuge in Deut 4:41; Deut 19:2,7.[58] The notion of separating Israel from the peoples

---

[57] The verb also appears, although not with God as subject, in connection with the Nazirite vow (Numbers 6) and the separation of the Levites (Numbers 8).

[58] The verb also appears in post-exilic literature in connection with the demand that Israel separate itself from the people of the land; Ezra 1:11; 6:21; 10:8; Neh 9:2; 10:29

appears also in the Holiness Code where it operates on analogy with separating clean from unclean, holy from profane.[59]   Consider Lev 20:24, 26:

24 ואמר לכם אתם תירשו את־אדמתם ואני אתננה לכם
לרשת אתה ארץ זבת חלב ודבש אני יהוה אלהיכם
אשר־הבדלתי אתכם מן־העמים

26 והייתם לי קדשים כי קדוש אני יהוה
ואבדל אתכם מן־העמים להיות לי

In the verses from Leviticus, however, Israel is not referred to as God's inheritance, נחלה , as in 1 Kings 8:53. Rather, that term derives from the Deuteronomistic literature. The term appears in the prayer of Moses in Exod 34:9, for instance: "If now I have found favor in your sight, O Lord, I pray, let the Lord go with us. Although this is a stiff-necked people, pardon our iniquity and our sin, and take us for your inheritance." The phrase is also found in Deut 4:20; and the ancient farmer's "credo" in Deut 26:5–9. The fusion of two theological traditions in the exilic verses of 1 Kgs 8:52–53 marks an important trend in the scripturalization of prayer.

Before concluding our examination of 1 Kgs 8:22–53, we should point out one more important element in this prayer. 1 Kgs 8:47 contains an imbedded, hypothetical "confession." It states that if the people should be taken captive in a foreign land and they repent and say the following confession: "We have sinned; we have done wrong; we have acted wickedly," they will be assured of forgiveness. This suggests that the use of a standard confessional form had developed by the time this prayer was written. Brettler also points out that a similar formula is found in Psalm 106:6, which is commonly held to be an exilic psalm.[60] The use of such a standard formula marks a significant development in liturgical expression.

1 Kings 8 became an important prayer in the body of Israelite tradition. One way to assess its impact is by looking at references to this prayer in later literature.[61] In hindsight, it is easy to understand

---

[59] The holy/profane, clean/unclean dichotomy of course runs through all of the Holiness Code. Cf. Lev 10:10, 11:47, 20:25; similar terminology appears in Ezek 22:26, 42:20.

[60] Brettler, "Interpretation and Prayer," 31.

[61] 2 Chr 20:5–12 is Jehoshaphat's prayer to God which quotes in verse 9 a part of 1 Kings 8, the divine promise to hear and save the people. "You have built a temple for your name, saying "If disaster comes upon us, the sword,

its importance. After the destruction of the First and then the Second Temple, Judaism was forced to make major adjustments in which the practice of prayer eventually assumed a central importance. 1 Kings 8 is the only passage in the Bible that makes the explicit connection between the Temple in Jerusalem and prayer, even providing specific cases in which prayer would be answered. Solomon's prayer occurs at the dedication of the Temple at a point when Israel was unified and at its strongest; its international influence in the ancient Near East was at a peak; and its borders greater than they would ever be. We should point out that Solomon's "prayer" is not so much a petition as a programmatic statement issued by an Israelite king that God should respond in a certain way and help the Israelites in certain situations. As Weinfeld observes, "The prayer of Solomon in 1 Kgs. 8:15ff is in fact not a prayer but a discourse on the function of prayer in Yahweh's chosen place, which sees the temple as an immense house of prayer with its doors open equally to foreigners coming from distant lands (vv.41–3; cf. Isa. 56:6–7)."[62] But for a people in exile or for a people for whom the practice of daily prayer comes eventually to replace the practice of sacrifice, *de facto* if not *de jure* in later rabbinic thought, Solomon's prayer of dedication seemed to offer the reassurance that their own prayers would be answered by God.

Conclusion

How did scripturalization in prayers begin? The evidence from the earliest prayers provides us some hint of how the process first

---

judgment, etc., you will hear and save." Fishbane also mentions this prayer as a notable example of the redeployment of 1 Kings 8:22–53. "Among the variations, one will observe that whereas Solomon refers to himself as the Temple-builder (cf. 1 Kgs. 8:13, 27, 43), Jehoshaphat reflects the Chronicler's all-Israel interest and refers to the Temple as having been built by the people. (cf. 2 Chr. 20:8.)" Fishbane, *Biblical Interpretation*, 386–387, n. 12.

1 Macc 7:37–38 also alludes to 1 Kings 8: "You chose this house to be called by your name, and to be for your people a house of prayer and supplication. Take vengeance on this man and on his army, and let them fall by the sword; remember their blasphemies, and let them live no longer." 2 Macc 2:8 "Then the Lord will disclose these things, and the glory of the Lord and the cloud will appear, as they were shown in the case of Moses, and as Solomon asked that the place should be specially consecrated." Verses 9–12 go on to liken the prayers and the sacrifices offered by Moses to those offered by Solomon. As will be elaborated in chapter 4, 3 Macc 2:10 also makes reference to two passages in 1 Kings 8 as well as 1 Kings 9:3–9. 3 Macc 2:10 calls on God to remember his promise to listen to the prayers made by a repentant people in their distress.

[62] Weinfeld, *Deuteronomy*, 37.

took shape. The roots of scripturalization are to be found in the earliest literary source, the Jahwist literature. The process seems to have started as an attempt by authors or editors to connect various figures or events, focusing on the divine promises made to the patriarchs about land and progeny. Two of the prayers, Gen 32:10–12 and Exod 32:11–13, contain quotations of the divine promise to the patriarchs. One factor involved may be the author's concern to carry a theme through an entire "epic" or literary piece. But we also see the divine promise to the patriarchs alluded to in a Deuteronomic prayer, Deut 9:26–29. Here, the appearance of the promise to the patriarchs in this prayer may simply indicate that the formula had wide currency in Israel and served a different theological *Tendenz*. Another piece of evidence for the earliest scripturalization of prayer appears in the quotation of the divine attribute formula from Exod 34:6–7 in the prayer in Num 14:13–19. The author of Num 14:13–19 was even so bold as to truncate the original divine attribute formula to emphasize God's mercy and compassion rather than God's punishment of human iniquity in succeeding generations. From his perspective, why bring up a sore subject when the pray-er is in dire need of assistance?

A crucial step in the trajectory of scripturalization occurs when the prayer recalls not just an event from the individual pray-er's life experience, but remembers an event from the corporate life of Israel, from the traditional history of the people. Corporate memory separates the remembered past of a people from the lived past of an individual. This remembrance of community history is embodied in all the prayers we have reviewed that contain the seeds of scripturalization, Gen 32:10–12; Exod 32:11–13; Num 14:13–19; and Deut 9:26–29; 21:7–8; and 26:5–10. Pride of place is reserved for divine promises to Israel's ancestors, either the patriarchs or David, for divine self-revelation such as the divine attribute formula of Exod 34:6–7, or remembrance of the Exodus event, the central divine act of redemption on Israel's behalf. We have seen that in the pre-exilic prayers in the earliest strands of the Bible, a major feature of the "scripturalization" of these prayers is the use of promise-and-fulfillment language with an interest in quoting divine speech.

Yet this explanation of the reasons for the earliest scripturalization cannot account for the nature of the scripturalization of 1 Kings 8. What accounts for the great differences between the simple prayers we examined at the outset of the chapter and such long prayers as 1 Kgs 8:23–53? Another crucial step in the trajectory of scripturalization is the conscious process of regarding earlier tradition as written scripture and taking the appropriate step of preserving it or sometimes even revising it in light of new theological insights. In 1 Kgs 8:25, we noticed that such revision had occurred in qualifying the Davidic promise as a result of the Exile. We have discussed the prayer in 1 Kings 8 in depth because it provides a prime example of conscious scripturalization that includes such a compositional process of revision and interpretation of earlier written traditions. The accrual of liturgical traditions around the Temple dedication ceremony proved an important milestone in the evolution of scripturalization in prayer. Moreover, as Levenson points out in his discussion of 1 Kings 8, this prayer marked a significant transition in Judaism. Judaism becomes a tradition of synagogue and house of study, of prayer and learning as opposed to Temple and sacrifice. "Prayer and learning were viewed as the temporary and imperfect continuation of the sacrificial practices once the destruction of the Temple rendered the latter incapable of literal fulfillment."[63] The Talmud mentions that the statutory prayers were established to correspond to sacrifice. Indeed, as Levenson points out, this equation is implicit in 1 Kings 8. In that prayer, the Temple is a house of prayer to which all must turn as they petition God. As Brettler notes, Solomon's prayer functions as a "timeless paradigm" applicable to any period in history.[64]

As we shall see in the post-exilic literature, something clearly seems to have happened in the Jews' relationship to the written word and tradition that resulted in even more dramatic changes in how prayers were composed and the reasons for using earlier traditions. In other words, there are precedents for scripturalization in the pre-exilic period, but the reasons the post-exilic authors used scripture are different from the pre-exilic authors. These are the issues we will address in coming chapters as we look at the scripturalization of prayers in Nehemiah 9, Judith 9, and 3 Maccabees 2.

---

[63] Levenson, "Between Synagogue and Temple," 165.
[64] Brettler, "Interpretation and Prayer," 85.

Chapter 2

Scripturalization in the Telling of History
Nehemiah 9

At the beginning of each summer when the harvest was just beginning to ripen in ancient Israel, each farmer was enjoined to offer some of his first fruits and to recite a prayer before God at the central sanctuary. Considering the circumstances under which it was offered, one might expect this prayer to focus on thanksgiving to God for providing the rich soil, rain, and sunshine necessary to grow these crops.[1] Instead, the prayer begins, "A wandering Aramean was my father, and he sojourned there, few in number; but there he became a great people, mighty and populous." The prayer in Deut 26:5–10 begins in the first person singular, but it is not the story of one individual, rather it evokes the past history of the entire people: their origins, their time in slavery in Egypt, their deliverance and entry into the promised land of milk and honey. The farmer does not just make reference to his individual situation or current events, for the good health that permitted him to cultivate his family's plot of land, for example. He prays in a way that ties him inextricably to a particular history that God has shaped for Israel. Finally, in the last verse, he acknowledges his indebtedness to God directly in the second person: "And now I bring the first fruit of the ground that you have given me, O Lord." This prayer was discussed briefly in the first chapter as one of the forebears of scripturalization. Deut 26:5–10 is a

---

[1] Moshe Weinfeld touches on this point in discussing the "liturgical oration" in the Deuteronomic literature. *Deuteronomy and the Deuteronomic School* (New York: Oxford University Press, 1972) 33.

simple prayer that offers a barebones history of Israel from Abraham
to the entry into the promised land.[2]

The post-exilic prayer of Nehemiah 9:5–37 offers both an
element of similarity and a striking contrast to the prayer of first
fruits offered in Deuteronomy 26. Nehemiah 9 contains a historical
retrospect, yet the prayer is baroque in its intricacies and dimensions.
The task of this chapter is to argue that written traditions—and
interpretive traditions—have become the means by which the past is
recalled. As will become evident, the thirty-three verse composition in
Nehemiah contains numerous allusions to earlier biblical traditions,
as well as interpretations, and citations from scripture. The prayer is
also replete with formulaic biblical phrases describing various divine
attributes. In short, it is steeped in biblical language and is quite
different in form and content from the prayer offered up with the
first fruits of the harvest. The bulk of the chapter will illustrate the
ways in which the prayer in Nehemiah 9 uses earlier scripture in
each section of its historical retelling by providing a nuanced
assessment of its interpretive character. Yet Nehemiah 9 does not
stand alone. The final part of the chapter will situate Nehemiah 9 as
one representative from a flock of Second Temple era prayers that
manifest such scripturalized history.

Nehemiah 9:5–37

The exact relationship of the prayer in Nehemiah 9 to its larger
context rests on a number of disputed questions. The biggest of these
is the relationship of Ezra-Nehemiah to the books of Chronicles.
Second to this is the nature of the composition of Ezra-Nehemiah and
the interrelationship of its parts and their relative sequence. A
complete discussion of the issues in the debate cannot be attempted
here.[3] As for the prayer's more immediate context, yet another

---

[2] Gerhard von Rad viewed this prayer as an ancient "credo" that
summarizes God's divine acts in history on behalf of the Israelites; *Old
Testament Theology*, Vol. 1 (New York: Harper & Row, 1962) 121–128.

[3] There is no consensus on the central issue of whether or not one person or
group of people was responsible for composing all of Chronicles and Ezra-
Nehemiah or whether the outlooks of these compositions, the vocabulary used
within them, and so forth, is sufficiently different to preclude a unitary
authorship. Scholarship on Ezra-Nehemiah has evolved quite dramatically
over the past twenty-five years or so. Sara Japhet and H.G.M. Williamson
overturned the scholarly consensus of a unified authorship for Chronicles and
Ezra-Nehemiah, though their positions have most recently been challenged by
Henri Cazelles and A.H.J. Gunneweg. For the argument against a unifed
authorship based on a careful linguistic study of these books, see Japhet, "The

question remains, was it original to the narrative section in Nehemiah 8–10? H.G.M. Williamson, for instance, argues that the prayer in Nehemiah 9 is an independent composition interpolated into Nehemiah 8–10 at some point.[4] Yet this question, while relevant to the issue of an exact dating of the piece, does not affect the observations in this chapter about the content of the prayer and its use of scripture. Because of internal references to the return from exile and the post-exilic community, it is clear that the prayer dates from that period, perhaps to the mid-fifth century.

The longer narrative section, Nehemiah 8–10, describes a series of acts of public worship in Jerusalem by the reconstituted Jewish community. The context of the prayer in Nehemiah 9 is worth noting because it differs from many of the prayers that will be considered in the course of this study by virtue of the fact that the prayer is offered in a liturgical context. Nehemiah 8 recounts that

---

Supposed Common Authorship of Chronicles and Ezra-Nehemiah Investigated Anew," *VT* 18 (1968) 330–371; as well as her more recent study, *The Ideology of the Book of Chronicles and its Place in Biblical Thought* (Beiträge zur Erforschung des Alten Testaments und des Antiken Judentums 9; Frankfurt: Peter Lang, 1989). So too, H.G. Williamson, *Israel in the Book of Chronicles* (Cambridge: Cambridge University Press, 1977). For counter-arguments, see Henri Cazelles' review of Williamson, *VT* 29 (1979) 375–80 and A.H.J. Gunneweg, "Zur Interpretation der Bücher Esra-Nehemia," *Congress Volume Vienna, 1980* (VTSup. 32; Leiden: Brill, 1981) 146–161.

More recently, in his commentary for the Old Testament Library series, Joseph Blenkinsopp stakes out a position closer to the unitary authorship theory. Japhet and Williamson argue on the basis of linguistic and stylistic reasons as well as divergences in ideology that the two compositions reflect distinctive authors. As his starting point, Blenkinsopp calls into question their methodology for linguistic analysis, in part arguing that because sources constitute 70% of the total narrative in Chronicles, the data base on which they rely is insufficiently large to prove their point. While some of his arguments are sound, he cannot entirely refute strong evidence proffered by Japhet for two distinct authors, including the great divergence in views of the northern tribes, as well as the extraordinary stress on David in Chronicles as opposed to his almost total absence from Ezra-Nehemiah. Though there is not space here to review all the evidence, it seems most likely that the two compositions were authored/shaped by different people or groups, though perhaps editing by a single hand occurred at some point, which would account for certain similarities in ideology between the two (elaborated by Blenkinsopp in his commentary on pages 53–54). For Blenkinsopp's discussion of the relationship of Chronicles to Ezra-Nehemiah, see his commentary, 47–54.

[4] H.G.M. Williamson, "Structure and Historiography in Nehemiah 9," *Proceedings of the Ninth World Jewish Congress.* (Jerusalem: Magnes, 1988) 117; and also in his commentary, *Ezra, Nehemiah* (Waco, TX: Word, 1985) 300ff.

Ezra reads from "the book of the Torah of Moses that the Lord had commanded Israel." And while Ezra reads before the people, the Levites act as interpreters (מבינים) to clarify its sense. This activity in itself reflects a significant stage in the process of the rise of scripture in early Judaism, that is, the importance of an authoritative text from which rules for behavior or norms for festivals are derived, as well as a reliance on oral interpretation that accompanies the written text. On the day after the public reading, there is a study session involving all the people, the priests, and the Levites, during which they realize that they should be observing the festival of Sukkoth.[5] The rest of Nehemiah 8 elaborates on this observance.

Nehemiah 9:1–5 describes a day of confession some days after Sukkoth. On the twenty-fourth day of the month, the people are gathered again and the narrative relates that they separate themselves from foreigners (as part of the preparation for the worship to follow). They then read from the Torah for one-fourth of a day and for another quarter of a day, they confess their sins and pray. It is at that point that the Levites initiate the prayer. Eight Levites recite a blessing (Neh 9:5) which continues with the lengthy prayer of praise and repentance in Neh 9:6–37.

There is one textual problem with significant implications for the rhetorical impact of this prayer. Who leads the prayer, the Levites or Ezra? The answer also determines where the prayer begins, in verse five or verse six. There is evidence on both sides of the question. In the MT, the prayer begins in Nehehiah 9:5b with the Levites exhorting the people to "Rise and bless the Lord your God from everlasting to everlasting," and ostensibly continues through 9:37. The Greek inserts καὶ εἶπεν Εσδρας, "and Ezra said" at the beginning of 9:6. Are we to accept the MT that omits the first phrase of verse 6, "and Ezra said," which would in fact change the force of the prayer? Without these words, which appear only in the Greek, the prayer is left as a continuation of the Levites' praise to God in 9:5. Is it the leader of the community, the priest-scribe Ezra, who is depicted in Nehemiah 9 as offering a prayer of penitence for the community, or are the Levites leading the group in prayer?

Joseph Blenkinsopp offers an observation about the relationship between Nehemiah 9:4–5, the two verses that are clearly pronounced by the Levites, and verses 6–32, the rest of the prayer.

---

[5] The similarity between this "discovery" of the book of Torah with a subsequent observance of a "forgotten" festival and the description of events leading to Josiah's reform in 2 Kings 23 is no doubt not coincidental.

Neh 9:4–5 contains a blessing that is found also at the end of some psalms (see esp. Pss. 41:14; 106:48; 45:18; 72:19; 89:53; 115:18). He suggests that Neh 9:5 was actually distinct from the prayer, which he thinks begins at verse 6: "Since the only example of a similar formulation at the beginning of a psalm or prayer occurs in C's history (1 Chr 29:10), it may also be suggested that the present arrangement of the text is the work of C."[6] Was the placement of this psalm verse a stylistic autograph of "C" (the Chronicler)? On the surface, it seems like a plausible suggestion, but closer examination of the evidence reveals that in fact the opposite may be true, that Neh 9:5 may well be the original beginning of the prayer. This draws into question his secondary conclusion, that the text is necessarily the work of C. He neglects to mention one significant feature of the psalm verses he cites. In each of the verses, the psalm concludes with a few words, either "Amen, Amen" (Ps 41:14, 72:19, 89:53) or "Praise the Lord" (Ps 106:48, 115:18). Thus, although the verses may be similar in form and content to Neh 9:5, they contain formal markers that signal the conclusion of the psalm. A second point to be made against his conclusions is that there are other prayers/blessings, not noted by Blenkinsopp, that *begin* with phrases similar to Neh 9:5. Compare the following:

> Stand up! Blessed are you, O Lord our God, from everlasting to everlasting and blessed be your glorious name, which is exalted above all blessing and praise. (Neh 9:5)[7]

> Blessed be the name of the Lord from now and forevermore. (Ps 113:2)

The prayer in Tobit 3:11–15 begins:

> Blessed are you, merciful God. Blessed is your name forever; let all your words praise you forever.

Tobit 8:5–7 starts in almost the same way:

---

6 Blenkinsopp, *Ezra-Nehemiah*, 296–7.

7 My translation follows H.G.M Williamson's convincing reconstruction of the verse, reading ברוך אתה יהוה אלוהינו for the MT's ברכו את־יהוה אלוהיכם. The first person plural ending, "our God" is supported by the Greek. He also views ויאמר עזרא as a later insertion on internal grounds, because the narrative context emphasizes the role of the Levites, and not Ezra, as contrasted with Nehemiah 8 in which Ezra does play a big role. See Williamson's article "Historiography" 117–118, note 3.

> Blessed are you, O God of our ancestors, and blessed is your name in all generations forever. Let the heavens and the whole creation bless you forever.

So also the blessing in Dan 2:20–23:

> Blessed be the name of God from everlasting to everlasting.

The list could be lengthened, but four examples should demonstrate that this verse is equally at home at the beginning of a prayer and that, in fact, the later literature seems to show a preference for placing such a blessing at the beginning of a prayer.[8] Equally plausible, then, is the theory that the prayer originally did begin with the Levites' call in Neh 9:5 and that this introduction had already become a standard way of beginning a prayer/blessing by the post-exilic period. The occurrence of this verse at the end of numerous Second Temple and Christian prayers thus suggests that there may even have been a shift from placing this blessing at the end to placing it at the beginning of a prayer.

The major English translations have all followed the Greek that portrays Ezra as leader of the prayer. They reflect the consensus view that Nehemiah 9 is part of Nehemiah 8–10 which was originally part of an "Ezra biography," and these three chapters were "misplaced" from their logical place at the end of the book of Ezra. From its current redaction, the readers must understand that Ezra and Nehemiah were contemporaries in Jerusalem and that the Levites offered this prayer to God. The Greek translator read something else, or else had a different text. There is no neat solution to this textual problem, but I accept the shorter reading of the MT as more authentic.[9]

> 5. And the Levites, Jeshua, Kadmiel, Bani, Hashabneiah, Sherebiah, Hodiah, Shebaniah, Pethahiah said: "Stand up!"
>
> Blessed are you, O Lord our God, from everlasting to everlasting and blessed be your glorious name, which is exalted above all blessing and praise. 6. You are the LORD, you alone. You have made the heavens, the heaven of heavens and all their host, the earth and all

---

[8] Cf. also Tob 11:14–15, 13:1; PrAzar 1:4.

[9] See also the discussion of Williamson, who argues that the Hebrew is primary, *Ezra, Nehemiah*, 304.

that is upon it, the seas and all that is in them. You have given life to everything. The host of the heavens worships before you.

7. You are He, the LORD God who chose Abram and brought him out of Ur of the Chaldeans and you made his name Abraham. 8. You found his heart faithful before you and established the covenant with his people, to give the land of the Canaanites, the Hittites, the Amorites, the Perizzites, the Jebusites, and the Girgashites to his descendants. And you established your word, because you are righteous.

9. And you saw the misery of our ancestors in Egypt and heard their cry before the Red Sea. 10. You set signs and miracles before Pharaoh and before all his attendants and before all the people of his land because you knew they acted arrogantly against them [our fathers] and thus you made a name for yourself as it is to this day. 11. You split the sea before them and they crossed in the middle of the sea on dry land, but their pursuers you cast into the depths, like a stone in powerful waters. 12. With a pillar of cloud by day you guided them and a pillar of fire by night to illuminate for them the way they should go. 13. You came down upon Mount Sinai and spoke with them from heaven. And you gave them just ordinances and true laws, good statutes and commandments. 14. Your holy sabbath you made known to them. Commandments and statutes and torah you commanded them by the hand of Moses your servant. 15. You gave them bread from heaven for their hunger and you brought forth water from a rock for their thirst. You told them to enter and possess the land that you had sworn to give them. 16. But they and our ancestors were arrogant and stiffened their necks and did not obey your commandments. 17. They refused to obey and they did not remember the wonders that you performed for them. They stiffened their necks and appointed a leader to return to their servitude in Egypt. But you are a God of forgiveness, gracious and merciful, long-suffering and of abounding faithful love. 18. Even when they made for themselves a molten calf and they said "This is your God who brought you up out of Egypt;" and they did great blasphemies. 19. But you in your great mercy did not abandon them in the desert. The pillar of cloud did not depart from them during the day to guide them on the way and the pillar of fire by night to illlumine for them the path they should travel. 20. You gave your good spirit to give them insight and you did not withhold your manna from their mouths and you slaked their thirst with water. 21. Forty years in the desert you sustained them; they lacked nothing. Their clothes did not wear out; their feet did not swell.

22. You gave them kingdoms and peoples and you apportioned them a corner. They possessed the land of Sihon, the king of Heshbon, and the land of Og the king of Bashan. 23. You multiplied their children like the stars of the heavens and you brought them to the land that you had told their ancestors to enter and possess. 24. The

descendants entered and took possession of the land and you subdued
before them the inhabitants of the land. You gave into their hand the
Canaanites, their kings and the peoples of the land to do with them
according to their whim. 25. They captured fortified cities and fertile
land and they seized houses full of goods: hewn cisterns, vineyards,
olive orchards, and fruit trees in abundance. They ate and were
sated and grew fat. They languished in your great goodness.

26. They were disobedient and rebelled against you and they threw
your torah behind their back and they slew your prophets who
admonished them to return to you and they did great blasphemies.
27. So you gave them into the hand of their oppressors who made
them suffer. And in the time of their suffering they cried out to you
and you heard from heaven. According to your great mercy you gave
them saviors who rescued them from the hand of their oppressors.
28. But when they had rest, they returned to doing wickedness before
you so you abandoned them into the hand of their enemies who
subdued them. They turned and cried out to you. You heard them
from heaven and you delivered them many times according to your
great mercy. 29. You admonished them to make them return to your
torah but they were arrogant and did not listen to your
commandments. They sinned against your ordinances by which a
person shall live if he observes them. But they turned a stubborn
shoulder and they stiffened their neck and did not obey. 30. You were
patient with them for many years. You admonished them by your
spirit through your prophets, but they did not heed so you gave them
into the hand of the peoples of the lands. 31. But in your many
mercies you did not bring an end to them and you did not abandon
them because you are a gracious and merciful God.

32. And now, our God, the great God, the powerful and the awesome,
keeping covenant and faithful love, do not minimize all the hardship
that has come upon us, upon our kings, our officials, our priests, our
prophets, our ancestors and upon all your people from the days of the
kings of Assyria until today. 33. For you are righteous in all that has
come upon us because you have acted faithfully but we have behaved
wickedly. 34. Our kings, our officials, our priests, and our ancestors
did not observe your torah and they did not heed your
commandments and the warnings with which you charged them.
35. Even in their own kingdom and in the great goodness that you
gave them, in the broad and fertile land that you set before them, did
not serve you and they did not turn from their wicked deeds. 36. And
now look, we are slaves today, and the land that you gave our
ancestors in order to consume its fruits and its goodness; lo, we are
slaves upon it. 37. Its great yield goes to the kings that you set over us
for our sins. They rule over our bodies and our livestock according to
their whim and we are in dire straits.

The prayer is divided most broadly into two major parts. 9:5–31
contain a historical retrospect, from the creation to the exile,

highlighting God's role in preserving the Israelites through even their most recalcitrant periods. 9:32–37, which is introduced by the transition, וְעַתָּה, contains a request for God's recognition of their current difficulties and thus, an implicit petition for help.[10]

Summary of contents:

9:5	Levitical exhortation and introductory blessing
6	affirmation of God as creator
7–8	God's choice of Abraham and covenantal grant of land
9–12	account of the Exodus from Egypt
13–14	gift of the Torah at Sinai
15–21	wilderness wandering, Israelite disobedience with molten calf incident
22–25	conquest and settlement of the land
26–31	disobedience during period of judges and monarchy leading to exile
32–37	present circumstances of slavery in their land leads them to confess their sinfulness in the present as in the past

This summary indicates at a glance the prayer's emphasis by the choice of elements that are included in the retelling of history and the amount of space devoted to each. The prayer moves from an affirmation of God as creator of heaven and earth, to the divine choice of Abraham and the promise of the land, to a lengthy account of the Exodus-Sinai-wilderness wandering. Then follow a short account of the conquest, an abbreviated description of the period of the judges and the monarchy with a reference to the exile, and finally a transition to the present period of affliction. The prayer is characterized predominantly by two emphases: the greatness and transcendence of God and the failure of the Israelites to uphold the covenant and their resulting need for repentance.

Scripturalization in Nehemiah 9

While the general thrust of the prayer is clear from looking at its principal elements, the finer points regarding its use of scripture and its scriptural interpretation are not. The prayer is a deftly woven fabric of scripture and traditions. Although many scholars have referred to this prayer, along with the "late prose prayers" in Daniel 9, Ezra 9, and Baruch 1–2 as Deuteronomistic, this characterization

---

[10] Blenkinsopp terms this part of the prayer a petition, *Ezra-Nehemiah*, 301.

is true only in terms of the prayer's most prominent themes.[11] The reasons generally given for this description are the prayer's use of Deuteronomic language and its theme that ties Israelite obedience or disobedience to the possession or loss of the land.[12] This influence cannot be denied, yet to describe the prayer simply as Deuteronomistic is to mischaracterize it by anachronism. The prayer draws on a wide range of scripture and themes and thus any reference to the prayer as "Deuteronomistic" requires considerable qualification. In an attempt to locate the segment of the Judean community responsible for its composition, H.G.M. Williamson has carefully qualified how Nehemiah 9 differs from deuteronomic ideology. He recognizes the term deuteronomistic as a notoriously "elastic designation."[13] The prayer also reflects a development of

---

[11] Martin Noth views Ezra-Nehemiah as the work of the Chronicler. Sara Japhet, who called into question the unified authorship of Chronicles-Ezra-Nehemiah, views Nehemiah 9:9–21 as a piece written in the spirit and style of Deuteronomy; *The Ideology of the Book of Chronicles and Its Place in Biblical Thought*, (New York: Peter Lang, 1989) 384. Japhet goes on to suggest, however, that the view of the Exodus as a principle of faith and testimony to God's greatness that is suggested by Nehemiah 9, is in sharp contrast to that presented by the Chronicler who downplays the significance of the Exodus, 385–386. For an overview of the problem of reconstructing the chronology of Ezra-Nehemiah, see Ralph Klein, "Ezra and Nehemiah in Recent Studies," *Magnalia Dei: The Mighty Acts of God* (Garden City, NY: Doubleday, 1976) 361–376.

[12] This shorthand description of the prayer is found in most introductions to the Bible in which Nehemiah 9 is grouped together with Ezra 9, Nehemiah 1, Daniel 9 and Baruch 1:15–3:8 under the same rubric, but the characterization is often found even in commentaries and specialized articles on the book of Nehemiah. Too often, this characterization is derived from an excessively broad generalization about the character of "Deuteronomistic." For instance, Joseph Blenkinsopp suggests that a basic theme of the Deuteronomistic history is shared by the prayer in Nehemiah 9, namely that "God is faithful to his covenant commitment and that therefore the disasters of history must be due to human failure not divine indifference." *Ezra-Nehemiah*, (OTL; Philadelphia: Westminster, 1988), 307. This generalization might be helpful as a way of categorizing a work as Deuteronomistic, but it calls into question its utility. Outside of the books of Job, Qohelet, and Esther, the theme of human finitude and failure in the face of divine commitment and subsequent disappointment is a dominant theme in the Bible. The Jahwist's portrayal of Adam and Eve's escapade in Eden might also fall under Blenkinsopp's general rubric, as might portions of the book of Numbers (clearly not Deuteronomistic material) in which the Israelites rebel in the wilderness.

[13] See his article, "Structure and Historiography in Nehemiah 9," in *Proceedings of the Ninth World Jewish Congress*. He also contrasts the character of the prayer in Nehemiah 9 with the rest of Ezra and Nehemiah,

interpretive tradition that takes it beyond Deuteronomistic bounds and gives the prayer its own unique flavor that reveals a more complex relationship to scripture and tradition than is suggested by the oft-used description, "Deuteronomistic" or "late prose prayer." Jacob Myers lists some of the many scriptural parallels to each verse of Nehemiah 9:6–37.[14] His list does in fact contain a disproportionate number of citations from the book of Deuteronomy and the Deuteronomistic history, but it also contains allusions to the Priestly literature, from the latter prophets, and the Psalms.[15] Alone among modern commentators, Joseph Blenkinsopp has noted the significance of the inclusion of Priestly traditions in this prayer. The prayer also contains some extra-biblical elements that reflect a certain degree of growing interpretive tradition that accompanied the transmission of Israel's scripture. A closer examination of how the reinterpretation of scriptural tradition occurs will thus illuminate the precise character of the prayer.

Creation
> 6. You are the LORD, you alone. You have made the heavens, the heaven of heavens and all their host, the earth and all that is upon it, the seas and all that is in them. You have given life to everything. The host of the heavens worships before you.

The retelling of history in the prayer that begins with an account of God as creator reflects the author's familiarity with the priestly account of creation. This is where scripture, and in it the story of the post-exilic community, begins. The verse contains no overt citations from Gen 1:1–2:4, but the phrase "heavens and all their host" derives from Gen 2:1. The understanding of what happened at creation goes beyond what lies in the priestly account. It incorporates elements from elsewhere in scripture, in particular, the

arguing that its distinctiveness suggests authorship by a poorer part of the Judean community that was never exiled to Babylon, 129–130.

[14] Jacob M. Myers, *Ezra-Nehemiah*, (AB; Garden City, NY: Doubleday, 1965), 167–169.

[15] In his commentary, Jacob Myers provides a partial list of biblical sources used in each verse of Nehemiah 9:6–37; however, he does not discuss the nature of the sources and how they are reemployed in the prayer. Michael Fishbane discusses many different kinds of inner-biblical interpretation in his lengthy treatment of the phenomenon, but although he deals with the issue of the reuse and transformation of liturgical formulae in the Bible, he does not treat the reinterpretation of haggadic material found in prayers. Michael Fishbane, *Biblical Interpretation in Ancient Israel* (New York: Oxford University Press, 1985), especially 329–334.

Deuteronomistic literature. The prayer begins with a monotheistic affirmation that the Lord is God alone, an assertion common in the late biblical material. It appears in Hezekiah's prayer during the siege of Sennacherib (2 Kgs 19:15, 19) as well as in the exilic framing chapters of the book of Deuteronomy, (Deut 4:35).[16] Not only is the "incomparability" of God suggested, as many commentators point out, but the word לבדו points to a radical monotheism. Thus the greatness and transcendence of God as the one responsible for the created order is already emphasized in the first verse of the prayer. Israel's God is not only the national deity of a particular people known through covenant, but in fact the creator of the entire cosmos, the universal God.[17] Another phrase also reflects a reliance on phraseology outside of the creation account: את־השמים שמי השמים. This is a distinctive phrase found only in three places: Deut 10:14, 1Kgs 8:27, and its parallel in 2 Chr 6:18, Solomon's prayer of dedication for the Temple. It thus qualifies as having a Deuteronomistic character. The phrase here in Nehemiah is slightly modified to include both the heavens *and their host*. The mention of the creation of the צבאם also sets up the final phrase of the verse which contains a subtle but significant trace element of interpretion.

The final phrase of the verse requires special attention: "The host of the heavens worships before you," וצבא השמים לך משתחוים. Verse six presupposes the priestly creation account of Gen 1:1–2:4a, yet celestial beings worshipping the creator are not found in any part of the priestly or Jahwistic creation accounts in Genesis 1–3. Rather, this image is the trace of an interpretive tradition that the "host of heaven," here meaning the angels, was created for the purpose of praising God continuously. By the post-exilic period, this tradition was already well-developed, but its roots can be discerned in earlier biblical texts.

The reference to heavenly creatures surrounding God has hoary ancient Near Eastern origins in the polytheistic concept of a divine council. A number of scholars have devoted considerable attention to the evaluating the relationship between Mesopotamian

---

[16] The same concept in different words is expressed in Second Isaiah (e.g., Isaiah 45:22 ואין עוד).

[17] Moshe Weinfeld suggests that the creation element became important in "the exilic and post-exilic liturgy," citing Jer. 32:17, Neh 1:5, Neh 9:6, 1 Chr 29:2, 2 Chr 2:11; 20:6; 3 Macc 2:3; *1 Enoch* 84:2–6 and the doxologies of Isaiah; *Deuteronomy*, 39. Weinfeld uses the term liturgy loosely and does not indicate in what ways these various pieces would have been incorporated into actual religious services, communal or individual.

texts describing the council of the gods and the Israelite adaptation of it.[18] Ugaritic literature in particular contains descriptions of the divine retinue—whose job is a *judicial* one—to assist the chief god El in rendering judgments and deciding the fate of the world.[19] As it appears in this verse, however, the ancient Near Eastern roots are completely obscured. The divine beings have been transformed, so that the council is now a host of subservient and worshipful beings whose premier task is to glorify God in response to the divine act of creation. The interpretive transformation of the Ugaritic divine council into the angelic hosts proclaiming the glory of God is complex and cannot be detailed here. What is important to mention, however, are some earlier and contemporaneous texts that depict this presumed divine liturgy.

There are a number of biblical texts that contain references to the angelic praise of God in connection with the creation. Psalm 148 calls on all the created order to praise God, in the first verse calling on those in the heavens. The second verse continues: "Praise him, all his angels; praise him all his host." Psalm 103 contains a similar theme.

---

[18] See the seminal studies of Thorkild Jacobsen, "Primitive Democracy in Ancient Mesopotamia," *JNES* 2 (1943) 159–172 and F.M. Cross, "The Council of Yahweh in Second Isaiah," *JNES* 12 (1953) 274–277. See also Patrick D. Miller, Jr., *The Divine Warrior in Early Israel* (Cambridge, MA: Harvard University Press, 1973) especially 12–23; 66–73. For a thorough discussion of many aspects of the relationship between Canaanite and Israelite literatures, consult Cross's study *Canaanite Myth and Hebrew Epic* (Cambridge: Harvard University Press, 1973). For a discussion of the appropriation of the concept of the Council of Yahweh in prophetic literature, see H. Wheeler Robinson, "The Council of Yahweh," *JTS* 45 (1944) 151–157. For a more recent treatment of the divine council, see E. Theodore Mullen, Jr. *The Divine Council in Canaanite and Early Hebrew Literature* (HSM 24; Chico, CA: Scholars Press, 1980) and his article, "Divine Assembly," *ABD* II, 214–217.

[19] The Ugaritic term for the divine assembly appears variously as *pḫr bn ʿilm* (e.g., KTU 1.47.29; 1.148), *mpḫrt bn ʿill* (e.g., KTU 1.65, 1.40), *pḫr mʾd* (KTU 1.2), and *dr ʿil/dr bn ʿil* (e.g., KTU 1.65, 1.41). The biblical references to the divine assembly do not use a cognate to *pḫr*, but rather *ʿedâ*, or *dôr*, cognate to the Ugaritic *dr*.

1 Kgs 22:19–22 is one biblical passage that scholars have suggested reflects the Ugaritic conception of the divine council. In the Israelite appropriation of the divine assembly, the prophet is understood to have taken over the function of the messenger of the assembly to the human sphere. In this pericope, the prophet Micaiah ben Imlah as the divine messenger reports his vision of the heavenly throne to King Ahab and King Jehoshaphat. In that case, צבא שמים, the host of heaven, is not described as worshiping (משׁתחוים) God; rather, they stand (עמד) before God who consults them about how to waylay King Ahab. Psalm 82 also describes the scene of God holding court with the divine council.

Although it does not state explicitly that the heavenly hosts have praised God from creation, the psalmist does call upon the angels, his hosts, his ministers, and all his works to join in the heavenly liturgy and bless the Lord (vv. 20–22). God's so-called "answer" to Job in chapter 38 also contains a reference to this heavenly liturgy. In Job 38:7, God responds to Job's complaints with a question, asking Job where he was at the time of creation, when "the stars of the morning sang together and all the sons of God raised a joyous sound." Psalm 29 also contains an image of the בני אלים, the sons of God, worshiping the Creator. The later stages of the transformation, which occur mainly in later Second Temple literature, rely on the two prophetic call narratives that depict scenes of the divine throne, Isaiah 6 and Ezekiel 1.

The significance of this interpretive tradition in the context of our discussion of Nehemiah 9 is twofold.[20] The first point relates to the question of the "Deuteronomistic" character of the prayer. There is clear Deuteronomistic influence on the attributes used to describe God as creator; however, by including the recognition of angelic beings, the prayer departs from what might be called "Deuteronomistic theology," which is strictly monotheistic, and opposes any hint of idolatry. A comment in this regard should also be made about the use of the Hebrew צבא השמים, the host of heaven, in this context. Of the seventeen times the phrase appears in the Bible, fourteen of them use the phrase in a negative context, in reference to idolatrous worship.[21] They appear primarily in the Deuteronomistic literature.[22] The transformation here is especially striking when compared to 2 Kgs 17:16, part of the passage describing the sins of the Israelites during the time of Ahaz, in which the Israelites are condemned for worshiping all the host of heaven.[23] The phrase in

---

[20] Moshe Weinfeld argues that in expositing Exodus 14 and 23, the author of Deuteronomy 4 and 7 purposely omits the role of a mediating angel in the Exodus in keeping with the strict monotheism Deuteronomic theology embodies. Weinfeld suggests that Nehemiah 9 is one of what he calls late "liturgical orations" in which the Deuteronomic emphasis on the Exodus-election-covenant is supplemented with the creation motif; *Deuteronomy* 34.

[21] The fourteen instances where the host of heaven appears as threat of idolatry: Deut 4:19, 17:3; 2 Kings 17:16; 21:3,5; 23:4,5; Isa 34:4; Jer 8:2; 19:13; 33:22; 2 Chr 18:18; 33:3; Zeph 1:5. One other is the occurrence in 1 Kings 22, when Micaiah ben Imlah sees the heavenly court; the other is a reference in Daniel 8 that occurs in the context of Daniel's vision of a goat.

[22] Other phrases for the divine council can be found in Ps 89:7–8, בני אלים, "sons of God," and סוד קדשים, "council of holy ones."

Nehemiah thus suggests a new use of this phrase; in a sense the host of heaven has been domesticated, robbed of its threatening role as an idolatrous temptation, and placed at the service of the Divine King himself.[24]

The inclusion of this tradition is also significant because it indicates that the author of the prayer was aware of an interpretive motif that linked God's creation with an angelic liturgy. It is impossible to know exactly how well-developed the interpretation was at the point when Nehemiah 9 was written. The references to the angelic liturgy from earlier and contemporaneous texts adduced above suggest that it was a well-known tradition by the time this author wrote. The reference in the prayer's account of the creation appears almost offhand, suggesting that it had already become a well-integrated part of the tradition by this point. A long list of texts could be compiled, from the Apocrypha, from Qumran, from early Christian and rabbinic writings, all of which postdate Nehemiah 9, that contain more elaborate descriptions of the angelic praise than appears in this terse phrase in Nehemiah 9.[25] The point here is to

---

[23] So too in 2 Kgs 21:3//2 Chr 33:3, Manasseh is described as worshiping the host of heaven as his father Ahaz had done.

[24] It is important to note the unique and subtle interpretive use of this image by the author. Elsewhere in this interpretive tradition, God is depicted as a king, the visions in Isaiah 6 and Ezekiel 1 are of the divine throne—royal imagery is an integral part of this tradition. Yet this royal element is missing from the creation account in verse 6. In fact, God is never referred to as king in the entire prayer. It seems that this royal theology has become an embarrassment to the author, perhaps in the absence of any clear successor to the Davidic throne and in the Jews' situation of subjugation to foreign kings in the post-exilic period.

[25] There are many other references to this interpretive tradition in Second Temple texts. The Prayer of Manasseh, which also describes God's role in creation, states toward the end that "the host of heaven sings your praise." Later Second Temple literature contains a more elaborate description of the angelic worship of God. The book of *Jubilees* presupposes an angelic hierarchy. According to *Jub.* 2:1–3, all of the different ranks of angels were created on the first day and their immediate response upon seeing the divine creation was to worship God: "Then we saw his works and we blessed him and offered praise before him on account of all his works because he made seven great works on the first day." The interpretive tradition of heavenly worship was also well known at Qumran, evidenced in the *Hodayot*, and in full-blown form in *11QShirShabb*. The *Angelic Liturgy*, thought to date to the first century B.C.E., reflects an elaborate form of this tradition, which is based on imaginative interpretations of biblical passages that depict the heavenly throne. The liturgy contains the angelic songs of praise for God assigned to the first thirteen sabbaths of the year, but it also contains obscure descriptions of

indicate that Nehemiah 9 shows clear signs of familiarity with this tradition. This "evidence" can be understood in one of two ways: either the author knew of much more elaborate traditions regarding the angelic liturgy and chose to include only this brief reference to it, or at the time Nehemiah 9 was composed, this interpretive tradition was still in its early, formative stages.

Abraham and the Divine Promise

> 7. You are He, the LORD God who chose Abram and brought him out of Ur of the Chaldeans and you made his name Abraham. 8. You found his heart faithful before you and established the covenant with his people, to give the land of the Canaanites, the Hittites, the Amorites, the Perizzites, the Jebusites, and the Girgashites to his descendants. And you established your word, because you are righteous.

The prayer moves from the creation tradition to speak of Abraham, and Abraham alone, among the patriarchs. The presentation of the Abraham tradition is interesting in a number of ways. Four incidents in Abraham's life are alluded to in verses 7–8, recognizable either by the distinctive vocabulary used or the particular incident mentioned in each. Their order is as follows: God chose Abraham and brought him out of Ur of the Chaldeans (Genesis 12); God changed Abram's name to Abraham (Genesis 17); and found Abraham's heart faithful before him (Genesis 22); and God

---

the heavenly Temple, the divine throne chariot, and the different groups of beings participating in this collective praise. See Carol Newsom, *Songs of the Sabbath Sacrifice: A Critical Edition* (Harvard Semitic Studies 27; Atlanta: Scholars Press, 1985).

This tradition became widely accepted in Christian and gnostic circles as well. The introduction to the Magnificat in Luke 2:13 reflects this background: "And suddenly there was with the angel a multitude of the heavenly host, praising God and saying . . .". For more, see Karl Erich Grözinger, *Musik und Gesang in der Theologie der frühen jüdischen Literatur* (Tübingen: Mohr-Siebeck, 1982), chapter 2.

Cf. also such liturgical poems (still in use today) in which each word begins with a successive letter of the [Hebrew] alphabet: Blessed God, great of knowledge/ prepared and wrought sun's brilliance// Formed skillfully glory for His Name/ placed luminaries about His Might// Chiefs of holy throngs/ praising God endlessly / recount to God His holiness. Translation from James L. Kugel, *The Idea of Biblical Poetry* (New Haven: Yale University Press, 1981), 312. The motif has continued to be a part of worship in Judaism and Christianity in which human participation in the divine liturgy is signaled by recitation of the Qedushah in traditional Jewish prayer and the Trishagion in traditional eucharistic liturgies.

made a covenant with Abraham to give to his descendants the land of
the Canaanites, Hittites, Amorites, Perizzites, Jebusites, and the
Girgashites (Genesis 15). The order thus does not follow the sequence
of events as they are narrated in the book of Genesis. The alteration of
the biblical order suggests that the final "punchline" of the Abraham
traditions for the author lies in the promise of the land. The
possession of the land is a major concern of the prayer, one that is
reiterated throughout the prayer.

There are numerous subtle interpretive changes knit into the
presentation. The first relates to the choice of Abraham, specifically
the use of בחר with Abraham as the object. The verb calls upon the
election language that is used in certain sections of the Bible, almost
exclusively in the book of Deuteronomy and Second Isaiah. Yet
nowhere else in the Bible is this verb coupled with Abraham as its
object. The seed/progeny of the patriarchs is mentioned twice in
Deuteronomy as the object of the divine choice. So too in the book of
Deuteronomy and three times in Second Isaiah, Israel/Jacob serve
the same role. Just as frequently, the divine choice refers to the place
of sacrifice in which God chooses to make his name dwell, in other
words the Temple, or the city of Jerusalem. But overwhelmingly in
the Bible, David is referred to as the chosen one (eleven times), as in
Psalm 89:4 in which the Davidic covenant is also recalled. The phrase
in Neh 9:7 is therefore anomalous. In Neh 9:7, however, God is
described with the relative clause אשר בחרת באברם. What is the
significance of the unique use of בחר? It suggests for one that the
author was not relying solely on the text of Genesis 12 in writing the
verse, although the reference to the departure from Ur is described
in that chapter. Rather, the author knows the story well but wants to
put a distinctive spin on the tradition. The rest of the character of this
spin will become clear by examining other parts of the Abraham
tradition appropriated by Nehemiah.

These two verses emphasize the divine agency guiding
Abraham's life. God is the subject of all the verbs in Neh 9:7–8, not
Abraham. Abraham does not leave Ur of the Chaldeans on his own;
rather, God brings him out from Ur. The wording of 7c is not actually
found in Genesis 12. At the beginning of that chapter, God simply
commands Abraham to leave, and Abraham gathers his family and
obeys. Though Neh. 9:7 refers to the events of Genesis 12, the actual
wording in clause 7c והוצאתו מאור כשדים shares the language of

Gen 15:7a.[26] In Genesis 15, the phrase appears as part of God's self-identification to Abram, "I am the Lord who brought you out of Ur of the Chaldeans. . ." In Neh 9:7, the phrase occurs in the second person; the prayer identifies God as the one who brought Abram out of Ur. God's self-identification in Gen 15:7 concludes: ". . . in order to give you this land to possess." The promise of the land is also emphasized in Neh 9:8, although there, the promise is not narrowly focused on Abraham, but extended to his descendants. It cannot be stated with certainty that in using this phrase, "who brought you out of Ur of the Chaldeans," the author intended to allude to the entire passage in Genesis 15 detailing God's covenant with Abraham and gift of the land. Yet this allusion seems likely, given the emphasis on the gift of the land not just in verses 7–8 but throughout the entire prayer. Another reason to support this source identification is that Gen 15:7 is divine speech to Abraham. As will be illustrated, the prayer reflects a pattern that draws upon divine promises and divine speech in order to "play back" some of these promises in the course of this petition. Neh 9:8a reads "and you found his heart faithful (לבבו נאמן) before you." This reference is ambiguous. On one hand, the source seems to lie in the wording of Gen 15:6, והאמן ביהוה ויחשבה לו צדקה.[27] Yet when this phrase is compared with later Second Temple interpretations of the Abraham tradition, the reference points to Genesis 22, when Abraham obediently moves to sacrifice his son when God tests him. In fact, the reference to being found faithful may well allude to the larger interpretive tradition developing alongside the Genesis literature that Abraham was tested by God not once, but a number of times.[28] This is suggested in a number of other

---

[26] Jacob Weingreen suggests that the use of the word הוצאתיך in regard to Abraham is meant specifically to connect Abraham's trek out of Ur with the Exodus event as "part of the stock of traditional terms used to convey the Exodus;" as noted in Michael Fishbane, *Biblical Interpretation*, 376. This is quite likely because of the frequency with which God is used as subject of the verb in reference to the Exodus event. The Hiphil form of the verb is used over sixty times throughout all strata of the Pentateuch and the former prophets in reference to God's action in delivering the people from Egypt, far outweighing its use in other instances.

[27] This is how the reference is understood by Jon D. Levenson, *The Death and Resurrection of the Beloved Son* (New Haven: Yale University Press, 1993) 175.

[28] At the annual meeting of the SBL, November 1996, Gerald T. Sheppard presented a paper on Nehemiah 9 that confirmed a number of my own insights contained in this chapter, including the perception that Neh 9: 8 makes reference to the Akedah.

books. In extolling Abraham as one of Israel's great heroes, Ben Sira 44:20 states that "he (God) established the covenant in his flesh, and when he was tested he was found faithful." The Greek here is καὶ ἐν πειρασμῷ εὑρέθη πιστός. Ben Sira refers to two different matters: the covenant of circumcision in Genesis 17 and either the sacrifice of Isaac in Genesis 22, which in the first verse states that God tested Abraham (והאלהים נסה את אברהם), or more generally the testing tradition as a whole. Although Abraham is never explicitly called "faithful" in Genesis 22, more support for this connection between Abraham's "test" with the near-sacrifice of Isaac as a sign of his faith can be found in other late literature.

Jubilees contains the earliest most complete account of the purported testing of Abraham. *Jubilees* 17:15–18:19 recounts the sacrifice of Isaac. In this version, however, the test of Abraham is precipitated by a wager that the satanic figure Mastema makes with God, a scene likely influenced by the prologue of Job: "Behold, Abraham loves Isaac, his son. And he is more pleased with him than everything. Tell him to offer him as a burnt offering upon the altar. And you will see whether he will do this thing. And you will know whether he is faithful in everything in which you test him."[29] Jub 17:16 makes an explicit connection between Abraham's faithfulness and his testing in the affair with Isaac. The passage mentions six other such "tests" of Abraham, that God tested him with his land (Genesis 13), and with famine (Genesis 12), with the wealth of kings (Genesis 14), with his wife when she was taken from him (Genesis 12, 20), with circumcision (Genesis 17), and with Ishmael and Hagar, in sending them away (Genesis 16). According to *Jubilees*, the sacrifice of Isaac is the seventh test of Abraham. There is no specific mention of the eighth and ninth tests, but the tenth test is Abraham's behavior in buying the cave of Machpelah for Sarah's burial place. In connection with the final test mentioned, *Jubilees* 19:8–9 contains language close to Nehemiah 9:8a.

> This is the tenth trial with which Abraham was tried. And he was *found faithful*, controlled of spirit. And he did not say a word concerning the rumor which was in the land that the LORD said he would give it to him and to his seed after him, but he begged a place there so that he might bury his dead because he was *found faithful* and he was recorded as a friend of the LORD in the heavenly tablets.

---

[29] This excerpt is taken from Orval Wintermute's translation of the book of *Jubilees*, in Charlesworth's *Old Testament Pseudepigrapha*, II (Garden City, NY: Doubleday, 1985) 92.

This passage underscores the connection between Abraham's faith and the trials he endures for God. More evidence for this interpretive tradition is found in 1 Maccabees, which dates from the late second/early first century B.C.E. In 1 Maccabees 2:52, when Mattathias is ready to die, he exhorts his children to remember the deeds of their ancestors: "Was not Abraham found faithful when tested, and it was reckoned to him as righteousness?" (Αβρααμ οὐχὶ ἐν πειρασμῷ εὑρέθη πιστός, καὶ ἐλογίσθη αὐτῷ εἰς δικαιοσύνην;) The last clause comes directly from Gen 15:6. The origin of the first clause is not so clear because it contains a reference both to testing (Gen 22:1) and to Abraham's faith, which seems to echo Gen 15:6a. Yet there is another way of understanding this reference to testing in 1 Maccabees. Like the more explicit passage reviewed above in *Jubilees*, this verse could be a construal of the Abraham tradition in which a number of events in the life of Abraham are considered tests, including the war with the foreign kings in Genesis 14, for which he was "rewarded" in Genesis 15. While it is difficult to know what the author of 1 Maccabees had in mind, the verse clearly contains a studied reflection on the stories of the Abraham traditions.

The New Testament also contains this depiction of Abraham as a knight of faith though not with this "ten trials" tradition explicitly stated. Hebrews 11 contains a list of Old Testament exemplars of faith. As examples of his faithfulness, the chapter includes Abraham's departure from Ur (Genesis 12/Heb 11:8); his sojourn in Canaan as a tent-dweller (Genesis 12/Heb 11:9); his ability to have a son with Sarah (Genesis 21/Heb 11:11); and finally, the sacrifice of Isaac (Genesis 22/Heb 11:17a: "By faith Abraham, when put to the test, offered up Isaac." (Πίστει προσενηνοξεν Ἀβραὰμ τὸν Ἰσαὰκ πειραζόμενος καὶ τὸν μονογενῆ προσέφερεν.)

Having reviewed texts that link the tests of Abraham to his faith, the oblique reference in Nehemiah 9 that God "found his heart faithful before him" would seem to refer either to the episode in Genesis 22 or perhaps to the developing interpretive tradition about Abraham's ten tests. Given the fact that the three other clauses in verses 7–8 refer specifically to discrete incidents in Abraham's life, it would seem likely that the author had in mind one specific incident in mentioning Abraham's "faithful heart."

The second half of verse 8 mentions God's covenant with Abraham in which God promises to give him and his descendants the land. The literal expression "to cut a covenant" כרת ברית, which is found in Neh 9:8, also occurs in Gen 15:18.[30] In Neh 9:8, God is also affirmed as righteous and hence as a sound guarantor of the covenantal agreement.[31] The description of God's relationship with Abraham and especially the gift of the land sets the tone for the rest of the prayer in which a concern with the Israelites' possession of the land is a recurring theme.[32] An important feature of this interpretation is that God's covenantal grant of the land is not described as contingent on behavior. In Genesis 17, circumcision of all males is required as the Israelite part of the covenant, yet even in that version of the covenant the penalty for failing to observe the commandment of circumcision is for an individual to be cut off from the people, not loss of the land. Though the Israelites' disobedience and subsequent punishment is mentioned at regular intervals throughout the prayer (9:26–27; 28–34), the punishment never entails the loss of the *proprietorship* of the land. Although the Exile is mentioned euphemistically in Nehemiah 9:30 in terms of the Israelites' being placed in the hands of the peoples of the lands (ותתנם ביד עמי הארצת), the prayer still affirms the Israelites' ancestral claim to the land even as its fruits are being taken by foreign overlords. According to the prayer, punishment for disregarding the divine commandments entails living under foreign domination, as opposed to losing "title" to the land.

The alteration of the Abraham tradition as it occurs in Neh 9:7–8 is subtle, yet it sets the tone for the rest of the prayer. The author demonstrates intimate knowledge of the scripture of Israel. The importance of Abraham in Israel's history is that through him God forged an agreement giving Israel inalienable claim to the land with the security that the claim would be safeguarded by a true and righteous God. The point is underscored in Nehemiah 9:7 by the use of the verb choose, בחר, in reference to Abraham. As noted above, God's special choosing was reserved for objects of great importance to

---

[30] There are two terms for establishing the covenant in the Priestly version. Gen 17:14 uses the expression "to set up a covenant," נתן ברית. "To establish a covenant" הקים ברית occurs in Gen 17:7, 19.

[31] The affirmation צדיק אתה occurs also in Jer 12:1, Psalm 119:137, Ezra 9:15. It occurs in the third person in Lam 1:18. Cf. also *1QH* 14:15. J.M. Meyers, *Ezra-Nehemiah* (AB 14; Garden City, NY: Doubleday, 1965) 167.

[32] Maurice Gilbert counts thirteen occurrences of "the land" in the prayer, "La place de la loi dans la prière de Néhémie 9," in M. Carrez, J. Doré , and P. Grelot, eds. *De la Tôrah au Messie. Mélanges Henri Cazelles* (Paris: Gabalda, 1981) 310.

the history of Israel. The verb is used most frequently in reference to the choice of David, the people, and the central place of sacrifice. The choice of word used here thus carries weighty significance. The theme of the unique possession is reinforced throughout the prayer by repeated mention of the land as a promised gift. In this post-exilic piece, an inalienable claim to the land has become a crucial issue, as does the continued obedience of the people as a necessary condition to independence on that land, free from foreign domination. The land is mentioned in several additional places throughout the prayer:

9:15a:
And you told them to enter and possess the land that you had sworn to give them;

9:22b–24a:
And they possessed the land of Sihon and the land of the king of Heshbon and the land of Og, the king of Heshbon. And you multiplied their children like the stars of the heavens. You brought them into the land that you had told their fathers to enter and possess. So their children entered and possessed the land and you subdued before them the inhabitants of the land, the Canaanites.

and 9:35–36:
Even in their own kingdom and in the great goodness that you gave them, in the broad and fertile land that you set before them, they did not serve you and they did not turn from their wicked deeds. And now look, we are slaves today, and the land that you gave our ancestors in order to consume its fruits and its goodness; lo, we are slaves upon it.

The repetition of the promise and conquest of the land reinforces the prayer's theme that the land is an inalienable possession that is introduced so prominently in the beginning of the prayer. The divine promise to the ancestors, which as we saw in the previous chapter, had a special pride of place in many pre-exilic prayers, continues to be cited in this post-exilic prayer.

Exodus

9. And you saw the misery of our ancestors in Egypt and heard their cry before the Red Sea. 10. You set signs and miracles before Pharaoh and before all his attendants and before all the people of his land because you knew they acted arrogantly against them [our fathers] and thus you made a name for yourself as it is to this day. 11. You split the sea before them and they crossed in the middle of the sea on dry land, but their pursuers you cast into the depths, like a stone in powerful waters. 12. With a pillar of cloud by day you guided

them and a pillar of fire by night to illuminate for them the way they should go.

The prominence given to the Exodus-Sinai-wilderness wandering complex of traditions is clear from the number of verses devoted to it, namely twelve, or roughly half of the entire historical retrospect. There are a number of noteworthy features in the description of the Exodus that illustrate the different ways the prayer as a whole has appropriated scripture. The clearest way to present the scripturalization in these verses is to begin with the most explicit use of earlier textual material and move toward the less distinct borrowings from tradition.

Verse 9 contains language very close to Exod 3:7 which is part of the divine commissioning of Moses at the burning bush:

Neh 9:9 ותרא את עני אבתינו במצרים ואת צעקתם שמעת על ים סוף
Exod 3:7 ויאמר יהוה ראיתי את עני עמי אשר במצרים
ואת צעקתם שמעתי מפני נגשיו כי ידעתי את מכאביו

The prayer does not quote God's words verbatim, but the reference to this divine speech to Moses in Exodus is clear. Beyond the shift from first-person speech to third-person, there are two other differences. In Nehemiah, God sees the affliction of "our ancestors," as opposed to the affliction of "my people." The second change involves the replacement of "on account of their taskmasters," with the phrase "before the Red Sea." Mention of the Red Sea at this point in the prayer is sequentially misplaced. The Israelites' cry to God at the Red Sea (Exod 14:10) does not occur until after God works through the ten plagues and the Israelites exit from Egypt. The plagues are not mentioned until the next verse in Nehemiah 9. This phrase occurs in verse 9, before reference to the signs and miracles performed as a means of getting them out. The mention of God's hearing the Israelites at the Red Sea raises the question of another textual reference. Indeed, it is possible to understand 9b as a reference to Exod 14:10b:

וייראו מאד ויצעקו בני ישראל אל יהוה

Neh 9:9 thus seems to be a fusion of two verses from the Exodus account, Exod 3:7 and 14:10b. Before continuing, let us pause to consider the significance of God's response to the Israelites' cry. There are 26 occurrences of the term Red Sea, or more literally Sea of Reeds, ים סוף, in the Hebrew Bible. Of these, only one aside from

Neh 9:9 mentions that the Israelites cried to the Lord, but it is a
notable one because it also appears in a historical retrospect. Josh
24:6–7 reads:

> When I brought your ancestors out of Egypt, you came to the sea; and
> the Egyptians pursued your ancestors with chariots and horsemen to
> the Red Sea. When they cried out to the Lord, he put darkness
> between you and the Egyptians, and made the sea come upon them
> and cover them; and your eyes saw what I did to Egypt. Afterwards
> you lived in the wilderness a long time.

These verses appear as part of the first-person divine oracle
delivered by Joshua which recounts God's beneficence toward Israel
from the time of Terah to the conquest. The historical retrospect in
Joshua 24 also views God's parting of the Red Sea as a direct reaction
to the distressed cry of the Israelites before their Egyptian pursuers.
In other words, that is how the "divine memory" preserved the
account. Beginning with the narrative of the crossing of the Red Sea
itself in Exod 14:10 and then remembered through divine oracle in
Josh 24:7 and recurring here in Neh 9:9, God's deliverance was a
direct response to the human cry of lament.

God's motivation in carrying out the Exodus is stated clearly in
Neh 9:10, "and thus you made a name for yourself as it is to this day."
This echoes the motivation stated in Exod 9:16:

ואולם בעבור זאת העמדתיך בעבור הראתך
את־כחי ולמען ספר שמי בכל־הארץ

The same motive, if not the exact wording of Neh 9:10, appears
also in Exod 14:15–18, where God's stated motive for delivering the
Israelites at the Red Sea is so that the Egyptians might know the true
God, thereby gaining glory over Pharaoh and his retinue. This
motive recurs in exilic and post-exilic books: Jer 32:20; Ezek 20:9, 14;
Isa 63:12,14; and Psalm 106:8. The verses in Jeremiah, Isaiah, and
the Psalms are, significantly, all prayers. Ezekiel 20 is a first-person
divine oracle. Daniel 9:15, also found in a prayer, shares the exact
language with Neh 9:10 ותעש־לך שם כהיום הזה. The same motive
occurs in 2 Sam 7:23, in David's prayer offered in response to
Nathan's oracle establishing the Davidic dynasty: "Who is like your
people, like Israel? Is there one nation on earth whose God went to
redeem it as a people, and to make a name for himself, doing great
and awesome things for them, by driving out before his people

nations and their gods?"[33] All but one of these mentions of the divine
intention behind the deliverance of the Israelites appear in prayers,
which suggests that it has become an important motivational clause
in prayers. Indeed, once loosed from their moorings in narratives, the
scripturalized description of history in liturgical prayers would
eventually become a vehicle by which the fame/name of the Lord is
rehearsed and spread.

Neh 9:12a contains a nearly exact citation from Exod 13:21;
only the syntax and the verb stem have been changed:
יומם בעמוד ענן לנחתם הדרך ולילה בעמוד אש להאיר להם
Missing is the beginning of the verse in Exodus: ויהוה הלך לפניהם,
which lends an anthropomorphic cast to the verse which the author
of Nehemiah 9 may have wanted to avoid. The pillar of cloud and the
pillar of fire appear in a number of passages as the Israelites make
their way through the desert (Exod 13:22, 14:19, 24; Num 14:14, Deut
31:15).

The wording in verse 11, "You split the sea before them" derives
from the book of Exodus, but with a slight difference. God instructs
Moses in Exod 14:16: "But you, lift up your staff, and stretch out your
hand over the sea and divide it, that the Israelites may enter in the
midst of the sea on dry ground." When the actual event is described,
the narrative in Exod 14:21 reads: "Then Moses stretched out his
hand over the sea. The Lord drove the sea back by a strong east wind
all night and turned the sea into dry land; and the waters were
divided." In the Exodus account, Moses plays an important role. In
fact, according to Exod 14:16, it is Moses' action that precipitates the
splitting of the waters. Of course, in Exod 14:21, God is the agent who
drives the sea back by blowing a strong wind to move the waters,
nonetheless, the verb בקע occurs in Exodus as a passive. Neh 9:11 by
contrast makes perfectly explicit that divine agency produced the
miracle. A close parallel to Neh 9:11a lies in the reference to the
crossing of the sea found in Psalm 78:13 בקע ים ויעבירם. Moses is
ignored in the Exodus account of Nehemiah 9; his rather limited
involvement occurs with the Sinai event.

Much of the rest of the account of the crossing of the Red Sea
contains wording found in the original account as well as in later
biblical references to the Exodus. ביבשה, a distinctive word in Neh

---

[33] An alteration appears in both the Greek versions of this verse and in the
Chronicler's version of this verse in 1 Chr 17:21 in which the phrase becomes
"making a name for *yourself*," thus making this phrase consistent with the
rest of the prayer that is addressed to God in the second person.

9:11a, occurs in Exod 14:16, 22, 29; 15:19a. It also appears in Gen 1:9, 10 in the Priestly creation account. Indeed this verbal coincidence is no coincidence. Because the word occurs only fourteen times in the Bible, all but one of which have some resonance with either the creation account or the Exodus account, it is probably an allusion made by the author.[34] There is a mythic resonance between the creation account and the Exodus-Red Sea crossing account as a "new creation."[35] The word occurs in Psalm 66:6, where it appears in a reference to the Exodus. In Josh 4:22 it recurs as part of the passage in which Joshua instructs the Israelites to teach their children about the entry into Jordan by likening it to the Exodus event. It is worth recounting the context because it, too, appears in a historical retrospect. After the Israelites have set up twelve stones to commemorate the crossing of the Jordan, Joshua enjoins them:

> When your children ask their parents in time to come, "What do these stones mean?" then you shall let your children know, "Israel crossed over the Jordan here on dry ground." For the Lord your God dried up the waters of the Jordan for you until you crossed over, as the Lord your God did to the Red Sea, which he dried up for us until we crossed over, so that all the peoples of the earth may know that the hand of the Lord is mighty, and so that you may fear the Lord your God forever. (Josh 4:21b–24)

Neh 9:11b uses language taken from Exod 15:5, though there is not an exact correspondence between the two. "Their pursuers you cast into the depths" echoes Exod 15:5b "they went down into the depths like a stone." One distinctive term used in Nehemiah 9:11b, "mighty waters," מים עזים is not found anywhere else but Isa 43:16, where it is also used in reference to God's work in saving the Israelites from pursuing chariots and horsemen. What can we make of this commonality? It is a rough approximation of the phrase מים אדירים in Exod 15:10. There is no other clear indication of direct borrowing from Isaiah so it can be considered only as an inadvertent

---

[34] "Dry land" appears in the book of Jonah three times. In Jonah 1:9, the prophet introduces himself to the foreign sailors as a Hebrew, "I worship the Lord, the God of heaven, who made the sea and the dry land." Soon, Jonah's very life is threatened by the destructive force of the sea and he is only delivered back to the dry land after he prays to God for deliverance. Here too land/sea are set up in mythic contrast. The only instance in the Bible where dry land is not used with some resonance to the creation or exodus accounts is in Isaiah 44:3, where it is used figuratively to mean existence without the spirit of the Lord.

[35] On this point, see Jon D. Levenson, *Creation and the Persistence of Evil* (New York: Harper & Row, 1988) especially 75–76.

echo, as another term for "powerful waters" such as appears in Ps 77:19, מים רבים, in reference to the raging waters of the Red Sea during the Exodus.

The phrase "signs and wonders," אתת ומפתים, appears nine times in the Bible in connection with the deliverance from Egypt. Its use in Neh 9:10a resembles most closely Deut 29:2 and 34:11. Deut 34:11 mentions that God sent signs and wonders in the land of Egypt, against Pharaoh, against all his servants, and against the entire land. The other occurrences are Exod 7:3; Deut 4:34, 7:19, 26:8; Jer 32:20,21; and Psalm 135:9. From its relative frequency in Deuteronomy and Jeremiah, the phrase rightly deserves to be called Deuteronomistic.[36]

Having examined the language of these verses, some preliminary conclusions are warranted because several ways in which the prayer as a whole appropriates scripture are illustrated by its construal of the Exodus tradition. One use of scripture is an exact or nearly exact citation. The appropriation of Exod 13:21 concerning the pillar of cloud and and pillar of fire in Neh 12a is an illustration of such a use. Explicit citations are the easiest to identify because their sources are clear. Another example is the combined use of Exod 3:7 and 14:10 in Neh 9:9.

A second kind of scripturalization, near kin to the first, is represented by the reuse of a phrase whose source/s is/are identifiable and that later comes to be used as a stock phrase in the interpretation of a particular tradition complex. An example is found in Neh 9:10d, that God "made a name for himself, [as it is to this day]." This is also found in a number of other contemporaneous passages, in Jeremiah 32, Psalm 106, Daniel 9, and Isaiah 63, all of which are prayers. The phrase can thus be regarded as having entered the liturgical idiom. The phrase becomes a theological affirmation of sorts. The expressed motivation suggests that God rescued the Israelites in part for God's own glory, in order to be recognized worldwide as punisher of injustice and redeemer of those unfairly subjugated. Another example of this sort of idiom is the promise to the ancestors, discussed in reference to the Abraham traditions above. An important feature of both of these reuses is that in their first appearance in the Pentateuch, both were originally divine speech, direct divine

---

[36] For the frequency and distribution of this phrase and many others characteristic of the Deuteronomistic literature, see Appendix A "Deutero-nomic Phraseology," in Weinfeld, *Deuteronomy and the Deuteronomic School,* 320–365.

statements, made to Abraham, Isaac, Jacob on the one hand, and Moses on the other. As indicated in the first chapter, divine promises and divine speech seem to have had a special status in the scripturalization of prayers in the pre-exilic period. In our discussion below of the use of the divine attribute formula in Nehemiah 9, it will become clear that this continues to be a feature of the scripturalization of prayers in the post-exilic period.

A third use of scripture is more diffuse. Some verses contain distinctive language that recurs in various sources, but that is not clearly dependent on any one narrative. In other words, it is derived from no specific narrative context but nonetheless has meaning in its new setting that derives from its use elsewhere in the Bible. The semantic field of reference from which its meaning is drawn is thus established by its use in various settings throughout the Bible. An example is the term "dry land" set in contrast to "mighty waters" that was discussed above in relation to its appearance in Neh 9:11. This evokes the mythic priestly creation account, itself derived from ancient Near Eastern mythic sources, but also the deployment of this language in the ancient Song of the Sea. Both draw from the same semantic well of mythopoetic water.

Yet other kinds of scripturalization, not clearly in evidence in the verses of Nehemiah 9, could be delineated. There is the use of biblical language, perhaps common to many psalms, or perhaps found elsewhere in many places in the biblical literature, that is not dependent on any one original narrative context for its meaning. In such "biblicizing," a distinction needs to be drawn between language that can be traced to one particular tradition complex: the pillar of fire and the pillar of cloud is immediately identifiable as coming from the Exodus/wilderness wandering traditions as discussed above; and language that cannot be pinned down, like God-language that has more diffuse origins. A "land flowing with milk and honey" would be an example of the latter. The latter category verges on not being dependent on written texts at all, but on the oral formulations of people passing traditions down through the ages. This category, admittedly a catch-all for wayward biblical phrases, will gain more clarity as we are able to add examples to illustrate it. Let the close scrutiny of the first eight verses serve as *pars pro toto*, because throughout the prayer, these various uses of scripture recur.

Sinai

13. You came down upon Mount Sinai and spoke with them from heaven. And you gave them just ordinances and true laws, good

statutes and commandments. 14. Your holy sabbath you made
known to them. Commandments and statutes and torah you
commanded them by the hand of Moses your servant.

For the author of the prayer, the Sinai and wilderness
experience is the paradigmatic example of God's providential care
for the Israelites despite their recalcitrance and continued
disobedience. The source material for Neh 9:13a is straightforward.

Exod 19:11b כי ביום השלישי ירד יהוה לעיני כל העם על הר סיני

Exod 19:20a וירד יהוה על הר סיני אל ראש ההר

Exod 20:19b אתם ראיתם כי מן־השמים דברתי עמכם

As is evident from the above comparisons, the wording of Neh
9:13a is close to that of Exod 19:11, 20, and Exod 20:19. The name of
the holy mountain mentioned in Neh 9:13 reflects not Deuteronomic
traditions, which refer to the mountain as Horeb, but use the
Jahwistic/Priestly designation Sinai.[37] Neh 9:13a nonetheless
presents a paradox. Did God come down to Mt. Sinai or did God
remain in the heavenly abode to speak with the Israelites? In a
similar contradiction, verse 13 suggests that God spoke directly to the
Israelites, but verse 14 suggests that Moses conveyed the divine laws
to the people. Stephen Geller has considered a similar question
relating to the divine theophany at Sinai as it is interpreted in
Deuteronomy 4.[38] According to Geller, the author of the framing
material of Deuteronomy had somehow to reconcile two conflicting
traditions regarding the lawgiving at Sinai from an exilic theological
perspective that permitted no anthropomorphic, immanental
depictions of God. As evidence of the author's careful reworking of
earlier traditions, Geller discusses especially Deut 4:36: "From the
heavens he let you hear his voice to instruct you, and on earth he let
you see his great fire, and his words you heard from the fire." Geller
argues that the author of the framing material in Deuteronomy was
trying to override earlier traditions, such as Deut 5:4, which state

---

[37] For the source-critical argument that associates the term Horeb with the
Deuteronomistic literature and Sinai with the J/P traditions, see Martin Noth,
Exodus (OTL; Philadelphia: Westminster, 1962) and Lothar Perlitt, "Sinai und
Horeb," *Beiträge zur alttestamentlichen Theologie.* (Göttingen: Vandenhoeck
& Ruprecht, 1977) 302–322. Horeb is used in Deut 1:2,6,19; 4:10, 15; 5:2; 9:8;
18:16; 28:69.

[38] Stephen A. Geller, "Fiery Wisdom: Logos and Lexis in Deuteronomy 4,"
Prooftexts 14 (1994) 103–139.

that God actually was present on the mountain. For the author of Deuteronomy 4, "the new point is the idea of absolute divine transcendence even if mitigated by a possible hint of actual immanence at Horeb."[39] Given that the author of Nehemiah 9 reflects a certain post-exilic Deuteronomistic *Tendenz*, we might ask if Neh 9:13 was also trying to reconcile two discordant traditions about the law-giving by subsuming one to the other. But if this is the intention of the author of Neh 9:13, he is not as successful at masking the reference to divine immanence at Sinai. Neh 9:13 explicitly uses the verb ירד for God's descent. Unlike Deut 4:36, Neh 9:13 does not speak of the divine voice emanating from the midst of a fire or, like Exod 34:5, in a cloud. The only possibility for understanding the two halves of Neh 9:13a as harmonious is if the top of Mt. Sinai is conceived as reaching to heaven itself, so that God's descent to Mt. Sinai was simply a lower level of heaven, the divine abode. The other holy mountain of Israel, Mt. Zion, had such ethereal connotations attached to it. Zion, as the site of the Temple, was considered in some traditions as the dwelling of God and the meeting point between the heavenly and earthly spheres.[40] Yet this verse in Nehemiah 9 shows no evidence of such mythopoetic appropriation of tradition. We must accept, as did the author of this prayer, that two seemingly contradictory traditions can stand side by side. It is notable that the author chose to preserve them both.

The Sinai formulation of Neh 9:13–14 as a whole has a sandwich structure:

(13b) [ותתן להם] משפטים ישרים ותורות אמת חקים ומצות טובים

(14a) ואת־שבת קדשך [הודעת להם]

(14b) ומצוות וחקים ותורה [צוית להם ביד משה עבדך]

The two outside clauses refer to the law in more general terms; 13b contains positive adjectives that modify these terms; 14b includes the phrase "you commanded them *by the hand of Moses your servant*." The center clause specifies one particular legal observance, the "holy Sabbath." This could be viewed as a redundant couple of

---

39 Geller, "Fiery Wisdom," 138, n.13.

40 For a thorough discussion of the Canaanite mythic origins of the cosmic mountain conception in Israelite literature, see the study of Richard J. Clifford, *The Cosmic Mountain in Canaan and the Old Testament* (HSM 4; Cambridge: Harvard University, 1972). See also the discussion of Jon Levenson, *Sinai and Zion: An Entry Into the Jewish Bible* (New York: Harper & Row, 1985), especially 122–126.

clauses in which the multiplication of legal terms is meant simply to give a sense of the sheer amount of legal prescriptions that made up the revelation at Sinai.[41] But if this were the case, why is the listing of legal terms interrupted by the phrase about the Sabbath? Given the evidence garnered so far of the author's careful attention to wording, it seems more likely that there is a specific rationale for the phrasing. 13b–14 suggest that God presented the Israelites with one set of legal statutes, including the Sabbath, and then another collection is given by the hand of Moses. Maurice Gilbert views this difference as two distinct references, one to the Decalogue, which God communicated directly with the people (v.13) and the Mosaic law (v.14b).[42]

The exact formulation in Neh 9:13b, in which the ordinances, laws, statutes, and commandments are qualified as just, true, and good, is unique.[43] Throughout the Bible, these terms are used in different orders and combinations. חקים ומשפטים is the combination most frequently found in Deuteronomy. The prayer in Nehemiah 1 uses the combination "commandments, statutes, and judgments," את המצות ואת החקים ואת המשפטים (v.7). The three verses that offer the closest parallels are found in post-exilic literature:

Mal 2:6a   תורת אמת היתה בפיהו ועולה לא נמצא בשפתיו
Ps 119:137   צדיק אתה יהוה וישר משפטיך
Ps 119:142   צדקתך צדק לעולם ותורתך אמת

Yet Psalm 119, a composition that offers an extended reflection on the worthiness of the divine law, contains no single verse that lists the various types of law with these particular modifying adjectives. The use of the legal terms in Neh 9:13–14 thus would fall into the category of "biblicizing" language, with no special narrative context from which it is derived other than the very general Sinai experience.

The only specific divine legal prescription mentioned in Neh 9:13–14 is the "holy sabbath," שבת קדש, a term found only once aside from Nehemiah, in Exod 16:23, a passage from the Priestly source. The stress on Sabbath observance in Neh 9:14 represents an interpretation that relies on priestly narrative in the Pentateuch in

---

41 See, for example, the editor's note in the apparatus of the *Biblia Hebraica Stuttgartensia*, which suggests the commandments and statutes of 14b were reproduced mistakenly from verse 13.

42 Maurice Gilbert, "La place de la loi dans la prière de Néhémie 9," 317.

43 Cf. also Ps 119:75a, 129, 144, 151, 160, and 164.

which the holiness of the Sabbath is stressed. The priestly creation account depicts the Sabbath as the ultimate response to the work of God, in which Sabbath observance is an institution established as part of the natural order of creation. God explicitly sanctifies the Sabbath in Gen 2:3. The priestly account of the Sinai covenant concludes with the institution of the Sabbath (Exod 31:12–17).

The strongly worded concern that the day be sanctified and not defiled is also found in Ezekiel 20. Ezek 20:13:

> But the house of Israel rebelled against me in the wilderness; they did not observe my statutes and rejected my ordinances, which by doing a man might live, and they greatly defiled my sabbaths so that I said 'I will pour out my anger upon them in the desert and make an end of them.'

The language used here, that the Sabbath is something to be consecrated (expressed by the Piel form of קדש), is found predominantly in the Priestly literature, and in Ezekiel which itself stands in the Priestly stream of tradition.[44]

It is instructive also to compare the two versions of the decalogue. The holy character of the Sabbath is emphasized also in the J version of the decalogue in Exod 20:8–11. God's rest after creation is cited as the motive for observing the Sabbath. Holiness is mentioned twice in the commandment and the verse concludes with that verb: על־כן ברך יהוה את־יום השבת ויקדשהו

By contrast, the motive for Sabbath observance in Deut 5:12–15 is God's deliverance of Israel from Egypt. The exhortation to sanctify the Sabbath occurs only once in verse 12. The point of this review is to illustrate once again that the priestly narrative was part of the variegated palette of scripture from which the author drew in composing the prayer.

Wilderness Wanderings

> 15. You gave them bread from heaven for their hunger and you brought forth water from a rock for their thirst. You told them to enter and possess the land that you had sworn to give them. 16. But they and our ancestors were arrogant and stiffened their necks and did not obey your commandments. 17. They refused to obey and they did not remember the wonders that you performed for them. They stiffened their necks and appointed a leader to return to their servitude in Egypt. But you are a God of forgiveness, gracious and

---

[44] Cf. Exod 16:22–26, a priestly passage that depicts the Israelites already observing the Sabbath in the wilderness.

merciful, long-suffering and of abounding faithful love. 18. Even when they made for themselves a molten calf and they said "This is your God who brought you up out of Egypt;" and they did great blasphemies. 19. But you in your great mercy did not abandon them in the desert. The pillar of cloud did not depart from them during the day to guide them on the way and the pillar of fire by night to illlumine for them the path they should travel. 20. You gave your good spirit to give them insight and you did not withhold your manna from their mouths and you slaked their thirst with water. 21. Forty years in the desert you sustained them; they lacked nothing. Their clothes did not wear out; their feet did not swell.

The section describing the Israelites' wandering in the wilderness is the longest single tradition complex elaborated in the prayer. The seven verses devoted to the wilderness experience stand in contrast to the succinct half-verse devoted to this period in the retrospect of Josh 24:7b: "Afterwards you lived in the wilderness a long time." As commentators have pointed out, the author seemingly abandons strict adherence to the biblical sequence of events in which God first provides manna and water for the Israelites soon after crossing the Red Sea (Exodus 16–17) before Sinai.[45] The incident in which the Israelites want to appoint a leader to take them back to Egypt, found in Numbers 14, is here mentioned in verse 17, before the reference to the story of the golden calf, which is found in Exodus 32. Instead, the order presents a certain scheme: divine providence (12–15), Israelite rebellion (16–18), and renewed divine mercy (19–21). At its center lies the main theme of the prayer: God's gracious mercy and providence in the face of continuing apostasy and disobedience on the part of Israel.

Let us trace some more of the scriptural references. Neh 9:15, which mentions God's provision of food and drink for the Israelites, contains a combination of phrases from two verses at some distance from one another. Neh 9:15a לחם משמים נתתה "bread from heaven" is a phrase found in Exod 16:4. Although one of the two incidents in which Moses produces water from the rock occurs in Exod 17:1–7, the phrase found in Neh 9:15 ומים מסלע הוצאת derives from Num 20:8.

The second half of Neh 9:15 refers to the conquest using Deuteronomistic language: ותאמר להם לבוא לרשת את־הארץ "To possess," ירש, is a verb used nowhere in the book of Exodus but which occurs fifty-two times in the book of Deuteronomy and seventeen times in Joshua-Judges. Deut 1:8 contains similar wording: ראה נתתי

---

[45] Blenkinsopp, *Ezra-Nehemiah*, 304.

לפניכם את־הארץ באו ורשו את־הארץ אשר נשבע יהוה לאבתיכם
The phrase having to do with possessing the land occurs five times in this prayer, which clearly reflects a principal theme of the prayer, the possession of the land.

Though the sources for the language of Neh 9:16 are biblical and parallels to it can be found, the language does not allude to any single event. For example, the phrase "stiffened the neck" (ויקשו את־ערפם) is found three times in the prayer, Neh 9:16, 17, 29. It is Deuteronomistic; see e.g. Deut 10:16; Jer 7:26, 17:23, 19:15, 2 Kgs 17:14. It is meant rather to convey a general impression of the recalcitrant behavior of the Israelites in the wilderness. The use of scripture here can thus be described as a kind of Deuteronomistic "biblicizing," meant to be evocative of the Israelites' general behavior during the wilderness experience.

In Neh 9:17, however, there is distinctive language in which the use of scripture is different: the first half of the verse refers to a particular episode in the wilderness tradition. The expression in Neh 9:17b ויתנו ראש לשוב לעבדותם במצרים, "And they appointed a captain to return to their slavery in Egypt," refers to one episode in the wilderness, drawing from language that is found in Num 14:4: ויאמרו איש אל אחיו נתנה ראש ונשובה מצרימה. The statement in Numbers does not mention slavery, however. The slight modification serves to introduce this subject of slavery, thus hinting at the nature of the Jews' current distress in the post-exilic period, the subjugation mentioned in Neh 9:36. In that verse, the fact of their current status as "slaves," subjugated in their own land to kings, is mentioned twice.

Neh 9:17 is important for another reason. Five verses in the prayer (9:17, 19, 27, 28, and 31) make reference to the divine self-disclosure passage that occurs in Exod 34:6–7 and occurs again, in what is likely a later tradition, in Num 14:13–19. Indeed, both of the incidents that provoked the use of the divine attribute formula—the Israelites' quest to return to Egypt and the incident with the golden calf—are included in verses 17 and 18. One incident is mentioned before the first appearance of this formula, and the other immediately after.

The divine attributes' use in the prayer as a kind of refrain ties it more closely to later liturgical formulae.[46] The most complete reference is the first one in the last half of Neh 9:17b. It reads:

---

[46] Though it is beyond our scope here to delve into putative influences of this liturgical phrase and Nehemiah 9 on later Jewish and Christan liturgies, it is worth mentioning that Leon Liebreich has suggested that this prayer had a

ואתה אלוה סליחות חנון ורחום ארך־אפים ורב־חסד ולא עזבתם

But you are a forgiving God, gracious and merciful, long-suffering and of abundant faithful love. And you did not abandon them.

The other references appear at intervals throughout the retelling of history in this prayer. The affirmation of divine mercy occurs as part of the larger pattern narrated in the retelling of history that recounts Israelite disobedience: the Israelites long to return to their slavery in Egypt, but God is *ready to forgive, gracious and merciful*, etc. (17) They make a calf for themselves, but God in his *great mercies* did not abandon them. (19) During the period of the judges, they threw the Torah behind their backs and killed the prophets, but God in his great *mercies* gave them saviors/judges to rescue them. (27) During the period of kingship, they again rebelled, and God had *mercy* (28). The final affirmation of these divine attributes occurs at the very end of the historical review, after the Israelites had rebelled and been exiled from the land. Verse 31 reads: "However, in your *great mercies*, you did not make an end of them and you did not destroy them, because you are a *gracious and merciful God*." The verse marks the transition in the prayer to the current period of distress, which is followed by a brief confession and a petition for help.

Two larger issues about the appropriation of the divine attribute formula as it appears in the prayer are worth noting. The first was

---

direct influence on the Sephardic liturgy for Yom Kippur. See his article, "The Impact of Nehemiah 9:5–37 on the Liturgy of the Synagogue, *HUCA* 32 (1961) 227–237. Ismar Elbogen also notes the widespread use of this passage already in biblical times as a significant step in the development of the liturgy. "The Thirteen Attributes revealed to Moses when he received the second set of tablets (Exod 34:6–7) are called סדר סליחה "rite of forgiveness;" they belong to the ancient heritage and were very widespread, as shown by the frequency with which they are quoted in the Bible. 'God showed Moses the order of prayer. He said to him, 'Whenever Israel sins, let them perform this rite before Me and I shall forgive them'; 'There is a covenant that the Thirteen Attributes do not return unanswered' (Babylonian Talmud Rosh Hashanah 17b) This rabbinic conception explains how the Thirteen Attributes became the nucleus of all prayers for atonement, so that they serve to this day as a refrain constantly repeated in all the selihot." Elbogen, *Jewish Liturgy: A Comprehensive History* (Raymond P. Scheindlin, trans., Philadelphia: Jewish Publication Society, 5753/1993) 177.

The liturgical setting and the role of the Levites in the narrative led von Rad to suggest that this prayer, which does in fact seem to be secondarily inserted into the book of Nehemiah, lived a double life as a part of a liturgical rite of confession or penitence.

mentioned above. In its most complete citation in verse 17, the formula appears out of chronological sequence when compared to its use in the book of Exodus. In other words, there seems to be a conscious rhetorical strategy at work in the way it is positioned in this prayer. Another important feature of this interpretation is that the formula in its entirety as it appears in Exod 34:6–7, and again in Num 14:18–19 does not occur in Nehemiah 9. Only 34:6 is quoted, though with several slight modifications. The order of the adjectives חנון ורחום has been reversed. This is true in other exilic and post-exilic appearances of this phrase.[47] Since Exod 34:6–7 occurs in conjunction with the revelation of the divine name, it begins with a twofold repetition of the Tetragrammaton. In Neh 9:17, God is affirmed as אלוה סליחות, a forgiving God. Another minor change is that the end of the clause in Exod 34:6 is ורב חסד ואמת; Neh 9:17 ends ורב חסד ולא עזבתם. The last two alterations serve to stress to an even greater extent the merciful aspects of God: God forgives and God did not abandon the Israelites.

The omission of the second half of the divine attribute formula as found in the Pentateuch is striking. God is not described in this verse as "not clearing the guilty, but visiting the sins of the parents on the children and the children's children to the third and fourth generation." The notion of punishment down through the generations is missing. Michael Fishbane has discussed the reuse of this attribute formula in post-exilic literature. Although he does not treat its appearance in Nehemiah 9, his insights echo what I have observed here. He suggests, quite plausibly, that the appearance of the first part of Exod 34:6–7 in a number of other late biblical texts without the punishment/reward clause is an aggadic reuse designed to evoke the gracious properties of God and avoid reminding God about divine judgment and retribution.[48] Given the alteration of the formula in 17b to stress the loyal/faithful character of God who will not forsake Israel, ולא עזבתם, Fishbane's suggestion makes sense. This notion is also reinforced by at least two other aspects of this prayer: the prayer emphasizes God's *inalienable* gift of the land to the

---

[47] Cf. also Joel 2:13, Jonah 4:2, Pss 145:8; 11:4, 112:4, and 2 Chr 30:9. It is important to note however, that all post-exilic literature does not follow this reversal. The Exodus 34 order obtains in *1QH* 12:14, 16:16; *1QS* 4:4, 5.

[48] Nahum's emphasis on divine punishment is "to a degree, an exception; for it is the theme of divine mercy that is generally stressed in inner-biblical reuses of the divine attribute formulary, particularly liturgical petitions, be these from the Pentateuch [like Num 14:17–19] or from the Psalter." Fishbane, *Biblical Interpretation*, 347.

Israelites; and the punishment of exile is downplayed so there is only a vague hint of life outside the land in verse 30.

As was the case with the angelic liturgy mentioned in reference to Neh 9:6, there are a number of other late biblical texts that reflect an interpretive reuse of the divine attribute formula. Fishbane has noted that many of them reflect an emphasis on divine attributes of compassion.[49] (See for instance 2 Chr 30:9, Joel 2:13, or Mic 7:18–20.) Its appearance in prayers, including Nehemiah 9, Jonah's prayer in 4:2, and in such psalms as 86:15, 103:8, 145:8 and in partial form in the acrostic psalms 111 and 112, strongly suggests that from an early period this formula had become a stock phrase used in composing liturgical texts.

The only time human speech is quoted in the prayer is in Neh 9:18 which refers to the Israelites' apostasy in the episode of the golden calf in Exodus 32. This appears in the middle of the historical retrospect, which is fitting, because idolatry lies at the heart of the author's concern. The wording is carefully chosen to suggest the people as a whole are to blame for the episode. Aaron's role is omitted in Nehemiah. Nehemiah states that the people themselves made a molten calf. In fact, according to Exod 32:1–4, it is Aaron, at their urging, who organizes the project, makes the calf, and declares a festival. Exod 32:4a thus reads ויעשהו עגל מסכה and the end of the verse contains their response which is quoted in Neh 9:18b:

ויאמרו אלה אלהיך ישראל אשר העלוך מארץ מצרים.

The only alteration in Neh 9:18b is a change to "this is your god" in the singular.[50] This reference which depicts the Israelites themselves making the calf actually seems to derive from God's retelling of the episode in Exod 32:8, where the Israelites' words are again quoted. The direct involvement of the Israelites is also echoed in Deut 9:16 and Psalm 106:19. The use of scripture in the verse thus serves the larger theme of the prayer: undeserving and apostate Israelites.

God's gift of the "good spirit" to instruct the Israelites, mentioned in Neh 9:20, could only refer to Num 11:16–25 in which

---

[49] Fishbane mentions a number of psalms that he thinks use this formulary as an organizing principle: 40, 78, 79, 85, 99; *Biblical Interpretation* 347. While I disagree with his understanding that these psalms are somehow organized or structured around this formula in a conscious exegetical process, there was clearly an appropriation of some of the divine attribute terminology in these psalms.

[50] The Greek reflects the third person plural to accord with Exodus 32.

God transfers some of the spirit placed on Moses to the seventy elders for prophesying. This expression "good spirit" is unique to Nehemiah 9.[51] Verse 20 also repeats that God provided the Israelites with manna (referred to as "bread from heaven" in v.15) and water. As has been pointed out by commentators, this cyclical portrayal of divine providence—Israelite rebellion—divine providence was deliberately shaped. God's anger, which is in fact also a recurring part of the wilderness experience, is omitted.

The Israelites' experience in the wilderness is summarized in Neh 9:21. The reference is taken from Deut 8:4 and Deut 29:4 as a comparison of these verses shows:

Neh 9:21   וארבעים שנה כלכלתם במדבר לא חסרו
שלמתיהם לא בלו ורגליך לא בצקו
Deut 8 : 4   שלמתך לא בלתה מעליך ורגלך לא בצקה זה ארבעים שנה
Deut 29:4   ואולך אתכם ארבעים שנה במדבר לא־בלו שלמתיכם
מעליכם ונעלך לא־בלתה מעל רגלך

The verse in Neh 9:21 emphasizes God's continuing care during the forty years in the wilderness. The mention of God's provision of food for the Israelites appears in both the first verse of the section describing their wilderness wandering (15) and here again in this last verse. Neh 9:21 extends the image of divine care by mentioning that their clothes were maintained and their feet did not swell. The image of God as provider and comforter contrasts with the anger of God that is also found in the wilderness narrative in Exodus-Numbers. Num 32:13–15 presents the forty years in the desert as punishment, a temporary abandonment served on the Israelites for their apostasy. So too, Josh 5:6 suggests that the period of forty years was a result of the Israelites' disobedience. Neh 9:21, by contrast, emphasizes divine mercy in another example of the selective interpretation of scriptural traditions employed by the author.

Conquest/Bequest of Land and Settlement
22. You gave them kingdoms and peoples and you apportioned them a corner and they possessed the land of Sihon the king of Heshbon, and the land of Og the king of Bashan.* 23. You multiplied their children like the stars of the heavens and you brought them to the

---

[51] Blenkinsopp suggests the connection between the Holy Spirit and prophecy is a Second Temple phenomenon; *Ezra-Nehemiah*, 305. Compare also Isa 63:11–14 which contains two mentions of God's spirit in reference to the wilderness period.

land that you had told their ancestors to enter and possess. 24. The
descendants entered and took possession of the land and you subdued
before them the inhabitants of the land. You gave into their hand the
Canaanites, their kings, and the peoples of the land to do with them
according to their whim. 25. They captured fortified cities and fertile
land and they seized houses full of goods: hewn cisterns, vineyards,
olive orchards, and fruit trees in abundance. They ate and were
sated and grew fat. They languished in your great goodness.

* Omitting "the land of" (the king of Heshbon) as a dittography, with
the Greek.

The three verses that describe the conquest continue in the
same vein. It is only through direct divine agency that the land is
won: ותכנע לפניהם את־ישבי אל־הארץ הכנענים. The conquest as
described in Neh 9:24–25 is a leaderless movement into the promised
land. Joshua is not mentioned, rather the descendants, הבנים [of the
wilderness generation] enter the land to possess it. To the author of
this prayer, it is as if the book of Joshua, indeed, the man Joshua, did
not exist. According to this account, the entry into the promised land
was a bloodless affair and proceeded completely through divine
agency.

The first words of verse 22 set the tone: "you gave them." The
verse refers to the events described in Num 21:21–35 and again in
Deuteronomy 2–3 in which the Israelites gain possession of the
territories of Sihon and Og.[52] These two kings were accorded more
attention in the tradition than Balak of Moab (who in fact features
even more prominently in Numbers 22–24) and the kings of Midian.
Yet the language has no exact biblical parallels. One scholar has
suggested that these two were included because they were the first
kings conquered.[53] It is difficult to determine what influenced the
author here in this aspect of the conquest. Blenkinsopp views the
mention of Sihon and Og here and elsewhere in the late biblical
interpretations of the conquest (Pss 134:10–12; 136:17–22) as
examples of "twinning" in ancient traditions.[54]

Neh 9:23a—ובניהם הרבית ככוכבי השמים. The phrase is a
reference to the promise to the ancestors, though only specifically in
reference to multiplying descendants. Another element of the

---

[52] Sihon and Og are also singled out for mention in Ps 136:17–22.

[53] F.C. Fensham discusses Y. Aharoni's view (*Land of the Bible*, 187) in
"Nehemiah 9 and Pss. 105, 106, 135 and 136. Post-Exilic Historical Traditions
in Poetic Form," *JNSL* 9 (1981) 44.

[54] Blenkinsopp, *Ezra-Nehemiah*, 305.

promise, the gift of the land, appears in the reference to the Abraham traditions in Neh 9:8. The promise recurs many times in the Pentateuch (Gen 15:5, 22:17, 26:4; Deut 1:10, 10:22, 28:62). Although the promise refers to certain specific incidents in Genesis, it no longer requires its original narrative context for meaning. As we saw in the first chapter, the use of this formula in prayers dates back to the pre-exilic period. The rest of verse 23 describes the approach to the land, again with God as agent, "you brought them to the land," which is the realization of God's promise of the land to their ancestors.

Verses 22–23 take place on the east bank of the Jordan. Verses 24–25 describe the entry into the land on the western side of the Jordan. Here again, one might expect some mention of Joshua and the renewal of the covenant made at the river in Joshua 24, but the prayer is silent concerning Joshua. Instead, verse 24 speaks of the descendants' (of the wilderness generation) entry into the land, the wilderness generation having been punished for expressing their desire to return to Egypt (Num 14:20–35). Verse 24 also mentions in summary the events of the conquest with wording that cannot be traced to any single passage in the Pentateuch or Deuteronomistic History. The last phrase in this long verse, stating that the Israelites were able to do with the kings and peoples of the land "according to their whim," כרצונם, is not found in any account of the conquest. It seems rather to be the author's addition to the conquest account which serves a particular rhetorical purpose in the prayer. The phrase recurs in 9:37, the last verse of the prayer, when the pray-er laments their oppression under foreign kings who treat them "according to their whim," כרצונם. Like the careful use of "slavery" in both Neh 9:17 and 36, this comparison highlights the fact that in the post-exilic period the tables have been turned; the former conquerors have become the vanquished at the mercy of foreign powers. The contrast is made even more striking by the first half of verse 25 which specifies the riches of the land that the Israelites came to possess. The wording comes from Deut 6:11, although it has been modified in the new context. Deut 6:11 emphasizes that Israel was not responsible for the riches they were to inherit: houses they did not build, cisterns they did not hew, and so on, whereas Nehemiah simply lists the items the Israelites inherited in the land. The emphasis for the author of this prayer lies in the progressive decline of the Israelites that came as a result of possessing these riches during their time in the land: "They ate and were sated and grew fat. They languished in your great goodness." Deut 6:11 ends with "they

ate and were sated." The wording for "they grew fat" וַיִּשְׁמַנוּ, seems
to reflect the influence of Deut 32:15, which paints a portrait of Israel
gorging on the fruits of the land:

וַיִּשְׁמַן יְשֻׁרוּן וַיִּבְעָט שָׁמַנְתָּ עָבִיתָ כָּשִׂיתָ

This section of Deuteronomy 32 also shares the same view of
the Israelites as having fallen into apostasy in tandem with their
increasing overweight. The prayer thus extends Deut 6:11 by adding
a word used in Deuteronomy 32 and then a word that is unique to
Nehemiah 9, וַיִּתְעַדָּנוּ, to underscore the point and to provide a segue
to the decline that is described in the succeeding verses.

Israel in the Land

26. They were disobedient and rebelled against you and they threw
your torah behind their back and they slew your prophets who
admonished them to return to you and they did great blasphemies.
27. So you gave them into the hand of their oppressors who made
them suffer. And in the time of their suffering they cried out to you
and you heard from heaven. According to your great mercy you gave
them saviors who rescued them from the hand of their oppressors.
28. But when they had rest, they returned to doing wickedness before
you so you abandoned them into the hand of their enemies who
subdued them. They turned and cried out to you. You heard them
from heaven and you delivered them many times according to your
great mercy. 29. You admonished them to make them return to your
torah but they were arrogant and did not listen to your
commandments. They sinned against your ordinances by which a
person shall live if he observes them. But they turned a stubborn
shoulder and they stiffened their neck and did not obey. 30. You were
patient with them for many years. You admonished them by your
spirit through your prophets, but they did not heed so you gave them
into the hand of the peoples of the lands. 31. But in your many
mercies you did not bring an end to them and you did not abandon
them because you are a gracious and merciful God.

The prayer continues with a description of the Israelites' life
once on the land, God's continuing providence for them despite their
rebelliousness, and their gradual demise. Neh 9:26–31 comprises the
periods of the judges, kings/prophets, and exile. By comparison with
the other sections of the prayer, this section gives a greatly
abbreviated account of the history which characterizes the period in
very general terms.

The first half of 9:26 does not contain any references to specific
scriptural passages.[55] The wording "they cast your Torah behind

---

[55] Blenkinsopp suggests that the source for this section (vv 26–31) is derived
from Judg 2:11–23, supplemented by themes from prophetic preaching,

their back" is found only here, although Jeroboam is described as having thrust God behind his back (1 Kgs 14:9) and Oholibah, the metaphorical figure of Judah, is said to have done the same (Ezek 23:35). The second half of the verse contains a reference to the murder of prophets. Jezebel is reported to have been responsible for killing prophets (1 Kgs 18:4, 13). So too King Jehoiakim is said to have killed the prophet Uriah (Jer 26:23) and Joash commands that Zechariah be killed (2 Chr 24:22). In Neh 9:26, however, "they," that is, the Israelites, are held responsible for murdering prophets. The verse accords with 1 Kgs 19:10,14 in which Elijah twice repeats the claim: "I have been zealous for the Lord the God of Hosts because the Israelites have abandoned your covenant and thrown down your altars. They have slain your prophets by the sword. I alone remain and they are seeking to take my life." The Hebrew Bible itself presents slim evidence for this accusation against the Israelites, but later tradition expands on this idea.[56]

Another phrase in Neh 9:26 merits additional discussion because it reflects a theological perspective that becomes even more fully developed in the rabbinic period. The verse states that "the prophets warned them to return to you," העידו בם להשיבם אליך. Sara Japhet has pointed out that this prayer contains the beginning of the rabbinic view that God does not punish without warning.[57] This notion was premised on the belief that God, being just, would not punish anyone for having committed an unintentional sin, that is, without having been forewarned of the consequences of wrong behavior. In cases of punishment described in the Bible, therefore, whether the supposed warning is found in the biblical text or not, the

---

especially Ezekiel 20. He does not adduce any specific parallels to support the claim, however, though he is correct about the general theme of Israelite rebellion-divine intervention contained in the passages.

[56] The assertion that the Israelites killed prophets is found in *Jub* 1:12–13; see note 54 below. It is also found as anti-Jewish polemic in the gospels (Luke 11:47–51, Matt 23:29–36) and Acts 7:51–53. The recontextualization of this tradition from Nehemiah to the New Testament is ironic. In Nehemiah, it is part of a prayerful confession, an admission of wrongdoing; whereas in the New Testament it becomes a way of condemning the contemporary generation of Jews for their ancestors' actions.

[57] For her discussion of rabbinic concept of the warning, see Sara Japhet, *The Ideology of the Book of Chronicles and Its Place in Biblical Thought*, (Frankfurt: Peter Lang, 1989) 185–191. She points out that the term העיד ב- is found already in a number of biblical texts (Gen 43:3; Exod 19:21, 23; 21:29), though it is expressed more fully as a theological idea in the late literature (187). See also the discussion of "Fair Warning" by James L. Kugel, "The *Jubilees* Apocalypse," *DSD* 1 (1994) 322–337, especially 328–331.

rabbis assumed its existence and the midrashic mind sometimes invented the perfect warning to fit the crime.[58] She argues that this is one example of an outlook that crops up already in the late biblical literature and developed as a result of the influence of the prophetic literature.[59] The prophets' role in this regard is thus to warn people and call them to repentance.

Literature produced in the late pre-exilic and exilic periods testifies to the existence of the idea. Jer 11:7 refers to the wilderness wandering as a time during which God warned the people to obey his commands but they were continually disobedient: "I certainly warned your ancestors on the day that I brought them out of the land of Egypt until today, warning frequently, saying: 'Obey my voice.'"[60] Their disregard of the covenant results in punishment. The role of the prophet as professional warner arose after the Israelites settled in Israel. Ezek 33:1–9 states pointedly that it is the duty of the prophet to warn the wicked about the consequences of their wrongdoing.[61] Second Temple literature also contains this fully developed idea.[62] In

---

[58] This principle was a hallmark of the rabbinic view of punishment and proved a spur to some creative midrash in cases of biblical punishment where no "warning" was found in the written text. It is also evident in some early Christian literature. Early interpretations of the flood story reflect a concern that this punishment was meted out without the proper forewarning. This led some interpreters to depict Noah as a preacher who warned the wicked in his generation to repent in order to ward off the imminent disaster (2 Pet 2:5; *Sibylline Oracles* I 125–131, 149–51; *1 Clement* 7:6). These interpretations may well reflect the influence of Josephus, cf. *Jewish Antiquities*, 1.73–75.

[59] Japhet notes that this view is absent from the book of Ezekiel and that, in fact, Ezek 3:15 contains a different view in which the sinner is punished even if he or she had been warned. Although she leaves Jonah unmentioned, the book of Jonah is an extended illustration of the principle (as well as an example supporting her argument that this concept of warning is more fully developed in the late literature). According to the book of Jonah, non-Israelites/non-Jews are clearly included in God's principle of warning before punishing.

[60] Cf. also 2 Chr 24:19, Jer 25:4.

[61] This passage uses the verb זהר rather than עדה to express the sense of warning.

[62] The book of *Jubilees* is another Second Temple composition that contains this tradition. In the beginning of the book, God reveals to Moses both past and future history, including an account of the pre-exilic period: *Jubilees* 1:12 states, "And I shall send to them witnesses so that I might witness to them, but they will not hear. And they will even kill the witnesses." The "witnesses" mentioned here are the prophets so the verse reveals its debt to this interpretive tradition. The word translated by O. Wintermute as "witnesses" is עדים, according to the corresponding Qumran fragment of *Jubilees*. The very term used by the author to indicate the biblical prophets suggests that the prophets were commonly understood to function as "warners." By

sum, aside from the reference to killing the prophets in 1 Kings 19, there is no clearly identifiable scriptural source for this verse; nonetheless, the appearance of this tradition in Neh 9:26 represents a studied reflection on the general role of the prophet in Israelite society.

The story of life in the land after the conquest continues in Neh 9:27 with a reference to the period of the judges. The beginning of the verse refers in a general way to the cycle recorded in the book of Judges and its language contains echoes from that book. The Israelites cry out to the Lord (Judg 3:15; 4:2, 10:12) in the time of their distress (Judg 3:5, 19, 31; 10:1, 14). God sends saviors (Judg 3:19, 18; 3:9, 15, etc.) who rescue the people from the hand of the enemy.

Both verses 27 and 28 contain the Deuteronomistic phrase "to hear from heaven," with God as subject. In the Priestly literature, God's presence is in the Temple, not heaven, and imagery relating to God tends to be visual, not auditory.[63] The phrase is most reminiscent of the prayer in 1 Kings 8. In that prayer, the plea that God should "hear from heaven" is repeated eight times as a kind of refrain (1 Kgs 8:30, 32, 34, 36, 39, 43, 45, 49). This verse also repeats a phrase found in verses 19, 27, and 31, a phrase that is related to the divine attribute phrase of 17b: כרחמיך. As expounded above, the theme of divine mercy in the face of human apostasy lies at the heart of the prayer.

Consonant with the entire section describing the period of the judges and the monarchy, Neh 9:29 contains phrases that do not refer to any individual incident; rather, it is composed of a pastiche of biblical phrases. The notion that God warned the Israelites repeatedly to obey the law, discussed above in regard to verse 26, recurs in this verse and the next. The phrase ויתנו כתף סוררת is found only in Zech 7:11 outside of this prayer. There is some Deuteronomistic wording, for instance, the phrase וערפם הקשו "stiffened their

---

"witnessing" (presumably to the demands of the covenant), the prophets served to warn the Israelites that punishment was imminent unless they repented. Although properly warned, the Israelites disregarded the threat and even killed the witnesses. Thus, just divine punishment in the form of Exile ensued. This verse from *Jubilees* succinctly illustrates this principle lived out in the history of Israel.

[63] For a more complete discussion of the idea of God's presence in heaven and the emphasis on audition in the Deuteronomic literature, see Weinfeld, *Deuteronomy and the Deuteronomic School* 191–198; and Tryggve N.D. Mettinger, *The Dethronement of Sabaoth* (Lund: CWK Gleerup, 1982), especially 46–50.

neck."[64] As Blenkinsopp has pointed out, the phrase describing the law as life-sustaining אשר־יעשה אדם וחיה בהם , calls to mind Deut. 30:15–20; however, the exact wording is very close to two P-related texts:

Lev 18:5 ושמרתם את־חקתי ואת־משפטי אשר יעשה אתם האדם
וחי בהם אני יהוה

Ezek 20:11 ואתן להם את־חקותי ואת־משפטי הודעתי אותם
אשר יעשה אותם האדם וחי בהם

This provides evidence anew that the author was well-versed in a wide range of scriptural traditions.[65]

Neh 9:30 contains the only reference to the exile; yet the exile is not described explicitly; there is no mention of deportation or life outside the land; rather, the verse states that God gave them into the hands of the "peoples of the lands," עמי הארצת.[66] This circumlocution contrasts with explicit descriptions of the loss of land and deportation found in the Deuteronomistic History as well as in other later Second Temple literature.[67] The reason for the de-emphasis would seem to lie with the author's desire to establish an inalienable claim to the land, a claim writ large in this prayer. How better to

---

[64] Cf. Deut 10:16, 2 Kgs 17:14; Jer 7:26, 17:23, 19:15, Neh 9:16,17, 29; 2 Chr 30:8, 36:13; Weinfeld, *Deuteronomic School*, 341.

[65] Blenkinsopp, *Ezra-Nehemiah*, 306.

[66] This phrase, with both nouns in the plural, appears only in three places, here, Neh 10:29, and 2 Chr 32:13 and is thought to refer generally in the post-exilic literature to the heterogeneous population of the land in contrast to the returnees from Babylon. A.H.J Gunneweg has argued that this term changes meaning over time in ancient Israel. In the post-exilic period, this terms comes to have a theological meaning of those who are not the true Israel and that this negative meaning is taken up and developed in rabbinic literature. See his article, "'AM HA'AREṢ—A Semantic Revolution," *ZAW* 95 (1983) 437–440.

[67] A strong contrast lies in the review of Israelite history by Achior the Ammonite in Jdt 5:17–18: "As long as they did not sin against their God they fared well, for the God who hates wickedness is with them. But when they departed from the way that he had established for them, they were defeated in many battles and were led away enslaved to a foreign country; the temple of their God was razed to the ground, and their cities were captured by their enemies." This is quite clear about exactly what happened and why. It stands in marked contrast to the prayers in Ezra 9 and Daniel 9, in which the loss of land as punishment for the Israelites' sins is explicit as part of lengthy confessions.

establish such a claim than to mitigate the aspect of the Exile having to do with the loss of the land as punishment?[68] Here the punishment for disobedience lies in the fact that the Israelites were put under foreign rule.

The verse also says that God warned "by his spirit" through the prophets. The particular expression is found only in one other late text, Zech 7:12, which makes the same point:

ולבם שמו שמיר משמוע את־התורה ואת־הדברים
אשר שלח יהוה צבאות ברוחו ביד הנביאים הראשנים
ויהי קצף גדול מאת יהוה צבאות

This second reference to God's warning through the prophets underscores the point made in the discussion of Neh 9:26 above. The author wants to make clear that not only were the Israelites warned once at the beginning of their time on the land but repeatedly about the risks of disobedience. The final verse of the section contains a reaffirmation of the merciful character of God, demonstrated by the fact that God did not destroy completely, nor even abandon, the Israelites. לא־עשיתם כלה echoes wording found in Jeremiah (Jer 4:27, 5:18, 30:11, and 46:28). The belief that God did not abandon the Israelites in their dire straits is found also in 9:17, 19 and constitutes a major part of the theme of the prayer along with the divine affirmation that follows in this final clause. The last phrase of this section, which concludes the historical retrospect of the prayer, is אל־חנון ורחום אתה. This is another partial reference to the divine attribute formula, found in more complete form in verse 17, and the phrase offers an appropriate transition to the description of the Jews' current straits.

Life in the Land after Exile

32. And now, our God, the great God, the powerful and the awesome, keeping the covenant and faithful love, do not minimize all the hardship that has come upon us, upon our kings, our officials, our priests, our prophets, our ancestors and upon all your people from the days of the kings of Assyria until today. 33. For you are righteous

---

68 Japhet has argued that it was also the aim of the Chronicler to minimize the effects of the Exile in comparison to the Deuteronomistic History and for that matter the period in Egypt preceding the Exodus. The latter claim she demonstrates in part on the basis of the genealogies in 1 Chronicles 1–9 that suggest continuous settlement of the land of Israel from the period of Jacob through David. Her arguments for the former seem to me more persuasive than the latter. (Japhet, *Ideology*, 364–373).

in all that has come upon us because you have acted faithfully, but we have behaved wickedly. 34. Our kings, our officials, our priests, and our ancestors did not observe your torah and they did not heed your commandments and the warnings with which you charged them. 35. They, in their kingdom and in the abundant goodness that you gave them, in the broad and fertile land that you set before them, did not serve you and they did not turn from their wicked deeds. 36. And now look, we are this day slaves, and the land that you gave our ancestors in order to eat its produce and enjoy its goodness; look, we are slaves upon it. 37. Its great yield goes to the kings that you set over us for our sins. They rule over our bodies and our livestock according to their whim and we are in dire straits.

The final section of the prayer describes the current plight of the returnees to the land. The author draws upon the Israelites' relationship to God in the past and God's abiding patience and mercy in that relationship. The request for help is not explicit. It is implied through analogy. Just as God did not abandon the Israelites in the past, so too, divine concern is alive today and help can be obtained through confession and cries of despair. As one might expect, the last section contains relatively fewer allusions to scripture in comparison with the historical retrospect found in this prayer; nonetheless, these six verses are also infused with biblical language.

Neh 9:32 begins with the word "and now," which marks the transition to the author's current concerns. The phrase is used to introduce a shift in many other prayers, early and late (cf. Num 14:17, Dan 9:15, Ezra 9:10). The first half of the verse is another invocation of God which contains divine attributes in adjectival and participial form. האל הגדול הגבור והנורא: Deut 10:17 contains the identical phrase, without plene spellings. Jer 32:18 contains similar wording: האל הגדול הגבור. The appearance of this phrase in Nehemiah 9 does not represent an interpretion or an allusion to the passage in Deuteronomy so much as simply a set liturgical phrase. This is clear from comparing the context of the two phrases. In Deuteronomy, the phrase occurs in a longer description of God (10:17–18), as part of an exhortation by Moses to the people of Israel to be obedient to the stipulations of the covenant. The verse continues by describing God as keeper of the covenant and faithful love, שומר הברית והחסד. This phrase occurs in Deuteronomic literature: Deut 7:9, 12; 1 Kgs 3:6, 8:23. The comparable phrase in Priestly literature is זכר ברית.[69] In late literature, this phrase is found in

---

[69] See Gen 9:15; Exod 2:24, 6:5; Lev 26:42; Weinfeld, *Deuteronomic School*, 330.

prayers as a liturgical formula, here, in Neh 1:5, and Dan 9:4. Both Nehemiah's prayer in Neh 1:5–11 and Daniel's prayer in Dan 9:4–19 begin with phrases nearly identical to this. Compare the following:

Neh 9:32a ועתה אלהינו האל הגדול הגבור והנורא
שומר הברית והחסד אל־ימעט

Neh 1:5 ואמר אנא יהוה אלהי השמים האל הגדול והנורא
שמר הברית וחסד לאהביו ולשמרי מצותיו:

Dan 9:4 אנא אדני האל הגדול והנורא שמר הברית והחסד
לאהביו ולשמרי מצותיו

The repeated occurrence of this phrase in prayers seems to indicate that it has already become a liturgical formula by the post-exilic period.

There are no identifiable quotes in this verse, nor even phrases or wording that are derived clearly from another particular biblical verse. In contrast to other late prayers, the confessional element is decidedly muted.[70] Verses 34–35 continue the confession. The list of people who are held culpable for sins, "our kings, officials, priests, and ancestors," appears to be a feature of late confessions. Similar lists are found in Jer 44:17, Dan 9:6,8; Ezra 9:7. So too, as discussed above in connection with verse 26, the use of the term עדותיך, "your warnings," is language used in late literature.

The last two verses of the prayer turn to the current situation in which the people are described as עבדים, slaves. Those who refused to serve God in the pre-exilic period (v.35 לא עבדוך) are now reduced to serving foreign overlords. The main concern of the prayer is reflected in these verses: they are not free on the land that God gave their ancestors and its produce goes to foreigners. The language used about the land here is reminiscent of wording in Deuteronomy (e.g., Deut 6:23, 19:8, 26:9) and Jer 2:7 (לאכל את־פריה ואת־טובה). The prayer thus ends much more abruptly than it begins, closing with a lament about the situation in the present.

The Use of Scripture in Nehemiah 9

Our long sojourn in the prayer in Nehemiah 9 offers a strong contrast to the pre-exilic prayer in Deuteronomy 26, where we

---

[70] Cf. Daniel 9, for example, which consists almost entirely of expiatory breastbeating.

started this chapter. While it is true that both recount the history of Israel in an abbreviated form, the elements that compose that history are very different, and more striking is the *way* in which Nehemiah 9 recounts this history: by recourse to scriptural traditions and scriptural interpretations, both fixed and fluid. The prayer in Nehemiah 9 is allusive, interpretive, and uses a full range of sources. There is evidence not only of the author's familiarity with the Deuteronomic literature, but of all the Pentateuch, including the late priestly source, as well as the latter prophetic literature with which there are a number of thematic and textual parallels.

   The preliminary assessment of the uses of scripture in the prayer made in reference to the description of the Exodus in Neh 9:9–12 above can now be reaffirmed and elaborated. The most overt way in which scripture is used in Nehemiah 9 is in direct biblical quotes. The two longest direct quotations in Nehemiah 9 appear in verses 17 and 18 in the center of the long prayer:

> Neh 9:17 "You are a God ready to forgive, gracious and merciful, slow to anger and abounding in steadfast love." (quoting Exod 34:6a)
> Neh 9:18 "This is your God who brought you up out of Egypt."
> (quoting Exodus 32:4b with minor modifications as noted above.)

These two citations reflect the major themes of the prayer, the forgiving, compassionate nature of God and the apostate nature of the people of Israel. These quotes also share another feature in common: in the original text in Exodus, both are divine or human speech and not third person narrative. In the first case, this is divine speech and, more important from the perspective of its liturgical use, divine revelation about God's own character made to Moses. Its use in prayers is thus significant. It indicates that Israelites/Jews know that they can believe God to be merciful, forgiving, and gracious because it was revealed directly by God. The prayer thus calls on the "truest" divine characteristics. By contrast, the prayer's citation of Exod 32:4b also shows the Israelites' "true colors" as idolatrous calf worshippers, at least according to the author. The Israelites can thus depend on the graciousness of God to forgive them even as they are recurrently in need of forgiveness for transgressing the rigorous monotheistic demands of the covenant.

   There is a continuity between the use of these quotes and the use of citations in the pre-exilic prayers discussed in the previous chapter. Pride of place goes to divine speech or promises that were revealed directly to a notable biblical ancestor. For instance, the prayers discussed in the last chapter recurrently quote the promise of land and progeny to Abraham, Isaac, and Jacob. The prayer in 1 Kings 8 cites the Zion covenant to David of 2 Samuel 7. Their appearance in Nehemiah 9 is slightly different, however. It is likely that a single tradent was responsible for tying together the narrative by reiterating divine promises in various narrative forms, including prayers. The author of Nehemiah 9, by contrast, was not the author of the original promises, but is rather drawing upon these written traditions explicitly. There are in total six instances aside from the five-fold reference to the divine attribute formula in which the author makes reference to what was originally divine speech.[71] They are not introduced by a formula such as "it is written . . ." as found in the New Testament or analogous formal markers in Qumran *pesharim*; but they are nonetheless identifiable.[72] Thus a distinct "scripture consciousness" marks the difference between the use of quotes in this post-exilic prayer from earlier prayers.

A second use of scripture is one that involves a certain degree of interpretation of the narrative, though at times the interpretation is subtle or slight enough better to be termed "spin." These extra interpretive elements have worked their way into the warp and woof of the prayer. The overt interpretation might be hidden from view and we see only the proverbial tip of the iceberg. For example the phrase in Neh 9:6 that "the hosts of heaven worship you" reflects an interpretation of the Genesis account that extends more deeply and broadly than that phrase would indicate. Another example of such interpretation appears in 9:26 in which God is said to have warned the Israelites about their punishment through the prophets. Some of the interpretations can be seen more fully developed in later Second

---

[71] The divine attribute formula or phrases from it occurs in Neh 9:17, 19, 27, 28, and 31. The six other references to divine speech follow. Neh 9:7 refers to Gen 15:7 in which God brought Abraham out of Ur of the Chaldeans. Neh 9:9 refers to Exod 3:7 in which God says that he has heard the cry of the Israelites. Neh 9:10 refers to Exod 9:16 in which God gives the reason for the Exodus, "to make for himself a name." Neh 9:15a refers to Exod 16:4 when God tells Moses that he will rain bread from heaven" for the people. Neh 9:15b makes reference to Num 20:8 in which God tells Moses and Aaron to bring water from the rock. Neh 9:23a makes reference to the promise to the ancestors, whose distinctive phrasing to make "descendants like the stars of heaven" recurs in the ancestral literature.

[72] For a listing of the variety of formulas in *pesharim*, see Maurya P. Horgan, *Pesharim: Qumran Interpretations of Biblical Books* (CBQMS 8; Washington, D.C.: Catholic Biblical Association, 1979) 239–244.

Temple literature or in collections of midrash. We shall also examine their appearance in later prayers.

An example of the more subtle form of interpretation, or "spin," can be found in the use of the verb "to choose," with God as subject, in reference to Abraham. Because the divine choice refers normally to David or Jerusalem, the semantic range of this verb adds regal standing to the status of Abraham. Perhaps also the association with the eternal choice of the Davidic dynasty and Jerusalem suggests the immutability of the divine promise made to Abraham and his descendants. Another such slight adaptation of the tradition lies in Neh 9:13 in which God "gives" the Israelites the law at Mount Sinai with the gracious gift of the holy sabbath included along with it.

A third kind of scripturalization has at least three subcategories. Most broadly it is the knitting together of biblical wording found in scripture, in a style that might best be termed "biblicizing." The use of biblical phrases or terms is not surprising in a review of history found in the post-exilic period, but this "biblicizing" is characteristic of late prayers in general as we shall see in other chapters. As other scholars have discovered long since, this language can be difficult to categorize because at times it is difficult to decide how the author meant to use these phrases and terms or they may be employed in an interpretive sense.[73] For instance, the use of the verb בחר, discussed above in reference to God's choice of Abram in verse 7, is both a kind of "biblicizing" because it does not involve explicit citation of scripture that is tied to one particular biblical narrative, and also represents an interpretive "spin" on the word normally used with Jerusalem or David as its object. Another difficulty inherent in this category is that the line between what is properly written scriptural text and oral tradition can be fuzzy. While the author knew the biblical text, it is not at all clear whether or not this particular tradent was looking at a scroll when composing the prayer. It seems that the author just had considerable biblical jargon or entire stories knocking around in his head which were retrievable without reference to a written text.

Some concrete examples will help to clarify the issues involved in making distinctions. One type would include distinctive language

---

[73] As mentioned in the introduction, Bonnie Kittel's discussion of the various uses of scripture in the Qumran Hodayot overlaps in certain respects with the findings here and was helpful to me in clarifying my own categories, except for the fact that she does not treat interpretive uses of scripture as a category. See her book, *The Hymns of Qumran* (Chico, CA: Scholar's Press, 1981) 48–55.

that refers to one particular episode in the Bible and does not recur
elsewhere. For instance, the reference to the Israelites' desire to
return to slavery in Egypt (Neh 9:17) derives from one specific text
as it is described in Numbers 14. The allusion to the incident, as well
as its notable interpretive expansion, is unmistakable.

Another use of biblical phrasing is a reference to a particular
tradition in which the language is already repeated within the Torah,
e.g., make descendants as "numerous as the stars of heaven." The
phrase is used in the promise to the ancestors and is used in general
to refer to that promise. In the first articulation of the promise, in Gen
15:5, that exact phrase is not used, but it is used subsequently in Gen
22:17, 26:4 and then in Exod 32:13, Deut 1:10, 10:22, 28:62, and 1 Chr
27:23. The phrase is used in the Bible only in reference to the great
population of Israel as a result of the divine promise, but because the
promise was reiterated twice to Abraham and once to Isaac, it is not
tied to one passage of scripture as, for instance, a reference to splitting
the Sea refers only to one narrative in Exodus 14–15. Another use of
biblical language that falls into this subcategory is language typically
employed by a certain tradition in the Bible, such as characteristic
phraseology employed by the Deuteronomistic tradents. Moshe
Weinfeld's work has identified many such Deuteronomic phrases.
Weinfeld identifies as Deuteronomic the phrase "to stiffen the neck",
which is found three times in the prayer (Neh 9:16, 17, 29).[74] An
example of distinctively Priestly language would be חקת עולם which
recurs throughout Leviticus. So, too, the distinctive phrase ברית עולם
occurs only in the Priestly stream of tradition, including Ezekiel.

A third variation of "biblicizing" is one in which there is no
single clearly recognizable referent. Rather the phrase is simply
recognizable as scriptural. For instance, the oft-repeated duo,
"statutes and ordinances" (משפטים and חקת), especially as it occurs
with an injunction to the Israelites to observe or keep them, recurs
throughout the biblical literature. Another recurrent term found in
Nehemiah 9 is עם הארץ, found here in the plural. The exact
meaning of the "people of the land" changes in the post-exilic period.
The larger point is nonetheless that this phrase is a decidedly biblical
one.

In addition to these three major categories, it is important to
note another use of biblical language in which scripturalized phrases

---

[74] The phrase actually occurs more in the prose sections of Jeremiah (three
times) than in the book of Deuteronomy, where it appears only once, Deut
10:16. (Weinfeld, *Deuteronomy*, 341).

seem to have been added to a liturgical idiom. This claim is warranted because of their frequent, specialized use in late prayers and psalms. These overlap with the three primary uses outlined above. In this prayer there are a number of such liturgical phrases, many of which are divine titles or actions relating to God. One example from Nehemiah 9 are the references, in whole and part, to the divine attribute formula of Exod 34:6–7. The phrase "in your many mercies" in verse 31 is one such partial form of the divine attribute formula. The attributive adjective "merciful" רחום is used, with one exception, exclusively of God and predominantly in prayers or psalms.[75] The divine action of שׁומר הברית והחסד, "keeping covenant and steadfast love" is another such liturgical phrase. It is associated with the Deuteronomistic literature and used as a formula in prayers of the post-exilic period.[76] Though neither one occurs in this prayer, such divine addresses as "God of Abraham, Isaac, and Jacob" or "Lord God of Hosts" are to a degree scripturalized. The first alludes to the special relationship of God to the pray-er based on the patriarchal accounts. The second concerns God's role as creator of the heavens and all their hosts based on the priestly creation account.

One fact related to the uses of biblical language reviewed above is indubitable: the author was not simply composing scripture *de novo*. By contrast, the author of Deut 26:5–9 recounts history in a way that is almost entirely unmarked by stereotyped phrases or expressions found elsewhere in the Bible. "A wandering Aramean" occurs in Deut 26:5 and there alone. The prayer does contain two Deuteronomic formulas "mighty hand and outstretched arm" and a "land flowing with milk and honey," and these phrases seem to have been traditions preserved orally, but the prayer as a whole retells history in a unique way.

The crucial difference between von Rad's historical "credo" in the Deuteronomic literature and the historical recital in the prayer under consideration in this chapter lies in the evolving role of scripture throughout the Second Temple period. The retellings found in the later literature contain more than the bare bones of what von

---

[75] The one exception is Ps 112:4, a wisdom psalm, in which righteous God-fearers who obey the commandments are described as gracious and merciful, echoing the preeminent divine attributes of Exod 34:6. The verbal form of this root also usually occurs in reference to God's relationship to Israel, though it is also used with humans as the subject.

[76] Weinfeld cites this as a Deteronomic phrase that is used as a liturgical formula in the post-exilic literature: Dan 9:4; Neh 1:5; 9:32. (*Deuteronomy*, 330). It also appears in 1 Kgs 8:23.

Rad believed to be Israel's core beliefs. It is also necessary to part company with von Rad's theological assessment of these compositions. He viewed later, more expansive retellings of Israel's history as gothic embellishments around a pure core of authentic memory, rather than the view taken here that the later retellings, too, are legitimate acts of reconstructive memory and interpretation that are an equally important part of the religious traditions of Israel.[77] In this prayer in the book of Nehemiah, even as scripture is being written for the first time, scripture preys on scripture as grist for a new composition. There is no clean divide between a canon of fixed scripture and its interpretation; rather, the two are enmeshed in this prayer. The process of tradition has long since begun.

Related Prayers Containing Historical Reviews

We noted at the outset of the chapter that Nehemiah 9 is not without precedent in pre-exilic literature. The cultic recital of Deuteronomy 26 also includes a brief review of Israel's history. Gerhard von Rad, who played a significant role in drawing attention to that recital, also observed that historical retrospects had continued relevance for later biblical authors. He noted especially an influence on a number of psalms that tend to expand and interpret the earlier "confessions." Psalms 78, 105, 106, 135, and 136 all contain such recitations of biblical history which appropriate scripture and tradition. They have been the focus of much scholarship for that reason.[78] There are also two prophetic prayers that contain long

---

[77] Von Rad found what he considered to be the most ancient and succinct form of the "holy history" in Deuteronomy 26:5–9 and Joshua 24:2–12. In both of these passages the divine acts mentioned are limited to three: the promise to the patriarchs, the deliverance from Egypt, and the conquest. Von Rad's description of these passages as "credos" that concentrate on "the objective historical facts" is open to question because it is clear that already by the time Joshua 24 was written, it was covered with an interpretive film that obscured the "historical acts" underlying it.

[78] The Scandinavian Myth-and-Ritual school located the *Sitz-im-Leben* of these liturgical pieces in a cultic New Year's Festival that was a way of making past events "live" in the present (Sigmund Mowinckel, Johannes Pedersen). While this is an attractive theory in many respects, there is scant positive evidence from the Bible to support such a view. No such festival is ever mentioned or described; scholars have rather inferred its existence on the basis of texts and Ugaritic parallels and on analogy with the Babylonian Akītu festival.

Other scholars have looked at these particular psalms with an eye to how the history of Israel is described. See for instance, Claus Westermann's *Praise and Lament in the Psalms* (Keith R. Crim and Richard N. Soulen, trans.;

reviews of history, Jer 32:16–25 and Isa 63:7–64:12. Examples of historical restrospects among the Qumran prayers include 4Q504, the *Words of the Luminaries* and, though not as comprehensive as other retrospects, 1QM, the *War Scroll*, cols. X-XI. These compositions were not of course all written at the same time. Psalm 78 is a pre-exilic psalm that narrates the story of Israel from the exodus to the early monarchy. It dates no earlier than the division of the kingdom because the psalm mentions the rejection of the "tent of Joseph" and the "tribe of Ephraim" which most understand to be a reference to the northern kingdom. It thus may postdate the fall of the northern kingdom to Assyria in 722 BCE. It is similar in theme to Nehemiah 9 in that it focuses on divine providence and Israelite apostasy particularly during the wilderness period. Another similarity with Nehemiah 9 is the occasional disregard for chronological sequence. For instance, the wilderness experience is mentioned in verses 14–31, but the subsequent verses 42–51 recount the plagues in Egypt.

Jer 32:17–25 is also a pre-exilic composition. The basic structure of the prayers in Jeremiah 32 and Nehemiah 9 is the same. There are three elements; each begins with a formal address to God, then is followed by praise to God based on divine activity on Israel's behalf throughout history, and concludes with an element of complaint or lament related to the current situation.[79] The historical review in Jeremiah 32 focuses on the elements of exodus, conquest, and possession of the land using language characteristic of the Deuteronomistic historian. It is more abbreviated than the review in Nehemiah 9, comprising only five verses in comparison with the 26

Atlanta: John Knox, 1981), *ad loc,* and Westermann's *Elements of Old Testament Theology* (English transl. Atlanta: John Knox, 1982; orig. pub. Göttingen: Vandenhoeck & Ruprecht, 1978). F.C. Fensham has also written on the connection of these psalms to the prayer in Nehemiah 9 examined in this chapter and in particular the rationale behind the particular events included in the compositions. He reaches the rather general conclusion that Nehemiah 9 and Psalm 105 stress the disobedience of the people and thus function as confessional pieces in the cult. He does not specifically discuss the use of scripture in these compositions in his article, "Nehemiah 9 and Pss. 105, 106, 135 and 136. Post-Exilic Historical Traditions in Poetic Form," *Journal of Northwest Semitic Languages* 9 (1981) 35–51.

[79] Patrick D. Miller provides a structural outline of some of the biblical prayers for "help and intercession" in an appendix to his book, *They Cried to the Lord: The Form and Theology of Biblical Prayer* (Minneapolis: Fortress, 1994). He includes Jer 32:16–25. Miller groups Neh 9:6–37 with other "late prose prayers of confession."

verses in Nehemiah. Neh 9:5–37 also contains a brief element of communal confession in verses 33 and 37 which differentiates it from Jer 32:17–25. The prayer in Jeremiah combines the themes of God as creator with God as redeemer from Egypt.[80] Indeed, the first verse of the prayer addresses God as the creator of heaven and earth who made them "with your great power and outstretched arm." The latter phrase is Deuteronomistic and used elsewhere to characterize God's work in the Exodus. Its combination here in a single verse with priestly creation language thus represents a marriage of two themes, identifying the God who created the world with the God of the Exodus, a combination found in Nehemiah 9. The prayer in Jeremiah 32 should thus be understood as an intermediate stage between the prayers in Deuteronomy 26 and Nehemiah 9 in terms of the degree of its scripturalization and its structural development.

Psalms 105, 106, 135, and 136 offer interesting parallels to Nehemiah 9. Although he does not examine the particular language each author uses and its relationship to earlier scriptural language, F.C. Fensham has assessed more broadly the shared traditions among these compositions.[81] This group of psalms is mainly concerned with the history of Israel from the time of the patrarchs to the entry into the land. The historical retrospect in Nehemiah 9 is more embracing than that. A thorough study of each of these psalms cannot be undertaken here, so we will let Psalm 105 stand for the group.

Psalm 105 is a psalm of thanksgiving that recalls God's deeds on Israel's behalf. It contains mention of the patriarchs including Joseph, the plagues, the Exodus, the wilderness wandering, and the entry into the land. One significant feature of the prayer is that pride of place goes to divine speech in a way similar to the pre-exilic prayers discussed in the previous chapter and Nehemiah 9. The first mention of divine speech is in Ps 105:10–11, which reiterates the part of the Abrahamic covenant promising the inalienable gift of the land: "And he affirmed this statute to Jacob; to Israel, an everlasting covenant, saying: "To you I give the land of Canaan, a portion for your inheritance." It is important to note that this "quote" is not a

---

[80] Moshe Weinfeld suggests that this creation element becomes important in "the exilic and post-exilic liturgy," citing Jer 32:17, Neh 1:5, 9:6, 1 Chr 29:2, 2 Chr 2:11; 20:6, 3 Macc 2:3; *1 Enoch* 84:2–6 and the doxologies of Isaiah; *Deuteronomy,* 39. Weinfeld uses the term liturgy loosely and does not indicate in what ways these various pieces would have been incorporated into actual religious services, communal or individual.

[81] Fensham, "Nehemiah 9 and Pss. 105, 106, 135 and 136."

verbatim quote from anywhere in Genesis. The everlasting covenant ברית עולם is mentioned in Genesis 17:7, 13, 19, but the phrase with the words חבל נחלה in juxtaposition occurs only in Deut 32:9 and Ps 78:55. In both of these instances, the term refers to the people as God's own possession, rather than the land as a possession of the people Israel, which is the sense of Ps 105:11. The "quote" is thus an invention by the author, albeit based on biblical phrasing. Like the mention of the patriarchal covenant in Neh 9:8, this does not include the promise of numerous descendants; the land is the preeminent concern both here and in the psalm as a whole. The historical retrospect begins with a description of God's covenant with Abraham in verses 8–11 with a clear emphasis on the land grant. The psalm also ends with the entry into the land in verses 44–45 as the fulfillment of the divine promise.

A second "quotation" of divine speech occurs in 105:15 in a passage that refers to the ancestral period. Verse 14 mentions that God "rebuked kings on their account." And verse 15 continues, "Do not touch my anointed ones; do not harm my prophets." This seems to allude to Gen 20:7 in which God appears in a dream to King Abimelech of Gerar and God refers to Abraham as a prophet. But it occurs in the singular and there is no mention in Genesis 20 of "anointed one." Ps 105:15 is the only occasion on which the patriarchs are identified as "anointed ones." Like the "quote" in verse 11, this does not correspond to the divine speech in Genesis 20. Both quotations of divine speech have been embroidered. The rhetorical function of the quotes is to emphasize God's gift of the land to Israel as well as the special status of the patriarchs.

The history recounted in Psalm 105 focuses on individual figures in biblical history—Abraham, Joseph, Moses and Aaron—to a greater extent than does Nehemiah 9, which downplays the role of Moses and omits mention of Joshua or Aaron; but like Nehemiah 9, the psalm is rife with biblical phrases. In recounting the plagues in Egypt, the author uses distinctive expressions from that narrative: "waters into blood" that result in dead fish (Exod 7:20–21), the land that "swarmed with frogs" (Exod 7:28), and "swarms of flies and gnats" (Exod 8:13,17). Only eight plagues are mentioned in this psalm, but their wording nonetheless demonstrates knowledge of the Exodus account of the plagues. As in the other psalms with historical retrospects, Psalm 105 remembers history through scriptural references and interpretation much in the same way as in Nehemiah 9.

Isaiah 63:7–64:12 also contains a historical retrospect. The prayer dates from the sixth century, though a reference to the devastated Temple would suggest that the composition was written before its rebuilding by Zerubbabel.[82] Commentators have categorized this piece as a communal lament and related it form-critically to a psalm lament.[83] It combines both third-person description with second-person address to God. The prayer begins, "I will recount the gracious deeds of the Lord, the prayers of the Lord." Isa 63:7–14 contain the historical recital recalling the "gracious deeds." God is not addressed in the second person until 63:15. The rest of the prayer, Isa 63:15–64:12, contains direct address to God focusing on the current situation of despair the community finds itself in, with the concern that God has abandoned them to excessively harsh punishment.

The character of the retold history in this lament is different from Nehemiah 9.[84] The author is lamenting the current desolation of Jerusalem and desecration of the Temple. Two remarkable verses pose questions as a way of lamenting God's seeming lack of involvement in the current situation of despair. Isa 63:11–12 reads:

> Then they remembered the days of old, of Moses his servant. Where is the one who brought them up out of the sea with the shepherd of his flock?[85] Where is the one who put within them his holy spirit? Who causes his glorious arm to march at the right hand of of Moses? Who divided the water before them to make for himself an everlasting name? Who led them through the depths?

These questions point to the God who has intervened in the past for the Israelites. Each of them is a "scripturalized" question,

---

[82] H.G.M. Williamson argues that the passage dates to the exilic period. Moreover, he hypothesizes on the basis of the affinities among the passage in Isaiah, Psalm 106, and Nehemiah 9 that they were used in penitential liturgies that took probably place on the ruined site of the temple during the exilic period; "Isaiah 63,7–64,11: Exilic Lament or Post-Exilic Protest?" *ZAW* 102 (1990) 58. His proposal is quite interesting, albeit speculative.

[83] Claus Westermann, *Isaiah 40–66* (Philadelphia: Westminster, 1969) 386 and Paul D. Hanson, *Isaiah 40–66* (Louisville, KY: John Knox, 1995) 235. Westermann suggests the *Sitz-im-Leben* of the piece is "a hymn to be used by the community in worship."

[84] According to Paul Hanson, "One of the functions of the historical resumé in the lament was to create intolerable tension between things as they were in the recalled past and as they were in the present as a means of shocking alienated parties into an honest confrontation with the causes of the tragic impasse." (*Isaiah*, 237).

[85] Reading singular רעה with the Greek for the MT רעי.

although they also contain embroidery, wording that does not occur in the original biblical narrative itself. For instance, the phrase "the shepherd of his flock" is not contained within the Exodus account. The phrase "holy spirit" occurs only here and in Ps 51:13. Other phrases are clearly derived from the book of Exodus: "divided the sea" (Exod 14:16), the divine motive for dividing the Red Sea, "to make for himself an everlasting name" (Exod 9:16). This wording, or a rough approximation of it, is also used to describe the exodus in Nehemiah 9. Williamson has pointed out that only in Isa 63:11 and Neh 9:20 is there a reference to God's spirit in association with the wilderness traditions.[86] The form is novel, occurring as it does here in a series of questions, but the phrasing is easily recognizable. Isa 63:7–64:12 thus provides another example of a scripturalized prayer.

Let us also linger briefly with the Qumran composition, *Words of the Luminaries*, because 4QDibHam is thoroughly scripturalized. Although only two of the fragments have an explicit indication of the days on which they are to be recited, Esther Chazon argues that the *Words of the Luminaries* contains a series of prayers for each weekday deliberately composed by one author.[87] A notable feature of these weekday prayers is the historical retrospect they contain, stretching from the creation of Adam on the first day to the exile and return. Whether or not we accept her suggestion that the fragments comprise daily prayers for a full week, if we accept her stronger argument for unitary authorship which is in part based on internal linguistic parallels, 4QDibHam provides another example of a liturgical composition that includes a historical retrospect, akin to Neh 9:5–37. Chazon has pointed out some of the ways in which these prayers have appropriated biblical language.[88] One feature of the

---

[86] Williamson, "Isaiah 63,7–64,11" *ZAW* 102 (1990), 56.

[87] Chazon, "Prayers from Qumran and Their Historical Implications," *DSD* 1 (1994) 265-284.

[88] "4QDibHam: Liturgy or Literature?" 452–455. She also makes the observation that one way in which 4QDibHam differs from historical retrospects in biblical prayer (such as Psalm 106 and Neh 9:5–37) is that the former explicitly petitions God to remember his past acts, (454).

Weinfeld suggests that the dominant motif in 4QDibHam (as well as in the Prayer for Mondays and Thursdays) is the remembering of the covenant with the patriarchs; however, the citations from 4QDibHam Weinfeld adduces to prove this point do not clearly specify a particular covenant. Given the fragmentary state of the collection, it is certainly possible that the patriarchal covenant was originally mentioned, but on the basis of the extant remains, this is inconclusive; cf. Weinfeld, "Liturgical Practice," 249–250. For instance, he compares "And remember Your covenant, you who brought us out in the

prayers in particular is relevant to our larger discussion. Four times in the weekday prayers, the prayer of Moses in Num 14:18–19 is quoted.[89] For Chazon this serves as a piece of evidence for the prayers' unitary authorship. For our discussion, it serves to underscore the continued reuse of the divine attribute formula, first found in Exod 34:6–7. It recalls the formulaic repetition of the divine attribute formula in Neh 9:17, 19, 27, 28, and 31. Here again, divine speech and divine self-revelation are accorded a special place in this series of prayers. Many other interesting features of biblical interpretation are present in 4QDibHam, but a thorough discussion of these must await another study.[90] It is clear that additional research on the use of biblical citation and interpretation not only in 4QDibHam, but in the Qumran corpus of prayers and hymns as a whole is needed to discern how the legacy of Israel's scripture is recycled through particular biblical motifs.

Conclusion

A few conclusions are warranted. We have seen that the historical review occurs not only in Nehemiah 9 but in psalms and prayers found in prophetic literature. It thus seems to have become a generally accepted compositional element in prayers. Although a number are laments or confessions, Psalm 105 reviewed above, is a psalm of thanksgiving, so we cannot say that the historical recital was restricted to one form of prayer.

What was the purpose of including the historical element in the prayer? The rhetorical effect of historical retrospects that occur in prayers is different from historical recitals found elsewhere in narratives. Judith 5:5–18, for instance, is one such review placed in the mouth of a foreigner, Achior the Ammonite. In that passage, he

---

eyes of the nations" (4Q504 1–2, V 9–10) with the phrase from the Tahanun for Mondays and Thursdays in the Siddur, "Have mercy upon us for the sake of your covenant." By contrast, the covenant at Sinai (4Q504 3 ii 6–19) and the covenant with David (4Q504 iv 6–8) are clearly recalled.

[89] (4Q504 1–2 ii 7–8; 4Q504 7 13–14; f. 6 10–11; and f. 3 ii 7); Chazon, "Liturgy or Literature?" 452.

[90] Chazon notes that a phrase concerning the ingathering of the exiles, derived from Isa 11:12; 56:8, that occurs in several apocryphal prayers from the Second Temple period (Sir 36:13–19; *Pss. Sol.* 8:28; 2 Macc 1:27) also appears in DibHam (4Q504 1–2 vi 12–14) and the *Festival Prayers* (4Q509 3 3–4). It is also seen in later rabbinic sources and part of rabbinic liturgy; "Prayers from Qumran," 278–279. She does not explore specifically how the biblical sources, if they are sources, relate to their use in the non-biblical literature.

tells the Assyrian general Holofernes about the nature of the people he is about to confront by recounting God's role in Israelite history from Ur to the post-exilic period. Placing such a confession in the mouth of a non-Israelite serves to emphasize for the reader the possibility of a universal recognition of Israel's God. By contrast, the role of the historical retrospect when it is found in prayers offered by Israelites, whether in the Psalms or in narratives, is to affirm a community's self-understanding in relation to God. The purpose of this reappropriation in the psalms and prayers was to make the character praying self-consciously associate him- or herself with the ongoing history of Israel, just as the farmer offering a prayer and a portion of his first fruits was connecting himself to the history of his people. Indeed, the people as a whole was constituted in part by shared historical memory, in particular, memories of God's promises and actions on their behalf in the past.

How was history retold in these prayers? It was recalled through the lens of scriptural memory, using the words of a sacred text that was itself shared by a people. Israel's expectations were established by how God had acted in the past as well as by divine promises made in the past. In the post-exilic period, the record of these acts and promises lay in texts and so the remembrance of history was shaped by the words in those texts. We have seen, in particular, how the divine attribute formula in Exod 34:6–7 shaped the expectations of the prayer in Nehemiah 9. This ancient formula, crystallized and bound up with other sacred scripture over time, came to be used as a focus and refrain in this prayer as a true representation of God's gracious and compassionate character. For the author of Nehemiah 9, there was divine self-revelation to this effect in the past as well as evidence from divine salvation during the course of Israelite history. The internalization of the "word of God" by this learned author of the post-exilic period resulted in a composition that is permeated with textual references, allusions, and citations. Nehemiah 9 uses scriptural traditions from all parts of the Bible including the priestly source, not just the Deuteronomistic material, although the latter strongly influenced the author. Some of the uses of scripture, as in the case of the divine attribute formula, seem to be conscious structural exegetical uses of earlier textual traditions. There are some overt citations of earlier biblical material. There are interpretive elements, such as the use of "the host of the heavens worships before you" that hints at the divine liturgy, ongoing from creation. Such elements suggest a knowledge of interpretive traditions associated with the creation account. In other instances, the appropriation of scripture seems less conscious and suggests an author who is simply using the language of scripture as a native tongue. But behind all of these multifarious appropriations lies the text, in a way strikingly different from the simple prayer of the farmer offering his first fruits, as described in the book of Deuteronomy. As we turn now to consider other prayers from a later period in the Second Temple era, we will see how the use of scripture continues to shape the composition of prayers.

Chapter 3

The Past as Blueprint for Present
Salvation by Typology in Judith 9

The author of Second Isaiah had an analogical imagination. With sensitivity to the agency of God in human events, he vividly portrayed the return from exile in Babylon using language linking the post-exilic restoration to the primordial creation account and the crossing of the Red Sea. Consider the following petition that appears in Isa 51:9–11:

> 9. Awake, awake, don strength, O arm of the Lord. Awake as in days of old, generations from eternity. Are you not the slayer of Rahab, the one who speared Tannin? 10. Are you not the one who dried up Yamm, the waters of the great deep? Did you not make a path through the channels of the sea where the redeemed could cross? 11. The ransomed of the Lord will return and enter Zion with singing. Joy will be upon their heads forever. Gladness and rejoicing will be carried away; and sorrow and sighing shall flee.

The prophet's address identifies God as the one who has created the world by drying up Yamm and in similar fashion making a path through the waters so that Israel might be created out of a redeemed band of slaves. As many scholars have pointed out, Deutero-Isaiah is replete with language that makes such typological associations between events.[1] In the book of Judith, we encounter a second

---

[1] Michael Fishbane points out the prayer in Isa 51:9–11 as an example of the typological "historicization of myth" in Israelite thinking. For a discussion of the use of typologies within the Bible, see the section of Fishbane's book dealing with typological interpretation (*Biblical Interpretation in Ancient Israel*, 350–379). Fishbane identifies four different types of typologies in the Bible: cosmological-historical, historical, spatial, and biographical. See also Bernhard W. Anderson, "The Exodus Typology in Second Isaiah," in *Israel's*

117

century author who could also peer across the gulf of time and see contemporary events mirrored in the life and times of ancient Israel.

The previous chapter illuminated the careful way in which the author of the prayer in Nehemiah appropriated biblical language in its retelling of history from creation to the contemporary period of Persian subjugation in early post-exilic Israel. The focus of this chapter, the prayer in Jdt 9:2–14, shares in some aspects, and indeed, intensifies, some of the uses of the Bible that we saw in Nehemiah 9. On one hand, there is an intensification of the use of scripture and midrashic interpretation. The second century author of Judith 9 crafted a prayer that contains biblical allusions and citations as well as interpretive motifs not found in the Bible, but that can be seen in other contemporaneous works. Yet Judith 9 owes a different debt to scripture from Nehemiah 9 that is not explained simply by the fact that it was written in a different era: Judith's is a distinctively typological appropriation of scripture. As opposed to using scripture from all parts of the Torah, Judith 9 reflects the special influence of three sections of the Bible: Genesis 34, the story of Dinah's rape and her brothers' revenge; the book of Isaiah, especially the narrative concerning the siege of Jerusalem by Sennacherib in Isaiah 36–39; and Exodus 15, the Song of the Sea. This chapter seeks to show that Judith's appropriation of scripture represents a typological understanding of people and events in the Bible. Judith's typological perspective is not entirely new, however, because the author found ample precedent for this kind of thinking in the book of Isaiah itself, with its understanding of the return from exile as a new exodus.

The prayer makes the most explicit use of Genesis 34 in order to justify Judith's violent attack on a foreigner who threatens to "rape" the innocent. The debt is revealed not only in the forthright appropriation of the story of Dinah, but also in the theological motifs and larger thematic concerns contained in the prayer. The prayer and the book as a whole draw other implicit analogies that are apparent in certain structural similarities as well as a web of biblical allusions. The devastation wrought by a foreign army marching through the land and the threat of the desecration of the Temple by a foreign ruler had happened a number of times in the history of the Jewish people. The author of the book of Judith conceived of these incursions not as distinctive events but as a recurrent pattern in which the same constellation of forces were arrayed against the

---

Prophetic Heritage (B.W. Anderson and W. Harrelson, eds.; New York: Harper and Row, 1962) 177–195.

Jewish people. Thus the author thought of the current situation in terms of a previous biblical event in which the country and the Temple were threatened in a similar manner: the seventh century rampage of Sennacherib through Judah. The structure and contents of the prayer itself are modeled after Isa 37:16–20/2 Kgs 19:15–19, Hezekiah's entreaty to God during the Assyrian siege of Jerusalem. The prayer partakes of the pre-exilic ideas that developed as part of "Zion theology," and Judith can be said to wrestle—quite literally if we consider her tumble on the couch with Holofernes—with the notion of the inviolability of Zion traditions that likely grew around Israel's Solomonic Temple in Jerusalem during the period of the United Monarchy. In fact, it can be stated even more pointedly that the tale as a whole can be understood as a lengthy post-exilic parable of a particular genre: the inviolability of Zion as it should be construed in the post-exilic era. The moral of the story is that God will protect the holy city, Jerusalem; however, divine aid will only be offered if the entire community remains faithful to the covenant. Moreover, divine protection arrives only through the agency of a faithful, covenant-upholding human servant. In this case, the agent is a widow, a member of the Simeonite clan. This explains the overarching rationale behind the biblical passages the author uses.

The prayer draws from a narrower range of biblical sources than does the review of history in Nehemiah 9, but it also differs in a more profound way. The prayer reflects a different hermeneutic at work. The author of Nehemiah 9 understood the contemporary history of post-exilic Judah as a continuation of the pre-exilic history of Israel. The immediate situation of the people in Nehemiah is different, yet the relationship to an unchanging God who is always faithful to the divine covenant remains the same. In contrast, Judith's overall appropriation of scripture represents a typological understanding of biblical characters and events with an understanding of history that is not so much linear and continuous, but cyclical, manifesting recurrent patterns. I would suggest it is this underlying assumption that leads the author to portray a contemporary situation as analogous to a number of biblical ones.

The book of Judith is not unique in this kind of scriptural appropriation among books of the Second Temple period. For example, the book of Tobit seems to have been shaped by numerous images and themes from the Bible—Job's suffering and perseverance; the Joseph story of the role of the Israelite in a foreign land, as well as the betrothal scenes of Isaac and Jacob.[2] DiLella has suggested that the placement of the final prayer of praise in chapter 13 of the book of Tobit, coming as it does right before the narration of Tobit's death, is modeled after the Song of the Sea in Exod 15:1–21. Clearly, the author of Tobit also drew on scenes and characters from the Bible that he viewed as prototypes on which to pattern his own principal characters and the narrative events. There are also a number of prayers that date from the Second Temple period that reinterpret one episode from biblical history, as does Judith 9 in its redeployment of Genesis 34. We will discuss some of these prayers briefly at the end of the chapter.

Our discussion of the prayer in Judith 9 requires consideration of two ways in which the books of Judith and Nehemiah differ. One difference derives from the relation of each prayer to the larger composition. Nehemiah 9 is not connected integrally to the narrative course of events in the book of Nehemiah, which some scholars have pointed to as evidence that the prayer is an interpolation. In Judith, the prayer is integrally connected to the narrative as a whole and no one questions that the author of Judith 9 is also the author of the entire book. The prayer is linked to the narrative action—Judith prays for help in delivering her people from foreign aggressors and the prayer is answered in the unfolding drama. Discussion of Nehemiah 9 therefore did not require discussion of its larger context. Judith 9, however, is related in a number of ways to its narrative context, and some discussion of the book as a whole helps illuminate parts of the prayer.

Specific literary issues relating to the book's composition as a whole and its relationship to the prayer will be considered *ad loc* in the course of the chapter, but the second difference between the two works, the historical character of each book, warrants attention at the outset. Ezra-Nehemiah was written to chronicle a particular period in Israelite/Jewish history, the reconstitution of the Jewish community after the exile, and to depict its tribulations under the new leadership. Although there are continuing scholarly arguments

---

[2] Carey Moore suggests that Tobit's plot and structure were influenced not only by the plot and details of the Joseph story (Ruppert, 1972) and the betrothal scenes of Isaac and Jacob, but also by many other elements in the book of Genesis; however, it is the book of Deuteronomy that provides the basic theology for the book of Tobit in general (DiLella, 1979) and for Tobit's farewell discourse in particular (Tobit 14). See Moore's entry "Tobit," *Anchor Bible Dictionary* (New York: Doubleday, 1992) vol. VI, 585–594 and his commentary *Tobit* (AB 40A; Garden City, NY: Doubleday, 1996).

over the nature of the conflation of the stories of Ezra and Nehemiah and the sequence of the return from the exile, no one disputes the essential historicity that lies behind the events narrated. But Judith's origins are less obvious. Some scholars have assumed that the author of Judith was simply ignorant on historical matters.[3] Attempts at a precise dating have stumbled over the fact that the seeming "historical" references in the book, when understood as masked references to real people and events, remain indecipherable. Scholars have tried to discern the traces of an actual historical invasion of Israel by a foreign army, by reading Holofernes and "Nebuchadnezzar" as ciphers variously for Assyrian, Persian, or Greek invaders. But some details of the scenario are contradictory. For instance, the purported "invasion" of the land by Holofernes' troops seems to be described as coming from the south (7:17–18) and elsewhere from the north (4:6; 8:21;11:14,19). Though many have tried to isolate the particular historical situation that prompted the author of Judith to write this book, the exact historical moment has proven elusive. In fact, the very number of proposals for the historical circumstances giving rise to its authorship and the consequent attempts to posit a number of redacted editions of the book of Judith —none of which has met with any consensus—suggests the futility of such a project. Moreover, such an attempt misses the larger meta-historical point the author most surely meant to convey, that the Jews had faced and would continue to face recurrent threats to their physical safety and to the sanctity of the Temple. One imagines that the author might be quite amused at the attempt of historical-critical scholars to locate the setting and personages so precisely when these were so purposefully camouflaged. The book itself militates against such an attempt by veiling its characters as pseudo-historical individuals. Nebuchadnezzar, that Babylonian king who rained terror on sixth century Israel, is vividly alive in the book and in the biblical memory of second century Jews. In the book of Judith, Nebuchadnezzar represents Everyking, that perennial historical threat to the safety and well-being of the Jews in their Temple on their land. There is no need to give an exact name; it need not be Sennacherib or Antiochus IV Epiphanes, because a new one will

---

[3] So says Otto Eissfeldt: "It can be seen how little the author knew history from the fact that he makes Nebuchadnezzar (604–562) king of the Assyrians with his residence in Nineveh which had been destroyed in 612, and show him still ruling even after the restoration of the Jewish religious community (520–516)." Quotation from his *The Old Testament: An Introduction* (Peter Ackroyd, trans.; New York: Harper & Row, 1965) 586.

come along to threaten the Jews, if not in this generation, then in the next or the succeeding one. As Carey Moore has suggested, even in the first verse of the book of Judith, the author seems to be winking to his audience that the tale to be told is not to be taken as a verifiably historical account by locating the setting during the period when Nebuchadnezzar ruled over the Assyrians from his capital Nineveh.[4] Indeed, it seems likely that the book of Judith was not intended primarily to relate any one actual crisis in the history of the Jews, but instead seeks to convey a set of moral ahistorical truths like any good work of fiction. This understanding of the narrative aims of the book of Judith is necessary to appreciate fully the way in which Judith 9 makes use of the biblical past to construct a biblicized present. A close examination of the prayer, as well as its relation to the larger purpose in the book of Judith, will thus reveal this typological mind at work.

Jdt 9:2–14:

9:2. Lord, God of my ancestor Simeon, into whose hand you gave a sword for revenge against foreigners, who loosed the head covering of a virgin for disgrace and laid bare the thigh for shame and polluted the womb for defilement, for you said, "This should not be" but they did it; 3. in return for which you gave their rulers over to murder, and their bed, which was abashed at their seduction/ deception, over to blood, and you struck slaves with rulers and rulers on their thrones. 4. And you gave their wives over to plunder and their daughters over to captivity and all their spoils over for apportionment among the sons beloved by you, whose zeal for you was great and who detested the profanation of their blood and who called upon you for help. O God, my God, listen to me also, a widow.

5. For you have done those former things and those afterward and those that are now and those that are coming. Those things that you had in mind came to happen 6. and those which you wished presented themselves and they said: "Behold, here we are;" for all your paths are prepared and your judgment is with foreknowledge.

7. For behold, the Assyrians have multiplied in their power. They have been exalted with horse and rider; they prided themselves in the arms of couriers; they hoped in shields and in javelins and in bow and sling, and they did not recognize that you are the Lord who crushes wars, 8. the Lord is your name. Dash their strength in your power and smash their rule in your rage; for they desire to desecrate your sanctuary, to defile the dwelling place of your name of glory, to cut down with the sword the horn of your altar. 9. Look on their arrogance. Send down your wrath on their heads; put into my hand, the widow's, the strength for what I have devised. 10. Through my

---

4 Carey A. Moore, *Judith* (AB; Garden City, NY: Doubleday, 1985) 46–47.

lips of deception/seduction, strike down slave with ruler and ruler with his servant. Shatter their haughtiness by the hand of a female.

11. For your strength is not in a multitude, nor your sovereignty in might, but you are God of the humble; you are the helper of the poor, protector of the weak, guardian of the despairing, savior of those with no hope. 12. Please, please, O God of my father and God of the inheritance of Israel, Lord of the heavens and the earth, creator of the waters, king of all your creation, listen to my prayer.

13. Trade my speech and deception/seduction for their wound and welt, they who would do harsh things to your covenant and your sacred house and Mount Zion and the house of your sons' possession. 14. And do this before your entire nation and every tribe, make it known because you are the God of all power and might and there is no other who safeguards the people of Israel but you.

Summary of contents:
  2–4   invocation and reinterpretation of events in Genesis 34
  5–6   abstract and generalized characterization of divine power
  7–10   description of present situation of distress Judith's request
         for divine intervention and divine empowerment
  11–12 characterization of divine power through divine titles
         request for God to hear Judith
  13–14 Judith's specific petition, a request for deception
         and additional motivation clause

Judith 9 and Genesis 34

In contrast to the other more implicit uses of scripture in this prayer, the first three verses of Judith's petition refer overtly to one biblical episode, the rape of Dinah and the revenge of her brothers in Genesis 34. The author draws on this particular story to provide an example of how God works on Israel's behalf and how Israel should respond to outside intrusions. This recollection of one significant moment in Israel's past sets the tone for the rest of the prayer. It is both a request for divine help and a call to action. The biblical interpretation in this representation of the story of Dinah contains motifs that can also be found in other compositions of the same period: the *Testament of Levi*, *Jubilees*, and a composition by Theodotus (as well as some writings from a later period, in Josephus' *Antiquities* and *Joseph and Aseneth*).[5] The way the biblical story is

---

[5] James L. Kugel has disentangled the many interpretive strands relating to the rape of Dinah in Second Temple literature in "The Story of Dinah in the *Testament of Levi*," *HTR* 85 (1992) 1–34. Cf. also Devorah Dimant's treatment of the appropriation of Genesis 34 in Judith 9, *Jubilees* 30, and *T. Levi* in her article "Mikra in the Apocrypha and Pseudepigrapha," *Mikra*, especially 396–

appropriated in this prayer is unique nonetheless because it serves a larger function in the book; namely, justifying Judith's act of violence against Holofernes by portraying it as an act analogous to Simeon's vengeance against the Shechemites, which was divinely sanctioned, according to Judith's interpretation. Another aspect of her interpretation of this story that sets it apart from other Second Temple interpretations is the typological/allegorical representation of Dinah, referred to as "the virgin" in verse 2. The sexual violation of an Israelite woman is here viewed as equivalent in moral terms to the violation of the Jerusalem Temple precincts. These two elements of the interpretation will become more clear after a closer look at Jdt 9:2–4.

> 9:2. Lord God of my ancestor Simeon, into whose hand you gave a sword for revenge against foreigners, who loosed the head covering of a virgin for disgrace and laid bare the thigh for shame and polluted the womb for defilement, for you said, "This should not be" but they did it; 3. in return for which you gave their rulers over to murder and their bed, which was abashed at their seduction/deception, over to blood, and you struck slaves with rulers and rulers on their thrones. 4. And you gave their wives over to plunder and their daughters over to captivity and all their spoils over for apportionment among the sons beloved by you, who burned with zeal for you and who detested the pollution of their blood and called upon you for help. O God, my God, listen to me also, a widow.

First, let us compare the appropriation of the rape of Dinah episode in Jdt 9:2–4 with its biblical forebear in Genesis. The comparison will reveal that, like the prayer in Nehemiah 9, the author of Judith employs elaborate expansions of the biblical tale, midrashic embroidery, as it were, but to an even greater extent than is found in Nehemiah.

In Genesis 34, the story comprises an entire chapter. In Judith, the reference to this episode is only three verses long, yet the differences reveal a considerable amount about how the author understood the story. More important for our immediate purposes,

---

399. She notices some of the most important similarities and differences, although she is not attentive to the specifically *exegetical* origins of these interpretive motifs. Robert Kugler offers an illuminating study that traces the history of the Levi-priestly tradition from the biblical sources through *Aramaic Levi, Jubilees*, and the *Testament of Levi*. He cites but does not discuss Jdt 9:2–4; See his book, *From Patriarch to Priest: The Levi-Priestly Tradition from Aramaic Levi to Testament of Levi* (EJL 9; Scholars: Atlanta, 1996) 66–68.

the authority which the author gave to this tale provided a stamp of legitimation for the heroine's murder of Holofernes. A number of disparities between the two accounts raise the following questions, the answers to which demonstrate precisely how the author used the story in Genesis 34:

> 1. Why does the first verse suggest that Dinah was defiled by a host of "strangers," whereas in the Genesis account, Shechem alone rapes her?
> 2. Gen 34:25 states that each of the brothers took up his sword and came upon the city." Yet Judith clearly proposes that *God* provided Simeon with a sword to wreak vengeance on the Shechemites. In what sense did God provide the sword to Simeon?
> 3. Judith claims that God stated a prohibition "This shall not be done." Genesis 34 appears in the Pentateuch before God gives Israel the Torah at Sinai with its incumbent legislation. When, then, did God actually prohibit this behavior?
> 4. Jdt 9:4 states that the sons of Jacob "burned with zeal for you and detested the pollution of their blood and called on you for help." How does this motive for the revenge killing compare with that stated in Genesis 34?
> 5. Why are neither Dinah nor Shechem/the Shechemites mentioned by name, but referred to in verse 2 only as "the virgin" and "the strangers"?

1. A casual reading of Genesis 34 would suggest that the whole population of the Shechemites was punished for the wrongdoing of one individual. The thought that this corporate punishment was somehow terribly unfair was clearly on the minds of later interpreters which led them to search the scriptures for some explanation for this large-scale massacre. By the time our second century interpretations had been put in writing, two trends in the interpretation of this episode had developed which provided a better explanation for the punishment. One trend looked at the larger context surrounding Genesis 34 for justification of the violence. *T. Levi* 6:8–11 provides a justification for the murder of all of the Shechemites by claiming that the Shechemites had caused serious problems for the Israelites over a period of time. Shechem's violation of Dinah was only the latest in a series of offensive violations of decency that finally culminated in divine retribution.

The other trend in interpretation looked to the narrative itself for some rationale. Interpreters could find justification in the text itself. Gen 34:27 states: "The sons of Jacob came upon the slain and they despoiled the city, because *they had defiled* (טמאו) their sister."

The third person plural conjugation of the verb "defile" suggested to later interpreters a corporate responsibility for the rape of Dinah. *Jubilees* 30:3 reflects the understanding that all the men of Shechem were responsible:

> And he [Shechem] begged his father and her brothers that she be given to him as a wife, but Jacob and his sons were angry at the men of Shechem because *they defiled Dinah*, their sister. And so they spoke treacherously with them and defrauded them and seduced them.

Jdt 9:2–4 clearly follows this trend which places the blame on all of the Shechemites. This particular interpretation in the prayer is used to legitimize the murder of the Assyrians. In Jdt 15:5–7, we find that the Judahites slaughter the Assyrians and plunder their camp, the exact fate that the Judahites had been anticipating from the invaders (Jdt 8:21).

2. As Kugel has carefully laid out, the mention of God's handing a sword to Simeon in Jdt 9:2 reflects an interpretive motif that is shared with *T. Levi* and probably *Joseph and Aseneth* 23:14, in which God in fact did provide a heavenly sword to accomplish the mission.[6] *T. Levi* 5:1–3 reads as follows:

> And the angel opened the gates of heaven to me, and I saw the holy temple and the Most High upon a throne of glory. And he said to me: To you, Levi, have I given the blessing of the priesthood, until I come and dwell in the midst of Israel. Then the angel brought me to earth and gave me a shield and a sword and said: Take revenge on Shechem because of Dinah, and I will be with you, for the Lord has sent me.

Kugel suggests that the exegetical origins of this motif lie in the use of a single word in Gen 34:25 which states that the two brothers "each took his sword and came upon the city in security," בטח. Some later tradents seem to have understood this verse to mean that the brothers felt secure as a result of their possession of the swords, which indicated that the weapons had some special power. As Kugel also points out, the swords were viewed by the author of *Joseph and Aseneth* as the instruments of God in punishing the Shechemites. As we shall see in considering the next question, the motif of the

---

[6] Kugel, "The Story of Dinah," 3–7.

heavenly sword was closely tied to the understanding that God disapproved of the actions of Shechem and his clan.

3. A careful examination of Genesis 34 reveals that this phrase occurs in verse 7: "And the sons of Jacob returned from the field when they heard the men gathered together and they were very angry because an outrage (נבלה) was done in Israel; viz., to lie with a daughter of Jacob because *this should not be done*."[7] The author of the prayer in Genesis has quoted the very last phrase, understanding the narrator's voice to be God's own speech.[8] This is the linchpin of the interpretation and it reveals the degree to which scripture was understood as having a commanding hold on the lives of Second Temple Jews. The author's construal of Gen 34:7 permitted him to view the revenge in which Simeon participated as divinely ordained, because in fact, God had stated that "this," presumably referring to the outrage of lying with a daughter of Jacob, was not permitted. As will become apparent in our discussion of zeal, the understanding that God actually had issued such an edict came to influence later interpreters of this episode. Simeon is described here as "zealous," an epithet which can be considered a shortened form of "zealous for the law," and he is zealous for the particular divine law that was enunciated in Gen 34:7. As will become clear, "zeal for the law" had a particular resonance by the time of Judith's authorship in the Second Temple period.

4. The answer to the question concerning the exact motive behind the massacre demonstrates not only the author's careful exegesis of Genesis 34, but also the influence of other biblical traditions on this portrayal of the incident. The precise motive for the revenge killing in Genesis 34 is stated in 13: They answer him "deceitfully" (במרמה) "because he had defiled their sister Dinah" (אשר טמא את דינה אחתם); LXX: ὅτι ἐμίαναν Διναν τὴν

---

[7] The Lucianic recension of the Septuagint inserts εἶπον before οὐχ οὕτως, understanding this phrase to have been spoken by the brothers. Clearly, the author of Judith was not reliant on the Greek for the construal of this phrase.

[8] To my knowledge, only three scholars have noted this aspect of the scriptural appropriation in Judith 9 or noted its significance for the author's view of scripture: Ernst Haag, *Studien zum Buche Judith* (Trierer Theologische Studien 16; Trier: Paulinus Verlag, 1963) 44–45; Dimant "Mikra in the Apocrypha and Pseudepigrapha," 397; and Kugel, "The Story of Dinah," 25–28.

ἀδελφὴν αὐτῶν). Gen 34:27 states that the sons of Jacob plundered the city "because their sister had been defiled" (אשר טמאו אחותם). After Jacob complains to his sons that he is in danger because of their rash and violent actions, they justify their behavior by saying in Gen 34:31 "Should our sister be treated like a whore?" (הכזונה יעשה את־אחותנו).[9] In Judith, the motive stated in 9:4 is slightly different. The sons are described as having great zeal for God and as detesting the profanation of their blood: ἐβδελύξαντο μίασμα αἵματος αὐτῶν. Their reaction is one step removed from avenging acts motivated by the intimate horror of having one's own sister raped and abused. Here, the disturbing aspect of the affair for the brothers is that their blood, their "line" as it were, has been sullied by contact with non-Israelites/Jews.

And in fact the aspects of the story that would be the most disquieting to twentieth century readers, namely, the violence of the act and the question of volition on the part of Dinah, do not seem to be the issue here. For a number of later interpreters, the issue of exogamous intercourse is the heart of the problem, for if another Israelite had "lain" with Dinah, an unmarried Israelite woman, there would have been no need for capital punishment. The penalty for an Israelite man would have been an obligation to take her as a wife (Deut 22:28–29). The understanding of women as property in ancient Israel deemed: you break it; you buy it. Furthermore, as Kugel points out in this regard, the Israelites were forbidden specifically from intermarrying at all with the Canaanites, of which the Shechemites were a subgroup.[10] So the salient issue for later interpreters in the story of the rape of Dinah was the fact of exogamous intercourse itself. That a foreigner, an uncircumcised one, had intercourse at all with an Israelite woman is understood as the grave violation, at least according to our later interpreters. For in

---

[9] There is a common reading of this story that Jacob objects to the vengeance on *moral* grounds. This interpretation is found not only in contemporary commentary on this chapter but in some Second Temple works. In *T. Levi* 6:7, for instance, Jacob is described not only as angry, but also filled with sorrow because newly *circumcised* individuals, that is, new members of the covenant, had died. In fact, according to a literal reading of Gen 34:30, Jacob appears only to be concerned with the physical safety of himself and his household. Simeon and Levi's response to him thus serves as a reproach for their perception of Jacob's inaction and parochial self-concern in the face of Shechem's grave misbehavior. See also Meir Sternberg's nuanced discussion of this passage in *The Poetics of Biblical Narrative* (Bloomington, IN: Indiana University Press, 1985) 445–475.

[10] Kugel, "The Story of Dinah," 17.

Judith we find that this is the source of the outrage: the pollution introduced into their bloodline by this act of intercourse. The wording in verse 4 is explicit on this count: "the sons . . . detested the profanation of their blood." There is no explicit word of concern for the physical or psychic harm done the actual victim; rather, the sons of Jacob have become the "victims" because it is their bloodline that has been tainted. The word used in Judith 9:4 for profanation, μίασμα, is another form of the word used in the Greek of Gen 34:5, ἐμίανεν: Shechem had defiled Jacob's daughter. As described above, according to our interpreter, this was contrary to divine fiat, and so Simeon was zealous to avenge this wrong.

The "beloved sons" who make off with plunder are described as motivated by zeal for God. Yet nowhere in Genesis 34 is the term zeal ζῆλος/קנאה used to describe the motivations of Simeon, Levi, or any of Jacob's sons. When Jacob's sons learn of the rape, they are described in Gen 34:7 as indignant and angry, (ויחר להם מאד, λυπηρὸν ἦν αὐτοῖς σφόδρα) at such an outrage/disgrace. ἄσκημον/נבלה is not done in Israel. 34:14 uses the word reproach or insult, ὄνειδος/חרפה. Zeal appears twice in this verse of the prayer of Judith and nowhere else in the book; nonetheless, the word has powerful connotations stemming from the use of this word in the Bible that reverberate throughout other Second Temple literature.[11] Another book roughly contemporaneous with Judith shares some of the interpretive aspects that evolved from the biblical concept of zeal. The most prominent passage that depicts Jews as "zealous for the law" (ὁ ζηλῶν τῷ νόμῳ) is 1 Maccabees 2. This chapter, in which zeal is mentioned no less than eight times, is also the one scholars hold up as evidence that "zealots" constituted a special class of Second Temple Jews. In 1 Macc 2:24–26, Mattathias, seized by zeal when a fellow Jew makes an idolatrous sacrifice on the altar in Modein, kills him along with the Greek official who was enforcing the sacrifice. The text goes on to say that "Thus he burned with zeal for the law,

---

[11] For more on zeal and the zealots as a class of people in later Second Temple times, consult David Rhoads entry on "Zealots," where he provides a helpful bibliography on the subject. According to Rhoads, zeal for the law included a number of offenses that warranted action by zealots, including idolatry (1 Macc 2:24), intercourse with a Gentile woman (*T. Levi* 6:3, *Jub.* 30); profaning God's name (*Jub.* 30:15); and the presence of uncircumcised people in the land (1 Macc 2:44–46). David Rhoads, "Zealots," *ABD* vol. 6, 1045. Martin Hengel's book remains the most comprehensive treatment of the topic; *Die Zeloten: Untersuchungen zur jüdischen Freiheitsbewegung in der Zeit von Herodes I bis 70 n. Chr.* (Leiden: Brill, 1961; second edition 1976).

just as Phinehas did against Zimri son of Salu." As will become clear below, the author is drawing on a *locus classicus* in which the Aaronite priesthood is established as a reward for Phinehas' zealotry.

As far as linking zeal with Genesis 34, Judith is not alone in describing "zeal" as the passion that motivated the brothers to revenge. In *T. Levi*, Levi is depicted as arguing against the plan that the Shechemites be circumcised. *T. Levi* 6:3 reads: "Then I advised my father and Reuben that they tell the sons of Hamor that they should not be circumcised, because I was filled with *zeal* on account of the abominable thing they had done to my sister."[12] The book of *Jubilees* does not use the term zeal in describing the motivation behind the brothers' attack on Shechem. The book does cite Levi's extreme zeal as the reason that Levi and his descendants are rewarded with perpetual priesthood in a passage that follows close upon the narrative regarding the attack:

> And the seed of Levi was chosen for the priesthood and levitical (orders) to minister before the Lord always just as we do. And Levi and his sons will be blessed forever because he was zealous to do righteousness and judgment and vengeance against all who rose up against Israel. (*Jub.* 30:18)

In the passage from *Jubilees*, zeal refers not just to a vigilance in upholding the law, but also in particular, to upholding the law against those who *rise up against Israel*, that is, foreigners, even to the point of vigilante-ism. *Jub.* 30:7–17, which follows immediately upon the passage describing Levi and Simeon's vengeance against the Shechemites, makes a special point of detailing a law that prohibits any intermarriage whatsoever. The penalty for both parties involved, gentile and Israelite, is death by stoning, because this is considered an act that defiles the holy Israelite people. Then follows *Jub.* 30:18–20, the description of God's covenant of perpetual priesthood with the Levites. Levi's behavior with regard to the Shechemites is not explicitly cited as the reason for this special honor; however, the author's placement of this passage, coming as it does immediately

---

[12] I am here following the translation of H.C. Kee, "Testaments of the Twelve Patriarchs," in *OTP* 1, 790. For a discussion of a variant in a number of manuscripts of the Greek text in which Levi agrees to the circumcision and arguments for the reading cited above, see J.L. Kugel, "The Story of Dinah," 6–12.

after the destruction of the Shechemites and the elaboration of laws prohibiting intermarriage, strongly suggests that this is the case.[13]

The origins of the use of the term "zeal" in Judith 9, *Testament of Levi*, and *Jubilees* deserve some further elaboration, because already by the mid-second century B.C.E., the term seems to have become almost a technical term, reserved for describing the motivation behind avenging certain violations of the law by means of physical violence. By the later Second Temple Period, "zealots," of course, constitute a special grouping of Jews, though the degree to which "zealots" comprised a separate sect apart from a putative mainstream Judaism remains an open question. There are, however, clear biblical origins for this trend in Second Temple Judaism. Two prominent biblical passages use the word zeal (קנאה, ζῆλος) in its various forms in reference to the motivation behind a certain response or behavior.[14] The first is Num 25:11–13 which describes the covenant of perpetual priesthood that God made with the Aaronite Phinehas:

> Phinehas, son of Eleazar, son of Aaron the priest, has turned back my anger from the Israelites by manifesting such zeal among them on my behalf that in my zeal I did not annihilate the Israelites. Therefore say, "I hereby grant him my covenant of peace. It shall be for him and his descendants after him a covenant of perpetual priesthood, because he was zealous for his God and made atonement for the Israelites."

Zeal, in all its forms, occurs four times in this passage. And how did Phinehas demonstrate his fervent zeal for the Lord? Remarkably enough, in a manner surprisingly similar to the situation confronting the sons of Jacob in Genesis 34, underscoring the probability of a direct connection in the mind of the author of Judith 9. In Num 25:6–9, the Israelite Zimri (it is ironic to note that he came from the clan of the Simeonites) and a Midianite woman

---

[13] This is in marked contrast to the account of Levi's elevation to the priesthood depicted in *T. Levi*, which is described *before* Levi participates in the attack against the Shechemites. In *T. Levi*, his elevation to the priesthood comes as a result of a prayer he offers to God. For a thorough discussion of the issues involved in Second Temple accounts of Levi's priesthood, including the aforementioned point, see James L. Kugel, "Levi's Elevation to the Priesthood in Second Temple Writings," *HTR* 86 (1993) 1–64.

[14] The term קנאה and its cognates also occurs in the more mundane sense of "envy" or "jealousy." It is used with that meaning in Gen 26:14; Gen 30:1; 37:11; Num 5:14; Num 11:29; Ps 37:1; 73:3; Prov 3:31; 4:14; 6:6.

Cozbi are killed by Phinehas *in flagrante delicto*. Indeed, it would appear that the author of Judith 9 had this biblical passage in mind with the careful use of the term "zeal." The linkage is based not solely on such verbal similarity, but on the larger interpretational context in which it appears.

The author of Judith is implicitly likening the act of vengeance undertaken by Simeon on the Shechemites to the murder accomplished by Phinehas, and by doing so, justifying the violence as God's will. Both of these events happened as a result of sexual "mixing." That the author understood God had prohibited this kind of union by divine command was made clear above, but the author has looked elsewhere for an analogy to the crime in order to discern the fitting punishment. Certain (Priestly) strands of biblical thinking are particularly concerned with maintaining strict boundaries between the holy and the impure. The passage from Numbers 25 cited above is one in which the sphere of holiness was understood to extend to the people of Israel. The reasoning behind this passage derives from a perceived threat of idolatry. The reasoning is based on the premise that for any male Israelite, the line between yoking oneself to a foreign woman and yoking oneself to a foreign god was a very thin one.[15] One entanglement frequently led to the other.[16] The situation in Genesis 34 is the same, *mutatis mutandis*, the threat now occurring with an Israelite woman and a foreign man. Zeal for maintaining a strict division between holy (the province of the Israelite who belongs to YHWH) and profane (the foreigner whose allegiance is to another god) on both counts is warranted and murder becomes divinely justifiable as lawful retribution. In post-exilic Judaism, the separation of the two spheres, holy and profane, permeated all aspects of life. The prohibition of intermarriage can be understood as an extension of other divine prohibitions of *kashrut* such as eating shellfish or pork or going near a corpse, all of which defile a Jew.[17] The threat posed by intermarriage and the possibility

---

[15] This episode and the episode narrated in Num 25:1–5 show sexual relations as closely linked to idolatrous behavior. The Israelite men at Shittim began having sexual relations with the Moabite women which led to their service to Baal, or, as some have suggested, ritual sexual activity was part of the worship of Baal.

[16] Cf. Deut 7:3.

[17] As Mary Douglas astutely expressed: "Defilement is never an isolated event. It cannot occur except in view of a systematic ordering of ideas. Hence any piecemeal interpretation of the pollution rules of another culture is bound to fail. For the only way in which pollution ideas make sense is in reference to

of defection from worship of YHWH was considered enormous with no less than the future of the community at stake. Thus, by drawing on the language of zeal, the author of Judith calls to mind the legitimation of this killing when it occurs in the name of keeping the Israelite/Jewish people pure from mixing with others.[18] Phinehas and his descendants were rewarded with perpetual priesthood for his demonstrable zeal. Within a certain strand of Second Temple thinking, reflected in the books of *Jubilees* and Judith and which can be viewed as a development of ideas found in priestly literature, Simeon and Levi were also lauded for the violence they initiated on behalf of their sister.[19]

The second biblical passage in which zeal is cited as a motivating factor in behavior is Isa 37:32. The verse occurs in a passage concerning God's protection of Jerusalem at the time of the reign of Hezekiah, when Judah was facing the historic siege by Sennacherib. Isa 37:31–32, paralleled in 2 Kgs 19:30–31, promises salvation from the Assyrian onslaught which will be marked by a sign:

> And this will be the sign for you: This year eat the grain that has grown by itself, and in the second year what has grown from that, but in the third year, sow, reap, plant vineyards, and eat their fruit. And a surviving remnant of the house of Judah will take root below and produce fruit above, for a remnant will go out from Jerusalem, and a number of escapees from Mount Zion. The zeal of the Lord of Hosts will do this.

The passage continues in vv.33–35 with a divine oracle proclaiming judgment on the Assyrians and pledging God's certain

---

a total structure of thought whose key-stone, boundaries, margins and internal lines are held in relation by rituals of separation." "The Abominations of Leviticus," *Purity and Danger: An Analysis of the Concepts of Pollution and Taboo* (New York: Ark/Routledge, 1984) 41.

[18] Fishbane makes a related point in his discussion of typologies that the prohibition of intermarriage in pre-exilic sources served as a typological prohibition for the post-exilic generation. "Moreover, just as the exodus generation and its descendants were warned not to intermarry with the Canaanites and to preserve their holy status (cf. Exod 34:15–16; Deut 7:1–6; cf. Judg 3:3–6), so was the post-exilic concern with intermarriage defined in the light of these prohibitions, and articulated with respect to the original, autochthonous Canaanites (Ezra 9:1–2)." *Biblical Interpretation* 363.

[19] Cf. also Sir 45:23–25 and 1 Macc 2:54 for references that tie the priesthood to Phinehas' zeal. Thanks to James D. Martin for drawing my attention to these two references (oral communication).

defense of Jerusalem. In this context, God's behavior is described as zealous, drawing on the ancient conception of YHWH as a zealous God who will not permit the Israelites to worship other gods. This characterization is evident in literary form at the beginning of the decalogue.[20] The two biblical passages that highlight zeal have one thing in common with our passage in Judith: they concern the threat of foreigners violating the sanctity of the people of Israel themselves or their sacred institutions located in the holy city, Jerusalem. Indeed, the preservation of holiness lies at the heart of the definition of zeal, according to these biblical passages. As will become clear as the chapter unfolds, this is not the only place in which Judith seems to be calling on traditions regarding the inviolability of Zion. But we see in Jdt 9:2–4 an interpretive melding of what were originally two distinct passages relating to zeal, each of which gave rise to interpretive traditions in the Second Temple period: the zeal shown by Phinehas in protecting the people of Israel against threats to its sanctity/purity, and the zeal shown by God in the theology surrounding God's promised defense of Jerusalem in the face of attack by an arrogant invader.

The above review of literature also indicates the close connection between zeal and obedience to the divine commandments embodied and embedded in the Torah. We see this clearly in Judith's interpretation of the Dinah episode in this prayer. The narrative voice in Gen 34:7 stating that "This should not be done" is construed as a divine command, and the sons of Jacob are *zealous* in punishing the Shechemites who violated this prohibition by (collectively, according to Judith) violating Dinah. The heroine in the book of Judith thus is praying to God for help so that in preemptively protecting the sanctity of Israel, she might play a role similar to that of her ancestor Simeon.

---

[20] Why are the Israelites supposed to worship Yahweh and Yahweh alone? Because, the Lord is a zealous God. In both versions of the decalogue in Deut 5:9 and Exod 20:5, the motivation clause describing the reason that Israelites should not worship other gods is that the God of Israel, Yahweh, is a zealous god אל קנא, in the Greek θεὸς ζηλωτής. Moreover, in Exod 34:14, the P covenant account, God's very name is "Zealous." The Israelites are warned in this Exodus passage not to make covenants with the inhabitants of the land because of the risk of idolatry associated with such relationships. For more discussion on the inseparability of divine zeal from God's holiness as reflected in the first commandment (according to the Christian enumeration), see Gerhard von Rad, *Old Testament Theology*, Volume 1 (D.G.M. Stalker, trans; New York, Harper & Row, 1962), 203–212.

5. As noted above, one unusual feature of Judith's interpretation of this episode is that both Dinah and Shechem go unnamed. As we will discuss at greater length below in considering the typology present in the prayer, the fact that neither Shechem nor Dinah is named in the account is significant and intentional. It serves the author's larger typological purpose of having biblical characters stand for figures, both human and non-human.

The author viewed the rape of Dinah as equivalent to the rape of the Temple/Zion. This is clear from the parallel terms used to describe both Dinah's rape in Jdt 9:2 and the violation of the Temple in Jdt 9:8. Consider the following correspondences:

9:2   loosed the hair covering for defilement
        ἔλυσαν μήτραν παρθένου εἰς μίασμα
9:8b   μιᾶναι τὸ σκήνωμα τῆς καταπαύσεως τοῦ
        ὀνόματος τῆς δόξης σου
        to defile the tabernacle where your glorious name rests

9:2   polluted the womb to disgrace her
        ἐβεβήλωσαν μήτραν εἰς ὄνειδος
9:8a   βεβηλῶσαι τὰ ἅγιά σου
        (who planned) to pollute your sanctuary

Judith's actions in order to protect her fellow Israelites and to safeguard the Temple in Jerusalem thus were based on an analogical equation. There are two interpretive steps necessary in setting up the analogy. The first involves conceiving of Jerusalem/Zion/Temple in female terms, as a female hypostatization. Judith had ample biblical precedent for viewing the city/Temple complex in terms of female metaphor, though sometimes the metaphor extended to the entire people of Israel/Judah. In the book of Lamentations, the devastated city of Jerusalem is referred to as "daughter Zion." This reference encompasses a larger entity than simply the city of Jerusalem or the Temple, extending to the people of the southern kingdom as a whole. Other books of the Bible reflect the tendency to metaphorize Zion as either one of two ideal "types": faithful wife of YHWH, or more frequently, unfaithful adulteress/whore, prostituting herself with foreign gods.[21]

---

[21] For the former, cf. Isaiah 62; for the latter, see Jer 3:30–31; 13:20–27; Ezekiel 16; 23; Hosea 3; Nahum 3.

The other requirement for the analogy is that the rape be seen in terms of purity/pollution language, in terms of a holy/profane dichotomy which attaches to people, places, and things. Although the interpretation of this episode in the book of *Jubilees* does not typologize Dinah as the Jerusalem Temple in the same way as Judith, the two books share the same sacral view of the universe in which the rape of Dinah amounts to the defilement or pollution of a holy person/rape. In the book of *Jubilees*, the view is even more extreme so that a foreigner's intermarriage with an Israelite is viewed as an abomination. *Jubilees* also shares with Judith the idea that the people as a whole will be held responsible if the Temple is defiled. *Jubilees* 30:15 states:

> For there will be plague upon plague and curse upon curse, and every judgment, and plague, and curse will come. And if he does this thing, or if he blinds his eyes from those who cause defilement and from those who defile the sanctuary of the Lord and from those who profane his holy name, then all of the people will be judged together on account of all of the defilement and the profaning of this one.

Just as in the prayer Dinah represents something other than Jacob's daughter, the sister of Simeon and Levi, so too, Shechem, the original perpetrator of the crime is understood typologically. Shechem functions as both person and place in Genesis 34. Indeed, Shechem is the eponymous ancestor of the Shechemites.[22] In Judith, Shechem represents the Shechemites who in turn are typologized as "the foreigners" of Jdt 9:2. In Judith, the rape of Dinah is not accomplished by one individual, but by a group. The punishment meted out by Simeon was visited upon "rulers, slaves, and princes on their thrones." Wives and daughters were not spared from the violence. The Shechemites have been turned into typological enemies—Everyenemy of the Jews.[23] This is true also in other

---

[22] This was not an uncommon way of viewing biblical figures in the Second Temple period. Look at the comments about the two ways in which Joseph is treated in Second Temple texts, either as an actual personage, upon whose story later tradents would reflect and include interpretation, or as a symbolic representation of the exiled northern tribes, a "reverse eponym." On this see the remarks of Eileen Schuller in "4Q372: A Text about Joseph," *Revue de Qumrân* 14 (1990) 367–369.

[23] Scholars have also understood the Shechemites of Judith as a cipher for the Samaritans, whose claim to be the true Jews rankled other Jewish groups. The ire this inspired among other Jewish groups eventually resulted in the destruction of the Samaritans' temple at Gerizim/Shechem by John

prayers (e.g., Sir 51:7 "They surrounded me on every side"). Unnamed generic enemies abound in the psalms, but in Judith the enemies are named.[24] In the book as a whole, the aggressors are a fusion of two historical enemies of the Jews: an "Assyrian" army is led by the "Babylonian" king Nebuchadnezzar (Jdt 1:7). In the prayer itself, Judith allows the Shechemites to go unnamed, but as "the foreigners" they represent a threat equivalent to the Assyrians, who are themselves referred to in Jdt 9:7 as the current threat to Israel's safety.

The foregoing review illuminates some of the more salient aspects of the use of Genesis 34 in this prayer. Let these serve to illustrate how complex the appropriation of biblical language is and what careful attention the author pays to the biblical text down to the most minute details. It is an exegetical use of the Bible; it is also a typological use of scripture. The character of the reinterpretation is premised on the idea that God had ordained the attack on the Shechemites and that, indeed, God has provided the very weapon by which the Shechemites were killed. Judith calls on this story as past

---

Hyrcanus. According to G.E.Wright's archaeological study of the site, John Hyrcanus destroyed the Samaritan temple on Mt. Gerizim in 128 B.C.E. and some years later brought about a final destruction of the city. "Thus our coins confirmed the conclusions already derived from pottery study: Shechem was resettled as a city not long before Alexander the Great and ceased to exist not long after ca. 110 B.C." G.E. Wright, *Shechem* (London: Duckworth, 1965) 172.

Veiled polemic is also reflected in the unique inclusion of the Shechemites in the list of peoples expelled from the land as a result of the conquest in Achior's historical retrospect: "They drove out before them the Canaanites, the Perizzites, the Jebusites, the Shechemites, and all the Girgashites, and they lived there a long time." (Jdt 5:16). The association of the Shechemites with the later Samaritans is also to be found in another text, the *Testament of Levi*, that we are considering in connection with the rape of Dinah in this chapter. *T. Levi* 7:1–4: "And I said to my father, Jacob, 'Through you the Lord will bring the Canaanites to nothing and will give their land to you and your descendants after you. For from this day forward, Shechem shall be called 'City of the Senseless,' because as one might scoff at a fool, so we scoffed at them, because by defiling my sister they committed folly in Israel and we left there and came to Bethel.'"

[24] Cf. the generic enemies in Pss 119:51, 69, 84, 85, 95, 115 or 133. Jon Levenson understands some of these references to persecution and oppression as influenced by the language of Jeremiah (cf. Jer 18:20–22); see his "The Sources of Torah: Psalm 119 and the Modes of Revelation in Second Temple Judaism," *Ancient Israelite Religion: Essays in Honor of Frank Moore Cross* (P.D. Miller, Jr., P.D. Hanson, and S. D. McBride, eds.; Philadelphia: Fortress, 1987) 563.

evidence that God will help when Israel is threatened and with the expectation that God will help in a similar situation in the present.

Judith 9 and Isaiah

As Devorah Dimant has discussed in her essay on the use of Mikra in the apocrypha and pseudepigrapha, the allusive quality in a text is frequently couched in its deployment of biblical models and motifs.[25] Such is the case with the relationship of Judith 9 to the book of Isaiah. Isaiah's influence on Judith 9 falls into these two categories: Isaiah 37 has been used as a model for the prayer in Judith 9, but there are also verbal and theological similarities that bespeak Isaiah's influence. In examining the connection between Isaiah and the prayer in Judith, it is also necessary to look at other parts of the book of Judith. The author of the book has clearly been influenced by biblical works in ways that go beyond the explicit citation of biblical scripture, although that, too, is part of the larger scripturalization of the book. Judith has been influenced by biblical motifs and patterns, as well as the theology of the post-exilic section of the book of Isaiah. Some of the allusions are quite subtle, but the accumulated weight of the allusions combines to make a strong case in favor of the argument that the author of Judith was influenced by these biblical passages. It will also become apparent in our discussion that the appropriation of language from Exodus 15 in this prayer cannot be discussed entirely apart from Judith's appropriation of Isaiah. Just as Isaiah looked to the past, specifically to the creation and to the Exodus from Egypt in order to describe the return from the Exile, so too,

---

[25] The book of Tobit, for instance, uses the model of Job yet nowhere explicitly cites Job as a model of behavior, as for instance, he mentions Abraham, Isaac, and Jacob as models of behavior in suggesting that his son go to his homeland to find a wife from his own people. The strongest similarities appear in the sequence of motifs that are shared with Job: e.g., Tobit is also a pious and wealthy man who is deprived of his possessions and must endure a number of physical afflictions, etc. For more, see the list in Dimant, "Mikra," 418.

Consider also the comment of Andrew Chester in an article that examines how a number of Qumran and apocryphal compositions use earlier scripture. He notes that " . . . [the author of Judith] has constructed the story skilfully, employing biblical traditions and allusions in a multi-layered and interwoven way" see his "Citing the Old Testament," *It is Written: Scripture Citing Scripture* (D.A. Carson and H.G.M. Williamson, eds.; New York: Cambridge University Press, 1988) 159. Chester discusses Judith and its use of scriptural models only briefly, and he admits that his treatment is incomplete.

Judith has taken up some of this Exodus language to describe her expectations for divine assistance in her own time.

Judith 9 and the Prayer of Hezekiah

Although there is no explicit mention of Hezekiah's prayer in Judith 9, there are a number of shared elements (Isa 37:16–20//2Kgs 19:15–19) that indicate that the author of Judith had this prayer in mind in composing Judith 9. Not only are there similarities in the structure and the contents of the prayer, but the larger context of the two prayers is similar and there are distinct parallels between the contexts that suggest that the author of Judith was in fact playing on the biblical theme of the inviolability of Zion.

Let us begin by looking at the prayer in Isaiah itself.

> Isa 37:16. O Lord the God of Israel who is enthroned on the cherubim, you are God, you alone, over all the kingdoms of the earth: you have made heaven and earth. 17. Extend your ear, O Lord, and hear; open your eyes, O Lord, and see; listen to all the words of Sennacherib, that he sent to mock the living God. 18. Truly, O Lord, the kings of Assyria have laid waste all the nations and their lands, 19. and have put their gods into the fire, though they were no gods but the work of human hands, wood and stone, and so they destroyed them. 20. So now, O Lord our God, save us, I pray you, from his hand, so that all the kingdoms of the earth may know that you, Lord, are God alone.

The correspondences indicate similarities in structure and content. The address to God contains similar theology. In Isa 37:15, God is described as the God of Israel, as King, enthroned above the cherubim, and as the creator of heaven and earth. Judith 9, although it contains different wording, emphasizes the same aspects of God. Jdt 9:2 contains the invocation to the Lord, God of Simeon, that is, a particularistic God of the people Israel. In Jdt 9:12 God is the "King of all creation" and "Lord of heaven and earth." The two prayers also share roughly the same kind of description of the enemy. In Isa 37:17–19, the threat posed by Sennacherib is described. His intent is to "mock the living God." The threat of arrogance by foreigners is echoed in Jdt 9:7–9: "Here now are the Assyrians . . . priding themselves in their horses and riders." The immediate threat is described somewhat differently in the two prayers, however. The "kings" of Assyria have thrown other nations' idols into the fire. Presumably Hezekiah fears a similar fate for the Temple environs: the destruction of the sanctuary and its religious paraphernalia. In

Judith's prayer, this fear is stated explicitly: "They intend to defile your sanctuary, and to pollute the tabernacle where your glorious name resides, and to break off the horns of your altar with the sword."

A third similarity is the motive expressed by the pray-er, stating why God should intervene on behalf of the people of Israel. In Isa 37:20/2Kgs 19:19 and in Jdt 9:14, both prayers assert that the reason God should intervene is for greater divine glory, and especially that the nations should know that YHWH *alone* is God. Hezekiah: "So now, O Lord our God, save us from his hand, so that all the kingdoms of the earth may know that you alone are the Lord." And Judith, "And do this before your entire nation and every tribe, make it known, because you are the God of all power and might and there is no other who safeguards the people of Israel but you." There are many passages in pre-exilic literature that express a similar motive, but without the affirmation that the God of Israel is the *only* God. For instance, throughout the plagues narrative in Exodus, the reason stated for God's performance of signs and wonders is so that "the Egyptians shall know that I am the LORD" (Exod 7:5).[26] In other words, the Egyptians might learn that Israel's God was a powerful force to be reckoned with, but monotheism was not the issue. This point is also illustrated by Jethro's affirmation after the Exodus: "Now I know that the Lord is greater than all gods, because he delivered the people from the Egyptians, when they dealt arrogantly with them." (Exod 18:11) Even the exilic book of Ezekiel does not emphasize the radical monotheism regarding Israel's God, although perhaps at this point in Israel's history, it is understood. Seventy-three times the phrase "you shall know that I am the Lord" appears in Ezekiel as a virtual refrain, but nowhere does the book specifically mention the exclusivity of YHWH, that God is Lord alone, as we find in the prayers in Isaiah 37 and Judith 9. The emphasis on divine monotheism does appear in another late prayer. A similar claim appears as part of a blessing in 1 Kings 8:

> Let these my words, with which I pleaded before the Lord, be near to the Lord our God by day and night, to maintain justice for his servant and for his people Israel day by day; so that all the peoples of the earth may know that the Lord is God; *there is no other*.
> (1 Kgs 8:59–60)

---

[26] Cf. Exod 6:7, 7:17, 8:22, 10:2, 11:7, 14:4, 14:18.

Nowhere is the claim of the universality and exclusivity of Yahweh made more clearly and forcefully than in Second Isaiah. The claim that there "is no other" (אין עוד) God but YHWH appears nine times, not counting other similar expressions about divine sovereignty and omnipotence.[27] The appearance of this formula in exilic or post-exilic literature suggests that the prayer in Isaiah 37 is also exilic.[28] It also underscores a certain thematic dependence of Judith on the book of Isaiah as a whole.

A fourth correspondence, the request to God, reveals not only a similarity but also a difference between the two prayers that can best be explained by elaborating on how the book of Judith as a whole was influenced by the narrative about the siege of Jerusalem by Sennacherib and specifically Hezekiah's response to it. The request in Hezekiah's prayer occurs in Isa 37:20//2 Kgs 19:19: "So now, O Lord our God, save us from his hand, so that all the kingdoms of the earth may know that you alone are the Lord." In Judith's prayer, the main request, aside from her plea for help in verse 4, occurs in verses 9–10, 13:

> Look on their arrogance. Send down your wrath on their heads; put into my hand, the widow's, the strength for what I have devised. Through my lips of deception/seduction, strike down slave with ruler and ruler with his servant. Shatter their haughtiness by the hand of a female . . . Trade my speech and deception/seduction for their wound and welt, they who wish to do harsh things to your covenant and your sacred house and Mount Zion and the house of your sons' possession.

In Hezekiah's prayer, the assumption is that the threat of devastation to Jerusalem and the Temple is occurring because of the people's sins. The situation in the book of Judith stands implicitly in strong contrast to this. The people have every reason to expect saving divine aid because their behavior during the time of dire distress has been impeccable. They have mourned by donning sackcloth and prayed intensely that they might be spared the onslaught threatened by the Assyrians.

The theology of the inviolability of Zion that is articulated in Isaiah 37 and 2 Kings 19 has been transformed into the theology of the eternal defense of Zion. Although the destruction of the Temple in Jerusalem is no longer outside the realm of possibility after the

---

[27] Cf. Isa 42:8; 44:8; 45:5,6,14,18,21,22; 46:9.
[28] Cf. also Joel 2:27.

devastation wrought by Nebuchadnezzar in 587, nonetheless, the theology persists in adapted form. Now, according to Judith, God will surely save the Temple and his virgin city Jerusalem, provided the people are obedient to the law of God. Another twist in the new concept of divine aid is that God puts the Jews to the test to see whether they are worthy of salvation. So states the crucial eighth chapter of the book of Judith. God will come to their aid, but only through a human agent, in this case, through an improbable heroine in the person of a childless widow.

The beginnings of this revised theology, with its view that the defense of Jerusalem is contingent on the behavior of the people of Israel, are already found in the post-exilic book of Zechariah 8:

> Thus says the Lord of Hosts: "I am zealous for Zion with great zeal and I am zealous for her with great wrath. Thus says the Lord: I will return to Zion, and will dwell in the midst of Jerusalem; Jerusalem shall be called the faithful city, and the mountain of the Lord of hosts shall be called the holy mountain. (v.2)

There follows in vv.4–13 a description of the restoration of Jerusalem, and then, in vv.14–16, a description of the new terms under which they have been restored to Jerusalem:

> For thus says the Lord of hosts: Just as I decided to bring disaster upon you when your ancestors made me angry, and I did not relent, says the Lord of hosts, so again I have decided in these days to do good to Jerusalem and to the house of Judah; do not be afraid. These are the things that you shall do: Speak the truth to one another, render in your gates judgments of peace that are true, do not plan evil in your hearts against one another, and do not love a false oath, for all these things are what I hate, says the Lord."

A similar modified view of the inviolability of Jerusalem can be seen in the following excerpt in Lam 4:12–13:

> 12. The kings of the earth did not believe, nor did any of the inhabitants of the world, that foe or enemy could enter the gates of Jerusalem. 13. It was for the sins of her prophets and the iniquities of her priests, who shed the blood of the righteous in the midst of her.

The contingency "spin" on the theology of the inviolability of Zion is not found in Judith's prayer itself. For this reason, recognizing allusions and biblical references contained within the prayer is not possible without sensitive attention to biblical patterns in the book as a whole. The book of Judith outside of the prayer in Judith 9 articulates three clear statements of this particular theology, which is also the central message of the book, a message echoed within the prayer itself. The first occurs in the speech that Achior makes before Holofernes, in which Achior recounts the history of the people of Israel up through the return from exile. In offering advice to the Assyrian general, he concludes by saying: "So now, my master and lord, if there is any oversight in this people and they sin against their God and we find out their offense, then we can go up and defeat them. But if they are not a guilty nation, then let my lord pass them by; for their Lord and God will defend them, and we shall become the laughingstock of the whole world." The second appears in Judith 8, which is the heart of the book, both in a structural and thematic sense. In a long speech, 8:11–27, Judith responds to what she views as the inadequate leadership of the elders of Bethulia. She begins by chastising them for their complete reliance on God to save them. Not only are they counting on God to save them from catastrophe, Judith contends, but they show great hubris by assuming they can know the plans of God. The latter point, as we shall see, is reiterated in verses 5–6 of Judith's prayer and strikes some resonances with the understanding of God found in Second Isaiah as well as Job. Judith goes on to affirm the essential piety and righteousness of her generation in comparison to the generation that preceded the exile (8:18–21, 24):

> For never in our generation, nor in these present days, has there been any tribe or family or people or town of ours that worships gods made with hands, as was done in days gone by. That was why our ancestors were handed over to the sword and to pillage, and so they suffered a great catastrophe before our enemies. But we know no other god but him, and so we hope that he will not disdain us or any of our nation. For if we are captured, all Judea will be captured and our sanctuary will be plundered; and he will make us pay for its desecration with our blood . . . Therefore, my brothers, let us set an example for our kin, for their lives depend upon us, and the sanctuary, both the temple and the altar, rests on us.

Judith closes her speech by stating a view that later becomes a standard part of rabbinic thinking, that God is testing Israel's righteousness by threatening them with the Assyrian invasion. Nonetheless, the essential point has been made, that the defense of Jerusalem will be safeguarded ultimately by God, but only if the people of Israel behave in accordance with the covenant and according to righteous expectations that they will use some of their own initiative to save themselves.

The third place in the narrative in which this essential message of the book is stated explicitly is also in a speech of Judith, when she is addressing Holofernes under her ruse of deserting from her fellow Bethulians. She tells them that she, too, has heard what Achior told Holofernes about her people and she affirms it all as true (Jdt 11:10): "Therefore, lord and master, do not disregard what he said, but keep it in your mind, for it is true. Indeed our nation cannot be punished, nor can the sword prevail against them, unless they sin against their God." She continues by spinning a web of deception. She claims that her people are about to commit exactly this kind of sin. They will transgress their dietary laws by eating their unfit livestock and will eat what should be set aside for God and the priests: the first fruits of the harvest and the tithe of wine and oil. This sin will inevitably result in their downfall, according to Judith, who goes on to tell Holofernes that she personally will lead him to triumph (Jdt 11:19a): "Then I will lead you through the middle of Judea, until coming to Jerusalem: there I will set your throne/chariot seat (δίφρον) in her midst."

These three passages, then, represent a transformed theology of the inviolability of Jerusalem, reshaped in light of the Deuteronomic theology of the exile. Sin and its consequences are understood as directly affecting the fate of the people and the larger area of Judea, but especially the city of Jerusalem and its Temple and sanctuary. Her speech to Holofernes reflects the narrative fulfillment of her entreaty to God in Jdt 9:13, that her deceitful words should bring about ruin to those who had plotted "against your covenant, against your sacred house, against Mount Zion, and against the house your children possess."

The theology reflecting the inviolability of Jerusalem is most clearly in evidence in the book of Isaiah. It is stated explicitly in the context of Sennacherib's invasion of Israel. Isa 37:33–35//2Kgs 19:32–34:

> Therefore, thus says the Lord concerning the king of Assyria: He will not come into this city, shoot an arrow there, come before it with a shield, or cast up a siege ramp against it. By the way that he came, by the same he shall return; he shall not come into this city, says the Lord. For I will defend this city to save it, for my own sake and for the sake of my servant David.

This statement of defense is echoed in Isa 38:6//2 Kgs 20:3. The foregoing discussion supports the notion that Judith 9 was written with Hezekiah's prayer in mind. There are four similarities in structure and content. One of these, the request to God, points to the larger issue about how the book as a whole is influenced by the entire narrative in Isaiah 37–39.

Judith 9 and Thematic Connections to Isaiah

Another general theme that the prayer, and moreover, the entire book of Judith, shares with Isaiah is the notion of reversal: the haughty and arrogant will be brought down; the lowly and humble will be exalted. That the proud will be brought low by divine might constitutes a virtual refrain in Isaiah. Isa 2:11–17 is a clear expression of this idea, as are Isa 5:15 and Isa 10:12. This last citation in fact sounds as though it might have been the inspiration for the book of Judith as a whole: "And when the Lord has finished all his doings on Mount Zion and in Jerusalem, he will punish the king of Assyria for his grandiosity and for his haughty arrogance." Compare also Isa 25:11 and 26:5. In Judith's prayer, this finds explicit expression in the theological affirmations of Jdt 9:11–12, but it also is expressed in the narrative by the fact that a widow, one of the weakest and most vulnerable members of society in the biblical view, is depicted as the savior of Israel by her singular act of derring-do. God will visit punishment on the Assyrians, they who pride themselves in their strength and force of arms, and this punishment will arrive by the hand of a woman. The theme appears again explicitly in the final hymn of thanks that Judith and the people of Judah sing to the Lord after their deliverance, in Judith 16. As the theme finds expression in this prayer, the mighty Assyrian was not done in by sturdy young men, nor towering giants, but by the hand of a widow. In fact, all the Judeans are characterized as underdogs, weaklings in the face of armed aggressors (Jdt 16:11):

> When my oppressed ones raised their war cry, and my weak ones shouted, the enemy was defeated, screamed, and ran. Sons of slave women slashed through them and wounded them like the children of deserters, and they died from the army of my Lord.

A similar list of divine epithets is found in the long penitential prayer in *Joseph and Aseneth* 12:13, in which Aseneth, in a manner akin to Judith, identifies herself as an orphan, a member of a group traditionally viewed as vulnerable in the Bible: "And I am now an orphan and desolate, and I have no other hope save in you, Lord, and no other refuge except your mercy, Lord, because you are the father of the orphans, and a protector of the persecuted and a helper of the afflicted."

Judith 9 and Exodus 15

A number of commentators have noticed the relationship of Exodus 15 to Judith 16, understanding the former as the model on which the latter is based. The basis for this assessment lies both in the context of the two: Judith sings a victory song after defeat of the enemy and salvation for Israel just as Miriam/Moses do, and also in the content of the prayer. Less attention has been paid the interconnections that extend to Judith 9 as well, especially as it relates to God's defense of Jerusalem as a warrior. I would suggest that is because there is an intermediate interpretive step involved, the fusion of the two themes of the Exodus and the defense of Jerusalem.

Judith also relies on the book of Isaiah for a number of its themes, as elaborated above. Second Isaiah contains the explicit combination of the exodus tradition with the creation theological traditions. God is understood as creator of the universe and a universal God of all people, as well as the warrior who brought Israel out of Egypt.

The following list shows the verbal correspondences between Judith 9, Exodus 15, Judith 16, and Isaiah 42–43:

> Jdt 9:7–8 You are the Lord who crushes wars; the Lord is your name.
> σύ εἶ κύριος συντρίβων πολέμους κύριος ὄνομά σοι
> Ex 15:3 (LXX) the Lord who crushes wars; the Lord is his name
> κύριος συντρίβων πολέμους κύριος ὄνομα αὐτῷ

> Jdt 16:2 For the Lord is a God who crushes wars;
> he sets up his camp among his people
> ὅτι θεὸς συντρίβων πολέμους κύριος,
> ὅτι εἰς παρεμβολὰς αὐτοῦ ἐν μέσῳ λαοῦ
> Isa 42:13 The Lord God of power goes forth; he crushes war;
> he stirs up zeal
> κύριος ὁ θεὸς τῶν δυνάμεων ἐξελεύσεται
> καὶ συντρίψει πόλεμον, ἐπεγερεῖ ζῆλον[29]

> Jdt 9:7 priding themselves in horse and rider
> ὑψώθησαν ἐφ᾽ ἵππῳ καὶ ἀναβάτῃ
> Exod 15:1 The horse and rider he has thrown into the sea.

---

[29] Note also the use of holy war terminology here, which includes a reference to the "zeal" of God.

ἵππον καὶ ἀναβάτην ἔρριψεν εἰς θάλασσαν
Isa 43:16–17 (Thus says the Lord, who makes a way in the sea,
a path in the mighty waters,)
who brings out chariot and horse, army and warrior;
ὁ ἐξαγαγὼν ἅρματα καὶ ἵππον καὶ ὄχλον
ἰσχυρόν

The verbal links above suggest that the author also had the Exodus account in mind when writing the book. The excerpts from Deutero-Isaiah represent later interpretations that combine an understanding of God's work in the Exodus with divine action in the present.

Another connection derives from Trito-Isaiah, one of the last parts of the book written. Isaiah 63–64 contains a precedent for fusing the concepts of Exodus 15 and the defense of Jerusalem. The following excerpts from the long prayer in Isa 63:7–64:11 resemble the themes in the prayer of Judith discussed above:[30]

Isa 63:11 Where is the one who brought them up out of the sea with the shepherds of his flock?
Isa 63:15 Where are your zeal and your might?

Is 63:18 Your holy people took possession for a little while, but now our adversaries have trampled down your sanctuary.

Isa 64:1a O that you would tear open the heavens and come down. . .

Isa 64:2b . . .to make your name known to your adversaries, so that the nations might tremble at your presence.

Isa 64:9–11 Your holy cities have become a desert; Zion has become a desert; Jerusalem a desolation. Our holy and beautiful house where our ancestors praised you has been consumed by fire, and all our pleasant places have become ruins. After all this, will you restrain yourself, O Lord? Will you keep silent, and punish us so severely?

The verses cited contain some similar wording to the prayer in Judith. We note in particular the mention of zeal (here in reference to God) in relation to holiness (of Israel). The prayer also makes reference to God's saving work in the Exodus. From the author's

---

[30] Paul Hanson characterizes this prayer as a communal lament which includes a recitation of the *magnalia dei*, likening it in some aspects to Psalms 44, 74, 79, and some of the prayers in Lamentations. For a discussion of this lament, focusing especially on its socio-political setting, see Hanson, *The Dawn of Apocalyptic: The Historical and Sociological Roots of Jewish Apocalyptic Eschatology* (2nd ed.; Philadelphia: Fortress, 1979) 79–100.

perspective, defilement of holiness requires a zealous response. The author laments the absence of God from Jerusalem and longs for God's advent as holy warrior to rescue them. The motive expressed is similar to that in Jdt 9:14 and Isa 37:20, that God should intervene forcefully so that the nations might know the divine name. Paul Hanson rightly notes the desperation found in these verses: "One can almost speak of the Third Isaiah group's concern with possession of Zion as an obsession from the early formulation of their program based on Second Isaiah . . . to the late polemical material."[31] Whether or not the precise social setting of the writers can be identified as Mushite Levitical priests in conflict with a returning exilic group as Hanson asserts, it is clearly the case that the author was alarmed at the situation involving the Temple, Jerusalem, and at their current state of destruction. In spite of the similarities between the excerpts from Trito-Isaiah above and Judith, we must also point out one strong difference. The lament in Isaiah 63–64 is passive, the lamenter awaits divine intervention as the pathway to salvation. By contrast, Judith expects to be part of Israel's own salvation, strengthened and emboldened by her faith in God as we elaborated above. Let us now consider how this salvation is effected.

Salvation by Typology

Our discussion up to this point has revealed that the author of Judith was immersed in the biblical traditions of Israel, so much so that she modeled characters and patterned the narrative after biblical prototypes. There are indeed more biblical influences on the book than there is space to detail in this brief chapter which focuses on one prayer.

Any discussion of biblical typology should draw distinctions between various appropriations of the biblical past, but the presupposition that lies at the root of all typological thinking in the Bible is that there is a sameness, a consistency that one can expect from God. Typological thinking originates in analogical thinking. An author thinking in analogical terms will see a correspondence between events, emphasizing similar aspects of them. In Israel, this reflects the view that God will work in some predictable pattern. A frequently cited example of this type of analogical thinking lies in Second Isaiah, where God's work in the first Exodus from Egypt is viewed as analogous to the return of the exiles from Babylon. The correspondence is inexact, of course. Instead of way down south in

---

[31] Hanson, *Dawn of Apocalyptic,* 97 n.61.

Egypt, the Israelites have been flung far to the east in Babylon. A strong commonality remains nonetheless: life outside the promised land, life among a foreign people that can all too easily deal roughly with the Israelites/Jews sojourning in their midst. So too there is no savior figure in the Egyptian exodus account who serves as a proto-typical figure for Cyrus. There is no clear statement that the Jews are enslaved in Babylon as they were in Egypt. Yet the author views the similarities as strong. The underlying pattern of divine rescue and restoration to the Promised Land is the same. In Isaiah, divine rescue is attributed to God by the hand of Cyrus; in the book of Judith, the heroine acccomplishes deliverance with the help of God. What salvation God has wrought for Israel in the past can be repeated in the present—and in the future—if the circumstances are roughly the same. Typology thus seeks parallels in ancient events and then extends their meaning through application to contemporary events.

The author of the book of Judith has put on such typological lenses, viewing the present situation in terms of repeated patterns from the past. We have seen how the "Assyrian" invaders of Judith are cast as types of sixth century Babylonians who are also cast as Shechemites from the time of the patriarchs. Judith 9 places Dinah in the role of the vulnerable Temple in Jerusalem. This literary move involves not only typology but also a kind of anthropomorphism. Aside from the prayer's internal typologies, Judith's prayer for help from God, viewed as a whole, has been influenced by the shape and theme of Hezekiah's prayer for the defense of Jerusalem found in Isaiah 37//2 Kings 19. Judith's prayer, like Hezekiah's, is spoken in a context in which the Temple is threatened anew. The active heroine Judith herself functions as a type on several levels. She is the "new Simeon," a reincarnation of her ancestor who acquired fame/ notoriety for the bloody avenging of his sister. This recasting is also influenced by the author's descriptive use of the word zeal which subtly links Simeon (and Judith typologically) with the positive post-biblical characterization of Phinehas as one who is possessed of zeal for the law and whose descendants were thus rewarded by God with perpetual priesthood. This subtle link thus serves to ennoble (in retrospect) Simeon's venture as well as the one Judith is readying to undertake. Judith is also a type of the female deliverer of Israel. As the bold savior of her people, she is an avatar of Deborah, Jael, perhaps in a certain sense even Miriam. There is yet a third sense in which she carries a mantle. As her name suggests, she can also be understood as representative of the Jews as a whole, who in times of dire distress must not only pray to God for help but also become partners in their own salvation. The author's use of all of these typologies reflects a belief in God's continuing relationship to Israel/the Jews. It also reflects the author's cherished hope that the underlying conviction related to all these correspondences will also hold true, that God's defense of Jerusalem and the people of Israel will remain true to type, and that God's relationship to Israel will ensure a steady defense.

Typology in Contemporaneous Prayers

The prayer in Judith 9 is unique because of its intricate connections with its context combined with its typological use of earlier scripture. We can nonetheless find other prayers from roughly the same period that share certain features of the scripturalization of the prayer in Judith 9, most notably its use and interpretation of one discrete biblical episode. Although parts of Isaiah and Exodus were in the author's mind in writing the book, Judith 9 alludes most clearly to Genesis 34, the rape of Dinah. There are a number of prayers that we might examine that would also illustrate an appropriation of scripture in which a single biblical episode is redeployed: Tob 3:2–6; 8:5–7; 1 Macc 4:30–33; 7:41–42; *1 Enoch* 84:2–6; *Bib. Ant.* 21:2–6; and 47:1–2; 11Q5 col. 26 (*Hymn to the Creator*), and 1QH, col. 11 (*Hodayot*). Let us review briefly two of these examples.

The prayer in Tob 8:5–7 is offered by Tobias and Sarah, the newly married son and daughter-in-law of Tobit. In it, Tobias blesses God and asks for a long life together:

> 5. And Tobias said: Blessed are you, O God of our ancestors and blessed is your name in all generations forever. Let the heavens and all your creation bless you forever. 6. You made Adam and you made for him as helper and support Eve his wife, and from the couple the seed of humanity has come. You said "It is not good for man to be alone, let us make for him a helper like himself." 7. And now I do not take this sister of mine on account of lust but from uprightness. Grant that she and I may obtain mercy and grow old in companionship.

The form of the prayer begins with a blessing, followed by an invocation to God and a petition. The prayer is much shorter and simpler than the prayer in Judith 9. The biblical episode that it alludes to is the creation of Adam's partner, Eve. Adam is mentioned only once in the Hebrew Bible outside the J creation account, in the genealogy of 1 Chr 1:1.[32] Eve is not named outside the Genesis account. Their reappearance in Tobit is thus notable. More significant is the specific use of the J creation account of humans in this prayer. Just as we have seen in Judith 9 and in other prayers we have examined, Tobit's prayer contains a quote of divine speech. This particular biblical citation comes from Gen 2:18. It appears in the Septuagint with a slight, though perhaps significant, divergence in wording.[33] Tobit's is the first recorded instance in which the creation of Adam and Eve is held up as the primal paradigm for marriage. It would not be the last, and indeed, Adam and Eve's creation and pairing became a frequently cited scriptural reference in prayers and blessings in Jewish and Christian marriage liturgies.[34]

One other Second Temple book warrants mention in this regard. The account of the creation of Eve in *Jub.* 3:4–7 contains a similar interpretation. In fact, *Jub.* 3:4 contains the same quote of divine speech from Gen 2:18 that we find in Tob 8:6. As a rewriting of the books of Genesis and part of Exodus, *Jubilees* includes much verbatim material from those biblical books, but *Jubilees* also includes much in the way of supplementation. The supplementation in *Jub.* 3:4–7 is the addition of Adam's carnal knowledge of his partner (a phrase in *Jub.* 3:6), which occurs well before the pair even entered Eden, and much longer before they ate the forbidden fruit and were expelled.[35]

Another example of such a scripturalized prayer is 1 Macc 4:30–33, which recalls the battle between David and Goliath. The

[32] Adam is mentioned in the Greek books of the Apocrypha, twice in Ben Sira, and ten times in 2 Esdras, though never in the context of his relationship to Eve.

[33] Eve is made not κατ' αὐτόν, "according to" or "corresponding to" her mate as appears in Gen 2:18, but ὅμοιον αὐτῷ, "of the same nature" or "like" him, a phrase that occurs in Gen 2:20.

[34] Early Christian marriage rituals are to thought to have been a borrowing or adaptation of Jewish ritual. Based on certain New Testament passages (e.g., Eph 5:22–24), the liturgy has also come to depict the marriage of a man and a woman as a type of the relationship of Christ to the Church.

[35] James Kugel suggests that *Jubilees'* supplemental interpretation of this episode derives from the author's understanding of Gen 2:24, "and they become one flesh" as meaning a consummation of their relationship. This interpretation, of course, stands in strong contrast to the predominant interpretation of the Fall and its aftereffects in the New Testament and in Western Christianity. For a discussion of the early history of interpretation of this episode in Judaism and Christianity, see Gary A. Anderson, "Celibacy or Consummation in the Garden? Reflections on Early Jewish and Christian Interpretations of the Garden of Eden," *HTR* 82 (1989) 121–148.

prayer is offered by Judas Maccabeus in the face of attack by the
Seleucid general Lysius. It appears before the climactic battle in
which the Israelites recapture Jerusalem and rededicate the Temple.
The prayer reads as follows:

> 30 And he [Judas] saw the strong army so he prayed and said:
> "Blessed are you, O Savior of Israel, who crushed the attack of the
> mighty one by the hand of your servant David, and gave the camp of
> the Philistines (ἀλλοφύλων) into the hands of Jonathan son of
> Saul and of the man who carried his armor. 31 Therefore, hem in
> this army by the hand of your people, Israel, and let them be
> disgraced by their forces and their horses. 32. Fill them with
> cowardice; melt the arrogance of their strength; let them tremble in
> their destruction. 33. Strike them down with the sword of those who
> love you, and let all who know your name praise you with hymns."

The prayer alludes to the battle between Goliath and David in 1
Samuel 17. In this prayer, Goliath goes unnamed. He is referred to as
the "mighty one" ὁ δυνατός.[36] This is similar to the anonymous
Dinah in Jdt 9:2, who is referred to only as "the virgin." In the prayer,
Judas Maccabeus, who must confront the greatest foreign power of
his time, stands for David, the archetypal Israelite leader.[37] Judas
offers the prayer because he, too, is facing a daunting opponent. The
interpretive formula is simple: "God, you saved David; you can save
us in like circumstances." But from what are they being saved? Not
only has the land been overrun with hostile Syrian troops, but the
Temple has been desecrated, and therein lies their greatest disgrace.
Like the prayer in Judith, some attention to the narrative context is
necessary to understand the full impact of this allusion. An important
part of the David and Goliath story is that David removes the
"reproach" ὄνειδος from Israel:

> David said to the men who stood by him, "What shall be done for the
> man who kills this Philistine, and takes away the reproach from
> Israel (καὶ ἀφελεῖ ὀνειδισμον ἀπο Ισραηλ)? For who is
> this uncircumcised Philistine that he should defy the armies of the
> living God?" (1 Sam 17:26)

---

[36] He is characterized using the same epithet in Sir 47:5.

[37] There is, of course, a certain irony in Judas' request that God strike
down the Syrians with the sword, because 1 Sam 17:47 states clearly that the
Lord "does not save by sword and spear." Clearly the author of 1 Maccabees
was not troubled by this nitpicking detail and, in fact, David uses Goliath's
own sword to kill and behead the giant (1 Sam 17:51).

David is remembered in the tradition for removing the reproach of the Philistine Goliath from Israel. The disgrace brought about by Goliath's bullying was considered severe and his death at the hand of the young shepherd was the greatest achievement in David's youth.[38] This view of David's slaying of Goliath is clear from two other Second Temple compositions. Ps 151:6–7, part of a psalm about David, reads: "I went out to meet the Philistine, and he cursed me by his idols. But I drew his own sword; I beheaded him, and took away disgrace (ἦρα ὄνειδος) from the people of Israel." A similar characterization is found in part of Ben Sira's description of David in the catalog of famous forebears. Sir 47:4–5 reads:

> In his youth did he not kill a giant, and take away the people's disgrace (ἐξῆρεν ὀνειδισμόν), when he whirled the stone in the sling and struck down the boasting Goliath? For he called on the Lord, the Most High, and he gave strength to his right hand to strike down a mighty man, and to exalt the power of his people.

This particular tale of David's courage as a young man gained epic proportions.[39] But what was the exact nature of the disgrace according to the author of 1 Maccabees? By looking at the immediate context of the prayer in 1 Maccabees 4, we see that after God grants Judas and his brothers victory over Lysias, they immediately set about restoring the temple in order to rededicate it. The "disgrace" is therefore the desecration of the temple and especially the defilement of the altar. This is evident from two references to disgrace found in the rest of the chapter. The first appears in connection with the renovation of the Temple and its trappings. The altar is considered so sacred that its defilement requires nothing less than to be remade. As expressed in 1 Macc 4:45: "And they thought it best to tear it down, so that it would not be a lasting shame to them that the Gentiles had

---

[38] The word for "disgrace" (חרפה, ὄνειδος) is used for only the most humiliating of circumstances in the Bible. Disgrace was generally considered some dreadful affront by non-Israelites or a situation in which the Israelites were disgraced by their own behavior before foreigners. Cf. the rape of Dinah in Gen 34:14; Isa 30:5; Jer 24:9. In Jer 20:8, Jeremiah goes so far as to call the word of the Lord, the divine message, a disgrace to the prophet because of the ridicule he is subjected to because of his preaching.

[39] This epic aggrandizement occurred even though a conflicting account in 2 Sam 21:19 attributes his death to Elhanan, the Bethlehemite. Another typological reference to David and Goliath appears in the Qumran literature; cf. the 1QM (*War Scroll*) xi, 2–3. For the Qumran community, young David represented the covenanters themselves; and Goliath, all those outside the group with whom God would wage war in the coming eschatological battle.

defiled it (αὐτοῖς εἰς ὄνειδος ὅτι ἐμίαναν τὰ ἔθνη αὐτό), so they tore down the altar." Not until this enormous task is accomplished is the disgrace left by the "Philistines" eliminated. 1 Macc 4:58 reads: "There was very great joy among the people and the disgrace (ὀνειδισμὸς) brought by the Gentiles was removed." We can thus see how the author of 1 Maccabees has scripturalized his prayer. He uses one well-known episode from ancient Israel, David's battle with Goliath, which removed the Philistine disgrace from Israel, and recontextualizes it to relate to a contemporary humiliation. Like the prayer in Judith 9, the prayer in 1 Maccabees 4 requires understanding the world in terms of sacral holiness versus defilement and disgrace. The author translates a tale of military victory into a tale of the triumph of holiness over the profane, defiling forces of the Seleucid invaders.

Conclusion

The prayers reviewed in this chapter provide more evidence for the scripturalization of prayer in Second Temple Judaism. They represent a particular hermeneutic, the reuse of one biblical episode as a typological retrieval of ancient traditions to apply to a contemporary situation. We have seen how divine speech found in the Bible is used to legitimate activity in the present, even when, as in Jdt 9:2, the "speech" is that of the narrator's voice. We have also seen how such retrievals often share other contemporary interpretations of biblical events. In Judith 9, Simeon was extolled for his valor and virtue in avenging the rape of his sister. This positive view of the brothers' violent acts is also reflected in the book of *Jubilees* and the *Testament of Levi*. The young David came to be thought of as the slayer of the mighty one, remover of Israel's reproach. This view is implicit in the prayer of Judas Maccabeus as well as in Psalm 151 and Ben Sira. Having now examined prayers that scripturalize history in chapter two, and prayers that view a single episode from the past typologically in this chapter, we will turn in the next chapter to consider a third way in which biblical traditions were used, in the delineation of character traits.

Chapter 4

Biblical Exempla
The Arrogance of Power in 3 Maccabees 2

The book of Ruth ends happily. Boaz, the wealthy land-owning relative of the widow Naomi, fulfills his obligation as next-of-kin and redeems Naomi's loyal daughter-in-law by marrying her. As part of the ceremony, the people and elders who act as witnesses call down a blessing on Ruth:

> And all of the people who were in the gate and the elders were witnesses and said: "May the Lord make the woman who is coming into your house like Rachel and Leah, the two of whom built up the house of Israel; and do valiantly[1] in Ephratha and make a name in Bethlehem. May your house be like Perez whom Tamar bore to Judah from the offspring that the Lord gives you from this woman." (Ruth 4:11–12)

In this exilic marriage blessing, family fertility is the theme. The people ask that God give Boaz a fruitful vine and olive shoots: that his wife may have many children and that their offspring be multiplied. It is similar thematically to such pre-exilic blessings for fertility and numerous descendants as Gen 24:60 and Gen 28:3–4, but there is an important difference. The blessing in Ruth 4 compares Ruth and Boaz to their renowned ancestors, Rachel, Leah, and Perez. The hope is expressed that Ruth will be as significant as the ancestors Rachel and Leah, two of the matriarchs of Israel's twelve tribes. The parallel between Ruth and Tamar is especially apt because each

---

[1] The only other occurrence of the expression "עשה חיל" is in Prov 31:29. "Many daughters have done valiantly, but you surpass them all." The exact meaning of this phrase is now lost to us.

woman was a non-Israelite who married into the Judahite tribe. Tradition remembers these two women for their contribution to Israel's royal line; both are part of the line from which King David descended.[2] Perez is likewise remembered in later scripture exclusively for his generative role.[3] It is significant the author distills and recalls only one notable aspect of these biblical characters. They are no longer multi-dimensional human ancestors, but uni-dimensional figures.

This chapter explores a related phenomenon in the prayer in 3 Macc 2:2–20, in which the Bible has become a source of moral, or in this case, immoral, exempla. As we shall see, the scripturalization of 3 Macc 2:2–20 is shaped in part by the influence of a Hellenistic rhetorical style. In 3 Maccabees 2, the high priest Simon prays that the Temple be spared desecration by the arrogant ruler Ptolemy Philopater who is planning to enter and desecrate the sanctuary. In 3 Macc 2:3–7, he recalls biblical exempla of arrogant and insolent characters: the giants who were destroyed by the flood, the Sodomites who were notorious for their vices, and the audacious Pharaoh who persecuted the Israelites in Egypt. The author's conception of the Bible's characters and stories is that they are primarily didactic. The behavior of individuals who are described in biblical narratives is understood as a kind of instruction, their actions either to be emulated (and so, by implication, have similar blessings brought down upon the heads of the pray-ers) or, as in this case, avoided. Although other Second Temple literature, and indeed some biblical literature as well, use examples from the past to exhort people to proper behavior or to extol renowned ancestors, the particular literary form of this section in the prayer bears a strong resemblance to a classical Greek rhetorical form. Yet in spite of this Hellenistic influence, the prayer retains a strongly traditional Jewish outlook. Even within the section with the suggested Hellenistic influence, 3 Macc 2:3–7, well-developed traditional interpretive motifs appear, including the ideas that the Nephilim and the *gibborim* mentioned in Genesis 6 were responsible for the corruption of the earth that resulted in the Flood, and that the Sodomites were egregious exemplars of wickedness. The prayer also includes the tradition that Jerusalem and the Temple were chosen and sanctified—long before the time of King David—at the time of the creation of the earth itself. Like the exogamous marriage between Boaz the Israelite and Ruth

---

[2] Cf. Ruth 4:18–22; 1 Chr 2:4, and in the New Testament, Matt 1:3.
[3] Cf. 1 Chr 2:4,5; 4:1; 9:4 and Matt 1:3,5; Luke 3:32.

the Moabitess, the scripturalization of 3 Macc 2:2–20 thus reflects the exogamous pairing of Greek style and Jewish biblical substance.

3 Maccabees 2:2–20

In contrast to the other prayers being considered in this book, the prayer in 3 Maccabees 2 has suffered from a lack of scholarly attention, in large part because to all religious communities with the exception of the Eastern Orthodox Churches, this book is not considered part of scripture. Even though it is considered extraneous by most modern religious communities, the book, and the prayer in particular, share many of the same marks of scripturalization that are apparent in other Second Temple works. John Collins, one of the few people who has remarked on the prayer at all, has suggested that 3 Maccabees 2 belongs to the same Deuteronomistic tradition of late biblical prayers as Nehemiah 9, Ezra 9, Daniel 9, and Bar 1:15–3:8.[4] Yet this attempt to categorize the prayer ignores its unique style and content and also overemphasizes the element of confession in the prayer, which is minimal. The prayer does suggest a vague connection between the Jews' sin and their supposed "punishment" by Ptolemy in his threat to the Temple in Jerusalem, but the confessional element is limited to parts of two verses (13 and 19). The focus of the prayer is not on the sins of the Jews but rather on the divine response to past abuses of power by non-Israelites. This

---

[4] *Harper Bible Commentary, ad loc.* As detailed in chapter 2, various scholars have drawn attention to the similarities among a select group of "historical psalms" and Nehemiah 9, as well as similarities among prayers lumped together under the rubric, "Deuteronomistic confessions." Collins does not mention important differences among these compositions. His criterion for categorizing 3 Macc 2:2–20 with the others is that it contains "Deuteronomistic theology," in other words, that the Jews are being punished for their neglect of their covenantal obligations. This, however, is not sufficient reason to categorize the prayer as a Deuteronomistic type alongside the other prayers he cites. He does acknowledge that the prayer contains a greatly muted confession of sin and that the punishment is not connected to the exile, both of which argue against his categorization. The focus of the historical retrospect is not on the sins of the Israelites as it is in Nehemiah 9, but rather on foreigners and their ill effects on Israelite/Jewish concerns. If it is any "type" at all, the prayer can be loosely categorized with such prayers as Judith 9 and 1 Macc 3:50–53, which are requests for divine aid to protect the Temple. They concern the sanctity of the Temple in the face of hostile attack by an idolatrous enemy. Thus the link to earlier biblical traditions lies as much with Priestly holiness laws as with Deuteronomistic literature. As this chapter is at pains to point out, the prayer reflects a complex and subtle melding of biblical traditions that goes beyond easy categorization.

concern with the relationship of Israel's God to non-Jews determines the list of exempla chosen in the beginning of the prayer. This and the related fear of the threat posed to the Temple by arrogant foreign powers are the central concerns reflected in the prayer. Here is the text of the prayer:

> 2. Lord, Lord, king of the heavens, and lord of all creation, holy among holy ones, sole ruler, almighty, give heed to us who are being tormented by this impious and profane man, who is haughty in his arrogance and power.
>
> 3. For you are the creator of all and the governor of all. You are a righteous ruler and you judge all those who have done things in hubris and pride. 4. You destroyed those who did unrighteousness beforehand, among whom were the giants, convinced of their strength and arrogance, whom you destroyed by bringing upon them immeasurable water. 5. You consumed with fire and brimstone the Sodomites, workers of haughtiness, who had become conspicuous because of their wickedness and you made them an example to future generations.
>
> 6. You put to the test the arrogant Pharaoh who enslaved your people, holy Israel, by manifold and multiple punishments through which you made known your great strength. 7. And when he gave chase with chariotry and a multitudinous throng, you overwhelmed him in the depths of the sea, and those who put faith in you, Sovereign of all creation, you carried through in safety. 8. And when they had seen the works of your hand, they praised you, the Almighty.
>
> 9. You, O King, when you had created the limitless and immeasurable earth, chose this city and consecrated this place for your name, although you are self-sufficient. And when you had glorified it by your majestic manifestation, you made the structure for the glory of your great and honored name. 10. And out of love for the house of Israel you promised that if it should happen that we turn away and anguish overcome us, if we should come into this place and pray, you would listen to our prayer.
>
> 11. And indeed, you are faithful and true. 12. When our ancestors were suffering persecutions, you came to their aid in their humiliation and you delivered them from great evils.
>
> 13. Behold now, Holy King, on account of our manifold and great sins, we are tormented and we are subdued by our enemies and we have become weak in our powerlessness. 14. In our downfall, this arrogant and profane man lies in wait to violate the holy place which is designated on the earth to the name of your glory. 15. For indeed your dwelling place, the heaven of heavens, is unapproachable by

humans. 16. But since you were pleased to situate your glory among your people Israel, you consecrated this place.

17. Do not punish us by the impurity of these people nor straighten us on account of this profanation, lest the law-breakers boast in their anger or exult in the haughtiness of their tongue, saying, 18. "We have trampled down the house of holiness, just as the houses of abominations are trampled down." 19. Blot out our sins, scatter our offenses, and manifest your mercy at this hour. 20. Let your compassion speedily overtake us and put praises in the mouth of those who are downcast and crushed in spirit, granting us peace.

Summary of contents:
3 Macc 2:

2–3	invocation to God, the divine King of heaven, ruler of creation
4–6	three paradigmatic examples of arrogance: the "giants," the Sodomites, and Pharaoh
7–8	the Exodus
9–11	Jerusalem and the holy site of the Temple chosen at creation
12	general statement about help in past
13	transition to present situation, muted confession
14–20	request for help against Ptolemy, recalling the divine promise to listen to prayers offered at the Temple

The Use of Examples

As became apparent in the previous chapter, the typologies found in the book of Judith suggest an understanding of the present that is in cyclical continuity with the biblical past, in which a recurrence of the biblical past was possible in the present. The prayer in Judith 9 portrays the events surrounding the rape of Dinah as happening again in the post-exilic period, if albeit on a more symbolic level, in which the Temple was threatened with rape through the entry into the sanctuary and its defilement by a foreign marauder.[5] 3 Maccabees 2 offers a certain degree of similarity with Judith 9. Not only does it share the same theme about the violation of the Temple, but its author also recognizes the past traditions of Israel as a crucial font from which to draw in understanding and acting in the present. Yet unlike the perspective of Judith, this prayer offers a perception of the past as over and done with, but from which instructive lessons can nonetheless be drawn. This brings us to the important feature of the prayer that distinguishes its use of scripture: it contains three

---

[5] Even the names of places and people in the book are symbolic. Judith herself represents a female hypostatization of the Jewish people and Bethulia, her town, is understood by most scholars as a play on the Hebrew word for virgin.

telescoped characterizations of personalities from the history of Israel, which we refer to as "exempla," that are used to understand behavior in the present.

Before proceeding with an analysis of the prayer itself, it is important to evaluate how examples are used not only in this prayer but in other Second Temple literature. Having suggested that there was a clear formal Hellenistic influence on part of this prayer, we should point out that there are various uses of "exempla" in Second Temple literature. A thorough study of the various types of biblical examples used in the body of literature deserves its own monograph, but building on the work of other scholars, we can assert some tentative conclusions about the nature of the paradigm list in 3 Maccabees 2 and its generic relationship to other examples lists. 3 Maccabees 2 and its kin comprise one of three general categories of exempla observable in this large corpus. One kind of list contains exemplary biblical characters, each with his or her own distinctive personality trait or a particular event in that person's life.[6] A second use of examples focuses on a virtue/vice or the specific actions of a single individual.[7] This can also be understood as a subcategory of lists

---

[6] Examples of this kind include *Jub.* 22:1–23, Sir 44–49, and *Hellenistic Synagogal Prayer* 12. *Jubilees* 22, Abraham's blessing upon Jacob, contains two distinct examples from the past. Abraham exhorts his son to avoid intermarriage with the Canaanites, because they are tainted "through the sin of Ham." He warns him not to commit idolatry and cites the Sodomites as paradigmatic idolaters, emulation of whose behavior is to be avoided. Ben Sira 44–49, the "hymn in praise of famous men," is a *locus classicus* of exempla, but its formal organization is different from 3 Maccabees 2. Ben Sira's list does not point out the same characteristic in all of the biblical "heroes," but suggests one outstanding quality that characterizes each one. *Hellenistic Synagogal Prayers* 12 recalls fifteen biblical "heroes" and lists their epithets including: righteous Noah, pious Lot, Joshua the soldier.

[7] There are many illustrations of this use. For instance, in order to illustrate the principle that intermarriage with Gentiles is prohibited, the angel/God instructs Moses in *Jub.* 30:17, "Therefore I command you, saying, 'Proclaim this testimony to Israel: 'See how it was for the Shechemites and their sons, how they were given into the hand of the two children of Jacob and they killed them painfully. And it was a righteousness for them and it was written down for them for righteousness.'" Simeon and Levi are cited here as positive examples, whose righteous zeal would be permanently commemorated. Another individual biblical example of zeal is cited in 1 Macc 2:26. The episode in which Mattathias kills a Jew who offers an idolatrous sacrifice on the altar in Modein is described in 1 Macc 2:15–25. Then verse 26 reads: "Thus he burned with zeal for the law, just as Phinehas did against Zimri son of Salu." Cf. also such New Testament passages as Jas 5:17–18; 1 Pet 3:5–6; or 1 John 3:12–15. The passage from 1 John appears as part of an

that multiply historical examples, but one that is concerned specifically with good or bad behavior as opposed to character traits. The third variety, which we will argue is closest to a particular Greek rhetorical style, cites biblical examples according to one specific principle that they are held to illustrate. In these lists, a principle is enunciated and then biblical examples of that particular principle are adduced as illustrations. The rhetorical function of the first category serves as a commemoration of biblical ancestors, a remembering of past heroes or villains. The purpose of the second and third categories is hortatory in order to dissuade contemporary readers from bad behavior or to reinforce positive behavior.

A number of scholars have discussed the use of examples in biblical and extra-biblical literature and its relationship to classical rhetoric.[8] Thomas Lee has studied the form of Ben Sira 44–50, the passage "in praise of honored men."[9] His form-critical assessment of

---

exhortation for people to love one another. That principle is stated in verse 11, and then in verse 12, Cain is cited as a negative example whose behavior should not be emulated: "We must not be like Cain who was from the evil one and murdered his brother. And why did he murder him? Because his own deeds were evil and his brother's righteous."

[8] In addition to the scholars discussed below, of special importance is the long article by Adolf Lumpe, "Exemplum," in *Reallexikon für Antike und Christentum* 6 (Stuttgart: Anton Hiersemann, 1966) 1229–1257. He treats the use of examples not only in classical Greek, but also in Jewish, Roman, and Christian literature. For later use of lists in the Ebionite Pseudo-Clementine literature, see Charles A. Gieschen, "The Seven Pillars of the World: Ideal Figure Lists in the Christology of the Pseudo-Clementines," *JSP* 12 (1994) 47–82. Gieschen understands a more broad "listing genre" that includes not only the *Beispielreihe* like that found in 3 Maccabees 2 and 6, but also more general lists with idealized biblical characters. He views their rhetorical function as polemic against Marcionite, Gnostic, Pauline Christian and other groups who denigrated Israel's scripture.

[9] His book focuses entirely on this and related questions: Thomas R. Lee, *Studies in the Form of Sirach 44–50* (SBLDS 75; Atlanta: Scholars, 1986). Compare also the earlier study by Burton Mack, *Wisdom and the Hebrew Epic: Ben Sira's Hymn in Praise of the Fathers* (Chicago: University of Chicago Press, 1985). Mack views Ben Sira 44–50 as a Second Temple epic written to encompass all of the history of the Jews. The passage was to serve the contemporary community as a kind of theory of origins. Mack's assessment of Lee's thesis corresponds with my own: "Ben Sira may have modeled his hymn with an eye to both genres [encomium and *Beispielreihe*], but neither literary form really is sufficient to account for the peculiar way in which his figures are characterized, linked, and used to trace a complete, schematic history" (135).

the piece is that it is composed of an examples list or *Beispielreihe* in
44:16–50:21 and a frame that includes 44:1–15 and 50:1–24. He
contends that this frame of the *Beispielreihe* transforms the entire
piece into an encomium celebrating the high priest Simon II. Simon
is the last in a long list of individuals from Israel's history who are
extolled for their achievements and contributions and the author
praises him in twenty-one verses, which is longer than the space
devoted even to Moses (eight verses) and David (eleven verses)
combined. The rhetorical end is to praise him for his achievements
and virtues and do this by lifting him up to the same status as Israel's
other "greats." Lee's thesis that Sirach knew of and employed a
Greek rhetorical form as a model is inconclusive, which he himself
admits. He suggests however that Greek influence was likely at
work, citing Hengel's work on the extensive and pervasive nature of
Greek culture in the third century B.C.E. My own view is that his
form-critical analysis of this passage does not define the *Beispielreihe*
form narrowly enough as a separate form. While it could be
conceded that there was Greek influence in his use of examples in
general and that the passage does function as an encomium, Lee's
claims for formal literary influence are less convincing because he
does not produce a sufficiently close classical analogue to this long
passage in Ben Sira.

Other scholars have succeeded in articulating more precisely
what constitutes formal Greek influence on the examples lists.
Devorah Dimant has written on the use of historical examples in the
literature of this period.[10] Dimant lists seven such examples that

---

[10] In an essay on the use of scripture in the Apocrypha and
Pseudepigrapha, she discusses three explicit ways in which scripture is used,
focusing in turn on biblical citation, catalogues of biblical individuals, and
isolated references to biblical individuals or circumstances. From our
perspective, Dimant sets up a somewhat artificial dichotomy between explicit
and implicit uses of biblical elements, when in fact they can be contained in
the same passage. For instance, Jdt 9:2–4 makes an explicit reference to the
rape of Dinah (Genesis 34) but it also contains an implicit allusion to Numbers
25 and Isaiah 37 in its use of the word "zeal," as detailed in the previous
chapter. She also does not mention that the evocation of the rape of Dinah is
found as part of a larger implicit use of biblical model. The prayer as a whole
is patterned after Hezekiah's prayer in Isaiah 37//2Kings 19. See "Use and
Interpretation of Mikra in the Apocrypha and Pseudepigrapha," *Mikra: Text,
Translation, Reading and Interpretation of the Hebrew Bible in Ancient
Judaism and Early Christianity*, (Compendia Rerum Iudaicarum ad Novum
Testamentum, M.J. Mulder, ed.; Assen: Van Gorcum/Philadelphia: Fortress,
1990) 379–420 and Chapter 2 above.

show signs of Hellenistic influence, including 3 Maccabees 2.[11] She defines them as "concise references to historical precedents grouped in a sequence of examples in a special literary structure, which is usually considered a distinct literary form."[12] Here is her evaluation of the way such lists composed of "historical examples" are used in certain Second Temple books:

> Each of these lists gives examples to butress [sic] the argument presented in the larger discourse. The role of the historical or mythical example in rhetorical argument was well-known in the ancient world, and was used extensively in biblical as well as in classical literature. This role consists of three functions: *the example establishes a general rule, or illustrates a rule already in force, or is a model or anti-model in order to recommend or condemn a certain type of behavior.* Our lists use examples in the second and third functions, usually combined. Such a combination is to be found mostly in discourses of a hortatory nature, whereas in prayers the examples are used only as illustration.[13]

She rightly distinguishes the lists of individuals that are ordered by one principle from other lists that occur in this literature like Ben Sira 44–49, which is a chronological recounting of all the most prominent biblical characters. The individuals mentioned are exceptional each for a different reason and there is no specific principle cited that works as a unifying thread, other than the very general membership in Israel's "Hall of Fame."

In her brief discussion of the literary form of such examples lists, Dimant makes reference to another scholar, Armin Schmitt, who has argued the most convincing case for Greek literary influence. In an article on exempla in Wis 9:18–10:21, he outlines four formal similarities between the material in Wisdom and Greek literature: 1) the list contains a heading with a focal point and goal of the *Beispielreihe*; 2) a number of individuals are adduced either to substantiate or illustrate this principle; 3) there is a compressed arrangement of these exempla so that only the "data" relevant to the principle are included; and 4) frequently, the wording of the heading

---

[11] The six other such lists are 1 Macc 2:49–64; 3 Macc 6:4–8; 4 Macc 16:18–23; Wis 10:1–21; Sir 16:6–10; and 4 Ezra 7:106–110 ("Use and Interpretation," 39).

[12] Dimant, "Use and Interpretation of Mikra," 392.

[13] Dimant, "Use and Interpretation of Mikra," 393. She is heavily dependent on the discussion of Ch. Perelman-L. Olbrechts-Tyteca for her definition of the three functions of these lists. Cf. *Traité de L'argumentation: La nouvelle rhétorique*, (Paris: Presses Universitaire de France, 1958) 149–170.

is repeated in the recitation of the examples chosen, which ties the piece together in a literary way as a unit.[14]

There was ample precedent for this use of exempla lists in classical literature. These kinds of lists appear in the work of no less an influential author than Homer. The use of exempla is apparent in the following passage from the *Odyssey*, in which Hermes has brought word from Zeus that Calypso should allow Odysseus to go free. In response, Calypso tells him:

> Oh you vile gods, in jealousy supernal!
> You hate it when we choose to lie with men—
> immortal flesh by some dear mortal side.
> So radiant Dawn once took to bed Orion
> until you easeful gods grew peevish at it,
> and holy Artemis, Artemis throned in gold,
> hunted him down in Delos with her arrows.
> Then Demeter, the tasseled tresses yielded
> to Iason, mingling and making love
> in a furrow three times plowed; but Zeus found out
> and killed him with a white-hot thunderbolt.
> So now you grudge me, too, my mortal friend.
> But it was I who saved him—saw him straddle
> his own keel board, the one man left afloat
> when Zeus rent wide his ship with chain lightning
> and overturned him in the winedark sea.
>   (*Odyssey* 5: 118–133)[15]

The passage illustrates the main features characterizing *Beispielreihe* pointed out by Schmitt. The principle that governs the choice of examples here is the gods' disapproval of divine-mortal intercourse, a principle stated at the beginning of the passage. This is then substantiated by drawing on mythic lore, the tales of Dawn and Orion, Demeter and Iason. The principle is then restated following the enumeration of examples ("So now you grudge me, too, my mortal friend") in reference to Calypso's own experience with Odysseus. There are many other instances of such exempla lists that could be adduced to demonstrate the point.[16]

---

[14] Armin Schmitt, "Struktur, Herkunft und Bedeutung der Beispielreihe in Weish 10," *Biblische Zeitschrift* 21 (1977) 1–22. His list of the four similarities appears on pages 18–19.

[15] This is the translation of Robert Fitzgerald.

[16] Lumpe cites many instances of examples lists from classical literature, including others from Homer: *Odyssey* 1:32–43; 21:293–310; 5:118–128. He mentions a number of instances in the *Iliad*, including 16:236–238, Achilles' prayer to Zeus in which Achilles recalls earlier divine responses to prayers.

Armed with a more narrow definition of what constitutes a particular form for *Beispielreihe* in Greek literature, it is possible to survey the landscape of Second Temple literature for such Hellenistic influence. A review of a few passages from various Jewish-Hellenistic works will help to establish some comparison.

One illustration of this literary form appears in Judith. Judith's exhortation to the people of Bethulia, spoken in order to reassure them about their ultimate fate, contains illustrations of the principle that God only tries the righteous:

> In spite of all these things, let us thank our Lord God who is testing us as he did our ancestors. Remember what he did with Abraham, and how he tested Isaac, and what happened to Jacob in Syrian Mesopotamia, while he was tending the sheep of Laban, his mother's brother. For he has not tried us with fire, as he did them, to search their hearts, nor has he taken vengeance on us; but the Lord scourges those who are close to him in order to admonish them. (Jdt 8:25–27)

The Greek for testing (πειράζειν) and the related word "try" (ἐτασμόν) are repeated to reinforce the general principle that is said to be upheld by this citation of historical examples. Another salient feature of this "examples list" in relation to 3 Maccabees 2 is its clear dependence on the Jewish interpretive tradition of the testing of the patriarchs. Abraham was tested with fire in that most fiery of cities, Ur of the Chaldees, that was ultimately punished by a fiery devastation, but this occurs only between the lines of the text in the imaginations of those who kept the traditional interpretive flame alive through the generations. So in this respect, the use of scripture in the passage from Judith 8 has two links with the *Beispielreihe* in 3 Maccabees 2: it reflects Hellenistic influence, but also contains traditional Jewish interpretive motifs.

1 Macc 2:51–60, which appears as part of Mattathias's death-bed testament, contains a list of biblical examples who are cited for their firm adherence to the covenant. The list includes Abraham, Joseph, Phinehas, Joshua, Caleb, David, Elijah, Hananiah, Azariah, Mishael, and Daniel. Mattathias's sons are exhorted in 1 Macc 2:51 to remember the acts of the ancestors, so that they too will receive great honor. Verses 50 and 64 form an inclusio, a statement and restatement of the principle that Mattathias's children should show zeal for the law/be courageous and grow strong in the law. Each verse in 51–60 cites one telescoped example of the biblical figure and his most outstanding deed that reflected his devotion to the Torah. As

Dimant has pointed out, in each verse the author uses one or two terms from an original biblical text that allude to the biblical character involved.[17] As in Judith 8 and 3 Maccabees 2, there are a number of traditional interpretations included. For instance, verse 53 reads "Joseph in the time of his anguish kept the commandment, and became lord of Egypt," which is surely a reference to Potiphar's wife's attempted seduction of Joseph. This episode had already begun to take on a life of its own in traditional interpretation by this time.[18] Here again, the list is a fusion of Hellenistic form with traditional Jewish characterizations of the heroes of the faith, chosen as scriptural examples with lessons the sons of Mattathias can extrapolate for daily life.

There are many other examples lists of this particular form that we could examine, but we will keep our focus now on the first six verses of the passage already cited above, 3 Macc 2:2–20.[19]

---

[17] The biblical terms used in reference to the particular biblical character do not in all cases derive from the primary narrative text devoted to that particular person. For instance, Joseph is referred to as the "lord of Egypt," a phrase derived from the Greek of Ps 105:21, which accurately summarizes his situation, but does not derive from the Genesis narrative. See Dimant, "Use and Interpretation of Mikra," 394.

[18] James L. Kugel has treated the history of interpretation of Joseph in the first half of his book *In Potiphar's House: The Interpretive Life of Biblical Texts* (San Francisco: Harper, 1990) 1–155. He makes a convincing case on the basis of later interpretation, which greatly expanded the significance of this event in Joseph's life, that the "commandment" referred to in this passage is the prohibition against adultery, and the specific instance in the life of Joseph was his experience with Zuleika. See in particular pages 20–26 on the extra-biblical treatment of Joseph.

[19] CD 2:14–3:12 is another clear example of a *Beispielreihe*. In the passage, ten biblical individuals or groups of people are evaluated on the basis of whether they "walked on the paths" of God or strayed. There are other lists. Wisdom of Solomon 10 has been thoroughly examined by Armin Schmitt, see note 14 above. 3 Maccabees 6 is another prayer similar in many respects to 3 Maccabees 2. 4 Macc 16:18–23 illustrates the principle that one ought to endure any suffering for the sake of God. The New Testament also contains a number of such examples lists. Hebrews 11, perhaps the most well-known *exempla* passage, is an encomium on the principle of faith and how different biblical characters embody this. Jas 2:21–26 illustrates the principle that faith without works is empty. The principle is the *inclusio* statement appearing at the beginning as a question in verse 21 and again in verse 26 as a conclusion to the pericope. The two examples chosen to illustrate this principle are Abraham and his "sacrifice" of Isaac as well as Rahab the prostitute in showing hospitality to the Israelite messengers. Jas 5:10–11 includes another such examples list that seeks to buttress the claim that patience and suffering will be blessed, invoking the prophets, Job, and the Lord himself. The last

2. Lord, Lord, king of the heavens, and lord of all creation, holy among holy ones, sole ruler, almighty, give heed to us who are being tormented by this impious and profane man, who is haughty in his **arrogance** and power. 3. For you are the creator of all and the governor of all. You are a righteous ruler and you judge all those

---

example of the patience of God is alluded to in a subtle way. Jas 5:11 states ". . . and you have seen the purpose of the Lord, how the Lord is compassionate and merciful." This is the first half of the divine self-revelation formula of Exod 34:6 and elsewhere, which continues "Slow to anger, and abounding in steadfast love and faithfulness." James seems to work under the assumption that his audience is quite familiar with the formula and thus needs only the first half to get the point. Cf. also Jude 5–7 and 2 Pet 2:5–10. Another quite interesting illustration of an exempla list, though thought to date from a later period (150–300 C.E.) is *Hellenistic Synagogal Prayer* 6, appropriated in the *Apostolic Constitutions*, which cites thirty examples of prayers that were answered in the Old Testament (one in 1 Maccabees), from the time of Abel down to Mattathias and Jael (this last appears out of chronological sequence) that were prayed by those who were "righteous in their generations." The prayer asks God on analogy to receive also the prayers of his people. A related examples list in 4 Ezra 7:106–110 cites biblical figures who successfully interceded for others.

As with any attempt at categorization of a body of evidence, there are always some defiant specimens. For instance, Tobit 4:12 contains a principle that is illustrated by a list of biblical exempla, but only their names are listed without specific narrative elaboration. In this particular passage, Tobit exhorts his son to emulate the heroes of Genesis by getting his wife from the mother country, Israel: "Beware my son, of every kind of fornication. First of all, marry a woman from among the descendants of your ancestors; do not marry a foreign woman, who is not of your father's tribe; for we are the descendants of the prophets. Remember, my son, that Noah, Abraham, Isaac, and Jacob, our ancestors of old, all took wives from among their kin. They were blessed in their children, and their posterity will inherit the land." In that verse, these individuals are viewed as models because they were showered with blessings by God, which presumably might accrue to Tobias if he behaves likewise. The principle underscored is: do not marry a foreign woman. The specific exhortation to "remember" (μνήσθητε/זכור) becomes characteristic of the particular Jewish appropriation of this examples listing. Perhaps Tobit's appropriation of such a list, if it does indeed betray the Hellenistic influence we have detected elsewhere, has consciously tried to "Judaize" it, in keeping with the highly traditional style of this book. Cf. the *Apocalypse of Zephaniah* 6:10, which might also be considered a subcategory because it concerns primarily God's action in relation to biblical characters as opposed to the character's behavior or virtues themselves. The passage contains such a chronicling of divine acts in a short prayer: "God saved Israel from Pharaoh, Susanna from the elders, the three holy men from the furnace; save me!" Other examples lists appear in 4 Macc 16:18–23; *T. Naph.* 3:1–5; and CD 2:14–3:12.

who have done things in **hubris** and **pride**. 4. You destroyed those who did unrighteousness beforehand, among whom were the giants, convinced of their strength and **arrogance**, whom you destroyed by bringing upon them immeasurable water. 5. You consumed with fire and brimstone the Sodomites, workers of **haughtiness**, who had become conspicuous because of their wickedness and you made them an example (παράδειγμα) to future generations. 6. You put to the test the **arrogant** Pharaoh, who enslaved your people, holy Israel, by manifold and multiple punishments through which you made known your great strength. 7. And when he gave chase with chariotry and a multitudinous throng, you overwhelmed him in the depths of the sea, and those who put faith in you, Sovereign of all creation, you carried through in safety. 8. And when they had seen the works of your hand, they praised you, the Almighty.

The principle that governs the choice of examples is God's disdain for human arrogance (θράσος), a word that is repeated three times in this prayer, as well as two times in this chapter outside the prayer, to characterize Ptolemy Philopater.[20] Other words included in the prayer are its near synonyms: hubris (ὕβρις), pride (ἀγερωχία) and haughtiness (ὑπερηφανία). The biblical figures chosen are all non-Israelites, which is of course fitting for the narrative situation in which a Gentile ruler is on the verge of desecrating the Temple. Each of the three biblical examples chosen succinctly illustrates this principle and, as will be detailed below, contains proto-midrashic extra-biblical interpretation. The *Beispielreihe* in 3 Maccabees 2 thus fits the same pattern observed in Judith 8 and 1 Maccabees 2.

Although we have looked at the Second Temple manifestation of this exempla list and stressed Greek influence, possible biblical roots of this phenomenon should not be ruled out. Indeed, having also noted the traces of traditional Jewish interpretation in some of these passages, the question should well be posed: are there any clear precedents for such examples lists in the canonical biblical literature? The question is best broken down into two subparts: Is there some evidence for the use of characters as moral or immoral examplars in biblical narratives? Are there analogies to the particular literary form outlined above? The second part of this question can be quickly answered in the negative. An examination of the biblical literature

---

[20] The theme of God's punishment of the arrogant is also featured in the prayer in 3 Maccabees 6, in which the word arrogance (θράσος) appears three times.

does not show any evidence to support the existence of this type of literary form, with a general principle stated at the beginning, followed by a number of examples from Israel's history, with perhaps a recurrent use of a particular term or set of terms that underscores the general principle. We should look then at the first question, and indeed there are certain signs of continuity with this particular consciousness and use of the past in the biblical literature. The chapter began with a discussion of the blessing in Ruth 4:11–12. Although Rachel, Leah, and Perez are not cited for any particular vice or virtue, their essential contribution to Israel was the reason for the comparison to Ruth and Boaz.

At first consideration another good precedent is the evaluation found in the Deuteronomistic History of certain virtuous and vicious kings. "Walking in the way of Jeroboam" or "following in the sins of Jeroboam" appears nineteen times in the book of Kings. His sponsorship of idolatrous worship is ultimately blamed for the exile. So too, David serves as the paradigmatic example of a good king, who, even when he does sin, as in the exceptional case of Bathsheba and Uriah the Hittite, nonetheless repents before God. On closer examination, however, this moral distillation of the kings' behavior is of a different order. These recurrent phrases are used as evaluative assessments about the other *kings* of Israel and they do not make reference to more than one example, nor do they mention other figures who are later esteemed in Second Temple literature, such as Enoch, Abraham, Joseph, Moses, or even Elijah, who also figures prominently in the Deuteronomistic History. The references to wicked Jeroboam function primarily as rhetoric to explain the ultimate fate of Israel in exile, although they do function secondarily to warn readers about the dangers of idolatry.

A better example is the reiteration time and again in prophetic literature of the fate of Sodom and Gomorrah as a warning to foreigners and also Israelites concerning their unhappy fate if they continue in their disregard of the divine will.[21] The fate of Sodom and Gomorrah is also mentioned in Deut 29:23. Deut 29:18–28 describes the dreadful fate that will result if Israel turns from obedience to the covenant. Deut 29:21–24 reads:

> The next generation, your children who rise up after you, and also the foreigner who comes from a distant land, will see the scourges of this land and the afflictions by which the Lord has afflicted it—all its

---

[21] E.g. Zeph 2:9–10 or Jer 23:14.

soil burned by sulfur and salt, nothing planted, unable to sprout, unable to support any plants, like the destruction of Sodom and Gomorrah, Admah and Zeboiim, which the Lord smote in his anger and rage. All the nations will ask, "Why has the Lord done such to this land? What caused this great scorching of anger? They will say, "It is because they abandoned the covenant of the Lord, the God of their ancestors, which he made with them when he brought them out of the land of Egypt."

The mention of the destruction of the cities of the plain does not provide an exact analogy, because here the destruction is recalled without specific reference to the nature of the sins that provoked divine punishment. It does, however, reflect the fact that the Sodomites were considered paradigmatic sinners fully deserving of divine wrath and were already by this time burned into the memories of biblical Israel as a moral lesson.

Another example that comes closer to the use we have observed in Second Temple literature lies in the legal material in Deuteronomy. Immediately after an injunction to guard against skin lesions (בְּנֶגַע־הַצָּרַעַת) in Deut 24:8, is Deut 24:9: "Remember what the Lord your God did to Miriam on your way out from Egypt." This brief allusion does not specify precisely, but it surely refers to Miriam's punishment with skin lesions (מְצֹרַעַת) when she and Aaron questioned the authority of Moses in his choice of a Cushite wife, an incident described in Numbers 12. This is a negative example, and although Miriam's punishment is cited nowhere else this way, unlike the legendary destruction of Sodom and Gomorrah, the rhetorical function of this historical example is much the same as the Second Temple exempla reviewed above.

The biblical examples reviewed above do not reflect exempla lists; all except the passage from the exilic book of Ruth cite one example from Israelite history in order to make a rhetorical point. And by and large, the distillation of the biblical literature for biblical character "types" who embody one particular virtue or vice is not seen extensively until the Second Temple period and is thus best understood as a product of Hellenization. As discussed and qualified above, the use of biblical exempla is largely missing even from the late pre-exilic literature, like the Deuteronomistic history. The DtrH contains a general assessment of the behavior of David and Jeroboam that is used for evaluative purposes. Jeroboam worshipped at the high places; idolatry for which he was condemned and the whole nation punished by exile. David followed in the way of the Lord except for the matter of Uriah the Hittite. But King Manasseh is never told by priest or prophet to behave like his faithful ancestor Abraham or to be valiant and brave on the battlefield like his forebear Joshua. The biblical literature thus contains only a very limited degree of moralizing by analogy such as we see in the Second Temple literature.

Before turning to a consideration of the use and interpretation of scripture in these examples and the rest of the prayer, a brief summary of our findings is in order. We have deduced that the exempla form detected in 3 Maccabees 2 likely reflects Hellenistic influence. One reason is the absence of the list form *per se* in any biblical literature. There are some references to individuals and their characteristic virtues or vices in the biblical literature such as we saw in Deut 29:21–24 and Ruth 4:11–12 in which earlier biblical personalities are viewed as models. This represents a shared rhetorical stance with the lists in Greek literature; nonetheless, in the Hebrew Bible, there is no special literary form for such exempla. Moreover, with the exception of the Sodomites and their paradigmatic sinfulness, the telescoped depictions of biblical characters found in later literature (Abraham the faithful or Phinehas the zealous) have not yet evolved. The other indication of Greek influence is the presence of this formal literary style in classical literature, as illustrated by the passage from the *Odyssey* and buttressed by the work of other scholars in this area, primarily Lumpe, Dimant, and Schmitt. The soundest conclusion, then, is that the use of biblical characters as moral exempla comes to the fore in the Second Temple period and is found predominantly though not exclusively (compare also the evidence from Qumran) in Second Temple literature of a Hellenistic bent. The Hellenistic influence that has been argued above is of great interest, though not in and of itself. Rather, it demonstrates that even with such a pervasive cultural influence as that exerted by Greek culture, Jewish literature nonetheless persisted in its traditional use and interpretation of scripture. We shall see Jewish tradition prominently displayed in this prayer for the safety of the Temple.

The Use of Scripture in Exempla

Having offered these conclusions about the origins and nature of exempla in this prayer, let us look at the concrete cases found in 3 Maccabees 2. The three scriptural examples illustrate the principle that God saves the chosen people from oppressive foreign enemies. Two derive from Genesis, and one from Exodus.

Giants Connected with Punishment by Flood

> 3 Macc 2:4: You destroyed those who committed injustice in the past, among whom were giants who trusted in their strength and arrogance (ῥώμῃ καὶ θράσει), upon whom you brought measureless waters.

The giants (γίγαντες or נבריס) referred to in Gen 6:4 are the first mentioned in this list. Direct mention is made of the cause of their downfall—their own strength and arrogance, as well as the specific punishment, the "measureless waters," brought upon them by God for their misdeeds. The first question to ask about this verse in 3 Maccabees 2 is: why are the "giants" indicted as unjust, possessed of strength and arrogance? The answer is important because it indicates how scripture is being interpreted in the prayer.[22]

Let us start with one of the biblical sources for this verse. Taken at face value, Gen 6:4 is hardly condemnatory of these great creatures: "The Nephilim were on the earth in those days and also afterwards, when the sons of God went into the daughters of man and they bore children to them; these were the *gibborim* that were of

---

[22] A preliminary note should be made on the Greek translation γίγαντες. The Greek translates the Hebrew words נפלים and נברים both as γίγαντες, reflecting an interpretive decision about the referent of "these" in the last clause and equating the *gibborim* and the *nephilim*. Why were they understood to be giants? The answer lies in two other passages in which *nephilim* and ʿanaq appear, Num 13:25–33 and Deut 1:28–2:21. The passage in Numbers describes the spies' report of their visit to Canaan. The men say that the people are extremely strong (אפס כי־עז העם, μεγάλαι σφόδρα; v.28), men of great size (אנשי מדות, ἄνδρες ὑπερμήκεις; v.33). They then report that they saw the Nephilim, translated here, too, as γίγαντες along with the explanatory comment that the "sons of Anaq," or the Anakim, come from the Nephilim, and that the Israelites seemed like grasshoppers to them. In other words, those Nephilim were enormous and strong, so presumably so were the Anakim. This is "confirmed" in Deut 2:10–11 which mentions the size of the Anakim, who are also identified as the Rephaim. The Numbers and Deuteronomy passages thus provide the exegetical underpinnings for the assessment in 3 Macc 2:4 that the "giants" were indeed not only "giant" but also strong. The association of the Nephilim with the great warriors the Anakim and the Rephaim also is reflected in Bar 3:26 in which the giants are described in terms similar to the Anakim in Numbers and Deuteronomy: "The giants were born there, who were named from the beginning, begotten of great size, expert at war."

old, men of renown."[23] On the contrary, not only is it not pejorative, but the final phrase used in the verse suggests a laudatory assessment of these super-human beings.[24] The answer, in brief, is that this is interpretively inferred from the context of Gen 6:4, in a manner akin to what is later known in rabbinic interpretation as *semichut parashiyot*, using neighboring passages of the biblical text to elucidate each other. In order to show how this is the case, we will first examine the biblical evidence itself in more detail, and then look at later literature relating to the supposed injustice of the giants which demonstrates more explicitly than the brief reference in 3 Macc 2:4 how interpreters interrelated the narratives about Enoch, the giants, and Noah in Genesis 5–9.

The first item to note is that the verse in 3 Maccabees mentions two biblical "events": the appearance of the giants described in Gen 6:2–4, who were understood to be the progeny of the sons of God and the daughters of humans, and their purported punishment in the Flood, found in Gen 6:5ff. These have been understood as two separate form-critical units by most modern commentators. Gen 6:2–4 is thought to be a fragment of an ancient myth, perhaps borrowed from a neighboring culture. The flood narrative is a spliced composite of the J and P versions of this event. Yet this modern propensity to disentangle literary strands stands at odds with the history of interpretation of the chapters concerning Enoch, the Nephilim/giants, and the Flood, including our specified verse here in 3 Macc 2:4, which portrays the events they narrate as if they are causally connected.

---

[23] The syntax of this verse raises a question about the peopling of the earth in those days. Are the *nephilim* the same as the children of the gods and women or are the *nephilim* to be understood as creatures separate from these divine-human offspring? The latter is the opinion of Speiser, *Genesis*, and E.G. Kraeling, "The Significance and Origin of Gen. 6:1–4," *JNES* 6 (1947) 197. Von Rad agrees, noting that verse 4 seems misplaced and perhaps occurred originally after verse 2 as an etiological story explaining the origin of such mythic and heroic superhumans; *Genesis* 115. Later tradents generally understood the offspring of the בני־האלהים and the women to be the "giants." See *Jub.* 5:1 and *1 Enoch* 7:1–5.

[24] This phrase is used nowhere else in the Bible. Some rabbinic interpretation of this phrase tries nimbly to connect the phrase אנשי השם with the Hebrew verb שמם, thereby asserting a negative connotation. (See for example *Gen. Rab.* 26:7). But of course, whenever two or three rabbis are gathered together, multiple viewpoints emerge. Another verse adduced to explain this phrase affirms its positive connotation. Job 30:8 asserts that those "without a name" are the equivalent of fools: "בני נבל גם בני בלי שם"

An early witness to this tradition, dating to the third century B.C.E., is the Book of the Watchers (*1 Enoch* 1–36).[25] *1 Enoch* contains an account of the fallen angels, their intercourse with women, their corruption of all humanity, and Enoch's attempted intercession on their behalf. Not content to let stand a general condemnation of the sins of the giants, as found elsewhere, *1 Enoch* elaborates in fine detail the specific nature of these "crimes against humanity" supposedly perpetrated by both the fallen angels and their progeny, the giants. Moreover, the "angels" are all named individually. The cast of characters has expanded greatly as has the scope of their activity and its implications for the fate of the world. Enoch is portrayed as a preeminently righteous man, which causes him to intervene, albeit unsuccessfully, on their behalf (*1 Enoch* 12–13). The giants are viewed as the origin of all evil in *1 Enoch* 15:8–12. This section of Enoch predates 3 Maccabees by over three centuries and represents an already fully developed interpretation of the material in Genesis 5–9, but Enoch is not the only witness to the interpretation found in 3 Macc 2:4.

Jubilees 4–6 also explains the text by means of *semichut parashiyot*, in that it interconnects the three pericopes from Genesis

---

[25] The dating of *1 Enoch* has changed since the discovery of the Qumran fragments. If we can accept the assessment of J.T. Milik that *1 Enoch* 6–11 (now part of what is known as the *Book of the Watchers*, Enoch 1–36) dates to the pre-Maccabean period, then this is indeed a very early witness. For his argument about dating 4QEn[a,b], see Milik's work, *The Books of Enoch: Aramaic Fragments of Qumran Cave 4* (Oxford: Oxford University Press, 1976). See also G.W.E. Nickelsburg, "The Epistle of Enoch and the Qumran Literature," *JJS* 33 (1982) 333–48 and James C. VanderKam, *Enoch and the Growth of an Apocalyptic Tradition* (CBQMS 16; Washington, D.C.: Catholic Biblical Association Press, 1984) 111–114. VanderKam expresses skepticism about Milik's contention that the Visions of Enoch antedates Gen 6:1–4, but he nonetheless accepts his dating of the *Book of the Watchers* to the third century (113–114).

Perhaps the earliest witness to these interpretive traditions lies in the Septuagint's translation of the sons of God as angels. There are two possibilities: either the translation of these creatures as angels helped to spawn the more full-blown interpretive expansions that appear in later narratives or the translation itself reflects a knowledge of an already existing interpretation.

Another passage from *1 Enoch* in the Dream Visions indicts the watchers as sinners responsible for bringing on the flood. In *1 Enoch* 84:2–6, Enoch offers a blessing and intercessory prayer to God, which includes this reference to angels committing sin on the earth. ". . .The angels of your heavens are now committing sin (upon the earth), and your wrath shall rest upon the flesh of the people until (the arrival of) the great day of judgment."

concerning Enoch, the Nephilim, and the Flood. As recounted in *Jubilees* 4:22, Enoch witnessed and recorded the activities of the "watchers," the fallen angels, "the ones who sinned with the daughters of men because they began to mingle themselves with the daughters of men so that they might be polluted."[26] *Jubilees* 5 also recounts the episode of Gen 6:1–5. Here the בני האלהים of Gen 6:1 are forthrightly translated as "angels of the Lord." The offspring of these angels and their human mates were the giants. Unlike *1 Enoch*, *Jubilees* does not detail the nature of all the sinful behavior that resulted except for mentioning one abomination particularly heinous to the author: cannibalism.

  Jub. 4:16 mentions the birth of Enoch. The author points out that he is a very righteous man, who judged the misdeeds of the Nephilim, and he was rewarded by God for his righteousness by being transported to the Garden of Eden (*Jub.* 4:22–25). Here already, we see the beginning of the interconnected interpretation of the Genesis material. Enoch is mentioned only in Gen 5:18–24; the story of the Nephilim is confined to Gen 6:1–4, yet the author of *Jubilees* has them living at the same time.[27] Aside from this anachronism, the author also offers an interpretive rendering of Gen 6:1–5:

> And when the children of men began to multiply on the surface of the earth and daughters were born to them, that the angels of the Lord saw in a certain year of that jubilee that they were good to look at. And they took wives for themselves from all of those whom they chose. And they bore children for them; and they were the giants. And injustice increased upon the earth, and all flesh corrupted its way; man and cattle and beasts and birds and everything which walks on the earth. And they all corrupted their way and their ordinances, and they began to eat one another. And injustice grew upon the earth and every imagination of the thoughts of mankind was thus continually evil. (*Jub.* 5:1–2)

  This passage is a tidy expansion of the Genesis passage. The author's modus operandi in writing this work is also clearly in

---

[26] This and all other text quoted from *Jubilees* is the translation of Orval Wintermute, *OTP* vol. 2, 35–142.

[27] The author of *Jubilees* uses a carefully exegetical "proof" in asserting that Enoch and the angels lived together on the earth at the same time. In Jub 4:15 states that Jared, the father of Enoch, was called by that name (ירד) "because in his days the angels of the Lord, who were called Watchers, *came down* to the earth in order to teach the sons of man, and perform judgment and uprightness upon the earth."

evidence there. It contains some of the precise biblical wording that is supplemented by additional interpretation.[28]

The *Damascus Document* (CD), thought to date from the late second century/early first century B.C.E., also contains an interpretation of antediluvian biblical narrative:

> Because having walked in the stubbornness of their hearts the Heavenly Watchers fell; they were seized because they did not observe the commandments of God. And their sons who were tall as cedar trees and whose bodies were like mountains also fell. All flesh on dry ground died; they were as though they had never been because they were doing their own will and did not observe the commandments of their creator so that his anger flared up against them. (2:17b–20)

The *Damascus Document* is written in part as an exhortation, and such a listing of examples of bad behavior is thus all part of the way the author seeks to encourage good discipline and right behavior.[29] The "sin" of the Watchers is here described in CD 2:17–18 as "walking in the stubbornness of their heart." (בלכתם בשרירות לבם נפלו עירי השמים).[30] This characterization is not exactly like 3 Macc 2:4, but close. The sons' strength and power is indicated by their size; they are as tall as trees and wide as mountains. God becomes angry with them because of the

---

[28] Moreover, *Jubilees* suggests not only that humans had become corrupt, but that all living creatures had become impure/wicked. This inclusive account of impurity which extends to all living creatures no doubt reflects a reading of the Priestly strand in Gen 6:11–12 that states that כל בשר, all flesh, on the earth was corrupt as opposed to the more restricted J assessment of Gen 6:5–7 in which it is humans, האדם, who have become corrupt. In fact, God's statement in *Jub.* 5:3, "And he said "I will wipe out *man* and *all flesh* which I have created from upon the surface of the earth," appears to be a conflation of these two J and P assessments in Gen 6:5, an attempt to harmonize two slightly discordant texts. From the perspective of the author of *Jubilees*, the moral turpitude of these angels was sufficient to pollute the whole earth and render it impure and worthy of punishment. It thus broadens the scope and implications of the wickedness.

[29] The recent work on the *Damascus Document* by Jonathan Campbell is helpful in tracing the sources of some of the allusions made in this passage; however, he does not treat any literature contemporary with CD. Jonathan G. Campbell, *The Use of Scripture in the Damascus Document 1–8, 19–20.* (BZAW 228; New York: de Gruyter, 1995). For his treatment of scripture in CD 2:14–4:12a, see pages 67–88.

[30] Campbell traces this phrase to the book of Deuteronomy (29:18) which he finds influential in this section of the *Damascus Document*. It also appears eight times in Jeremiah.

"stubbornness of their heart," a phrase roughly analogous to "arrogance" because both connote following one's own will as opposed to divine desires.

1 Enoch, Jubilees, and the Qumran material are all early witnesses to this interpretive trajectory that link the discrete narrative episodes in Genesis 5–9.[31] They all predate 3 Maccabees by some two centuries. Aside from these longer expositions on the sins of the Nephilim, there are briefer mentions of the giants/watchers/*nephilim* in Sir 16:7, Wisd 14:6–7, and Bar 3:24–28.[32] The first two are worth discussing because they share aspects of the characterization of the giants found in 3 Macc 2:4.

> Sir 16:7:
> He did not forgive the ancient giants who revolted in their might.

This verse from Ben Sira appears in a passage that also mentions the Sodomites, the Egyptians (another nation destroyed for their sins), and the first generation of Israelites out of Egypt who were not able to see the Promised Land because of their rebellious stubbornness. This short list of disobedient exempla ends with the punishment of a group of Israelites in order to underscore the point that divine anger will not be mitigated even by special covenant relationship. If these non-Israelites have been punished for disobedience, then even more punishment would ensue were the Israelites to rebel. From our standpoint, the verse stands as a shorthand witness to the development of this interpretive tradition. The Greek used for "might" here is ἰσχύι, not ῥώμῃ as in 3 Macc 2:4, but the general sense is the same and both reflect the same interpretive trajectory. The precise incidents giving rise to this

---

[31] The *Genesis Apocryphon* from Qumran also contains some traces of this interpretation. The fragment starts *in media res;* however, and no mention is made of the flood. Noah's father Lamech suspects that Noah himself may have been begotten by one of the Watchers or the Holy Ones or the Giants, all of whom were thus understood to be part of the general population in antediluvian times.

[32] Baruch is one of the few books that offers an alternative interpretation of the giants that is not utterly condemnatory. According to Bar 3:24–28, the giants were in fact born in the "house of God," "famous of old, great in stature, expert in war." Baruch suggests a more deterministic view of their end. God did not choose them or give them the way to knowledge, and that is why they ultimately perished. Their error resulted from their lack of wisdom, "they perished through their own folly." No additional information about their behavior is given.

characterization of the giants' wickedness are not indicated here, only the fact that the punishment came as a result of the misuse of their strength which implied a rebellion against God.

Wisdom 14:6:
καὶ ἀρχῆς γὰρ ἀπολλυμένων ὑπερηφάνων γιγάντων
ἡ ἐλπὶς τοῦ κόσμου ἐπὶ σχεδίας καταφυγοῦσα
ἀπέλιπεν αἰῶνι σπέρμα γενέσεως τῇ σῇ κυβερνη-
θεῖσα χειρί.

For even in the beginning, when *arrogant* giants were perishing, the hope of the world took refuge on a raft, and steered by your hand left to the world the seed of a new generation.

Here, in one sentence, the author of the Wisdom of Solomon has made a concise connection between the supposed sin of the giants and the righteous one Noah who was saved in the ark. Ben Sira mentions the giants' strength; this verse explicitly mentions their arrogance.[33]

The New Testament also refers to some of these traditions. Another, albeit more allusive, reference to the interpretation of events in Genesis 5–9 lies in the Epistle of Jude. Jude 6 makes allusion to the fallen angels and Jude 7 mentions Sodom and Gomorrah. Jude 5 makes reference to the exodus from Egypt and the destruction of the infidels. Thus the three examples we find in 3 Macc 2:4–7 also appear in the book of Jude. The exhortation in Jude serves the same kind of purpose as the other lists of exempla we are reviewing, to isolate one offensive kind of behavior, rebellion against God by ignoring divine commands, and to warn against emulating it.[34]

---

[33] The origins of the idea that the giants' were arrogant seems to stem from the characterization of Nimrod, described in Gen 10:8–14. Nimrod was one of the *gibborim*, a clan that included the Rephaim and the Anakites (see nn. 22–23 above), counting among their numbers Og of Bashan. Although Nimrod is described in Genesis positively as a strong hunter (גבור־ציד), in Jewish tradition he is blamed for rebelling against God (in part stemming from the etymology of his name) by planning the construction of the tower of Babel (cf. Jos. *Ant.* 1.4.2, Pseudo-Philo 6, *b. Ḥul.* 89a; *b. ʿAbod. Zar.* 53b). To presume to rebel against God was the epitome of arrogance. Given the misdeeds of the antediluvian giants and their descendants, Nimrod and later Og, King of Bashan, the whole "clan" of the *gibborim*/giants was tainted as arrogant.

[34] For a discussion of the use of Old Testament figures as ethical and religious models in some New Testament letters, see the article by Richard Bauckham, "James, 1 and 2 Peter, Jude," in *It is Written: Scripture Citing Scripture* (D.A. Carson and H.G.M. Williamson, eds.; New York: Cambridge University Press, 1988) 303–317. He offers the observation that the apostate

2 Peter, which is generally held by scholars to be dependent on Jude, also refers to the supposed sin of the angels. 2 Pet 2:4–10 contains a capsule version of this antediluvian history, mentioning in turn God's punishment of the angels for sinning (though the sin is not specified), Noah, who is lauded as a herald of righteousness, and Sodom and Gomorrah. According to 2 Peter, the special sins deserving of punishment are indulging the flesh in depraved lust and despising authority.

3 Maccabees, Ben Sira, Jude, and 2 Peter contain many of the same examples. Although the precise nature of the sin is somewhat different, the common element is the sinners' failure to recognize the rightful authority of divine commands. In 3 Maccabees 2, the problem is termed arrogance. In Ben Sira, the general problem is "disobedience" (16:6). The giants rebelled; the Sodomites were arrogant, and the stubbornness of the wilderness generation of the Israelites is likewise cited as a reason for punishment. For Jude, the problem is those who are unfaithful and licentious. For 2 Peter, like Jude, it is ungodliness which finds expression in licentiousness.

The inclusion of this bit of interpretation in the prayer in 3 Macc 2:4 suggests that the interpretation had developed to a great degree by the first century B.C.E. It contains a reference to the flood, perishing from "measureless waters" (ἀμέτρητον ὕδωρ) which does not reflect the actual biblical wording, but which serves to summon up vividly the threat of chaos overcoming the order of creation. Also of interest is that the interpretation of the giants as sinners who are blamed for the flood, found in short form in 3 Maccabees but in expanded form elsewhere, reflects a kind of interpretation of scripture that would later become known in rabbinic interpretation as *semikhut parashiyot*. The longer excerpts from *1 Enoch* and *Jubilees* contain extended interpretations of the events of Genesis 5–9 that reflects the broad hermeneutical principle of *semikhut parashiyot*. In Ben Sira and literature dating from a later period, 3 Maccabees 2, as well as the NT letters of Jude and 2

---

angels and the cities of the plain function as "types of the imminent eschatological judgment" in Christian literature. He makes the following remark about the examples in 2 Peter: "Thus it appears that the OT material in 2:4–10a is subject to the same eschatological hermeneutic as Jude's in line with the lively eschatological expectation which, contrary to common assertions, pervades the outlook of 2 Peter" (314).

Peter, brief allusions are sufficient to conjure up the full dimensions of the episode.

Sodomites Notorious for their Vices

3 Macc 2:5: "You consumed with fire and brimstone the Sodomites, workers of haughtiness (ὑπερηφανίαν), who had become conspicuous because of their wickedness and you made them an example (παράδειγμα) to future generations." The second group condemned in the prayer is the Sodomites. Not only is their behavior noted as egregiously wicked, but they are held forth as a casebook example of divine punishment, an example that could serve long into the future as a warning to other individuals. Just as the verse about the giants reflects a well-developed method of biblical interpretation, so too the interpretation of the Sodomites' downfall is shaped by an evolved interpretive method, one that seeks to harmonize divergent biblical passages relating to one incident or individual.[35]

This verse makes explicit reference to the punishment suffered by the inhabitants of the cities of the plain in Gen 19:24 with its mention of "fire and brimstone" (καὶ κύριος ἔβρεξεν ἐπὶ Σοδομα καὶ Γομορρα θεῖον καὶ πῦρ παρὰ κυρίου ἐκ τοῦ οὐρανοῦ) but the entire interpretation does not rely simply on Genesis 19. The inhabitants are here characterized as "workers of haughtiness," those who were notable examples of evildoing. Moreover, their sin is of such an extreme nature it has become truly "exemplary," as manifest in the Greek term παράδειγμα. According to this prayer, it was God's plan to make the Sodomites an example to future generations. Within the author's biblical frame of reference, the Sodomites had earned such a bad reputation that this brief mention in one verse could conjure up the depth of their depravity. In order for the author of this prayer to use the Sodomites as an example of wicked behavior on a par with the threat of Ptolemy Philopater's desecration of the Temple, their sin must have been considered grave indeed by the standards of traditional interpretation. Just as we asked in the case of the wicked giants, so too we should pose the question, what are the ultimate biblical origins of this characterization?

The Hebrew Bible outside of Genesis suggests a number of ideas about the exact nature of Sodom's sin: adultery, social injustice, arrogance, and oppression of the poor. Already in the prophetic

---

[35] The harmonization of biblical passages at a remove from one another is also found in the interpretation of the *gibborim* as arrogant giants, described in the previous section.

literature, the destruction of Sodom and Gommorah had become a shorthand way of referring to the deserved destruction of a wicked people. Outside the book of Genesis, there are twelve references to Sodom or the Sodomites, either paired with Gomorrah, or cited alone. Of these, seven function in a similar rhetorical way.[36] Ezekiel 16:49 is an important passage to consider because it contains an explicit list of the sins of the Sodomites. It also figures prominently in early interpretation of Genesis 19. In Ezek 16:49, Sodom's guilt rests in arrogance, surfeit of bread, prosperous security, and not helping the poor and needy. Arrogance, translated in the Greek as ὑπερηφανία, is the first offense listed. Zeph 2:9–10 also makes reference to the arrogance of the inhabitants of Sodom and Gomorrah. The prophet likens the fate of Moab and Ammon to the Sodomites' sorry end. They will live in "a land possessed by nettles and salt pits, and a waste forever." Zeph 2:10 then lists their sin: "This is what they will get in place of their pride (גאונם/ὕβρεως αὐτῶν), because they scoffed and boasted against the people of the Lord of hosts."

Other references to Sodom appear in the prophetic corpus, condemning Israelite behavior as analogous to the Sodomites' sins. The sins are listed variously as adultery, lying, strengthening the hands of evildoers (Jer 23:14), empty religious practices, and lack of social justice (Isa 1:10). Indeed, some scholars have suggested that two distinct traditions about the Sodomites were in circulation in ancient Israel, one reflected in the Genesis narrative, the other in the prophetic corpus.[37] What is clear from these abundant references

---

[36] Jer 49:18; 50:40, Isa 13:19, Amos 4:11, and Lam 4:6.

[37] Von Rad suggests that the story in Genesis about the violation of the law of hospitality was perhaps only secondarily connected with Sodom as the seat of all sin (*Genesis* 218). At least one modern scholar disagrees that the depiction of Sodom in Genesis and the prophets reflect different traditions. J.A. Loader has written a monograph on the early history of Jewish and Christian interpretation of the Sodom traditions that provides some revisionism of the common modern view that the "sin of Sodom" was simply homosexuality. He argues in part that Augustine was largely responsible for a shift in emphasis from the "social aspect" to the "sexual aspect" of the interpretive tradition; see his *A Tale Of Two Cities: Sodom and Gomorrah in the Old Testament, Early Jewish and Early Christian Traditions* (CBET 1; Kampen, the Netherlands: J.H. Kok, 1990).

The reader will note that the position taken in this study differs from Loader's work in at least two ways. I understand early Jewish interpretation of the Sodom episode *primarily* as an *exegetical harmonization* of all the biblical references to the Sodomites. Loader suggests that both the narrative in Genesis 18–19 and the references to Sodom and Gomorrah in the prophetic literature are "the same tradition with the same motifs and the same basic

with their strong condemnation of the Sodomites is that they had a singularly conspicuous reputation for doing evil. As we shall see, other post-biblical interpretation of the sins of the Sodomites reveals a range of opinion on the nature of Sodom's iniquity, but on one note they are in agreement: the Sodomites' sin was severe indeed. How did the Sodomites gain such a terrible reputation? The answer lies in the interpreters' synthesis of the variety of biblical references to the Sodomites.

Literature outside the Hebrew Bible for the most part construes the Sodomites' wickedness in one of two ways: arrogance or sexual misdeeds. Ben Sira and 3 Maccabees pick up the interpretive motif of arrogance mentioned in Ezekiel and Zephaniah. Sir 16:7 reads, "He did not spare the sojourners near Lot, whom he loathed on account of their arrogance." As noted in our discussion of the giants above, Sir 16:7–8 makes reference both to the giants and the Sodomites and shares a similar depiction of the giants and the Sodomites with 3 Maccabees 2. The giants are considered rebels and the Sodomites are notoriously arrogant. The common interpretations are worth noting because this suggests that some of the same examples were reused frequently in Second Temple literature. We have still not ascertained why the Sodomites are considered arrogant. Brief references to the Sodomites in the book of Genesis outside the narrative that describes its final destruction provide other clues for reconstructing its interpretive history.

In Gen 13:13, long before the episode of Lot and his visitors is narrated in Genesis 19, this evaluation of the Sodomites appears:

---

function . . . there is no fundamental difference in the view taken of Sodom and Gomorrah, of what their inhabitants did, and of what happened to them." *A Tale of Two Cities*, 73. My second major disagreement with Loader is over the relationship between Ezekiel 16 and Genesis 18–19, which he considers "the fountainhead" of the Sodom traditions. Here I would have to take strong issue with Loader's comment: "The gluttony, complacency and social irrespon-sibility should not be ascribed to a variant tradition as opposed to a 'mainline' tradition about the sexual sins depicted in Genesis 19." *A Tale of Two Cities*, 65. His attempt to argue that Ezekiel's depiction of Sodom relies on the same "complex of motifs" as does Genesis 18–19 is unconvincing. Granted, both passages understand Sodom to have been destroyed by God because of its wickedness, but divine punishment for wickedness is a theological constant in most of the Hebrew Bible. That alone does not function as a "motif." Specificity in details—in this case, the exact conception of Sodom's sins—marks one "motif" as distinct from another. Thus I cannot accept Loader's claim that "Ezekiel's social motif is essentially the same as that of the Sodom cycle."

ואנשי סדם רעים וחטאים ליהוה מאד

So too in Gen 18:20, before the events associated with the angelic visitors unfold, God makes the observation that the outcry against Sodom and Gomorrah is very great and their sin is very serious. For early interpreters, these editorial evaluations regarding the sinfulness of the Sodomites thus suggested the longstanding and particularly severe nature of their depravity. This is reflected in the Targums that elaborate on the translation of Gen 18:20.[38] It is also reflected in Josephus' account of the Sodomite kings.

Josephus provides a clue to understanding how the Sodomites were understood as arrogant on the basis of their great wealth. This is related to the narrative in Genesis 13–14. Josephus' description of the fall of Sodom in *Jewish Antiquities* (1. 194-95) begins with this "editorial comment" of sorts before the story of Abraham's encounter with the three messengers:

> About this time the Sodomites grew arrogant on account of their riches and great wealth (Genesis 13–14). They became unjust toward men, and impious toward God, in that they did not remember the advantages they received from him: they hated strangers, and abused themselves with Sodomite practices (Genesis 19).

Josephus' account of the destruction of Sodom is significant because it offers a "dirty laundry list" that conflates interpretive motifs in the biblical account but also includes an expanded account of their sins. Ezekiel's sin list includes arrogance and excessive wealth; Josephus here lists arrogance *as a result* of their great wealth. "Sodomite practices" seems to refer to sexual misdeeds, though Josephus does not state explicitly that the Sodomites abused *strangers* sexually. The latter inference appears in the *Testaments of the Twelve Patriarchs* and *Jubilees*, no doubt because of the Sodomites' intentions in regard to Lot's visitors.

---

[38] The Targums' translation of Gen 18:20 has specified the nature of the sins of the Sodomites, presumably reading it in light of the assumed characterization of the Sodomites in Genesis 14. *Targum Pseudo-Jonathan* to Genesis 18:20ff reads, "And the Lord said to the ministering angels, 'The cry of Sodom and Gomorrah, because they oppress the poor, and decree that whoever gives bread to the needy will be burned with fire, is therefore great, and their guilt is exceedingly heavy. I will now appear, and see whether like the cry of the young woman Peletith that ascends before me, they have completed their sins.'" *Targum Onqelos* also specifies the wrongdoing of the Sodomites as oppressing the poor and punishing those who give food to the needy.

The *Testaments of the Twelve Patriarchs* and the book of *Jubilees* refer to Sodom's sin as some kind of sexual misdeeds. *T. Benj.* 9:1 reads:

> From the words of Enoch the Righteous I tell you that you will be sexually promiscuous like the promiscuity of the Sodomites and will perish, with few exceptions. You shall resume your actions with loose women, and the kingdom of the Lord will not be among you, for he will take it away forthwith.

In this passage, the sin of the Sodomites is sexual promiscuity; homosexuality is not specified, rather, illicit sexual relationships with women seem to be at issue. Moreover, the fate of the cities of the Plain is not mentioned. *T. Benjamin* does not provide any context to this reference, and thus it is difficult to determine which biblical passages the author had in mind, if any, in including this exhortation. The author more likely included this warning against licentiousness and simply used a well-known example about other famed lechers that came easily to mind.

By its very nature as a rewritten account of Genesis and Exodus, the book of *Jubilees* reveals that the interpretation of the Sodomites' sin was based at least in part on Genesis 19. At the end of the narrative that recounts the destruction of Sodom and Gomorrah, the author of *Jubilees* adds this summation in *Jub.* 16:5–6:

> And in that month the Lord executed the judgment of Sodom and Gomorrah and Zeboiim and all of the district of the Jordan. And he burned them with fire and sulphur and he annihilated them till this day just as (he said), "Behold, I have made known to you all of their deeds that (they were) cruel and great sinners and they were polluting themselves and they were fornicating in their flesh and they were causing pollution upon the earth." And thus the Lord will execute judgment like the judgment of Sodom on places where they act according to the pollution of Sodom.[39]

Not only does the author of *Jubilees* point out that the sin of the Sodomites was fornication, but he also includes the more general assessment that they were great sinners. It is not clear from the passage if their denunciation as sinners included a wider variety of

---

[39] Abraham's blessing in *Jubilees* 22 also includes a brief reference to the Sodomites' punishment, again underscoring the paradigmatic character of their sin that should serve as a warning for future generations: ". . . Just as the sons of Sodom were taken from the earth, so too all of those who worship idols shall be taken away."

sins or if their sin consisted solely of their "sins of the flesh." In any case, it is clear that the author was most exercised by their sexual behavior, which constituted pollution. Here again, as in *T. Benjamin*, the fate of the Sodomites is to serve as an example for current and future generations who might be tempted to behave likewise. Thus, although the sin of Sodom is characterized differently from 3 Maccabees 2, the use of the Sodomites in exhortation as a negative example is the same.

We can also see such a use of exempla in the New Testament. Jude 7 contains this reference to the cities of the Plain:

> Likewise, Sodom and Gomorrah and the surrounding cities, which in the same manner as they, indulged in sexual immorality and pursued unnatural lust, serve as an *example* (πρόκειˊνται δεῖγμα) by undergoing a punishment of eternal fire.

Not only does Jude 7 contain an expanded and generalized version of the sin of the Sodomites, but it states that Sodom and Gomorrah should *serve as an example* by their destruction as a warning to future generations. 3 Macc 2:5 also makes explicit reference to their use as an example (παράδειγμα). The author of Jude thus shares the same perspective as the author of 3 Maccabees in regard to the use of these Old Testament figures. For the authors of 3 Maccabees, *Jubilees*, and Jude, the inhabitants of the cities of the Plain were not merely worn characters in a tale from the far distant past, but people whose fate might have some bearing on how Jews or Christians ought to live in the present. This is an essential trait of the hermeneutical perspective which is manifest in the exempla list and one which we shall discuss at greater length in the conclusion of the chapter.

Two points are worth underscoring at this juncture. The first is that the interpretation appearing in 3 Macc 2:5 reflects the tendency to harmonize divergent parts of the biblical text. The Sodomites have become known for their egregious depravity; in the words of our prayer, they had "become conspicuous for their wickedness." The punishment meted out, fire and brimstone, comes directly from Genesis 19, but the sin of arrogance derives from Ezekiel 16. As was evident from Josephus, the connection of the arrogance motif from Ezekiel 16 with references to the Sodomites in Genesis 13 was also being made during the first century C.E. Later Jewish interpretation in rabbinic sources also reflects the tendency to harmonize divergent biblical material about the Sodomites.[40] The second point is just as important as the nature of the exegesis that characterized the sin of the Sodomites. The hortatory use of the fate of the Sodomites to dissuade contemporary readers from similar behavior is evident not only in such texts as 3 Maccabees 2 and Jude that use the actual Greek term for example but also is implicit in *Jubilees, T. Benjamin*, and indeed, in the prophetic corpus itself. Let us turn now to the third example from the prayer.

Pharaoh as Arrogant and Audacious

The interpretive characterization of Pharaoh in 3 Macc 2:6 does not contain as much recognizable midrash as do the interpretations of the giants and the Sodomites. There is nonetheless an interpretive spin put on the story for the purposes of the prayer's rhetorical punch. Pharaoh is here "put to the test," which implies he had a choice whether or not to persecute the Israelites. The Greek verb used (δοκιμάζειν) normally translates בחן in the Hebrew Bible and refers to the kind of refining activity of smelters and miners.[41] The idea that Pharaoh actually had a choice in terms of his own role in the Exodus as opposed to being a foil in the grand divine plan stands in contrast to the biblical account. In the book of Exodus, a repeated refrain is that God hardens Pharaoh's heart in order to bring about signs and wonders and demonstrate his own magnificence and saving activity both to the Israelites and the Egyptians.[42] By portraying Pharaoh as someone who had a clear choice either to oppress the Israelites or to treat them justly, as opposed to the biblical account which does not elaborate on Pharaoh's motivation, the author of 3 Maccabees 2 enables the analogy to function as a cautionary notice to Ptolemy Philopater or any other oppressive overlord who might seek to harm the Jews. Our author equates such willful disdain for divine laws with arrogance.[43]

---

[40] Rabbinic literature depicts the Sodomites as arrogant, parsimonious, and cruel; see the discussion of Louis Ginzberg, *The Legends of the Jews* (Philadelphia: Jewish Publication Society, 1968) I.245–250.

[41] Another verb used for test is the Greek πειράζειν, Hebrew,נסה. This verb is used of God's testing of Abraham in Gen 22:1 and all references to the etiological "testing" incident at Massah and Meribah (Exod 15:25; 16:4; 17:2,7; 20:20, Num 14:22; Deut 8:2; 33:8).

[42] Cf. Exod 4:21; 7:3–5, 13, 22; 9:12; 10:1 and so on.

[43] There are a number of arrogant enemy "types" in the books of Maccabees. For instance, 1 Macc 1:20–21 describes Antiochus's arrogant desecration of the sanctuary. His arrogance is mentioned also in 2:47, 49, 50 in contrast to the

In the post-exilic period, we can see a trace of this characterization of the Pharaoh as arrogant. In a clause from Neh 9:10 Pharaoh and the Egyptians in general are noted for their insolence: ["And you set signs and wonders before Pharaoh and his retinue and all the people of his land] because you knew that they were acting arrogantly against them" (כי ידעת כי הזידו עליהם rendered in Esdras 19:10 as ὅτι ἔγνως ὑπερηφάνησαν ἐπ' αὐτούς).[44] This probably derives ultimately from Exod 18:10–11, Jethro's blessing in response to God's deliverance of the Israelites: "Blessed be the Lord, who has delivered you from the Egyptians and from Pharaoh. Now I know that the Lord is greater than all gods, because he delivered the people when they dealt arrogantly (זדו עליהם) with them." Exod 18:11 is the only other occasion in which this verb is used in connection with the Egyptians or Pharaoh.

Zion/Temple Chosen at Time of Creation

Having determined that the three exempla used contain traditional interpretation, we can now discuss other parts of the prayer that contain extra-biblical, proto-midrashic interpretation as well. One verse in particular reflects a long interpretive history. 3 Macc 2:9 reads:

> You, O King, when you had created the limitless and immeasurable earth, chose this city and consecrated this place for your name, although you are self-sufficient. And when you had glorified it by your majestic manifestation, you made the structure for the glory of your great and honored name.

---

zeal for the Torah displayed by Mattathias (1 Macc 2:24, 27). So also 2 Macc 9:4, 7 mention Antiochene arrogance.

[44] The verb זיד occurs only fourteen times in the Hebrew Bible; including three times in reference to the Egyptians and three times in reference to the Israelites. As discussed briefly in Chapter Two, two references to the Israelites' disdain/arrogance also occur in the prayer in Nehemiah 9, and are intended to compare the Israelites' behavior with that of the Egyptians. The Israelites are also mentioned as acting arrogantly in Deut 1:43, when they disregard God's commands not to venture into Amorite territory.

In rabbinic Hebrew the verb evolved to mean to sin consciously (e.g., *b. Šabb.* 69a; see Jastrow), which meaning obtains in modern Hebrew as well. It is possible that by the time Nehemiah 9 was composed, the verb already had this connotation, although clearly the translator of the Greek thought otherwise. The Greek writers translated the Hebrew roots זוד and גוה in their various forms with the verb ὑπερηφανεύεσθαι and its associated forms.

Two items about this verse should be noted to help focus the direction of our discussion. First is its location in the chronology of events in the prayer. The historical sequence of events contained in the verse up to this point is as follows: giants/flood, destruction of Sodom, Exodus, creation/choice of Jerusalem and site-plan of Temple. The last item is conspicuously out of order. The other feature of the verse worth exploration is the notion of God's presence in relation to the Temple. The verse states that God made a manifestation at the Temple, yet it was built for the glory of the divine name. Both of these are important features of the prayer with significance for the history of interpretation concerning the Temple.

Let us begin then with the question of sequence. What compelled the author to mention the choice of Jerusalem and the Temple in connection with the creation and to do so at this juncture in the prayer? The answer lies in the notion that the site of the Temple on Mount Zion was chosen by God at creation. This tradition has certain parallels in other Second Temple literature.[45] Moreover, other interpretive traditions attest to the notion that the virtual architectural plans date from creation. For example, Wis 9:8 states in a prayer for wisdom: "You have given command to build a temple on our holy mountain, and an altar in the city of your dwelling, an imitation of the holy tent that you prepared from the beginning."

Jubilees 1:27–28 contains this tradition, though in slightly different form. God is telling his angel to write for Moses a history of the world:

> And he said to the angel of the presence, "Write for Moses from the first creation until my sanctuary is built in their midst forever and ever. And the Lord will appear in the sight of all. And everyone will know that I am the God of Israel and the father of all the children of Jacob and king upon Mount Zion forever and ever. And Zion and Jerusalem will be holy."

Here the Temple itself is not built before creation but its planned construction is already clearly in sight. This passage shares two themes with our verse in 3 Macc 2:9. The first is that God will become manifest at this sacred place. The second is that the site, not just generally Jerusalem, but also more specifically Zion, presumably meaning the Temple Mount within the precincts of Jerusalem, is

---

[45] This conception is also found in rabbinic tradition. According to *b. Pesaḥ*. 54a, the Temple is one of the seven things created before the creation of the world.

chosen for consecration long before the construction of the Temple is allowed by God to take place. In other words, it is already in the eternal divine blueprints. The notion that the consecration of Zion/Temple/Jerusalem was planned from days of yore is also attested in *Jub.* 8:19, which comes immediately after Noah's blessing of Shem: "And he [Noah] knew that the garden of Eden was the holy of holies and the dwelling of the Lord. And Mount Sinai was in the midst of the desert and Mount Zion was in the midst of the navel of the earth. The three of these were created as holy places, one facing the other." Though not stated explicitly, the sense seems to be that these three sites were also created simultaneously to face each other, and thus because of the inclusion of Eden, this would indicate at the beginning of God's creation.

The association of the garden of Eden with the Temple is found elsewhere in the book of *Jubilees* in the seemingly unexpected connection with the laws of purification after childbirth. According to *Jub.* 3:9–14, these laws originated immediately after Eve was created from Adam's rib. Indeed, the regulations regarding the defilement of childbirth found in Lev 12:2–5 are here inserted into the narrative as *Jub.* 3:10b–11.[46] The passage in Leviticus prohibits a woman from entering the sanctuary in the Temple for a fixed number of days

---

[46] The reason for the insertion of the laws regarding purification after childbirth at this point is somewhat unclear, although it reflects the author's tendency to assume that all the Sinaitic legislation was manifest from the creation of the world. The author recasts Gen 2:18, 21–24 about the creation of Adam and Eve in *Jub* 3:4–7, the passage immediately preceding the discussion of childbirth laws. God makes Adam and then Eve from his rib and on the seventh day, the two form a perfect union, so to speak, by having intercourse (which serves the author as explanation of Adam's enthusiastic exclamation in Gen 2:23: "*This* at last is bone of my bones and flesh of my flesh.") One possible reason for the inclusion of the childbirth impurity laws immediately following this passage is that from the author's perspective, the purpose of intercourse was rightly procreation, so this became the proper place to reveal the laws concerning childbirth, which had been written from eternity on the heavenly tablets. Gary Anderson offers a different explanation for the inclusion of childbirth impurity laws at this point: "The situation in *Jubilees* does not quite fit the model of Leviticus 12, for Adam and Eve have had no children yet and will not have any until they are expelled from the Garden. But their own creation has become a model for the rite of purification enjoined on all subsequent parents" ("Celibacy or Consummation in the Garden?" 129). Anderson also makes the important point that the understanding of *zō't happaʾam* in *Jub* 3:6 to refer to the sexual pairing of Adam and Eve outside of the Garden is the earliest Jewish reference to pre-expulsion intercourse ("Celibacy or Consummation in the Garden?" 128).

depending on whether the baby is a girl or a boy. The garden's likeness to the Temple is clear from the analogy. According to the author of *Jubilees*, the garden of Eden, which was created on the third day, was a sanctified place within the larger land of Eden (*Jub.* 2:7). In other words, there were degrees of holiness in the world that God had created. Eve was forbidden from entering the garden of Eden until the eighth day after Adam entered because of the garden of Eden's extreme holiness, "more holy than any land," and *Jubilees* also cites a prohibition from entering the sanctuary for a prescribed number of days after bearing a child. *Jub.* 3:13 states "Therefore the ordinances of these days were ordained for anyone who bears a male or female that she might not touch anything holy and she might not enter the sanctuary until these days are completed for a male or female."

A passage with the most explicit articulation of the idea that associates the Temple with creation appears in a much later work, *2 Baruch*. In *2 Apoc. Bar.* 4:1–4, the Lord is speaking to Baruch about Jerusalem:

> And the Lord said to me: "This city will be delivered up for a time and the people will be chastened for a time and the world will be forgotten. Or do you think that this is the city of which I said: On the palms of my hands I have carved you? It is not this building that is in your midst now; it is that which will be revealed, with me, *that was already prepared from the moment that I decided to create Paradise*. And I showed it to Adam before he sinned. But when he transgressed the commandment, it was taken away from him—as also Paradise. After these things I showed it to my servant Abraham in the night between the portions of the victims. And again I showed it also to Moses on Mount Sinai when I showed him the likeness of the tabernacle and all its vessels."

This passage from *2 Baruch* delineates an interpretive tradition that jibes with 3 Macc 2:19. The Temple, which God planned even before the creation of Paradise, was revealed to three notable ancestors: Adam, Abraham, and Moses. It thus establishes a putative link between the "Heavenly Temple" and Mount Sinai, which would explain its placement at this point in our prayer after the mention of the Exodus.

This review of Second Temple interpretive traditions prompts another more basic question: what are the biblical origins of this interpretive tradition? Let us first reconsider the fact that in terms of sequence, the creation and choice of Temple site in 3 Macc 2:9

appears after God has rescued the people from Pharaoh (verses 6–7), and mention has been made of the song sung to God by the Israelites as a way of giving thanks for their redemption (verse 8). A closer look at the Song of the Sea provides an answer to part of our question. In Exod 15:13, 17, mention is made of the divine sanctuary: "You led them in steadfast love, you redeemed this people; you guided them in your strength to your holy habitation. . . You will bring them and plant them on the mountain of your inheritance, the place of your dwelling that you made O Lord, the Sanctuary, O Lord that your hands established." From a narrative perspective, mention of the Temple at this point does not immediately make sense. The verb used here is כוננו, a Polel perfect form, indicating a completed action. Some modern scholars have explained the anachronism by recognizing this ancient song as an interpolation later fitted into the prose narrative, and the mountain referred to in its verses as the mythic Mount Zaphon of Ugaritic myth.[47] Readers of the Second Temple period who recognized only one rightful temple, however, would have read this mention of the sanctuary as an overt reference to the Temple on God's mountain, Zion. Moreover, from the perspective of an ancient interpreter of this material, the Israelites' presumed knowledge of the existence of a temple, the place of God's dwelling, that God has already established, would have indicated the existence of the Temple already at the time of the Exodus. Of course, interpreters had to wrestle with the literal narrative in the Deuteronomistic History that described God's promise of a house to David and Solomon's subsequent carrying out of its construction, but this is where the notion of preexistent *plans* would come into play. God did not build the actual Temple at creation, but its divine conception had already occurred בראשית, in the beginning.

Other scholars have explored the connection between the Temple Mount/Zion and Paradise, especially as it occurs in Ezekiel.[48]

---

[47] See, for example, the discussion of F.M. Cross in *Canaanite Myth and Hebrew Epic*, 112–144.

[48] The connection between Temple and Eden can also be seen in Ezekiel 28, which is an oracle against the King of Tyre. He is descried for his arrogance (גבה לב) resulting from his assuming divine status (Ezekiel 28:2–6). In particular, his grave sin lies in his use of wisdom to amass excessive wealth through trade, this leading in turn to an arrogance that results in divine judgment against him. Much of the language used to describe the King of Tyre is taken from Gen. 2:4bff., but this language is also used in conjunction with the holy/profane language used about the Temple.

The connection between Temple and Eden can also by seen in Ezekiel 28, which is an oracle against the King of Tyre. Much of the language used to describe the King of Tyre is taken from Genesis 2, but this language is also used in conjunction with the holy/profane language used about the Temple. The king is described as a kind of Adam, a first man who originally walked blameless on the holy mountain of God. He is censured for arrogance (גבה לב) resulting from his presumption of divine status (Ezekiel 28:2–6). In particular, his gravest sin lies in his use of wisdom to amass excessive wealth through trade, this leading in turn to an arrogance that eventuates in divine judgment against him.

A major difference between the mention of the Temple in Exodus 15 and this prayer is the location of God in relation to the Temple. In Exodus 15, and in much other pre-exilic literature, God was thought to dwell in the Temple. This verse in the prayer makes a claim for a theophany in the Temple, but not for God's continuing immanence. In 3 Macc 2:15, the prayer explicitly states that God's dwelling place is the "highest heaven." Tryggve Mettinger has mounted a strong argument that the conception of divine transcendence and the "name theology" in which only the divine name inhabited the Temple was a reaction to the destruction to the first Temple and the Exile.[49] Whether or not Mettinger's evolutionary theory is correct, the contrast between the pre-exilic conception of a deity who abides in the Temple and a Temple sanctified only by the divine name is a strong one. The idea of a transcendent God whose Temple contains the divine name during the Second Temple period seems to accompany a heightened concern for the sanctity of the Temple. Certainly for the people living in the

---

See Jon D. Levenson, *Sinai and Zion*, (New York: Harper & Row, 1985), especially 127–134 for a discussion of the connection made between the Garden of Eden/paradise in Ancient Near Eastern mythic traditions and the site of the Temple/Mount Zion. See also his *Creation and the Persistence of Evil*, (New York: Harper & Row, 1988) 78–99. Gary Anderson has discussed the resonances between paradise as described in Genesis 2:4b–3, and later interpretations of this story found in the book of *Jubilees* and the *Hymns on Paradise* of Ephrem the Syrian. He points to significant similarities between *Jubilees* and Ephrem in their view of the purity/holiness accorded to Eden that is like the Temple; "Celibacy or Consummation in the Garden?," esp. 129–131 and 142–146.

[49] For more on the evolution of this concept in ancient Israel, consult Tryggve N.D. Mettinger, *The Dethronement of Sabaoth: Studies in the Shem and Kabod Theologies.* (Lund: CWK Gleerup, 1982).

land during the Second Temple period, the Temple was the center of religious life. Its security, that is, the maintenance of its inviolate holiness, was of supreme importance, as witnessed not only by this prayer, but by the prayers in Judith 9 and 1 Maccabees 2 .

Other Significant Citations and Allusions in 3 Maccabees 2

Aside from the interpretation of biblical narrative reviewed above, the prayer clearly alludes to other biblical verses and their contexts: 1 Kgs 8:33–34 in 3 Macc 2:10 and Ps 79:8 in 3 Macc 2:20. The salient feature of these verses in regard to their use in 3 Maccabees 2 is that the original context of both passages in which they occur relate to the Temple.

Prayer and the Temple in 1 Kings 8

3 Macc 2:10 reads:

καὶ ἀγαπῶν τὸν οἶκον τοῦ Ισραηλ ἐπηγγείλω διότι, ἐὰν γένηται ἡμῶν ἀποστροφὴ καὶ καταλάβῃ ἡμᾶς στενοχωρία καὶ ἐλθόντες εἰς τὸν τόπον τοῦτον δεηθῶμεν, εἰσακούσῃ τῆς δεήσεως ἡμῶν.

And out of love for the house of Israel you promised that if it should happen that we turn away and anguish overcome us, if we should come into this place and pray, you would listen to our prayer.

A number of scholars have suggested that 3 Macc 2:10 makes a clear reference to 1 Kgs 8:23–53, the long prayer offered by Solomon at the dedication of the Temple and discussed at some length in Chapter One above. There are three indications that the verse in 3 Maccabees makes reference to Solomon's prayer. The first is simply that 1 Kgs 8:23–53//2 Chr 6:14–42 is the only time that the subject of what prayers God might answer from the Temple appears in the Bible. The second indication for dependence is the circumstances surrounding the high priest's prayer in 3 Maccabees 2. The petition is offered at the Temple in the face of Ptolemy Philopater's invasion of Jerusalem and threatened desecration of the Temple. 1 Kgs 8:23–53 lists seven different "cases" of distress in which God should listen to the Israelites in their prayer. The fourth case in 1 Kgs 8:37–39 includes a situation similar to that of 3 Maccabees 2. The Jews are being besieged in not just one of their cities but in their capital, Jerusalem. The Temple itself is threatened. The situation thus fits a prescribed case. The third indication is a verbal coincidence. Both this prayer [3 Macc 2:10 (εἰσακούσῃ τῆς δεήσεως ἡμῶν), 3 Macc 2:15 (κατοικήτηριόν σου οὐρανὸς τοῦ οὐρανοῦ),] and the relevant portions of Solomon's prayer make a point of mentioning that God would hear from his dwelling place in Heaven (σὺ εἰσακούσῃ ἐκ τοῦ οὐρανοῦ). In fact, the phrase, "Then, you, hear in heaven" occurs seven times, acting as a kind of refrain (1 Kgs 8:32, 34, 36, 39, 43, 45, 49).[50]

Several distinct differences between the prayers are worth noting. God's motivation for responding to Israel's prayers is not specified in 1 Kings 8 or 2 Chronicles 6, but in 3 Macc 2:10, God's motivation is "for love of the house of Israel." Another difference from the prayer in the Deuteronomistic history is that there is no mention of the Davidic dynasty, as appears so prominently in the Temple prayer in both Kings and Chronicles. 1 Kings 8 does not address God as King. The only kings mentioned are David and Solomon. Yet this royal address for God has become the norm in 3 Maccabees 2, where he is addressed three times in this prayer as "King" (3 Macc 2:2, 9, 13) as well as sole ruler (μόναρχη). The portrayal of God as king played a part in Israelite religion from an early date and royal language used to describe God is found throughout later Jewish and Christian liturgies, yet relatively few of the prayers found in the Second Temple narratives of the so-called Apocrypha and Pseudepigrapha address God as king.[51]

One other difference calls for somewhat more disentanglement because it relates to the narrative following the prayer in 1 Kings 9. What should be made of the claim in 3 Macc 2:10 that God promised (ἐπηγγείλω) that he would hear and respond to certain prayers? A close examination of 1 Kgs 8:23–53 does not disclose the terms of the promise as they are indicated in 3 Macc 2:10, that if difficulties

---

[50] The instruction about prayer in the book of Kings specifies that if the people προσεύχονται καὶ δεηθήσονται, that is, pray and make supplication, they will be rescued from the enemy by whom they are being punished for their sins. 3 Macc 2:1,10 refer to this prayer as a supplication (δεήσιν). The prayer is also referred to in 3 Macc 2:21 as a "petition of the prescribed form" (ἐνθέσμου λιτανείας) The Greek λιτανείας appears only in 2 Macc 3:20, 10:16 and 3 Macc 2:21, 5:9. δέησιν appears more frequently in the Greek translation of the Bible.

[51] The epithet "king" in reference to God does not appear in the prayers of Ezra-Nehemiah, Daniel (or Additions to Daniel), Tobit, Prayer of Manasseh, Baruch, Susanna, *Letter of Aristeas*, 1 Maccabees, *Jubilees*, Pseudo-Philo, or *Testament of the Twelve Patriarchs*. It is found in nine prayers: Sir 51:1; Jdt 9:12, Add Esth 13:9, 15; 14:3, 12; 2 Macc 1:24; 3 Macc 2:2, 9, 13; 6:2; and *1 Enoch* 9:4; 84:2.

should overcome Israel, God would assuredly listen to their supplication if they should appear in the Temple and pray. The only divine promise appearing in the 1 Kings 8 prayer is the restatement of God's covenant to David promising eternal successors to the throne (1 Kgs 8:25) provided they continue to be faithful to the divine laws. There is a passage outside the prayer that provides more of a clue to this reference in 3 Maccabees. In 1 Kgs 9:3–9, God does indeed respond to Solomon's prayer, assuring Solomon that he has heard his plea and responding by reiterating the promise of the eternal Davidic covenant once again. God then warns Solomon about the threat of exile from the land if the stipulations of the covenant are not carried out. Yet 1 Kgs 9:3–9 does not include the promise contained in 3 Macc 2:10.

The answer to the question about the terms of the promise lies in the expanded account of God's answer to Solomon's prayer in 2 Chr 7:12–22. This passage nearly reproduces the account in 1 Kgs 9:3–9. The content of 1 Kgs 9:3–6 comes as a reminder to Solomon to observe the laws of God, lest he lose the throne of David, and it contains the stern warning that disobedience will result in the destruction of the Temple. But the Chronicler has edited and expanded the original version of God's response in 1 Kings 9.

1 Kgs 9:3 states:

> The Lord said to him, "I have heard your prayer and your supplication that you made before me; I have sanctified this house that you have built, and put my name there forever; my eyes and my heart will be there for all time."

Compare the Chronicler's version in 2 Chr 7:12–16:

> 12. Then *the Lord* appeared to Solomon in the night and *said to him*: "*I have heard your prayer*, and have chosen this place for myself as a house of sacrifice. 13. If I should shut up the heavens so that there is no rain or if I should command the locust to consume the land, or send a pestilence on my people, 14. if my people who are called by my name humble themselves, pray, seek my face, and repent from their wicked ways, then I will hear from heaven, and will forgive their sin and heal their land. 15. Now my eyes will be open and my ears attentive to the prayer in this place. 16. And now *I have* chosen and *consecrated this house so that my name will be there forever; my eyes and my heart will be there for all time.*

The italicized phrases in the passage from Chronicles indicate the shared elements with 1 Kgs 9:3. The author of Chronicles has softened the message by adding more specific details to the content of the divine response. 2 Chr 7:13 makes reference to just a few cases mentioned in the long list in 1 Kgs 8:31–50, including wording from the fourth case that covers the broadest range of circumstances in 1 Kgs 8:37–40. 2 Chr 7:14–15 then state unequivocally that God will listen to the prayers of the people provided they repent of their sins. This, then, is the basis for the claim in 3 Macc 2:10 that God promised to listen to the prayers of the Israelites made from the Temple. The wording that describes the circumstances compelling God to listen to Israel's petition in 3 Macc 2:10, "reverses and tribulation should overtake us" (ἀποστροφὴ καὶ καταλάβῃ ἡμᾶς στενοχωρία) is of sufficiently broad scope that it can be understood to encompass all the circumstances listed in Solomon's prayer in 1 Kings 8.[52] The reference in 3 Macc 2:10 thus includes an interpretive allusion to both accounts of Solomon's dedicatory prayer and the reassuring divine response to it using 1 Kings and the interpretive expansion in 2 Chronicles. The author thereby harmonizes the divergent biblical passages that mention God's response to prayer offered at the Temple and at the same time provides hope to a people in distress that their petition would be answered as God had "promised."

LXX Psalm 78:8

One more biblical citation warrants exploration. 3 Macc 2:20, the last verse of the prayer, reads: "*Let your compassion speedily overtake us* and put praises in the mouth of those who are downcast and crushed in spirit, granting us peace." The first clause of this verse is a direct citation taken from Ps 78:8 (MT 79:8): ταχὺ προκαταλαβέτωσαν ἡμᾶς οἱ οἰκτιρμοί σου. The clause occurs nowhere else in the Bible. Given the careful interpretive reference made to the Temple dedication prayer and its context, the citation from this particular psalm is surely not accidental. The larger context of this quote from Psalm 78 should be mentioned because the subject of the psalm as a whole is a request for divine intervention in the face of the desecration of the Temple in Jerusalem. The theme corresponds to the situation that has given rise to Simon's prayer in 3 Maccabees 2. Ps 78:1 sets the scene: "O God, the nations have entered into your inheritance; they have desecrated your holy Temple; they have demolished Jerusalem to ruins." The psalm continues with the

---

[52] Brettler, in fact, argues that case four, which contains the most comprehensive list of circumstances, was originally the end of the first edition of the prayer; see Chapter One above.

The request of the psalmist to save them from their enemies and to avenge the blood of the Israelites is made "for the glory of your name." The final verse of the psalm affirms that if God should rescue them, then Israel will give thanks to [God] forever, ". . . from generation to generation we will recount your praise." This response of praise to divine acts of salvation is echoed in the final verse of the prayer in 3 Maccabees 2 , in which Simon asks that God put praises in the mouths of those who are in distress. This is the most pious way of asking God to save the people, because it assumes that the natural response of the redeemed will be to sing God's praises. It thus marks a fitting end to the prayer. All of this contextual evidence points to a careful and deliberate appropriation of biblical wording on the part of the author of 3 Maccabees 2.

Conclusion

Our review of the prayer in 3 Maccabees 2 reveals a complex degree of scripturalization. The author uses a Greek literary form to shape part of the prayer, but also uses much in the way of biblical language and traditional interpretation.[53] Though this Jewish book may have been shaped by foreign influences, it nonetheless retained much of its distinctive imprint. What is most important to note in the scripturalization of this prayer in contrast to the use of scripture in 1 Kings 8 or Nehemiah 9 is the degree to which scripture *as interpreted* becomes a part of the composition. Traditional interpretation is so imbedded that it informs the depiction of biblical characters. The exegetical assumptions behind *semikhut parashiyot* and the harmonization of scripture have led to the characterization of the *gibborim* in Genesis 6 as giants and also as arrogant creatures whose misdeeds resulted in the devastation by the flood. Interpretation is an imbedded part of the negative characterizations of the Sodomites and Pharaoh as well. Aside from the exempla list, we see traditional interpretation in the conception that the Jerusalem

---

[53] That a work like 3 Maccabees which was written as a reproach to the Hellenes was shaped by Hellenistic literary forms should on first reconnaissance come as something of a surprise. Why should the Maccabees imitate cultural forms of the very people who tried to impose their alien culture on the Jews? As Martin Hengel comments in his discussion of this Jewish appropriation of Hellenistic forms, ". . . the fact should not be overlooked that these 'new' literary forms were predominantly used, at least after the Maccabean revolt, for the production of polemic, anti-Hellenistic, tendentious literature." Quotation from his *Judaism and Hellenism* (John Bowden trans.; Philadelphia: Fortress, 1974) 112.

of the Sodomites and Pharaoh as well. Aside from the exempla list, we see traditional interpretation in the conception that the Jerusalem Temple was planned, or even present, at creation. If we were to dig farther back into the ancient Near Eastern past, we could discover that this "traditional interpretation" itself reflects an appropriation of the myth of Marduk's creation of the world and subsequent building of his temple at Esagila, but as the tradition appears in Second Temple literature (particularly in *Jub* 3:9–14 which retrojects the laws of childbirth to the time of creation), it has been embellished with interpretive tradition and thus transformed. We also noted that the use of the one clear scriptural citation involves an awareness of the original context of a phrase in LXX Psalm 78 (79), a psalm in which the Temple has been desecrated and Jerusalem lies in desolation. The first century composition 3 Maccabees 2 thus exhibits a wide variety of scriptural appropriation.

We have focused particularly on the exempla list in this chapter. The use of these particular examples in this prayer might prompt the question: why choose these villains and not others? Pharaoh is an obvious choice, but Enoch is not a prominent figure in the Bible. Why not single out Cain or Shechem the Hivite for such malignity? The answer to this is not at all clear, but it seems to lie in the peculiar growth and persistence of particular traditions in the interpretive imagination. One might as well ask, "Why is Abe Lincoln eternally cast as honest?" when no doubt Millard Filmore was made of equally ingenuous substance. One possibility, to put it in terms of modern media, is because these particular villains had received slightly more "air time" than others. In the case of the Sodomites, other verses even in the book of Genesis outside the narrative of the cities' destruction, suggested their paradigmatic arrogance to later interpreters. But this explanation does not serve to explain the encrustation of interpretive tradition that developed around the figure of Enoch, whose story in the Bible is limited to four verses. James VanderKam has suggested that some early interpreters of the Bible were particularly interested in the antediluvian figures because they sensed the apocalyptic end of the ages was nigh. The flood story served as a type for the final judgment and the biblical characters described therein might also provide clues for how to behave in the present. "For writers who were convinced that the celestial court would soon convene, the legends about Noah, the angels and the deluge were of transparent hortatory value."[54] This provides a plausible, but only partial, explanation for the fascination with some of the exempla figures we have found listed in various Second Temple works. Moreover, as we saw in 3 Maccabees 2, the mention of the giants does not appear in a context of eschatological expectation. The question cannot be fully answered, though we can note that the same egregious "bad guys" are condemned elsewhere. These exemplars garnered such a bad reputation in their interpretive history throughout the biblical period and later that they were destined to be frequently used bywords for wickedness.

The use of exempla is prevalent throughout Second Temple literature, as we mentioned (though largely in footnote discussion) above. There are numerous instances in which only one biblical character is mentioned as a positive or negative example. The use of a single individual or group can be seen already in the Hebrew Bible itself. Exempla lists are also common and generally appear as part of an exhortation. While not all lists of examples focus solely on a shared common trait as does 3 Maccabees 2, we noted that kind of use, the *Beispielreihe*, in such writings as the Qumran composition CD 2:14–3:12 and in the New Testament writings Hebrews 11 and Jas 5:10–11. 3 Macc 2:2–8 is just one of a number of exempla lists that can be seen specifically in liturgical compositions such as 3 Macc 6:2–15; *Apoc. Zeph.* 6:10; *Hell. Syn. Prayer* 6; and 4 Ezra 7:106–110.

This chapter brings us to the end of our investigation of scripturalization in prayers, from its hazy beginnings in pre-exilic prayers to its full flowering in the Second Temple period. We have examined three different hermeneutical approaches to scriptural interpretation, all the while seeing some common uses of traditional biblical interpretation and some common trends in biblical citation.

---

[54] James VanderKam, "The Righteousness of Noah," *Ideal Figures: in Ancient Judaism: Profiles and Paradigms* (J.J. Collins and G.W.E. Nickelsburg, eds.; Chico, CA: Scholars, 1980) 25–26. Steven Fraade, commenting on ideas suggested by James VanderKam, states: "In an age of apocalyptic expectations, the antediluvian heroes were especially significant within such chains of righteous ancestors, since living during or in close proximity to the "golden age" of history and having been spared the destruction of the Flood, they were thought to have special claims to righteousness and esoteric knowledge." Quotation from his *Enosh and His Generation: Pre-Israelite Hero and History in Postbiblical Interpretation* (SBLMS 30; Chico, CA: Scholars Press, 1985) 229–230.

We have noted that each of these different hermeneutics—the retelling of history, the typological appropriation of biblical stories, and the hortatory use of biblical characters as role models—is common to a number of other Second Temple prayers. Our investigation is only a partial examination of the multifaceted use of scripture in prayers, but it serves as a solid beginning. It begins to answer the questions of how scripturalization began and how scripture is used in prayers during the formative Greco-Roman era. Two primary tasks remain for the concluding chapter. We must reflect on a more general question, the "why" of the scripturalization of Second Temple prayer, and we must consider how examining the use of scripture in prayers might be extended into the history of Jewish and Christian liturgy. To that dual focus we now turn.

Chapter 5

From Prayers to Liturgy

Scripturalization in Prayers

While conceding that psalms could become "worn out and petrified with use," Sigmund Mowinckel went on to make the following comment about the forms and traditional language of the psalms:

> But through all the various experiences and emotions associated with them through generations, they may also be able somehow to store the religious experience of the generations and become symbols and "ideograms," "words saturated with experience," as V. Grönbech calls them, words which only need to be mentioned to release a series of associations, of thoughts, experiences, and emotions. The words contain more than they seemingly contain.[1]

Mowinckel was referring to the use of the psalms in worship; however, his observations hold true for the use of scripture in prayers we have examined and the continuing function of scripturalized prayers in worship. We would only want to add 'words saturated with tradition and experience' to reflect the way in which traditional interpretations of scripture are incorporated into the prayers we have reviewed. The excerpt thus provides an appropriate note on which to begin our conclusions because it also points to the ongoing use of scripturalized prayers in Jewish and Christian liturgies, which is where we will end our remarks.

This book offers just a partial delineation of a broad-based trend, a first step in categorizing the ways in which scripture serves as the backdrop for prayers. We have reviewed prayers in literature

---

[1] *The Psalms in Israel's Worship* Vol. 1 (New York: Abingdon, 1962) 14–15.

spanning more than one thousand years and seen how scriptural tradition increasingly came to be woven into the fabric of many prayers. We have traced the scripturalization of prayers from its tentative beginnings in the pre-exilic literature to the first century C.E. In the introduction, we noted three major ways in which prayers are shaped by scripture. One is the emulation of successful scriptural models. Prominent examples of this trend can be seen in how the narrative circumstances giving rise to the song of praise in Judith 16 seems to be modeled after Exodus 15, the Song at the Sea, or the way in which the author of the Magnificat in Luke 1 is thought to have modeled his prayer after the Song of Hannah in 1 Samuel 2.[2] A second way in which scripture lies behind prayers of the Second Temple period is in the continuation of formal patterns from the biblical period: confessions, praise, thanksgivings, blessings, and petitions.[3] Our main focus has been on a third way in which prayers are influenced by scripture, their use of biblical wording, including the use of biblical citation, allusion, and interpretation. In addition to tracing a historical trajectory in the scripturalization of Second Temple prayers, we looked at three different ways in which Second Temple prayers use scripture: in the retelling of history, in the reuse of one biblical episode, and in listing examples of good or bad behavior. In order to provide a thorough examination of the use of scripture in the prayers, we examined one prime exemplar of each of these types, while noting other Second Temple prayers that comprise each category.

The first chapter traced the beginnings of scripturalization in a number of pre-exilic and exilic prayers. Although the use of the term scripture is an anachronism for prayers composed in the pre-exilic period, we noted some early prayers that included references to past

---

[2] On the dependence of Judith 16 on Exodus 15, see the comments of Carey Moore, *Judith* (AB 40; Garden City, NY: Doubleday, 1985) 256–257; Andrew Chester, "Citing the Old Testament," *It Is Written* 158–59; Toni Craven, *Artistry and Faith in the Book of Judith* (Chico: CA Scholars Press, 1983) 111–112 and Patrick Skehan, "The Hand of Judith," *CBQ* 25 (1963) 94–110. On the relationship of the Magnificat to the Song of Hannah, see Raymond E. Brown, *The Birth of the Messiah* (Garden City, NY: Doubleday, 1977) 357–360 and Paul Winter, "Magnificat and Benedictus," *BJRL* 37 (1954) 328–43.

[3] For a thorough discussion of the forms of biblical prayer, see Patrick Miller, *They Cried to the Lord*. See especially Miller's discussion of "The Aaronic Benediction as Paradigm of Blessing," 294–299. On the interpretive reuse of the Priestly Blessing, see Leon J. Liebreich, "The Songs of Ascent and the Priestly Blessing," *JBL* 74 (1955) 33–36; and Michael Fishbane, "Form and Reformulation of the Biblical Priestly Blessing," *JAOS* 103 (1983) 115–21.

history. Both Gen 32:9–12 and Exod 32:11–13 quote divine speech, specifically the promise of land and descendants to Abraham. Num 14:13–19 likewise recalls divine speech, the divine attribute formula revealed in Exod 34:6–7. The early use of these divine promises and revelations signals the beginning of an important trend in the continuing scripturalization of prayer. Solomon's long prayer of dedication in 1 Kgs 8:23–53 marks a significant transition, not only in the scripturalization of prayer, but in the status of prayer generally, vis-à-vis the Temple. Solomon's prayer quotes two divine promises, the covenant with David promising an eternal throne (1 Kgs 8:25) and the divine assurance that God's name would dwell in the Temple (1 Kgs 8:29). These two promises taken together were supposed to ensure that Solomon's petitions would be granted.

The first post-exilic prayer examined was Neh 9:5–37 with its long review of Israelite history. An early precedent for this kind of prayer is Deut 26:5–11 which recalls Israel's earliest ancestors and draws on continuities with the past. Nehemiah 9 reflects a reliance on written scriptural traditions as well as traces of midrashic elaborations on biblical stories. We noted a brief reference to the divine liturgy of angelic praise in Neh 9:6 and the testing of Abraham in Neh 9:8. The historical review stretches from creation to the contemporary period of Ezra. The author viewed the history of Israel as a linear, continuous one, in which the post-exilic community constituted the direct descendants of Abraham, and as such were heirs to the promise of the land. A significant feature of the prayer is its use of the divine self-revelation passage of Exod 34:6–7 as a device to punctuate the prayer and emphasize the gracious and merciful properties of the God being petitioned. Exod 34:6–7 functions prominently in shaping other biblical and Second Temple prayers such as the Prayer of Manasseh, Jonah 4, 1QH 10:14–35, 4Q504 (*Words of the Luminaries*), and the lament in *Joseph and Aseneth* 11. Another use of scripture that we noted in Neh 9:8 is the reference to the covenant with Abraham, which does not specifically mention the promise of many descendants, but only the promise of the land, which is a major theme of the prayer. The recollection of the Abrahamic covenant marks a continuity with pre-exilic prayers. Indeed, the use of divine promises, theophanies, and citations of divine speech is a recurring feature in many Second Temple prayers. One prominent passage that has been oft-noted is the theophany of Isaiah 6, which becomes the basis for the Qedushah/Sanctus, but there are many other instances in which divine speech is quoted in later prayers.

Judith 9 stands in a biblical tradition of prayer because it is modeled after a particular petition, Hezekiah's prayer imploring help from God in the face of the siege of Jerusalem in Isaiah 37//2 Kings 19. The most notable use of scripture in Judith 9 is the interpretation of the rape of Dinah story in Genesis 34. Jdt 9:2 quotes "divine speech" in order to justify Judith's attack on Holofernes; however, the divine speech is a construal of the narrator's voice in Gen 34:7. The scripturalization in Judith 9 is more complex than the use of scripture in Nehemiah 9. The prayer contains a distinctive typological approach to scriptural interpretation in casting the Dinah, "the virgin," as the contemporary Temple, and the Shechemites as the Assyrian army intent on violating the Temple. The prayer reflects a purity/impurity dichotomy that is drawn from priestly sources of the Bible, and that can be seen in contemporaneous descriptions of the rape of Dinah in the books of *Jubilees* and the *Testament of Levi*. Judith's zeal to save her people and the Temple from desecration from the foreigners is equated with her ancestor Simeon's efforts on behalf of his sister. The use of the term "zeal" also echoes a similar situation recounted in Num 25:11–13 in which the priest Phinehas is rewarded with the priesthood for his zeal in killing an Israelite man who has paired off with a Midianite woman.

The prayer in 3 Macc 2:2–20 exhibits still another use of scripture, in which the Bible is drawn upon as a source of moral or immoral exempla. The giants, the Sodomites, and Pharaoh are all condemned for their arrogance. We determined that the particular literary genre in which the negative examples appear was influenced by a Greek rhetorical form in which prominent characters from the past are used to illustrate one particular vice or virtue. The formal literary influence is Greek, but the didactic use of the Bible to provide cautionary or exemplary lessons about its characters can already be seen in the Bible itself. Deut 24:9, for instance, exhorts the Israelites to behave in order to avoid leprosy, citing Miriam as an example of what can happen to rebels. There is also a long tradition involving the condemnation of the Sodomites as paradigmatic evildoers. The prayer contains interpretive characterizations of the *gibborim* as arrogant, which is not at all obvious from the biblical text of Genesis 6. Likewise, the affirmation found in 3 Macc 2:9 that Jerusalem and Temple were chosen at the time of creation is a reflection of a midrashic interpretation.

Having reviewed some of the major conclusions of the study, it may also be helpful to restate exactly what this study has not attempted to do. I have not been concerned with form-critical study, that is, in determining genre and which prayers may have been used in what contexts. This is in part because the four prayers I have focused on are imbedded in narratives and seem for the most part to have been written with the particular narrative contexts in mind. Nehemiah 9 represents a significant exception because it is not well-integrated into the book of Nehemiah as a whole. I have also not tried to relate my discussion of prayers to the associated issue of actual practice of prayer during this era. These questions of practice and the prayers' *Sitz-im-Leben* are very important, but are not at the heart of my concern. The study of the scripturalization of prayer is parallel and complementary to such efforts.

I have assumed that the prayers imbedded in narratives of Second Temple literature are in some fashion verisimilar to prayers that would have been offered during this period, in particular *the ways in which and the degree to which they are scripturalized*. This sole focus has led me to bracket a number of interesting questions about the practice of prayer during this period. I have not attempted to answer the questions of what kinds of prayers were offered, by whom, and under what circumstances. My approach thus lies in strong contrast to recent work that explores the Qumran corpus of prayers, such as Bilhah Nitzan's extensive study of Qumran prayers, Esther Chazon's work on 4Q DibHam, as well as scholars like Carol Newsom, Eileen Schuller, Lawrence Schiffman, and Moshe Weinfeld who have also studied Qumran hymnic or liturgical materials.[4] I have also not been concerned primarily with the development of statutory prayer forms and the history of Jewish liturgy from a form-critical standpoint. In this respect, the goal of my work is markedly different from many Qumran studies of prayer.

The Changing Role of Prayer

The bulk of this study has been concerned with *h o w* scripturalization of prayers occurred. Before turning to the question of continuity between Second Temple prayers and later Jewish and Christian liturgies, we should mention some of the factors that relate to *why* scripturalization occurred and how the prayers relate to the increased emphasis on prayer during this period generally. The

---

4 The work of these scholars is treated in the Appendix.

aspect of Second Temple prayers that has concerned us throughout this study, the scripturalization of prayer, is but a subcategory of the general retrieval of biblical or classical sources and the flourishing of biblical interpretation in Second Temple Judaism. Nonetheless, the reuse of scripture in prayers is especially significant for two reasons. From a purely formal perspective, such "scripturalization" eventually becomes an unquestioned literary convention in the composition of liturgies. Below, we will point to some of the continuities in Jewish and Christian liturgies. But the scripturalization of prayer also suggests something important about the evolving status of scripture in Judaism, which may well have varied among different Jewish groups during this period. A rhetorical shift occurs when scripture is prayed. In the case of the reuse of psalms, the shift is not significant. David's songs, or the Levites' songs, were initially composed to be addressed to God. So, too, the reuse of divine promises is understandable. The covenant with Abraham or the Davidic covenant of an eternal throne are cited in order to "remind" God of past beneficence. But the reuse of narrative literature is more striking in its redeployment. The narrative sections of the Pentateuch chronicle events in the lives of Israel's ancestors. They contain history and genealogy and are for the most part written in the third person. In one case we have reviewed, Jdt 9:2, the narrator's voice itself is understood as the voice of God. Judith uses the "divine" admonition "This shall not be" in the story of the rape of Dinah in Genesis 34 as justification for the violent murder of Holofernes. We cannot make any more general statement about how Second Temple prayers view the status of scripture without a much more extensive study, but the question of how authors understood the nature and authority of scripture during this period is an important one.

Aside from the oft-noted rise of interpretation during the Second Temple period, we should consider the changing role of prayer in regard to sacrifice. Indeed, in order to understand the development of Jewish and Christian liturgies, and their eventual central role in these religions, the precise functional role of prayer during the Second Temple period must be determined. Such a complex question, really an interrelated set of questions, cannot be treated fully here, but ignoring the issue would be remiss. The degree to which prayer was a public activity or a private one, consisted of fixed wording or was more spontaneous, whether it was offered in the Temple or not, and its relationship to Temple sacrifice, are all relevant factors.

To what degree did prayer play a part in Temple sacrifice, if at all? The Mishnah states that prayers were offered by the priests as part of the daily Tamid sacrifice. According to *m. Tamid* 5:1, during the sacrifice, the priest would recite the Shema; moreover, assigned laypeople were called upon to recite scriptural verses while the Tamid was being offered.[5] Other scholars have contested the accuracy of this picture. Recently, Israel Knohl has built on the work of Yehezkel Kaufmann, who argued that the Israelite sacrifices were offered in silence in contrast to the sacrificial practices of other ancient Near Eastern temples.[6] Knohl allows for the offering of prayers, psalms, and hymns within the Temple courts, but this activity was only performed by the laity:

> As we have said, silence reigns only within the priestly realm of the Temple. Surrounding it, in the sphere of the turbulent folk cult, one can hear the voice of prayer, melody, and hymn. As may be seen from the combination of the testimony of the Priestly Torah and that of the non-Priestly strata, the Temple complex was constructed of a series of circles of voice and silence distinct from one another.[7]

---

[5] For a socio-historical reconstruction of sacrifice and worship during the Second Temple period, see Shaye Cohen, *From the Maccabees to the Mishnah* (LEC 7; Philadelphia: Westminster, 1987) 62–75. Cohen thinks sacrifice was originally offered in silence but that prayer gradually came to play a role in the Temple. He describes the contrast between sacrifice and the cult of the Temple vis-à-vis popular prayer and piety in terms similar to Moshe Greenberg, as one of "elitism and populism" (63).

[6]*The Sanctuary of Silence: The Priestly Torah and the Holiness School* (Minneapolis: Fortress, 1995), and especially "Between Voice and Silence: The Relationship between Prayer and Temple Cult," *JBL* 115 (1996) 17–30. Knohl bases his argument on a careful study of the Priestly materials, concluding there were in fact two Priestly schools, one (PT) responsible for much of the Priestly literature and one (HS) responsible for the Holiness Code and other "HS" materials that are interspersed in the Priestly material. He challenges accepted opinions on the relationship of P and the Holiness code by suggesting that H actually postdates P and that HS was responsible for the final editing of the Torah. Moreover, Knohl argues that each school reflected a distinctive philosophy: "The PT philosophy is focused on the priestly views of belief and ritual and on differentiating them from the beliefs and ritual of the masses, while the HS attempts to interweave and blend the priestly elements of belief and ritual with popular traditions and customs" (*Sanctuary of Silence*, 6–7).

[7] "Between Voice and Silence," 21. Menahem Haran understands prayer offered in the Temple in a similar way. Prayer was a kind of poor man's sacrifice. Prayer was offered in the courts of the Temple, on the periphery, whereas the priestly domain was sacrifice. See his "Temple and Community in Ancient Israel," *Temple in Society* (M.V. Fox, ed; Winona Lake, IN: Eisenbrauns, 1988) 17–25.

We cannot examine Knohl's thesis in its entirety here, but we present it as one of two divergent opinions about Temple worship. The question of what prayer was offered at the Temple remains open, as does the related question of what kinds of prayers may have been offered. Without trying to resolve the issue, we might add as one counterargument to Knohl that in 3 Macc 2:2–20, the high priest Simon offers the prayer "facing the Temple" (ἐξ ἐναντίας τοῦ ναοῦ). The prayer is referred to in 3 Macc 2:21 as a "lawful supplication" (τῆς ἐνθέσμου λιτανείας). Assuming some verisimilitude is attached to the narrative, this petitionary prayer suggests that at least by the late Second Temple period, there was a prescribed form for the high priest to request help from God at the Temple under certain circumstances. Although the description does not locate him in the Temple, the high priestly participation in the cult of Knohl's *hoi polloi* is notable. It is also not clear what significance Knohl attaches to such pre-exilic prayers accompanying sacrifices outside Jerusalem (e.g., 1 Sam 7:7–10, Samuel at Mizpah or 1 Kgs 18:36–37, Elijah at Mt. Carmel).[8] Knohl deals with such examples cursorily in footnotes and mentions the sacrificial dimension without mentioning the accompanying prayers.

Whether or not prayer actually accompanied sacrifice as part of priestly ritual and laying aside what kinds of prayers may have been offered in the Temple, an indubitable fact is the great increase of prayers in Second Temple literature. This trend too requires more of an explanation than can be given here, but one precipitating factor in this increase that has often been noted by scholars was the major disruption in the sacrificial rites after the destruction of the First Temple. The Judeans in exile necessarily had to find some alternate ways for offering gifts to God and atoning for sin other than through the sacrificial system in the Jerusalem Temple. The growing importance of prayer can be seen in exilic literature. As we noted in Chapter One, Solomon's long prayer of dedication for the Temple in the prayer in 1 Kings 8 does not once mention sacrifice, but specifies seven circumstances under which Israelites both in and outside the land might *pray* toward the Temple and expect divine help. This prayer, as noted by Jon Levenson, serves to mark the beginning of a

---

8 Cf. also Joel 2:17: "Between the vestibule and the altar let the priests, the ministers of the Lord, weep. Let them say, 'Spare your people, O Lord, and do not make your heritage a mockery, a byword among the nations. Why should it be said among the peoples, 'Where is their God?'"

transition from Temple to synagogue. It was a long and complicated transition, but there are other signposts that the transition was taking shape. Heinemann suggests that this association of prayer with sacrifice was in place during the Second Temple.[9] The Temple is called a "house of prayer" in Isa 56:7, at which all nations might worship. Based on evidence from Qumran, we can say that at least in the case of one sectarian group, prayer was viewed as a complete substitute for sacrifice and the active expression of faithfulness to God.[10] There is also interesting evidence outside of Qumran in a passage from 2 Maccabees. 2 Macc 2:9–12 consciously associates the prayer of Solomon with Moses:

> It was also made clear that being possessed of wisdom Solomon offered sacrifice for the dedication and completion of the temple. Just as Moses prayed to the Lord, and fire came down from heaven and consumed the sacrifices, so also Solomon prayed, and the fire came down and consumed the whole burnt offerings. And Moses said, "They were consumed because the sin offering had not been eaten." Likewise Solomon also kept the eight days.

This is an interesting typology because it reflects the same equivalency between prayer and sacrifice. Prayer is the *sine qua non* of sacrifice. According to the author of 2 Macc 2:9–12, the prayers offered by Moses and Solomon spur the acceptance of the offerings. Here the author legitimates it by associating the archetypal national founder Moses with the wise king Solomon.

Once reinstituted in the post-exilic period, the daily sacrificial system continued in full operation throughout the period of the Second Temple. However, the disruption that occurred in this perfected system was a major dislocator indeed, judging from the literature that was written in reaction to it (Daniel, Judith, 1, 2, and 3 Maccabees). The Exile had been the first trauma, but there was also the period when Antiochus Epiphanes desecrated the sanctuary. How did this second time of discontinuity affect a life of piety and

---

[9] He does not think that prayer took the place of sacrifice, but that it paralleled and complemented the daily sacrifices, quoting *b. Ber.* 26b to support this view. Joseph Heinemann, *Prayer in the Talmud: Forms and Patterns*. Richard Sarason, transl. (Studia Judaica, Bd. 9; New York: de Gruyter, 1977) 15. He may, however, overstate the evidence that "worshippers were scrupulous to recite their prayers at just those hours when the daily sacrifices were being offered up, and the incense burned."

[10] Chazon, "Prayers from Qumran," 265. Chazon mentions 1QS 9:3–5 and CD 11:18–21 in this regard.

worship? The issue of the exact relationship of prayer to sacrifice during the Second Temple period has yet to be resolved definitively, but it is clear that an equivalency between the two was understood in some Jewish circles long before 70 C.E.[11]

Implications of Scripturalization for the Study of Jewish and Christian Liturgy

The prayers in the Apocrypha and Pseudepigrapha show continuities with both New Testament prayers and later Jewish and Christian liturgies in a number of ways. This is evident in their use of biblical language and interpretative motifs, and more generally in the three representative ways in which scripture has been appropriated: in reviews of history, the appropriation of one event from the biblical period, and the use of biblical figures as exempla. We can also see that certain hermeneutical stances governing the appropriation of scripture persist as well, such as the typological interpretation of scripture in Christian liturgies.

Continuities with Jewish Liturgy

Although we have not focused our attention on form-critical elements of prayers, we can note one significant continuity. Many scholars have remarked on the petitionary-confessional form of a number of late biblical prayers.[12] David Flusser has been one of the most forceful in arguing that many prayers in Second Temple literature, including Jdt 9:2–14, Neh 9:5–37, and 3 Macc 2:2–20, all fit a basic pattern that recurs in the prayer in Jewish liturgy called the Taḥanun.[13] Three constituent elements combine in the pattern: 1.

---

[11] Consider the following comment of Joseph Heinemann: "From what we have said above, it becomes evident that prayer was regarded as ʿavodah, in a manner analogous to the sacrificial cult, not only in the period following the destruction of the Second Temple, but even during the period of the Temple itself—the only difference being that, in the Temple period, prayer did not take the place of the sacrifices, but rather paralleled and complemented them;" *Prayer in the Talmud,* 15.

[12] Cf. the discussions of Balentine, *Prayer in the Hebrew Bible,* 109–119; Miller, *They Cried to the Lord,* 255–259; Reventlow, *Gebet im Alten Testament,* 275–86; and commentaries on these biblical books.

[13] See his discussion of "Prayers in Distress" in "Psalms, Hymns and Prayers," *Jewish Writings of the Second Temple Period.* (M. Stone, ed.; CRINT II 2; Assen: Van Gorcum, 1984) 570–573. Flusser does not make reference in his discussion to the seminal article of Leon J. Liebreich on a similar topic, "The Impact of Nehemiah 9:5–37 on the Liturgy of the Synagogue," *HUCA* 32 (1961) 227–237.

a supplication to God for help; 2. remembrance of divine saving deeds in the past; and 3. repentance/prayer for forgiveness. In addition to our three exemplars, Flusser cites the prayers in Dan 9:4–19, Additions to Esther 13–14, the Prayer of Azariah, Bar 2:6–3:8, and 3 Macc 6:2–15 as examples of this form.[14] While Flusser is correct in discerning similar thematic elements, he does not differentiate among the precise contents of any of the prayers. Neh 9:5–37 in particular, stands out in this regard because as we demonstrated above, it uses parts of the divine attribute formula of Exod 34:6–7 as a kind of refrain five times throughout the prayer. The other prayers mentioned do not. It is that feature, as much as the common inclusion of the three constituent elements Flusser outlines, that links these prayers to later Jewish liturgical use.

Leon Liebreich has noted connections between Neh 9:5–37 and the Taḥanun that occurs after the Shemone Esrei on weekdays. Both the extended form of the Taḥanun on Mondays and Thursdays and the abbreviated form used on the other weekdays use the divine attribute formula. Both forms include the petition:

רחום וחנון חטאתי לפניך יי מלא רחמים

רחם עלי וקבל תחנוני

Merciful and gracious One, I have sinned before thee; O Lord, who art full of compassion, have mercy on me and accept my supplications.

In the long version, there are frequent appeals to God's gracious and compassionate nature, as we found to be the case in Neh 9:5–37. A major difference between the two is there is no long historical retrospect in the Taḥanun for the weekdays as there is in Nehemiah 9, but Liebreich points out other structural similarities as well.[15] While the thesis that Nehemiah 9 had a direct influence on the synagogue liturgy in this way is appealing, we should emphasize that it is likely that the entire history of interpretation concerning the use

---

14 Flusser, "Psalms, Hymns and Prayers," 570–571.

15 Liebreich points out three other major similarities. One is the interweaving of the affirmation of God's unity with benedictions praising God. Another is that the theme and order of three of the benedictions correspond to material in Nehemiah 9: God's revelation in nature, God's choice of Israel, and God's deliverance of Israel from Egyptian bondage. A third is the liturgic principle that laudation precedes supplication. These three similarities are not as convincingly argued as is the suggestion about the divine attribute formula.

of this formula should be taken into account in deciding on liturgical influence. For example, Liebreich nowhere notes a similar structural use of this formula in the affirmation of Ezra to his angel guide in 4 Ezra 7:132–140.[16]

Aside from this continuity in terms of formal elements in the Taḥanun, there are many continuities in the way scripture is cited and interpreted. To take just the use of the examples list, we can find numerous parallels, although they do not necessarily reflect the same appropriation of the*Beispielreihe* form that is apparent in 3 Maccabees 2. One of the earliest examples appears in *Hellenistic Synagogal Prayer* 6.[17] This prayer invokes the God of Israel in order to ask that God listen to the prayers of his people. As part of the prayer, the pray-er asks God to accept the prayers of his people just as God accepted the gifts of Israel's ancestors. The prayer includes a chronological listing of major figures, who had either offered sacrifice at altars (e.g. Abel; Noah; and Abraham, "after his coming out from the land of the Chaldeans") or who had prayed (e.g., David on the threshing floor of Ornan the Jebusite, Hezekiah in illness and concerning Sennacherib). The prayer is therefore significant not only for its didactic listing of biblical characters, but also for its association of prayer and sacrifice, as we discussed above. We might also point out a similar list of biblical heroes found in one of the *selichot* in the evening prayer for Yom Kippur: "He who answered Jacob in Bethel, He who answered Joseph in the prison," and it continues, ending with "He who answered all the righteous, the devout, the wholesome, and the upright, may He answer us." There are other such listings of biblical characters in the Jewish liturgy, especially among the *piyyutim*, although some of the prayers that list biblical characters emphasize divine action toward the individuals as opposed to focusing on the individual's behavior.[18]

---

[16] For a discussion of this passage as a midrashic exposition of the divine attribute formula, see Michael E. Stone, *4 Ezra* (Minneapolis: Fortress, 1990) 256–261. See also the discussion of Exod 34:6–7 and its various reuses in Jack Sasson, *Jonah* (AB; Garden City, NY: Doubleday, 1990) 279–283.

[17] For more information on the *Hellenistic Synagogal Prayers*, extant in the *Apostolic Constitutions,* see *OTP* 2, 671–697, and the discussion of Christian liturgy below.

[18] Cf. for example the formulaic blessings invoked for various occasions. On the occasion of naming a new-born daughter: "He who blessed our fathers Abraham, Isaac and Jacob, Moses and Aaron, David and Solomon, may he bless the mother — and her new-born daughter —. . ."

Another trajectory in Jewish liturgy in which the scripturalization of prayer deserves additional study is *piyyutim*, or liturgical poetry. This particular type of poetic insertion into the liturgy for festivals and other occasions makes many biblical allusions, sometimes very obscure, as well as references to later rabbinic writings. These compositions generally contain rhyme, acrostics, biblical metaphors, and other wordplay. A number of scholars have recognized that the origins of *piyyut* are quite ancient. Aharon Mirsky, for example, suggests that the origins of *piyyut* lie in the Bible itself, though it took later tradents to develop what was there in its earliest forms.[19] Ben Sira shows some of the trademark stylistic poetic flourishes that we see in later *piyyut*. Mirsky draws on Ben Sira's famous passage "In Praise of the Ancestors" to illustrate his point. One of his examples is Sir 44:17–18, which describes the covenant that God made with Noah after the flood. As Mirsky points out, nowhere is the actual sign of the covenant—the rainbow— mentioned specifically. Rather the allusion is made to the story of Noah by using the term ברית עולם, as well as a web of other terms that relate to the flood account and its aftermath.[20] We have remarked on the presence of extensive amounts of extra-biblical interpretation in the prayers we have examined, sometimes referring to these interpretations as "proto-midrashic." We have seen similar allusive features in prayers we have examined. Jdt 9:2 does not identify Dinah by name, but only as "the virgin." Other allusions to the story of the rape of Dinah in Genesis 34 appear in Jdt 9:2–4 in a concentrated way. Another forebear of a species of *piyyut*, the *kinnuy*, appears in a number of Second Temple texts. The *kinnuy* form comprises a series of questions or statements that point to an

---

[19] *Ha-Piyyut: The Development of Post Biblical Poetry in Eretz Israel and the Diaspora* (Jerusalem: Magnes, 1990) [Hebrew] 31. David Flusser also recognizes in this regard the importance of prayers in Second Temple literature: "Beyond the scope of this volume is the significance of these texts for the development of early synagogal poetry (piyyut). It is important to study the language and poetical style of these psalms, hymns and prayers, especially of those preserved in Hebrew, not only to enrich our knowledge of the various levels of post-biblical poetical Hebrew, but also to deepen our understanding of the various types of synagogal poetry and of private prayers" ("Psalms, Hymns and Prayers," 577). See also Ezra Fleischer's study of liturgical poetry, *The Yoṣer: Its Emergence and Development* (Jerusalem: Magnes, 1984) [Hebrew].

[20] Mirsky, 40. Jefim Schirmann also links the development of midrash with the development of *piyyut*, both animated by the same spirit of respect for the scriptures; see his "Hebrew Liturgical Poetry and Christian Hymnology," *JQR N.S.* 44 (1953) 123–161.

Praying By the Book

individual or God but does not name him. At least one example
appears in a prayer that we have discussed.[21] Isa 63:11–12 asks
"Where is the one who brought them up out of the sea with the
shepherds of his flock? Where is the one who put within them his
holy spirit? Who caused his glorious arm to march at the right hand
of Moses, who divided the water before them to make for himself an
everlasting name, who led them through the depths?" The answer to
these rhetorical questions is, of course, God. The pray-er's pointed
questions about the absence of God during a period of crisis makes the
prayer more poignant than a direct address.

Continuities in Christian Liturgies

Many issues in the early history of Christian liturgy remain
open questions, as Paul Bradshaw has recently made clear.[22] Because
so many issues relating to the origins of Jewish liturgy have yet to be
resolved and the seminal work of Heinemann has been considered by
only a few Christian liturgical scholars, Bradshaw thinks that the
reconstruction of early Christian liturgy must be undertaken with
due consideration of these issues. To provide an example of how
future work might be done in this area, we may consider one of the
most important sources for the history of Christian liturgy, the
collection of ancient church orders.[23] A number of prayers thought to
be originally of Jewish origin are included in Books 7–8 of the
Apostolic Constitutions.[24] These prayers are highly scripturalized and

---

[21] Cf. also the similar form in Bar 3:29–30 and the series of biblical
characters who go unnamed in Wisdom of Solomon 10.

[22] Bradshaw's recent book focuses on developing a clear and consistent
methodology for evaluating early liturgical texts; see his *The Search for the
Origins of Christian Worship: Sources and Methods for the Study of Early
Liturgy* (New York: Oxford University Press, 1992).

[23] The relationship of the various church orders to one another is very
complex. The various texts that have come to light include the *Apostolic
Constitutions*, the *Apostolic Church Order*, the *Didascalia Apostolorum*, the
Egyptian Church Order, the *Canons of Hippolytus*, the *Didache*, and the
Testamentum Domini. For an overview of these documents and a discussion
of their interrelationship, see Bradshaw, *The Search for the Origins*, 80–110.

[24] The so-called *Hellenistic Synagogal Prayers* extant in Books Seven and
Eight of the *Apostolic Constitutions* were likely written in the second to third
century C.E. See David Fiensy's introduction (*OTP* 2, 673) for a discussion of
the date. See also his discussion of the history of scholarship on the collection,
which he calls "the liturgical equivalent of Philo" because of the Greek
philosophical conceptions that inform the prayers; "The Hellenistic Synagogal
Prayers: One Hundred Years of Discussion," *JSP* 5 (1989) 17–27; also his book,
Prayers Alleged to Be Jewish: An Examination of the Constitutiones

they illustrate not only how the interpretive trends that we have outlined in this study continue in Jewish liturgy, but also how Christians appropriated and transformed Jewish prayers according to their own new beliefs.

In his discussion of Second Temple prayer, J.H. Charlesworth provides an excerpt from *Hell. Syn. Prayer* 5:1–7 in order to show how Christians adopted and adapted a Jewish prayer:

> O Lord, Almighty One,
> You created (the) cosmos *through Christ*,
> and marked out a Sabbath-day for a remembrance of this;
> because on it you rested from the works (of creation),
> in order to give attention to your own laws.
> And you appointed festivals for (the) gladdening of our souls,
> so that we may come into remembrance
> of the Wisdom created by you:
> *how for us he submitted to birth, that (birth) through a woman;*
> *(how) he appeared in (this) life,*
> *having demonstrated himself in (his) baptism;*
> *how he who appeared is God and man;*
> *(how) he suffered for us with your consent,*
> *and (how) he died and arose by your strength.*
> *Therefore, celebrating the resurrection festival on the Lord's Day,*
> *we rejoice over the one who indeed conquered death,*
> *having brought to light life and immortality.*

Charlesworth states the "The Christian redactor has clarified for a new liturgical *Sitz im Loben* [sic!] the means by which God has created the cosmos, identifies Wisdom with Christ, and rehearses the economy of salvation."[25] Charlesworth does not elaborate on this prayer. He uses it to illustrate the transition from Jewish to Christian prayers, but it also illustrates the scripturalization of prayer and its different uses by Jews and Christians. I use this example because those familiar with the prologue to the Gospel of John and the notion of the pre-existing Logos will readily be able to see the connection. We have extant only the Christian version, so that we can only hypothesize about the original form of the Jewish prayer. The

---

Apostolorum (BJS 65; Chico, CA: Scholars Press, 1985). He claims that "The most serious mistake . . . made by virtually all who have studied these prayers, is the failure to consider the theological tendencies and linguistic and literary conventions of the compiler of AC" (21).

[25] "A Prolegomenon to a New Study of the Jewish Background of the Hymns and Prayers in the New Testament," *JJS* 33 (1982) 285.

selection is an excerpt of a much longer prayer that contains a total of twenty-one verses.

Each one of the prayers in the collection is deserving of extensive treatment. We shall mention just two others. *Hellenistic Synagogal Prayer* 12 is a long hymn of praise to God that includes a review of history from creation (which alone is 34 verses) through the conquest. The prayer ends with a short description of the angelic worship and the Sanctus from Isa 6:3. *Hellenistic Synagogal Prayer* 2 is a prayer of praise. In five places it quotes divine speech and divine promises in a way similar to the first "scripturalized" biblical prayers in Gen 32:10–12 and Exod 32:11–13: an excerpt from the divine attribute formula (2:3), the covenant with Abraham (2:16), reiterated to Isaac (2:18), and to Jacob (2:20). The final citation contains God's words to Moses at the burning bush (2:22), "I am the Being, this is for me an eternal name, and a remembrance to generations of generations."

The point to be made in this discussion is that both Jewish beliefs and the Christian transformation of them can be understood most completely through a careful study of the history of interpretation. These prayers articulate an essential point of transition and the best way in which to understand their meaning is through the study of the reuse and transformation of biblical language and interpretive motifs.

Another area that warrants more diachronic research is how the three basic interpretive modes evident in the three Second Temple prayers we reviewed (linear historical continuity, typologies, and the didactic view of scripture implicit in the biblical exempla) continue to be employed in later prayers. For Christianity, of course, typology was one of the major ways in which the Old Testament was made to relate to the new revelation in Christ. This mode of interpretation thus entered into the understanding of two of the earliest sacraments in the Church, baptism and the eucharist. William Horbury summarized the situation as follows:

> Baptism and the eucharist became focal points in the complex of typological interpretation. Thus the baptismal ceremonies of dipping, anointing and the gift of milk and honey recalled the flood, the Red Sea, the priestly unction and the entry into the promised land; and the eucharistic bread, water and wine similarly evoked

Melchizedek, the manna, the banquet of Wisdom and the promised refreshment of the faithful.[26]

Already in the New Testament we can see certain paradigmatic Old Testament events interpreted typologically. 1 Pet 3:18–22, for instance, understands Noah and the ark as a type for the baptized Christian and the Church, just as it would eventually be construed in the thanksgiving over the water in many Christian liturgies.[27] From the standpoint of the history of Christian liturgy, a worthwhile study would be an examination of the history of interpretation of certain biblical motifs in late biblical, early rabbinic, and Christian literature to see how this informs their use in Christian liturgy. One such study has recently been published. Pierre Dumoulin has researched the use and significance of the gift of manna in Wisdom of Solomon. He argues that the use of the manna tradition in Wis 16:15–17:1, specifically the understanding of manna as a heavenly gift of nourishment from God, presages to some degree the understanding of bread in the Eucharist.[28] We have traced a very early use of typological interpretation in a prayer (Judith 9) that long predates any New Testament source, let alone any Christian liturgy, but it represents one of the beginnings of a very long trajectory in liturgical history.

We could mention a number of other related trajectories in which the study of the use of scripture in early liturgy could prove illuminating. The Syrian forms of Christianity in particular preserved elements of Jewish tradition that are not seen in other

---

[26] "Old Testament Interpretation in the Writings of the Church Fathers," *Mikra* 750.

[27] Many other types for the water of baptism were identified in Old Testament sources by the Church Fathers. The prayer over the water in the thirteenth century Sarum baptismal rite relied on interpretive references found in the Church Fathers and contained typological allusions to the waters of creation, the flood, the heavenly city, the womb, the rivers of Paradise, the water from the rock, and the wedding feast at Cana. See Marion J. Hatchett, *Commentary on the American Prayer Book* (New York: HarperCollins, 1980), 274–275. On the varieties of Christian initiation rites, see Bradshaw, *Search for the Origins*, 161–184.

[28] Pierre Dumoulin, *Entre la manne et l'eucharistie: Etude de Sg 16,15–17,1a: La manne dans le livre de la Sagesse, synthèse de traditions et préparation au mystère eucharistique* (AnBib 132; Rome: Pontifical Biblical Institute Press, 1994). See also the review of this work by Michael Kolarcik, *CBQ* 58 (1996) 310–311.

Western Christian traditions. Ephrem the Syrian is perhaps the most renowned liturgist of early Christianity. His work is richly allusive to the Old Testament and contains many such midrashic interpretations as we have explored in Second Temple prayers. We mentioned above the development of *piyyutim* in Jewish liturgy which also contains these characteristic midrashic interpretations. A comparison of some early *piyyutim* and hymns of Ephrem which explores their formal and interpretive similarities could shed new light on the relationship of early Christian and Jewish liturgies.[29]

In Summary

If one conclusion is indisputable from this book, it is that scriptural tradition became an integral part of prayers early in Israel's history and ultimately in Jewish and Christian liturgies. The precise delineation of how Jewish and Christian liturgies came into being is still ahead of us, but we hope this study has helped shape its contours. The ways in which scripture was used in these prayers became constitutive for early religious communities, both Jewish and Christian. Scripture was viewed as a source for moral lessons, a direct precursor to contemporary history, or a typological backdrop

---

[29] Jefim Schirmann has outlined some similarities between Jewish *piyyutim* and eastern Christian hymnody. His characterization focuses not only on formal similarities (such as the alphabetic acrostic form—its biblical origins and its subsequent appropriation by Jewish and Christian authors), but to a lesser degree on the contents of the *piyyut* and the midrashic biblical interpretation contained therein ("Hebrew Liturgical Poetry"). He notes not only Ephrem the Syrian, perhaps the best known of the eastern theologians, but also Romanos and Auxentius. Romanos authored some poems in the *kontakion* form, a relatively complicated poetical form containing a poetic homily, a hymn, and a dialogue. "It is therefore remarkable that the Jewish Qeroba like the *kontakion* could link up with a Bible text read as a lesson, paraphrase it, interpret it, invariably containing hymns and sometimes dialogues between the acting persons." A number of his pieces contain interpretive motifs similar to those found in midrashic collections and *piyyut* (sacrifice of Abraham, the chaste Joseph, three young men in the fiery furnace). Auxentius also used the *kontakion*. Schirmann is careful not to overemphasize the similarities between the *piyyut* and the *kontakion*; see especially pages 155–160 on this. The main problem with his analysis is that he does not draw on many examples to illustrate his points, which underscores the fact that more work should be done in this area.

We should also mention in this regard the classic study by Eric Werner that explores the interaction of Jewish and Christian liturgy, especially in music and hymnody, throughout the Middle Ages; see *The Sacred Bridge* (New York: Schocken, 1959).

to the current age, which reengaged ancient patterns. In different ways, prayers alluded to, quoted from and interpreted scripture. Not only was scripture read and studied in the religious communities, but equally important, scripture was *prayed*. The combination of scripture and remembrance of tradition was the regenerative force in which community self-understanding was reinforced through worship. This continues to be the case in Jewish and Christian communities that retain traditional liturgies in their worship. The present monograph is a modest beginning toward systematizing how scripturalization functions. Additional study of how scripture is appropriated in prayers can only deepen our understanding of how Jewish and Christian religious communities expressed their faith through prayer, while continuing to preserve and enhance their connection to the Bible.

APPENDIX

A Selective History of Scholarship on Prayer and Liturgy

Many readers of this volume are likely interested in biblical prayer or Jewish and Christian liturgy. I therefore include the following review of some of the principal works of scholarship on biblical prayer, Qumran prayer, and Jewish liturgy in order to situate my work on the scripturalization of Second Temple prayer in a broader context of scholarship. The review is not exhaustive, especially in regard to Jewish liturgy, but outlines the major currents in the history of scholarship in these areas.

While it is easy to understand why prayer in extra-biblical literature has been neglected, it is surprising that so little has been written on the topic of prayer in the Hebrew Bible itself. In the first half of the twentieth century, very few studies of biblical prayer appeared. John McFayden's 1906 book, *The Prayers of the Bible*, represents the first systematic examination. Its positive contributions are its insights into the meaning of the content of the prayers; however, the constraints of his methodology and hermeneutical assumptions limit its relevance to this study. His focus is restricted to the canonical books of the Protestant Old and New Testaments. The book does not participate in any larger scholarly dialogue and ignores historical-critical scholarship on the Bible which was still in its infancy at the beginning of the twentieth century. McFayden's view of prayer reveals a perspective shared by other scholars as well, which views spontaneity as the hallmark of "true prayer:"

> In particular it might be argued that the true Protestant not only feels the impulse, but is under the obligation, to pray in his own words. Just as he claims the rights and duty to think for himself, so it might be said that he has a similar right and duty to express his thoughts to God no less than to man, in his own way. . . . There can

be no doubt that free prayer is, on the whole, more consonant with
the idea of prayer than fixed. If prayer be a real intercourse of the
human heart with God, prescribed or studied words would seem to
be no more natural than in intercourse with men . . . [1]

This romantic view of the autonomous individual who
expresses a heartfelt spirituality in isolation from any larger religious
community points to a problem pervading his understanding of
biblical prayer; namely, the implicit hermeneutical assumptions
behind McFayden's remarks.[2] The starting premise is this: for the
Protestant Christian reader, the Bible is a document that is
authoritative for guiding people in their lives. The narrative of the
Bible depicts characters praying "spontaneously," that is, as a result
of some event or necessity that prompts such an outpouring. The
contents of these prayers are the characters' "own words." Thus
according to McFayden, reading the Bible is the equivalent of poring
over a roadmap to find directions, providing the pious reader with
guidance for daily living. The foregoing claims hinge on two corollary
assumptions. The narratives of the Bible were not shaped by any
literary hand, but reflect events "as they happened," as a mirror
record of historical events; and the words in these prayers are the
words of the characters themselves as they uttered them—they were
not composed or reshaped by anyone else. On this basis he claims that
the prayers are "spontaneous," reflecting no prescribed or set
liturgical pattern. The problem with McFayden's assessment of
biblical prayer is that in his desire to stress spontaneity as a primary

---

[1] John Edgar McFayden, *The Prayers of the Bible* (New York: A.C.
Armstrong & Son, 1906) 221.

[2] The study of biblical prayer in the early twentieth century was influenced
by certain romantic conceptions of prayer. The exact intellectual origins of this
bias cannot be detailed here, but certainly include the influence of Reformed
Protestantism. Friedrich Heiler's study of prayer, *Prayer: A Study in the
History and Psychology of Religion* (Oxford: Oxford University Press, 1931),
offers a representative view of the nature of prayer in the nineteenth century.
Heiler's highly romantic conception of prayer excluded written texts as
inauthentic, stultified, calcified expressions of the human need for
communication with the divine. According to Heiler, true prayer is the
spontaneous communion of humans with God. Sam D. Gill wryly points out
the inherent difficulty in Heiler's position: "Heiler held that prayer texts were,
in fact, not true prayers . . . Heiler's study of prayer therefore, was a failed
effort from the outset in the respect that he denigrated his primary source of
data for his study of prayer leaving him wistfully awaiting the rare occasion to
eavesdrop on one pouring out his or her heart to God" from his entry "Prayer,"
Encyclopedia of Religion (Mircea Eliade, ed.; NY: MacMillan, 1987) 11. 490.

characteristic of biblical prayer, he ignores their written character, mistaking literary depiction of spontaneity for actual spontaneity. This is not to say that the situations in which biblical characters uttered prayers were not verisimilar to actual circumstances in which prayers in ancient Israel were offered; however, McFayden does not consider any literary art to be involved in the prayers' composition and forms. Also unappreciated is the significance of the fact that many of these prayers are imbedded in stories. McFayden's book is not the only treatment of Old Testament prayer in the early years of this century, but in his idealized depiction of individual, "spontaneous" and non-ritual form of worship, he is representative of an era of Protestant biblical scholarship.[3]

Another early study and the only book-length treatment of prayers in the Apocrypha and Pseudepigrapha is a brief monograph by Norman Johnson published in 1948, *Prayer in the Apocrypha and Pseudepigrapha*. The book's primary virtue is that it is comprehensive, treating all of the relevant material available to him at the time, but it has two major problems. The first is that through his quest of locating one purported "theology," Johnson seeks to portray Judaism as a unified whole. This ideal is reflected in the book's organization. There are three principal chapters that discuss in turn the aims of the prayers, the means of inducing God to heed the prayers, and the divine responses. The result is a work that offers citations from the prayers without regard to their context or the date of the text from which they are culled. His treatment of the material is arranged to produce a "systematic theology" of Judaism, according to which his observations about the prayers provide evidence for the conceptual categories of divine omnipotence, omniscience, immanence, and omnipresence. His main conclusion is that Jewish "theology" of this period was inconsistent and contradictory—

---

[3] In his book on prayer in the Hebrew Bible, Samuel Balentine notes two other early studies by J. Hempel (1922) and H. Schmidt (1928). While both studies offer a more sophisticated methodological approach to the literature than McFayden, they both reveal a bias toward "spontaneous" prophetic prayers and a denigration of Priestly tradition and ritual in the form of prescribed prayer. On this topic, see the discussion of Balentine, *Prayer in the Hebrew Bible*, 226–230. Moshe Greenberg traces the origins of the heightened appreciation of "spontaneous prayer" in the work of Hempel and Schmidt to the influence of Heiler, the author of the classic work on prayer noted above. Heiler's book postdates McFayden's book and so of course could not explain McFayden's own predilection for spontaneous over fixed forms of prayer.

exhibiting what is now widely recognized as the great diversity of ideology and praxis in Second Temple Judaism.

A second methodological weakness is his underlying assumption about the degree to which prayer in the narrative reveals the faith and beliefs of characters who utter them, and, more than that, about the profile of a prototypical "Jew" of the period. The following remarks illuminate his understanding of the significance of prayers in narratives:

> If, unknown to him [the pseudepigraphal pray-er], we can invade the privacy of his chamber and hear the spontaneous outpouring of his own prayer, then we can truly overhear his beliefs. Nothing reveals them more honestly than does the catalog of (1) what he prays for, (2) the way he tries to induce God to grant the petition, and (3) the manner of response he expects.[4]

Like McFayden, Johnson views the narrative as an undistorted mirror of life in ancient Palestine, instead of an artifice with its own conventions. In other words, he mistakes drama for "real life." This point might seem an overly easy criticism of a study that only reflects a prevailing hermeneutical posture of the time in which it was written, but the methodological problem involving an implicit "hermeneutics of similitude" carries over into more recent studies of prayer as well, as we shall discuss below.

Though both books contain some interesting insights about the contents of biblical and extra-biblical prayers, the trailblazing efforts of Johnson and McFayden are outdated. One reason is that they were both written before the discoveries at Qumran opened up a wealth of material for the study of the Second Temple period. A second problem is that the authors neglect to engage historical-critical scholarship so that both books speak in monologues. If, for instance, McFayden had taken source criticism into consideration, if even to refute its results, his own work might have been more convincing. He would have been forced to argue against the idea that biblical texts were frequently written down long after the period they depict, and in stating and arguing his own position explicitly, he might have strengthened the thesis of his book.

A number of more recent studies provide research on prayer using historical-critical approaches to the literature. The second half of the twentieth century has seen increasing interest in the topic of

---

[4] Norman B. Johnson, *Prayer in the Apocrypha and Pseudepigrapha: A Study of the Jewish Concept of God* (SBLMS 2; Philadelphia: Scholars, 1948) 3.

prayer. Scholarship on prayer in the Bible can be generally divided into two camps: those works that focus predominantly on the Psalms and their *Sitz im Leben,* and those works that include serious consideration of prayers imbedded in biblical narratives as an independent witness to Israelite religion or biblical theology.

Henning Graf Reventlow's book *Das Gebet im Alten Testament* represents the former trend.[5] He builds on a long tradition of German historical-critical biblical scholarship on biblical psalmody. Categorizing psalms according to form and establishing their relationship to Temple worship have been the central results of this tradition in Psalms scholarship. His work reflects the influence of Mowinckel, who first theorized that the life setting of the Psalms was the Temple cult. Reventlow's discussion of prose prayers in particular builds on the work of A. Wendel and L. Krinetzki.[6] He also relies on the form-critical work of Gunkel, Begrich, and Westermann to inform his sorting of the psalms into different *Gattungen,* the major types being praise, lament, and thanksgiving, each with its particular structure and place in the cult. The bulk of the study is a form-critical discussion of biblical prayers, in which category he includes, and indeed stresses both the book of Psalms and other compositions of a hymn-like nature found inserted into biblical narrative, such as Exodus 15. His central thesis is that all prayers in the Old Testament originate from a cultic background. Reventlow thinks that the prose prayers found outside the book of Psalms in the narrative parts of the Bible contain structural elements similar to the psalms and reflect a dependence on them. According to Reventlow, Jacob's short prayer in Gen 32:10–13, for instance, represents an abbreviated form of the lament form found in the Psalms. He thus views prose prayers not as spontaneous outpourings of the pious soul, but as studied compositions.[7] His conclusion that all forms of prayer are dependent on the most formalized and structured specimens found in Psalms has shaped his assessment of the role of prayer in

---

[5] Henning Graf Reventlow, *Das Gebet im Alten Testament* (Stuttgart: W. Kohlhammer, 1986).

[6] Samuel Balentine offers a helpful review of scholarship on prose prayer in the second chapter of his study, *Prayer in the Hebrew Bible,* 19–32. There is no need to reduplicate his thorough discussion here, because from the perspective of this study, it is more important to establish the broader trajectories of scholarship on biblical prayer.

[7] Reventlow is sensitive to the literary function of the prayers in narrative and their conscious use by the authors of biblical narrative. See his discussion of the "early laments" in *Gebet,* 87–90.

the Bible and its implications for certain forms of Protestant worship, namely, that Old Testament prayer is not characterized by spontaneity, but rather is bound up in an established tradition. Reventlow's work on Old Testament prayer is concerned primarily with literary questions. Other recent attempts have been made to establish the social setting of the psalms by using form-critical studies and assessing Mesopotamian ritual parallels.[8]

Among scholars who take the non-psalmic prayers in narrative seriously as an independent witness to Israelite religion, Moshe Greenberg offers the most provocative thesis in his short book, *Biblical Prose Prayer*. The book explores biblical prayer from both literary and sociological angles.[9] He assesses not only the shape and content of prayers in the Hebrew Bible, but also what can be said about ancient Israelite religious practice based on these observations. His thesis is that the prose prayer found imbedded in narratives offers a look at a kind of grassroots, popular religiosity, a private prayer form on the part of the people that offered an egalitarian alternative to an officially sponsored hierarchical Temple cult. According to his count, there are ninety-seven prose prayers in the Bible, the equivalent of two-thirds the number of psalms in the book of Psalms. They issue from the mouths of kings, prophets, and in thirty-seven cases, from people who have neither special royal or cultic status.

According to Greenberg, these prayers are characterized by a lack of stereotyped and cultic formulae, and are patterned after interpersonal discourse, except with the purpose of communicating to the deity. Greenberg asserts that the imbedded prose prayers found in narrative texts closely reflect the spontaneous prayers that would

---

[8] On the basis of a form-critical distinction between individual and communal laments, Erhard Gerstenberger argues that there were two distinct worship settings for laments. The setting for the individual lament was the more intimate family or clan; the setting for the communal lament was the larger, more impersonal, national group associated with the Temple. See Erhard Gerstenberger, *Der bittende Mensch: Bittritual und Klagelied des Einzelnen im Alten Testament* (WMANT 51; Neukirchen-Vluyn: Neukirchener Verlag, 1980) 140–146. The work of Gerstenberger and others, such as R. Albertz, offers interesting hypotheses about the origins and development of Israelite prayer and ritual.

[9] Moshe Greenberg, *Biblical Prose Prayer* (Berkeley: University of California Press, 1983). The book represents the development of ideas found in his earlier article "On the Refinement of the Conception of Prayer in Hebrew Scriptures," *Association for Jewish Studies Review* 1 (1976) 57–92.

have been offered by "common people," that is, everyday Israelites who were not members of the priesthood or professional establishment of the Temple. Here Greenberg makes explicit a way of reading the text that was implicit in McFayden. He concedes that the prayers might in some way be shaped by the narrator's hand, yet he evaluates them as a *de facto* reflection of Israelite religious expression: this was the way the average Israelite prayed in biblical times, providing us with a window into the popular religion of ancient Israel (the subtitle of Greenberg's book). The depiction of these prayers as plebeian is not entirely accurate. One of his arguments is that many of the prayers offered in the Bible are offered by "lay people," those with no priestly status or royal credentials. His claim is misleading. One could easily counter that the prayers of Abraham and Jacob, for instance, are included in the Bible because they do have a special status as the eponymous ancestors of Israel. They do not represent "Everyman" but rather narratized traditional portraits of prominent biblical ancestors.[10]

Greenberg's rationale for associating the prose prayers in the Hebrew Bible with popular religious practice is evident in the following excerpt:

> To determine their verisimilitude we must ask: are the circumstances and formulations of prayer in the scriptures such as raise doubts as to whether they might have been so prayed in ancient Israel? Are the various literary prayers so conditioned by their narrative contexts as to be formally distinct, so that we must regard the art of the given narrator as decisive in their formulation? Can we find analogies in social speech for the forms of prayer, so that the notion that the narrators loosely and freely invented the prayers they put in the mouths of characters seems unlikely? If the answers to these questions support the view that the forms of Scriptural prayer represent the forms actually in use in ancient Israel, we shall have made an advance in our knowledge of ancient popular religion.[11]

---

[10] Consider in this regard the comments of Reventlow: "Die Beter sind in der Regel nicht Privatleute, im modernen Sinne. David ist ein König, Josua der Führer des Volkes, Simson ein volkstümlicher Held, Gideon der Offenbarungs-empfänger und Kultgründer, Rebekka die Ahnfrau, Jakob das Clan-Oberhaupt. . . . Die soziologischen Bedingungen, die sich in den Texten widerspiegeln, sperren sich gegen moderne Versuche, eine altisraelitische "Laienfrömmigkeit" zu isolieren." (*Gebet*, 99). He is reacting not only to the thesis of Greenberg, but also the work of Rainer Albertz, *Personliche Frömmigkeit und offizielle Religion* (Stuttgart: Calwer, 1978).

[11] Greenberg, *Biblical Prose Prayer*, 8–9.

The first question indicates that his point of departure is the assumption that the narrative can and should reflect the actual practice of prayer. I would argue that the burden of proof is on the social historian to prove that a written text does accurately depict ancient Israelite life. The biblical books were written in most cases long after the time they depict, so doubts about whether the circumstances and formulations are close to actual practice are valid. Even assuming a conservative tenth century date for the Jahwist epic, this would mean it was written several hundred years after the supposed ancestral era. Greenberg does not address the question of what period "ancient Israel" might actually depict. The last of the questions Greenberg poses concerns his theory about the composition of the prayers. The question suggests that there is a dichotomy between "social speech" and conventions and the free invention of an author. He in fact argues in his book that this is not the case. In his attention to the forms of the prayers, Greenberg offers some important observations. Greenberg resists dividing all prayer strictly into "spontaneous" and "prescribed" types. Rather he sees a mixture of the two as representing another form of biblical prayer, patterned prayer-speech, in which there are some conventions and formulae used, perhaps to govern openings and closings, but whose substantive content might vary. This flexible form lies in between the purely spontaneous extemporized phrasings that appear in narrative and that have no apparent convention, such as David's exclamation, "O frustrate Ahitophel's counsel, YHWH" (1 Sam 15:31), and such highly formalized works as appear in the Psalms—Psalm 119 for example, with its alphabetic form and regular strophes. According to Greenberg, "All three levels were available throughout the period of biblical literature, and narrators might choose to place their characters on any level according to circumstances."[12]

Greenberg's claim about prayer in biblical literature stands in strong contrast to the view of Claus Westermann who views the development of biblical prayer in evolutionary terms, moving from short prose prayers tied to the narrative to poetized psalms to long prose prayers.[13] Greenberg's observations about biblical prayer hold

---

[12] Greenberg, *Biblical Prose Prayer*, 46.

[13] Westermann's theory of the three developmental stages of prayer holds that the first stage comprises early, simple, prose prayers that are bound to the narrative and cannot be taken out of context therefore requiring no cultic framework. The second stage is represented by psalms, both in the book of Psalms and in other books. These psalms are not dependent on narrative context and their *Sitz im Leben* is the worship service. The final stage is

true for Second Temple literature, too. Interjections of the sort uttered by King David and short, prose prayers do not disappear from late post-exilic compositions. There is, however, a trend to include more long prayers, both in original compositions and in their editorial reshaping. Such compositions as the prayers of Mordechai and Esther, the Songs of Daniel and the Three Young Men, and the Prayer of Manasseh that were written to enhance and expand earlier books illustrate this tendency toward longer prayer compositions. It would seem that a theory between Greenberg and Westermann is true; that while short prayers continue to play a part in Second Temple literature, an evolutionary proclivity toward longer, elaborate, scripturalized prayers is evident.

Greenberg's study, with its emphasis on the importance of non-psalmic prayer in the understanding of Israelite religion, augured a new interest in such prayer among biblical scholars. Two books of more recent vintage offer interesting insights into the phenomenon of biblical prayer. Both Samuel Balentine and Patrick Miller have authored books on the theology of biblical prayer.[14] Balentine's book focuses only on prayer in the Hebrew Bible. Balentine's study seeks to redress the inattention given to prayers in the Hebrew Bible by previous scholarship, especially prose prayers in narratives. One of his central conclusions affirms the importance of laments deriving from the experience of human pain as a legitimate response to God.[15]

---

characterized by long prose prayers such as 1 Kings 8, Ezra 9, and Nehemiah 9 in which there is no longer any unity between the congregation in worship and the civil community sponsoring prayer compositions. The description of the final stage is not fully fleshed out. Westermann's developmental approach is limited in its usefulness because he only considers the canonical books of the Bible, which cannot give him an accurate picture of the historical development of prayers. His developmental theory is described in *Elements of Old Testament Theology* (Atlanta: John Knox, 1982) 153–174.

[14] Balentine, *Prayer in the Hebrew Bible*; and Miller, *They Cried to the Lord: the Form and Theology of Biblical Prayer.*

[15] In emphasizing the importance and legitimacy of laments as prayers to God, Balentine reacts against the neo-orthodox stance of Karl Barth and the biblical theology of Gerhard von Rad. Both Barth and von Rad view praise as the appropriate response of faithful human beings to a God who has acted in decisive ways in Israel's history. Balentine counters this notion by broadening the definition of theology to include the witness of the human side of the divine-human dialogue found in scripture whose end is to maintain the covenant relationship. He suggests that "theology" simply in its strict sense as knowledge or information about God is insufficient in constructing useful and authoritative constructs for the Church. Rather, the human part of the divine-human dialogue is equally important in discerning the Church's theology that

Miller, by contrast, looks at the form and theology of prayers in the entire Christian canon, including the New Testament, although his emphasis is decidedly on the Old Testament. As a starting point, he uses a comparative analysis of Mesopotamian prayer and ritual, but his primary concern remains the distinctiveness of Israelite worship and the theological meaning of biblical prayer. Both of these books are excellent studies that serve to redress the longstanding neglect of the topic. To the degree that the studies are synchronic accounts of biblical prayer, they are of limited use to this study which is concerned primarily with the historical development of prayers. This study argues that the increasing references to scripture in prayers do have implications for understanding the authority of the Bible, but that its authority for worship cannot be separated from the religious communities and the process of tradition within those communities that gave rise to the prayers, and later, liturgies. The Bible as it is interpreted in prayers of the liturgy continues to shape religious communities through their ongoing worship.

Our review of biblical scholarship on prayer reveals in main that the focus lies on canonical biblical literature and that extra-biblical literature has gone largely ignored. Aside from some individual articles on isolated prayers, the three exceptions that have tried to treat the extra-biblical corpus more systematically are Norman Johnson, as mentioned above, Günter Mayer, and David Flusser. Twenty-five years after Johnson's pioneering work, Mayer authored an article that treats prayer in the apocrypha from a different perspective.[16] He examines under what circumstances the prayers are offered by the characters in the narratives. He looks only at the books of Judith, 1 Maccabees, Tobit, and the Greek Additions to Esther. In all the prayers that consist of more than just a line or two, Mayer discerns three elements: a retrospective reference to the past, the specification of the enemy, and the articulation of a belief in God as the ultimate deliverer. He observes that prayer is found when the action turns or when it progresses, especially at the high points in the

---

it derives from scripture. Using what he considers to be a central insight of the biblical theologies of C. Westermann, W. Brueggemann, and P. Hanson that view the Bible not as a univocal theology but as dialectical theologies that lie in tension with one another, he suggests that lament is equally as important as praise in constructing an understanding of biblical theology.

[16] Günter Mayer, "Die Funktion der Gebete in den alttestamentliche Apokryphen"*Theokratia. Jahrbuch des Institutum Judaicum Delitzschianum II 1970–1972* (Leiden: Brill, 1973) 16–25.

narrative. His main conclusion is that the books examined all stress the immanence of God in mundane affairs and a confidence in the ultimate power of God to shape the events of history. Mayer's article offers a sound analysis of the question posed, but in the limited space of an article, he does not get beyond the more obvious literary features of the prayers in the narratives. Günther Mayer's article offers the only recent antidote to the neglect of prayer in the Apocrypha and Pseudepigrapha, but his treatment does not do justice to the breadth of literature in the Second Temple corpus. More recently, David Flusser has provided an overview of psalms, prayers, and hymns in the Second Temple period that points to some important features of selected prayers and suggests the need for additional study of the prayers in the Apocrypha, Pseudepigrapha, and Qumran sectarian writings.[17]

Jewish Liturgy

We now turn to consider scholarship on the origins and early development of Jewish liturgy. The review is admittedly selective, but is chosen to provide the reader with a sense of the major issues. Although the methods used to arrive at conclusions in Jewish liturgical scholarship sometimes overlap with those of biblical scholarship, the body of texts that are examined and the set of questions that are posed are different. Beginning in the nineteenth century, philology, and more recently, form-criticism, have been the chief methods used to discover when and how the Jewish liturgy, in particular, the statutory prayers (the Shema, the Amidah, and the Grace after Meals) originated. The texts that have been the focus of most scholarly attention are thus liturgical texts, whether in the form of existing liturgies, prayers contained in rabbinic literature, Cairo Genizah manuscripts, or Qumran liturgical material. Another related concern has been to establish the point at which obligatory daily prayer became a normative practice for adult males in the Jewish community. The first question posed in the study of Jewish liturgy, then, is more directly related to textual study. The second question involves some historical and sociological inquiry, and raises the thorny issue of normative religious practice in the Jewish community during the Second Temple period and later. As will become apparent in a review of some of the literature, opinions on these two questions differ.

---

[17] See Flusser's essay, "Psalms, Hymns and Prayers," in *Jewish Writings of the Second Temple Period.*

The earliest critical work on liturgy employed a philological-historical approach in an attempt to establish a putative "original" single text from which the many varieties of liturgical prayer stem.[18] This search for the Ur-liturgy has been called into question by a number of scholars, most notably Joseph Heinemann. With the publication in the mid-1960s of his first major book on liturgy, *Prayer in the Period of the Tanna'im and Amora'im*, he pioneered a new approach by applying form criticism to prayers.[19] As the title suggests, his work deals almost exclusively with rabbinic sources as opposed to prayers in extra-biblical (and non-rabbinic) books. With its different methodological underpinnings, Heinemann's approach resulted in a work that overturned the consensus by suggesting an alternate model for the development of statutory prayer. Instead of positing the existence of an Ur-liturgy, he argued that a more fixed and structured liturgy evolved slowly during the Second Temple period when a variety of prayers and liturgical structures were in use. His research suggests that there were four rough stages in its development: 1) free formulation, 2) development of common patterns of content though the exact formulation was not fixed and improvisation was permitted, 3) the fixing of common patterns by halakhic decision, and 4) the set formulation of prayer texts. The last

---

[18] Leopold Zunz was the first to approach the study of liturgy using the tools of *Wissenschaft des Judentums* in his book *Die gottesdienstlichen Vorträge der Juden*. Ismar Elbogen used philological methodology in his book, *Jüdische Gottesdienst in seiner geschichtlichen Entwicklung* (Grundriss der Gesamtwissenschaft des Judentums; Frankfurt am Main: J. Kauffmann, 1934; 3d ed.), as did Louis Finkelstein in his influential articles "The Development of the Amidah," *JQR* 16 (1925–1926) 1–43, 127–170; and "The Birkat Ha-Mazon," *JQR* 19 (1929) 211–262. For a thorough review of the history of Jewish liturgical scholarship, see Richard Sarason, "On the Use of Method in the Modern Study of Jewish Liturgy," *Approaches to Ancient Judaism: Theory and Practice* (W.S. Green, ed., Brown Judaic Studies 1; Missoula, MT: 1978, 97–172; reprinted in J. Neusner, ed., *The Study of Ancient Judaism* (New York, 1982) 1.107–79.

Other scholars have reacted to Heinemann's overemphasis on form-criticism. Stefan Reif has also pointed to new interdisciplinary paths for the future study of Jewish liturgy, using a combination of methods including philology and form-criticism; see his *Judaism and Hebrew Prayer: New Perspectives on Jewish Liturgical History* (Cambridge: Cambridge University Press, 1993). So too, Lawrence Hoffman suggests going beyond a textual focus to include sociological and political considerations in the shaping of the liturgy; see his *Beyond the Text: A Holistic Approach to Liturgy* (Notre Dame, IN: University of Notre Dame Press, 1987).

[19] Joseph Heinemann, *Prayer in the Talmud*. Originally published in Hebrew as *Prayer in the Period of the Tannaim and Amoraim,* 1964.

two stages occurred only late in the Amoraic period, the fourth stage probably not until the early medieval era, when in fact different versions became authorized for Babylonia and Palestine. In spite of Heinemann's significant achievements, the exact relationship of these later more fixed liturgies to earlier biblical and post-biblical forms of prayer is still unclear. Scholars have come to no agreement on the exact steps involved in the development of the liturgy, especially during the Second Temple period, from which there is scant documentary evidence that relates specifically to prayer.

Qumran provides an important witness to Second Temple Judaism, however, and an increasing amount of attention has been paid to liturgical texts and references to prayer in the Qumran literature.[20] On the basis of evidence at Qumran, Lawrence Schiffman has suggested that there was a greater degree of fixity to the elements of prayer at this stage than Heinemann's model would allow.[21] He determines this on the basis of parallels between the texts and practices found at Qumran and those of the early Tannaim, in particular, certain supplications (intended for use on Wednesdays and Saturdays) that are similar in theme and content to the rabbinic supplications for Mondays and Thursdays, daily prayers, and specific prayers for each festival.[22] He traces precursors to the first benediction before the Shema and to the blessing concerning the chosenness of Israel which is recited over the Torah reading.[23] Though there are significant differences between the order of liturgy Schiffman reconstructs from Qumran sources and the later liturgy

---

[20] For an informed *status quaestionis* piece on the Qumran liturgical texts, raising important methodological questions about how to treat this material and relate it to "non-sectarian" prayers, see Eileen M. Schuller's article "Prayer, Hymnic, and Liturgical Texts," *The Community of the Renewed Covenant: The Notre Dame Symposium on the Dead Sea Scrolls* (E. Ulrich and J. Vanderkam, eds.; Notre Dame, Ind: University of Notre Dame Press, 1994) 153–171.

[21] His arguments about the development of liturgy at Qumran can be found in *Reclaiming the Dead Sea Scrolls* (Philadelphia: JPS, 1994) 289–312 and "The Dead Sea Scrolls and the Early History of Jewish Liturgy," *The Synagogue in Late Antiquity* (Lee I. Levine, ed.; New York: Jewish Theological Seminary, 1987) 33–48.

[22] This insight did not originate with Schiffman. Moshe Weinfeld draws attention to an early article by Manfred R. Lehmann on this topic, "A Re-Interpretation of 4Q Dibrei Ham-Me'oroth," *RevQ* 5 (1964) 106–110, in Weinfeld's "Prayer and Liturgical Practice," *The Dead Sea Scrolls: Forty Years of Research* (D. Dimant and U. Rappaport, eds.; Leiden: Brill, 1992) 248 n.38.

[23] Schiffman, *Reclaiming*, 295.

as it took shape within rabbinic Judaism, he nonetheless is confident in asserting that there were essential commonalities that were inherited from an earlier era.

Ezra Fleischer's work has also challenged Heinemann's conclusions.[24] Unlike Schiffman, who views the Qumran material as an important witness to Second Temple Judaism, Fleischer discounts its evidence as a sectarian form of Judaism whose practices would not have reflected the Temple-centered activities of mainstream Judaism. Fleischer argues that there was no fixed prayer, either in the sense of daily obligatory prayer or in the sense of fixed wording of prayers, that pre-dates the destruction of the Second Temple. According to Fleischer, the synagogues were used as public gathering places and as locations for study and learning, but not for prayer. The requirement of thrice-daily prayer was only instituted at Yavneh as a way of adapting to life without the Temple. He also suggests that the order and wording of the prayers was instituted *de novo* at the same time. His position thus contrasts with that of Heinemann, who argues that although the exact order and wording of the prayers were not entirely fixed during the Second Temple period, the normative practice of daily prayer originated during that time.

Even more recently, Bilhah Nitzan and Esther Chazon have focused exclusively on the topic of prayer at Qumran, offering additional insights about the development of Jewish liturgy.[25]

---

[24] Cf. the discussion of Fleischer in Chapter Five above, 213-214.

[25] Aside from Nitzan and Chazon, who have devoted their full attention to prayer at Qumran, other scholars have also made contributions to the study of prayer and liturgy at Qumran. We cannot mention all of them here. Other important work on Qumran prayer includes scholarship on the Songs of the Sabbath Sacrifice most notably, John Strugnell, "The Angelic Liturgy at Qumran—4Q Serek Shirot 'Olat Hasshabbat," *Congress Volume: Oxford 1959* (VTSup 7; Leiden: Brill, 1960) 318–45, and Carol Newsom's *Songs of the Sabbath Sacrifice: A Critical Edition* (HSS 27; Cambridge, MA: Harvard University Press, 1985). Newsom suggests parallels between the Songs of the Sabbath Sacrifice liturgy, with its quasi-mystical vision of the angelic liturgy praising God in the heavens, and roughly contemporaneous apocalyptic literature, such as *1* and *2 Enoch*, the *Apocalypse of Abraham*, or parts of the *Testament of Levi*. At least one aspect of this liturgy is retained in Jewish liturgy, namely the recitation of the Qedushah (which is adopted and adapted in Christian eucharistic liturgies as the Sanctus), in which earthly participants take part with the angels in their continuous praise of God.

Moshe Weinfeld has pointed out some verbal parallels between the liturgies at Qumran and customs known from Pharisaic halakhah. He is careful to make the point that there was no orthodoxy in the Second Temple period such as developed in Pharisaic Judaism after the destruction of the Second Temple.

Nitzan's book, *Qumran Prayer and Religious Poetry*, is an ambitious project that seeks to present a comprehensive view of prayer at Qumran and its relationship both to biblical prayer and to Jewish liturgy. In brief, her study paints a picture of linear development, "namely, from free and variegated religious poetry in the Bible to ordered and structurally fixed prayer under rabbinic law."[26] The study is comprehensive in treating all the liturgical texts found at Qumran; however, two of the overarching categories she sets up in order to discuss Qumran prayer skew its results. Nitzan divides the Qumran liturgical texts into two groups: those that represent "sectarian" prayer with an ideological outlook distinctive to the Qumran community, and those prayers that represent a purported "mainstream" Judaism. She assumes a Jerusalem "mainstream" orthodoxy and does not make mention of such diverse groups as the community at Elephantine in Egypt, who had their own Temple, or the Samaritans in Shechem, who viewed themselves as the true descendants of biblical Israel. In other words, the notion of an unqualified "mainstream" Judaism at this stage is not accurate. Moreover, deciding which prayers were composed at Qumran and which were not, based on the degree to which they reflect "sectarian" ideas, is rather circular reasoning, yet this designation is the overarching principle that she uses to categorize the material. It preemptively forecloses the possibility that Qumran compositions may have been "orthodox," that is, that some prayers composed by the Yahad may not have contained any references to a solar calendar, the community's belief in two messiahs, or criticism of a corrupt Jerusalem priesthood.[27] One need only look at another group,

A recent contribution is "The Angelic Song over the Luminaries in the Qumran Texts," *Time to Prepare the Way in the Wilderness: Papers on the Qumran Scrolls by Fellows of the Institute for Advanced Studies of the Hebrew University, Jerusalem, 1989–1990* (D. Dimant and L.H. Schiffman, eds; STDJ 16; New York/Leiden: Brill, 1995) 131–157. See also the Appendix to his article, "Prayer and Liturgical Practice in the Qumran Sect," *The Dead Sea Scrolls: Forty Years of Research* (D. Dimant and U. Rappaport, eds; Leiden: Brill, 1992) 241–257. Earlier articles by Weinfeld also attempt to draw parallels; "Traces of Qedushat Yoser and Pesukei de-Zimra in the Qumran Literature and in Ben Sira," *Tarbiz* 45 (1978–79) 15–26 (Hebrew) and "The Prayers for Knowledge, Repentance and Forgiveness in the 'Eighteeen Benedictions'— Qumran Parallels, Biblical Antecedents, and Basic Characteristics," (Hebrew), *Tarbiz* 98 (1979) 188–200 (Hebrew).

26 Bilhah Nitzan, *Qumran Prayer*, 22.
27 For a discussion of the limitations of distinguishing sectarian from non-sectarian prayer, see Carol A. Newsom, "'Sectually Explicit' Literature from

a Jewish sect at the outset, Christianity, in order to discover that prayers need not be "sectarian" to have originated in a "sectarian" group. The Magnificat, Mary's prayer in Luke 1:47–55, the Benedictus, Zechariah's prayer in Luke 1:68–79, and even that most "Christian" of prayers, the Lord's Prayer, are all "sectarian" compositions that are still used in Christian worship, yet none betrays any Christological beliefs that would make them incompatible with Jewish teaching. Thus Nitzan's central organizing principle in categorizing the Qumran liturgical materials is flawed.[28]

Nitzan also draws a sharp line between prayer she designates as "occasional," that is, prayer that appears in a narrative, and "fixed prayer," so that she too readily dismisses the evidence from the Apocrypha and Pseudepigrapha as representing only "occasional prayer." Fixed prayer in her occasionally idiosyncratic lexicon refers both to prescribed times and prescribed wording. Here she confuses the narrative circumstances that give rise to prayers, which occur occasionally or spontaneously, and the wording of the prayers themselves, some of which could be reused on other occasions. While she is correct in asserting that many of the prayers in these books are intimately connected to the narrative situation in which they are offered (3 Maccabees and threat to the Temple), that does not mean there are not significant correspondences between the *texts* contained in the narratives and the *texts* that came to be included in formal, "fixed" liturgies. To underscore this point even more clearly, consider the prayer of Jonah 2:2–9. In the maw of the great fish, Jonah offers a prayer under "occasional circumstances" that is really a knitting together of parts of several different psalms, or prescribed words. Thus the wording of this prayer was not "spontaneous" but had some relationship to texts that had already been "fixed" as part of a collection of psalms in scripture.

These difficulties must be noted, but they in no way diminish the significant amount of work she has done on the Qumran material and the many valid observations she makes about the forms and contents of the prayers and their connections to later rabbinic liturgy. Nitzan's book does offer important observations about the use

---

Qumran," *The Hebrew Bible and its Interpreters* (W.H. Propp, B. Halpern, and D.N. Freedman, eds; Winona Lake, IN: Eisenbrauns, 1990) 167–87.

[28] Consider the comment of Eileen Schuller, who notes: ". . . although I applaud the attempt to distinguish sectarian and non-sectarian and am confident that we can and will refine our methodology in the coming years, I suspect that this body of texts will remain the most resistant to such a distinction" ("Prayer, Hymnic, and Liturgical Texts," 170).

of scripture in Qumran prayers. Her observation that ". . . scripture served as the basis for the religious cult of the entire Jewish people in all its different factions" undergirds our own study.[29] She points in particular to the use of scriptural models, such as the priestly blessing of Num 6:24–26 that influenced the authors of Qumran compositions.

Chazon's work more clearly grapples with methodological questions in her study of prayer at Qumran. Her aim is to contribute to "the single most important issue for the history of Jewish liturgy. . . the question of the existence of fixed, public prayer in non-sectarian circles prior to the destruction of the Second Temple."[30] In evaluating Qumran prayer as a whole, Chazon divides Qumran prayers into seven form-critical categories: liturgies for fixed prayer times, ceremonial liturgies, eschatological prayers, magical incantations, collections of Psalms, *Hodayot* hymns, and prose prayers. She also offers some carefully considered criteria for determining the liturgical function of prayers.[31] Chazon recognizes the complex relationship of Qumran prayers to a presumed "mainstream" Judaism:

> . . . even patently sectarian prayers witness nonsectarian liturgical practices to the extent that they draw upon a common liturgical heritage and incorporate elements common to that heritage. In fact, a constituent feature of sectarian prayers is their re-use of common liturgical language and forms.[32]

Her final criterion for assessing origin is negative: only prayers that contain ideas or terminology at odds with Qumranic theology

---

[29] Nitzan, *Qumran Prayer*, 13.

[30] E. Chazon, "Prayers from Qumran and Their Historical Implications," *DSJ* 1 (1994) 279.

[31] She qualifies even her tentative decisions about liturgical function: "Moreover, we must always consider the possibility that a prayer's function may have changed over the years and among different worshippers, and that while its content and form may refect the original function, they may not give accurate expression to its subsequent use." Chazon, "Prayers from Qumran," 275.

[32] E. Chazon, "On the Special Character of Sabbath Prayer: New Data from Qumran," *Journal of Jewish Liturgy and Music* 15 (1993) 1. See also her discussion of the issue in "Prayers from Qumran," 271–273 and her article "Is *Divrei ha-me'orot* a Sectarian Prayer?" *The Dead Sea Scrolls: Forty Years of Research* (D. Dimant and U. Rappaport, eds.; STDJ 10; Jerusalem: Magnes and Yad Izhak Ben Zvi, Leiden: Brill, 1992) 3–17.

and practice can be considered to have originated outside the sect.[33] But as she then goes on to point out, "With few exceptions (the ceremonial liturgies of benediction and malediction, the *Hodayot*, and probably the *Songs of the Sage*) such references are virtually nonexistent in the prayers."[34] Scholars have found very few liturgical compositions that qualify.[35] This is, in fact, one weak point in Chazon's careful argumentation. She argues for the non-Qumranic origin of 4Q503, "our first direct evidence of fixed public prayer outside of Qumran during the Second Temple period," even though Qumran provenance cannot be ruled out.

She admits that the system of liturgical practice against which Qumran prayer should be understood is unclear. While acknowledging the difficulty of the task of correlating Qumran prayer texts to Jewish liturgical history, she argues that based on her study of the *Words of the Luminaries* (4QDibHam), there is evidence for fixed public prayer outside of Qumran during the Second Temple period. Chazon finds shared times for prayer, shared themes and specific formulations in common between 4QDibHam and rabbinic prayers. Whether or not the prayers derive from Qumran, the parallels with later rabbinic prayer that she points out are striking: "In content, language, form and function, the benedictions of 4Q503 resemble the rabbinic *Benediction on the Luminaries* (*b. Ber.* 11a–12a)."[36] This

---

[33] Chazon also mentions certain other considerations, such as paleographical dating and distinctive linguistic features, that can sometimes shed light on provenance.

[34] Chazon, "Prayers from Qumran," 271.

[35] As Chazon notes, Carol Newsom reversed her original assessment that the Festival Prayers originated at Qumran because they begin the annual cycle in Tishri which contradicts the Qumran solar calendar ("Prayers from Qumran," 272).

[36] Chazon, "Prayers from Qumran," 282. Moshe Weinfeld has noted certain parallels between 4QDibHam and the Tahanun said on Mondays and Thursdays after the Amidah, although they do not seem particularly close. See Weinfeld, "Prayer and Liturgical Practice in the Qumran Sect," *Forty Years* 248–250. In this article, Weinfeld is less cautious than Chazon about asserting the existence of certain norms, liturgical and other, that were the common inheritance of the various streams of Judaism during this period. In most cases, however, he argues for the antiquity of normative prayer practices on the basis of parallels between Qumran prayer (or other Second Temple literature) and later rabbinic tradition. For instance, he states that rabbinic obligation to recite a blessing upon seeing a rainbow is already found in Sir 43:11: "Behold the rainbow and bless its maker," without considering the possibility that the rabbinic obligation may have been based in part on this phrase in Ben Sira ("Liturgical Practice," 241). The context of Sir 43:11 gives no indication that this was a normative practice in the second century B.C.E.

conclusion corroborates Heinemann's thesis about the gradual evolution of fixed, public prayer and weighs against the position held by Fleischer.

The form-critical examination of the Qumran corpus of prayers has produced fruitful results. The work of both Nitzan and Chazon buttress Heinemann's theory that the statutory prayers had established themes and patterns during the Second Temple period while the precise wording was still in flux. There are, nonetheless, difficulties in trying to reconstruct normative prayer practices of Second Temple Jews on the basis of the prayer practices of a group alienated from other Jewish groups of the period.

One paramount difficulty lies at the center of the discussion of Qumran prayer that neither Nitzan nor Chazon can completely overcome; namely, the relationship of Qumran prayer and liturgical practice to that of other contemporaneous Jewish practices. Eileen Schuller has noted that because of the very traditional nature of much liturgical and prayer literature, the body of prayers and hymns found at Qumran resists easy categorization into sectarian and non-sectarian categories.[37] Moreover, it is not exactly clear what is at stake in the attempt to differentiate between sectarian and non-sectarian. Is the designation "non-sectarian" as it is used in these studies to be associated with a putative "mainstream" Judaism that is the linear predecessor of rabbinic Judaism? For Nitzan, the answer is yes. Chazon offers a much more nuanced evaluation of this and

---

[37] Consider, too, the following comments and questions, which are not easily answered: "The very essence of prayer and prayer-hymnic discourse, whether sectarian or non-sectarian, is its dependence on a common stock of stereotyped and formulaic, biblical based phraseology. Those precise features that scholars have singled out as hallmarks in recognizing "sectarian"— whether institutional clues (Teacher of Righteousness, calendar) or theological concepts (predeterminism, dualism)—are least likely to come to expression in a prayer text. Although this is readily recognized on one level, I am afraid that at times we work with very outdated understandings of the function of liturgical language, still conceiving it as predominately cognitive and fundamentally a vehicle for polemical and theological discourse . . . Do the generating impulses that lead to division and a new self-identify necessarily find expression in "new" prayers? What are retained of 'old' prayers, and how are they understood?" Quotation from Eileen Schuller, "Prayer, Hymnic, and Liturgical Texts," *The Community of the Renewed Covenant: The Notre Dame Symposium on the Dead Sea Scrolls* (E. Ulrich and J. VanderKam, eds.; CJAS 10; Notre Dame, IN: University of Notre Dame Press, 1994) 170.

related questions than Nitzan, who seems to assume the existence of only two Jewish groups during this period.[38]

Building on earlier scholarship on Qumran prayer, the work of both Nitzan and Chazon has greatly contributed to our understanding of prayer at Qumran and its formal relationship to later rabbinic liturgies. Both scholars have examined this important evidence for the study of prayer and practice in Second Temple Judaism, while also taking into consideration the prayers in extra-biblical literature outside of Qumran to some degree. Their overriding focus on form-critical concerns and prayer's relationship to fixed public prayer in Jewish liturgy, however, leaves many questions unanswered and many issues about Second Temple prayer unexplored.

Implications for this Study

The survey of scholarship on biblical prayer and Jewish liturgy points to some unresolved problems. McFayden's book on the nature of biblical prayer represents one end of the spectrum: biblical prayers are spontaneous outpourings with no prescribed form. His work exposes the danger of reading the Bible too literally, assuming that prayer portrayed as spontaneous actually *is* spontaneous prayer. This assumption rules out consideration of such "spontaneous" prayer as a witness to the development of liturgical phraseology or patterns. It also eliminates the possibility that prayers can play a narrative function, as for instance, explored by Mayer in his article on prayer in the Apocrypha. Reventlow's work on prayer reflects a position at the other end of the spectrum: prayers in narratives are essentially loose variations of forms found in the book of Psalms. There is art to their composition that relies on a fixed body of conventional forms. Moshe Greenberg's work offers a middle ground by asserting that many prayers seem to reflect patterned prayer-speech in which there are some conventions and formulae used, perhaps to govern openings and closings, but whose content (particularly in terms of inner-biblical interpretation) varies according to the narrative situation in which they appear.

The review of scholarship also reveals that there is still work to be done before any consensus can be reached on liturgical

---

[38] Consider Nitzan's comment: ". . . one must remember that the people of Qumran constituted a distinct community, separate from the main body of the congregation of Israel, which necessarily developed its own practices in terms of prayer and literary creation" (*Qumran Prayer*, 5).

development during the Second Temple period. In liturgical scholarship, as in scholarship on biblical prayer, a number of positions are evident. Schiffman, by including Qumran material in his analysis, discerns an early, pre-Common Era fixing of prayer patterns and content. Fleischer, at the other extreme, suggests a much later date after the destruction of the Second Temple for both the institution of mandated daily prayers and their fixed sequence and wording. Heinemann's work represents another position. He believes that the practice of daily prayer began long before the rabbinic era, but that the precise formulation of these prayers developed slowly, with roots in the Second Temple period, crystallizing only in the Gaonic period. The specialized work of Chazon and Nitzan would support Heinemann's thesis. Yet one point of agreement among Heinemann, Schiffman, and Fleischer is that all prayer started out as a free-form phenomenon. Their disagreement lies not at the beginning, but at the end of developmental line, or more precisely, they disagree on when and how the fixed wording of prayers occurred. Although the present study certainly bears on these still unresolved issues, its point of departure and main focus is the scripturalization of prayer, a question largely ignored by previous scholars.

The summary of research also suggests that there has been little cross-pollination between biblical scholars and liturgical scholars. Although they work on some of the same issues, few scholars have made connections between the two sets of "data" for the study of prayer—biblical prayers and Jewish and Christian liturgies. Liturgical scholars such as Heinemann have been more active in making connections to prayers in biblical literature, though they have not generally used the tools of historical criticism to assess these sources. In addition, the wealth of prayers in extra-biblical, non-rabbinic literature of the Second Temple period has not been adequately examined. Even including research done on late biblical prayer, a great deal of preliminary work remains to be done in examining the language of prayers found in texts largely or wholly composed within the Second Temple period (from the 6th century B.C.E. through the 1st century C.E.).

Index of Ancient Citations

Biblical and Apocryphal Texts

Hebrew Bible

Genesis

1–3	66	12:20	73
1:1–2:4	65, 66	13–14	183
1:9, 10	80	13	73, 185
2	192	13:13	182
2:1	65	14	73, 74, 183
2:3	86	15	71, 72, 74
2:4bff	191	15:2, 3	23
2:18	4, 151, 189	15:5–21	23
2:21–24	189	15:5	94, 106
2:23	189	15:6	72, 74
2:24	151	15:7	72, 104
4:10–12	7, 23	15:7–8	72
4:13–14	7, 23	15:18	75
4:26	23	16	73
5–9	173, 174, 177–179	17	70, 73, 75
5	204	17:7	75, 111
5:18–24	175	17:13	111
6	197	17:14	75
6:1–5	175	17:19	75, 111
6:1–4	173–175	18–19	181, 182
6:1	175	18:20	7, 183
6:2–4	173	18:23–32	7
6:4	172	19	182, 185
6:5–7	176	19:18–20	23
6:5	176	19:24	180
6:5ff	173	20:7	111
6:11–12	176	21	74
9:15	102	21:16	21
10:8–14	178	22	70, 72–74
12	70, 71, 73, 74	22:1	74, 186
12:8	23	22:13	30
		22:17	32, 94, 106
		24:12	29

24:27	30	4:13	23
24:42	30	4:21	186
24:48	30	5:22	23
24:60	155	6:5	101
26:4	33, 94, 106	6:7	140
26:14	131	7:3–5	186
28:3–4	155	7:3	81
28:10	30	7:5	140
28:12	30	7:13	186
28:13–15	30	7:17	140
28:13	30	7:20–21	111
29:35	22	7:22	186
30:1	131	7:28	111
30:24	22	8:22	140
31:3	30	9:2	186
32:9–12	203	9:16	78, 104, 113
32:10–12	216, 225	10:1	186
32:10	31, 32	10:2	186
32:10–11	29	11:7	140
32:10–12	29, 32, 36, 53	13:21	79, 81
32:12	29, 32	13:22	79
34	118, 120, 123–125, 127, 130–132, 206, 213	14–15	106
		14	68
		14:4	140
34:5	129	14:10	77, 78, 81
34:7	127, 129, 134, 204	14:15–18	78
34:13	127	14:16	79, 80, 113
34:14	129, 153	14:18	140
34:25	125	14:19	79
34:27	125, 126, 128	14:21	79
34:31	128	14:22	80
34:30	128	14:24	79
37:11	131	14:29	80
43:3	96	15	118, 138, 192, 202, 225
48:14	22		
48:15–16	7	15:1–21	120
		15:1	146
Exodus		15:3	146
2:24	101	15:5	80
3:7	77, 81, 104	15:10	80
4	23	15:13	191

15:17	191	34:6–7	17, 36, 53, 88–90,
15:19	80		107, 114, 203, 211,
15:21	146		212
16–17	87	34:6	103, 167
16:4	87, 104, 186	34:9	35, 51
16:22–26	86	34:14	134
16:23	85	34:15–16	133
17	24		
17:4	23, 24	Leviticus	
17:1–7	87	9:24	25
17:2	186	10:10	51
17:7	186	11:47	5112 189
18:10–11	187	12:2–5	189
18:11	140, 187	16:21	25
19:11b, 20a	83	18:5	99
19: 21, 23	96	20:24, 26	50, 51
20:5	134	20:25	51
20:8–11	86	26:40	25
20:19b	83	26:42	101
20:20	186		
21:29	96	Numbers	
23	68	5:14	131
31:12–17	86	6	50
32–34	31, 35	6:24–26	7, 237
32	31–33, 38, 87, 91	8	50
32:1–4	91	10:11	23
32:4	91, 103	11:16–25	91
32:7–10	32	11:29	131
32:7–14	31, 32	12	20, 170
32:8	31, 91	12:13	19, 28
32:10	32	13:25–33	172
32:11–14	32	14	17, 35–37, 87
32:11–13	29, 31–33, 36, 53,	14:4	88
	216	14:13–19	29, 35, 36, 37, 53,
32:11	23, 32, 34		88, 203
32:13	32, 106	14:14	79
32:25–29	31	14:17–19	90
32:31–32	31	14:17	101
34:5	84	14:18–19	90, 114
34:6ff	35	14:18	37
		14:20–35	94

14:22	186
16:22	23
20:8	87, 104
21:21–35	93
22–24	93
25	132, 162
25:1–5	132
25:6–9	131
25:11–13	131, 204
27	38
32:13–15	92

Deuteronomy

1	46
1:2	83
1:6–4:40	38
1:6	83
1:8	87
1:10	94, 106
1:11	25
1:19	83
1:28–2:21	172
1:28	172
1:33	172
2–3	93
2:10–11	172
3:23–25	25
3:24–25	38
4	68, 83, 84
4:1–40	45
4:1–10	47
4:7	47
4:10, 15	83
4:19	68
4:20	47, 51
4:34	81
4:35	66
4:36	83, 84
4:39	47
4:41	50
5:2	83

5:4	83
5:9	134
5:12–15	86
6:11	94, 95
6:23	102
7	68
7:1–6	133
7:3	132
7:8	34
7:9, 12	102
7:19	81
7:20	48
8:1	33
8:2	186
8:4	92
9:8	83
9:16	91
9:20	25
9:25–29	25, 32
9:26–29	29, 31, 33, 34, 37, 38, 51, 53
9:26	34, 45
9:29	32, 45
10:14	66
10:16	88, 99, 106
10:17–18	101
10:17	101
10:22	94, 106
11:9	33
12:11	45
13:6	34
15:15	34
17:3	68
18:16	83
19:2, 7	50
19:8	102
21:7–8	25, 29, 37, 53
21:7	21
21:8	34
22:28–29	128
24:8	170

24:9	170, 204		
26	56, 103, 107, 108, 110	Judges	
		2:11–23	95
26:5–9	107, 108	3:3–6	133
26:5–10	25, 29, 37, 53, 55	3:5	98
26:5–11	203	3:15	98
26:8	81	3:18	98
26:9	102	3:19	98
28	44, 48	3:31	98
29:18–28	169	4:2	98
28:25	48	6:13	23
28:52	48	6:21	25
28:67	94, 106	6:22	21
28:69	83	10:1, 14	98
29:2	81	10:6–9	26
29:5	92	10:10	26
29:18	176	10:12	98
29:21–24	169, 171	15:18	23
29:21	47	16:29	25
29:23	169	21:3	23, 24
30:1	47		
30:10	47	1 Samuel	
30:15–20	99	2	202
31:15	79	7	38
32	95	7:7–10	208
32:9	111	12:10	26
32:15	95	12:13	27
33:8	186	15:31	228
34:4	33	17	152
34:11	81	17:26	152
		17:47	152
Joshua		17:51	152
4:21b–24	80		
4:22	80		
5:6	92	2 Samuel	
7:7–9	23	7	25, 42, 45, 50, 104
24	78, 94, 108	7:1–17	42
24:2–12	108	7:1–6	44
24:2–15	12	7:8–16	44
24:6–7	78	7:13	50
24:7	78, 87	7:14–16	49

7:18–29	24, 38	8:31	46
7:22b–24	38	8:32	47, 98
7:23–53	42–43	8:32	194
7:23	34, 78	8:33	48
12:13	26	8:33–34	193
15:31	27	8:34	47, 98
21:19	153	8:35	35
24:10	26, 27	8:36	35, 45, 47, 98, 194
24:17	26, 27	8:37–39	193
		8:37–40	45, 196
1 Kings		8:37	48
1:36–37	7	8:38	47, 98
3:6–9	24	8:39	47, 48, 194
3:6	102	8:40	46, 48
8	24, 25, 28, 38, 39,	8:41–43	44, 52
	42, 44, 51–54, 98,	8:41	47, 48
	104, 195, 196, 198,	8:43	47, 52, 98, 194
	229	8:44–53	44, 45, 47
8:6–13	43	8:44	45
8:12–21	44	8:45	47, 194
8:12	44	8:46–51	42
8:12–13	44	8:46–53	39, 47
8:13	52	8:46	45
8:14–21	44, 45	8:47	26, 47, 51
8:15ff	52	8:48	47
8:15–21	24, 39, 44, 45	8:49–50	47
8:22–53	24, 48, 51, 52	8:49	47, 194
8:22–44	44	8:51–53	45, 49
8:22	45	8:51	47
8:23–43	45	8:52–53	50, 51
8:23–53	19, 39–41, 43, 45,	8:52	47
	53, 193, 194, 203	8:53	35, 51
8:23	38, 47, 101, 107	8:54	45
8:24–25	49	8:55–61	24, 39
8:25	49, 50, 54, 195, 203	9	194
8:27	52, 66	9:3–6	195
8:28–29	49	9:3–9	52, 195
8:29	49, 203	9:3	195
8:30	35, 48, 98	12:28	31
8:31–50	196	14:9	96
8:31–40	48	17	19

17:22	19, 23	37	138, 204
18:4, 13	96	37:15	139
18:36–37	208	37:16–20	15, 119, 139
19	98, 204	37:17–19	139
19:4	26	37:20	140, 141, 148
19:10	26, 96	37:31–32	133
19:14	96	37:32	133
19:15–19	119	37:33–35	38, 144
19:30–31	133	38:6	144
19:33–35	133	42:8	141
22	68	42:13	146
22:19–22	67	43:16–17	147
		43:16	80
2 Kings		44:3	80
6:17	26	44:8	141
6:18	26	45:5	141
6:20	26	45:6	141
17:14	88, 99	45:14	141
17:16	68	45:18	141
17:36	32	45:21	41
19:15–19	15, 24, 38	45:22	66, 141
19:15	38, 66	46:9	141
19:19	66	51:9–11	117
21:3	68, 69	56:6–7	52
21:5	68	56:7	209
23:4, 5	68	56:8	114
		62	135
Isaiah		63	81
1:10	181	63:7–64:11	109, 112, 113,
2:11–17	145		147, 148
5:15	145	63:7–14	112
6	68, 69, 203	63:11–14	92
6:3	203	63:11–12	112, 214
10:12	145	63:11	113, 147
11:12	114	63:12, 14	78
13:19	181	63:15–64:12	112
25:11	145	63:15	112, 147
26:5	145	63:18	147
30:5	153	64:1	147
34:4	68	64:2	147
36–39	118, 145	64:9–11	147

Jeremiah

		20	78, 96
2:7	102	20:9	78
3:22–25	21	20:11	99
3:30–31	135	20:13	86
4:27	100	20:14	78
5:18	100	21:2	46
7:26	88, 99	22:26	51
8:2	68	23	135
11:7	97	23:35	96
12:1	75	28	191
13:20–27	135	28:2–6	191
15:18	23	33:1–9	97
17:20	23	40:6	46
17:23	88, 99	40:10	46
18:20–22	137	40:20	46
19:13	68	40:22	46
19:15	88, 99	41:12	46
20:8	153	42:7	46
23:14	169, 181	42:20	51
24:9	153	43:1	46
25:4	97	43:2	46
26:23	96	44:3	46
30:11	100		
32	81, 110	Hosea	
32:16–25	109	3	135
32:17–25	109, 110		
32:17	32, 66, 110	Joel	
32:18	101	2:13	90, 91
32:20	78, 81	2:17	35, 208
32:21	81	2:27	141
33:22	68	4:2	35
44:17	102		
49:18	181	Amos	
50:40	181	4:11	181
Ezekiel		Jonah	
1	68	1:9	80
3:15	97	2:2–9	236
8:5	46	4	203
16	135, 182, 185	4:2–3	26, 38
16:49	181	4:2	23, 90, 91

Micah	
6:4	34
7:18–20	91
Nahum	
3	135
Zephaniah	
1:5	68
2:9–10	69, 181
2:10	181
Zechariah	
7:11	98
7:12	100
8:2	142
8:14–16	142
Malachi	
2:6a	85
Psalms	
11:4	90
28:9	35
29	68
37:1	131
40	91
41:14	59
44	147
45:18	59
51	8
51:13	113
66:6	80
72:19	59
73:3	131
74	147
77:19	81
78/79 (LXX)	91, 108, 109, 147, 196, 198
78:1	196
78:4	196

78:8	193, 196
78:13	79
78:42	34
78:55	111
78:62	35
78:71	35
82	67
85	91
86:15	91
89:4	71
89:7–8	68
89:31–38	49
89:53	59
94:4, 5	35
99	91
103	67
103:8	91
103:20–22	68
105	93, 108–111, 114
105:8–11	111
105:10–11	111
105:11, 14, 15	111
105:21	166
105:44–55	112
106	81, 93, 108–110, 112, 113
106:6	51
106:8	78
106:19	91
106:40	35
106:48	59
111	91
112	91
112:4	90, 107
113:2	59
115:18	59
119	228
119:51	137
119:69	137
119:75a	85
119:84	137

119:85	137	4:12–13	181
119:95	137		
119:115	137	Daniel	
119:129	85	2:20–23	60
119:133	137	8	68
119:137	75, 85	9	63, 64, 81, 99, 102
119:142	85	9:4–19	102
119:144	85	9:4	102, 107
119:151	85	9:6, 8	107
119:160	85	9:15	78, 101
119:164	85	9:19	35
134:10–12	93		
135	93, 108–110	Ezra	
135:9	81	1:11	50
136	93, 108–110	6:21	50
136:17–22	93	9	63, 64, 99
148	67	9:7	102
145:8	90, 91	9:10	101
		9:15	75
Job		10:8	50
24:18	46		
30:8	173	Nehemiah	
38	68	1	64
38:7	68	1:5–11	102
		1:5	66, 102, 107, 110
Proverbs		1:7	85
3:31	131	1:10	34
4:14	131	5:19	27
6:6	131	8–10	57, 60
		8	58, 59
Ruth		9	8, 16, 17, 54, 56–58,
4:11–12	155, 169, 171		60, 63, 64, 68–70,
4:18–22	156		72, 74, 77, 79, 82,
			84, 88, 90–93, 101–
Ezra			104, 106–115, 118–
9	229		120, 124, 198, 204,
9:1–2	133		205, 229
		9:1–5	58
Lamentations		9:2	50
1:18	75	9:4–5	58, 59
4:6	181	9:5–31	62

9:5–37	17, 56, 60–62, 89,	9:25	94
	110, 113, 203, 210,	9:26–27	75
	21	9:26–31	95
9:5	58–60	9:26	95, 96, 98, 100, 102,
9:6	58, 59, 65, 66, 69,		104, 105
	91, 104, 110, 203	9:27	88, 89, 98, 104, 114
9:6–32	58	9:28–34	75
9:6–37	58, 65, 109	9:28	88, 89, 98, 104, 114
9:7	71, 72, 75, 104, 105	9:29	88, 98, 99, 106
9:7–8	70, 71, 74, 75	9:30	75, 91, 99
9:8	72–75, 94, 111, 203	9:31	88, 89, 98, 104, 107,
9:9–21	64		114
9:9–12	76, 103	9:32–37	63, 101
9:9	78, 81, 104	9:32	101, 102, 107
9:10	78, 81, 104	9: 33	110
9:11	79, 80, 82	9: 34–35	102
9:12–15	87	9:34–37	101
9:12	79, 81	9:35–36	76
9:13–14	82–85	9:35	102
9:13	83, 84, 105	9:36	88, 94
9:14–31	109	9:37	58, 94, 110
9:14	83, 85	9:42–51	109
9:15–21	86–87	10:29	50, 99
9:15	76, 87, 92, 104		
9:16–18	87	1 Chronicles	
9:16	88, 99, 106	1–9	100
9:17	35, 87, 88, 90, 94,	1:1	151
	98, 100, 103, 106	2:4	156
9:17	88, 89, 98, 104, 114	2:5	156
9:18–21	87	4:1	156
9:18	88, 91, 103	9:4	156
9:19–21	87	17:21	79
9:19	88, 89, 98, 100, 104	27:23	106
9:20	91, 92, 113	29:2	66, 110
9:21	92	29:10	59
9:22–23	94		
9:22b–24a	76	2 Chronicles	
9:22–25	92, 93	2:11	66, 110
9:22	93	6	194
9:23a	93, 104	6:16	40, 49
9:24–25	93, 94	6:18	66

7:12–22	195	7:132–140	212
7:12–16	195		
7:13	195	Judith	
7:14–15	196	1:7	137
14:11	27	4:6	121
18:18	68	5:5–18	114
18:43	46	5:16	137
20:5–12	51	5:17–18	99
20:6	66, 110	7:17–18	121
20:8	52	8:21	121
20:9	51	11:14	121
24:19	97	11:19	121
24:22	96	8	168
30:8	99	8:11–27	143
30:9	90, 91	8:18–21	143
32:13	99	8:24	143
33:3	68, 69	8:25–27	165
33:11–19	8	9	15, 38, 54, 118, 123,
36:13	99		133, 193, 204
		9:2–14	17, 118, 122, 123,
Apocrypha			210
Additions to Esther		9:2–4	124, 126, 134, 162,
13–14	211, 229, 230		213
13:9	194	9:2	135–137, 152, 154,
13:15	194		204, 206, 213
14:3	194	9:4	125, 128, 129
14:12	194	9:5–6	143
		9:8	135
Baruch		9:7	137, 146
1–2	63	9:7–9	139
1:15–3:8	64, 157	9:9–10	141
2:6–3:8	211	9:11–12	145
3:24–28	177	9:12	194
3:26	172	9:13	141, 144
3:29–30	214	9:14	140, 148
		11:10	144
2 Esdras		11:19	144
19:10	187	13:4	27
		13:17	27
4 Ezra		15:5–7	126
7:106–110	163, 167, 199	16	202

16:2	146
16:11	145

1 Maccabees

1:20–21	186
2	129, 168, 171, 193
2:15–25	160
2:24–26	129
2:24	129, 187
2:26	160
2:27	187
2:44–46	129
2:47	186
2:49–64	163
2:49	186
2:50	186
2:51–60	165
2:52	74
2:54	133
3:50–53	157
4:30–33	150–152
4:45	153, 154
7:37–38	52
7:41–42	150

2 Maccabees

1:24	194
1:27	114
2:8	52
2:9–12	52, 209
9:4	187
9:7	187

3 Maccabees

2	18, 54, 193, 196, 199, 212
2:1	194
2:2–20	156–159, 167, 168, 204, 208, 210
2:2–8	199
2:2	194

2:3–7	156
2:3	66, 110
2:4–7	178
2:4	172–174, 176, 177, 179
2:5	180, 185
2:6	186
2:6–7	191
2:8	191
2:9	187, 188, 190, 194, 204
2:10	52, 193–196
2:15	192, 193
2:19	190
2:20	196
2:21	194, 208
5:9	194
6	18, 166, 168
6:2–15	199, 211
6:2	194
6:4–8	163
7:23	27

4 Maccabees

16:18–23	163, 166, 167

Prayer of Azariah

1:4	60

Prayer of Manasseh

	203, 229

Psalm 151

6–7	153

Sirach

16:6–10	163
16:7	177, 182
16:6	179
36:13–19	114
43:11	238

44–49	160, 161, 163	2:13	70
44:1–15	162	3:32	156
44:16–50:21	162	11:47–51	96
44:17–18	213		
44:20	73	Acts	
45:23–25	133	7:51–53	96
47:5	152		
47:4–5	153	Ephesians	
50:1–24	162	5:22–24	151
51:1	194		
51:7	137	Hebrews	
		11	74, 166, 199
Tobit		11:8, 9, 11, 17a	74
3:2–6	150		
3:11–15	27, 59	James	
4:12	167	2:21–26	166
8:5–6	27	5:10–11:3	199
8:5–7	4, 59, 150	5:10–11	166
8:6	151	5:11	167
8:15–17	27	5:17–18	160
11:14–15	27, 60		
12:17	27	1 Peter	
13:1	60	3:5–6	217
		3:18–22	217
Wisdom of Solomon			
10	214	2 Peter	
10:1–21	163, 164	2:4–10	179
14:6–7	177	2:5–10	167
14:6	178	2:5	97
16:15–17:1	217		
		1 John	
New Testament		3:11	161
Matthew		3:12–15	160
1:3	156	3:12	161
1:5	156		
23:29–36	96	Jude	
		5–7	167
Luke		5	178
1	202	7	178, 185
1:47–55	236		
1:68–79	236		

Other Ancient Texts

Ugaritic
KTU 1.148   67
KTU 1.2   67
KTU 1.40   67
KTU 1.41   67
KTU 1.47.29 67
KTU 1.65   67

Pseudepigrapha
2 Apocalypse of Baruch
4:1–4   190

Apocalypse of Zephaniah
6:10   167, 199

1 Clement
7:6   97

1 Enoch
1–36   174
7:1–5   173
9:4   194
12–13   174
15:8–12   174
84:2–6   66, 174, 190
84:2   194

Hellenistic Synagogal Prayers
2   216
2:3   216
2:16   216
2:18   216
2:20   216
2:22   216
5:1–7   215
6   167, 199, 212
12   18, 160, 216

Joseph and Aseneth
11   203
12:13   145
23:14   126

Jubilees
1:12–13   96
1:12   97
1:27–28   188
2:1–3   69
2:7   190
3:4   151
3:4–7   151, 189
3:6   151, 189
3:9–14   198
3:10b–11   189
3:13   190
4–6   174
4:15   175
4:16   175
4:22   175
4:22–25   175
5:1–2   175
5:1   173
5:3   176
8:19   189
16:5–6   184
17:15–18:19 73
17:16   73
19:8–9   73
22   184
22:1–23   160
22:11–23   18
30   123
30:15   129, 136
30:7–17   130
30:17   160
30:18–20   130

Psalms of Solomon
8:28   114
Pseudo–Philo
Bib. Ant.
6   178
21:2–6   150
47:1–2   150

Sibylline Oracles I
125–131   97
149–151   97

Testaments of the Twelve
Patriarchs
T. Benjamin
9:1   184
T. Levi
5:1–3   126
6:3   129, 130
6:7   128
6:8–11   125
7:1–4   137
T. Naphtali
3:1–5   167

Qumran and Related Manuscripts

Damascus Document
2:14–3:12   166, 167, 199
2:14–4:12a   176
2:17–20   176
2:17–18   176

Daily Prayers
4Q503   238, 239

4Q Enoch   174

Festival Prayers
4Q509 3 3–4   114

Hodayot
1QH 10   203
1QH 11   150
1QH 12:14   90
1QH 14:15   75

1QH 16:16   90

Hymn to the Creator
11Q5 col. 26   150

Rule of the Community
1QS 4:4, 5   90

War Scroll
1QM 10–11   109
1QM 11:2–3   153

Words of the Luminaries
4Q504–506   109, 113, 114, 203,
                233, 238
4Q504 1–2 ii 7–8   114
4Q504 7 13–14   114
4Q504 f.6 10–11 114
4Q504 f.3 ii 7 114

Rabbinic Texts

b. ᶜAbod.Zar.
53b   178

b. Ber.
11a–12a   238
26b   209

b. Ḥull.
89a   178

b. Pesah.
54a   188

b. Šabb.
69a   187

Gen. Rab.
26:7   173

m. Tamid
5:1   207

Targum Pseudo-Jonathan
18:20ff.   183

            Classic Sources
Homer
Iliad
16:236–238   164

Odyssey
1:32–43   164
5:118–133   164
21:293–310   164

Index of Modern Authors

Albertz, Rainer 226
Anderson, B.W. 118
Anderson, Gary A. 13, 151, 189, 192

Balentine, Samuel 6, 25, 26, 28, 35,
    44, 210, 223, 225, 229
Barth, Karl 229
Bauckham, Richard 178
Beyerlin, Walter 37
Blenkinsopp, Joseph 22, 57-59, 63-
    65, 87, 92, 93, 95, 99
Bradshaw, Paul 214, 217
Brettler, Marc 44-48, 51, 54, 196
Brooke, George J. 17
Brown, Raymond E. 202
Brueggemann, Walter 230

Campbell, Jonathan 176
Carmignac, Jean 14
Cazelles, Henri 56, 57
Charlesworth, James H. 3, 8, 215
Chazon, Esther 6, 10, 17, 113, 114,
    205, 209, 234, 237-241
Chester, Andrew 138, 202
Childs, Brevard 21, 23, 31
Clifford, Richard J. 84
Cohen, Shaye 207
Collins, John J. 157
Corvin, J. 27, 28
Craven, Toni 202
Cross, F.M. 24, 44, 67, 191

Davies, Philip 22
Dentan, Robert C. 36
Dimant, Devorah 14, 15, 123, 127,
    138, 162, 163, 166, 171
Douglas, Mary 132-133
Dozeman, Thomas B. 36
Dumoulin, Pierre 217

Eissfeldt, Otto 121
Elbogen, Ismar 89, 232

Fensham, F.C. 93, 109, 110
Fiensy, David 215
Finkelstein, Louis 232
Fishbane, Michael 13, 36, 45, 51, 52,
    65, 72, 90, 91, 117, 133, 202
Fitzmyer, J.A. 14
Fleischer, Ezra 213, 234, 239, 241
Flusser, David 3, 4, 210-211, 213,
    230-231
Fraade, Steven 198
Geller, Stephen 83, 84
Gerstenberger, Erhard 226
Gieschen, Charles A. 161
Gilbert, Maurice 75, 85
Gill, Sam D. 222
Ginzberg, Louis 186
Gottwald, Norman 29
Gray, John 43
Greenberg, Moshe 6, 9, 21, 24, 28,
    207, 223, 226-229, 240
Greer, Rowan A. 13
Grözinger, Karl Erich 70
Gunkel, Hermann 12
Gunneweg, A.H.J. 56, 57, 99

Haag, Ernst 127
Halpern, Baruch 42
Hanson, Paul D. 112, 147-148, 230
Haran, Menahem 207
Hatchett, Marion J. 217
Hays, Richard 16
Heiler, Friedrich 222
Heinemann, Joseph 209, 232-233,
    239, 241
Hempel, Johannes 223
Hoffman, Lawrence 232
Holm-Nielsen, Svend 14
Horbury, William 216-217
Horgan, Maurya P. 104

Jacobsen, Thorkild 67
Jacobson, Howard 16
Japhet, Sara 56, 57, 64, 96, 97, 100

Jepsen, Alfred 45, 47
Johnson, Aubrey 25
Johnson, Norman 223–224, 230

Kaufmann, Yehezkel 207
Kelber, Werner 12
Kittel, Bonnie 14, 105
Klein, Ralph 64
Knohl, Israel 207–208
Knoppers, Gary 42-44
Koch, Klaus 12
Kraeling, E.G. 173
Krinetzki, L. 225
Kugel, James L. 9, 12, 13, 17, 70, 96, 123, 127–128, 130–131, 151, 166
Kugler, Robert 124

Lee, Thomas R. 161–162
Levenson, Jon D. 4, 43-47, 49, 54, 72, 80, 84, 191, 208
Liebreich, Leon 88, 89, 202, 211
Loader, J.A. 181–182
Lumpe, A. 161, 164, 171

Mack, Burton 161
Mathys, Hans-Peter 39
Mayer, Günter 230–231, 240
McCarter, P. Kyle 42
McFayden, John 221–222, 224, 227, 240
Mettinger, T.N.D. 43, 44, 98, 192
Milgrom, Jacob 36, 37
Milik, J.T. 174
Miller, Patrick D. 23, 28, 67, 109, 202, 210, 229, 230
Mirsky, Aharon 213
Montgomery, J. 45
Moore, Carey 120, 122, 202
Mowinckel, Sigmund 108, 201
Mullen, Jr., E. Theodore 67
Myers, Jacob M. 65, 75

Nelson, Richard D. 24
Newsom, Carol 70, 234–235, 238
Nickelsburg, G.W.E. 174
Nitzan, Bilhah 9, 10, 205, 234–237, 239–241
Noth, Martin 31, 35, 36, 38, 64, 83

O'Connor, Michael 9, 46

Olbrechts-Tyteca, L. 163

Patte, Daniel 13
Perelman, Ch. 163
Perlitt, Lothar 83, 84

von Rad, Gerhard 35, 56, 107, 108, 134, 173, 181, 229
Reif, Stefan 232
Reventlow, Henning G. 210, 225, 227, 240
Rhoads, David 129
Robinson, H. Wheeler 67

Sarason, Richard 232
Sarna, Nahum 30
Sasson, Jack 212
Scharbert, J. 36
Schiffman, Lawrence 10, 205, 233–234, 241
Schirmann, Jefim 213, 218
Schmidt, Heinrich 22, 223
Schmitt, Armin 163–164, 166, 171
Schniedewind, William 44, 49
Schuller, Eileen 136, 205, 233, 236, 239
Sheppard, Gerald T. 72
Skehan, Patrick 202
Smith, Jonathan Z. 46
Speiser, E.A. 173
Staudt, Edwin E. 5
Sternberg, Meir 128
Stone, Michael 212
Strugnell, John 234

Thompson, Thomas L. 21, 22

VanderKam, James C. 174, 198–199

Waltke, Bruce K. 45, 46
Weinfeld, Moshe 10, 32, 52, 55, 66, 68, 81, 98, 99, 101, 106, 107, 110, 113, 205, 233–235, 238
Weingreen, Jacob 72
Weitzman, Steven 13
Wendel, A. 225
Werner, Eric 218
Westermann, Claus 27, 28, 44, 108, 109, 112, 228–230

Williamson, H.G.M. 56, 59, 60, 64,
    112, 113
Winter, Paul 202
Wintermute, Orval 73, 97, 175
Wolff, Hans Walter 38, 47
Wright, George E. 137

Zakovitch, Yair 13
Zunz, Leopold 232

Bibliography

Aejmelaeus, Anneli. *Traditional Prayer in the Psalms*. (BZAW 167; Berlin: de Gruyter, 1986).

Albertz, Rainer. *Personliche Frömmigkeit und offizielle Religion*. (Stuttgart: Calwer, 1978).

Alexander, T. Desmond. "Lot's Hospitality: A Clue to His Righteousness." *JBL* 104 (1985) 289–291.

Anderson, Gary. "Celibacy or Consummation in the Garden? Reflections on Early Jewish and Christian Interpretations of the Garden of Eden." *HTR* 82 (1989) 121-148.
———. "Sacrifice and Sacrificial Offerings (OT)." *ABD* V, 870-886.

Ap-Thomas, D.R. "Notes on Some Terms Relating to Prayer." *VT* 6 (1956) 225-41.

Assmann, Jan. *Ägyptische Hymnen und Gebete*. (Zürich: Artemis, 1975).

Balentine, Samuel E. *Prayer in the Hebrew Bible: The Drama of Divine-Human Dialogue*. (Overtures to Biblical Theology; Minneapolis: Augsburg Fortress, 1993).
———. "Prayers for Justice in the Old Testament: Theodicy and Theology." *CBQ* 51 (1989) 597-616.
———. "Prayer in the Wilderness Traditions: In Pursuit of Divine Justice." *Hebrew Annual Review* 9 (1985) 53-74.

Bauckham, Richard. "James, 1 and 2 Peter, Jude." *It is Written: Scripture Citing Scripture*. (D.A. Carson and H.G.M. Williamson, eds.; New York: Cambridge University Press, 1988) 303–317.

Baumgarten, J.M. "The Essenes and the Temple: A Reappraisal." *Studies in Qumran Law*. (SJLA 24; Leiden: Brill, 1977) 57-74.

Baumstark, Anton. *Comparative Liturgy*. (London: A.R. Mowbray 1958).
———. "Das eucharistische Hochgebet und die Literatur des nachexilischen Judentums." *Theologie und Glaube* 2 (1910) 353-7.
———. "Trishagion und Qedusha." *Jahrbuch für Liturgiewissenschaft* 3 (1923) 18-23.

Beyerlin, Walter. *Herkunft und Geschichte der Ältesten Sinaitraditionen*. (Tübingen: J.C.B. Mohr, 1961).

The Bible in Greek Christian Antiquity. (Paul M. Blowers, ed. and transl.; Notre Dame: University of Notre Dame Press, 1997).

Biblical Perspectives: Early Use and Interpretation of the Bible in Light of the Dead Sea Scrolls. Michael E. Stone and Esther G. Chazon, eds. (STDJ 28; Leiden: Brill, 1998).

Blank, Sheldon. "Some Observations Concerning Biblical Prayer." *HUCA* 32 (1961) 75-90.

Blenkinsopp, Joseph. *Ezra-Nehemiah.* (OTL; Philadelphia: Westminster, 1988).
———. *The Pentateuch: An Introduction to the First Five Books of the Bible.* (ABRL; New York: Doubleday, 1992)

Boccaccini, Gabriele. *Middle Judaism: Jewish Throught, 300 B.C.E. to 200 C.E.* (Minneapolis: Fortress, 1991).

Boyce, Richard Nelson. *The Cry to God in the Old Testament.* (SBL Dissertation Series 103; Atlanta: Scholars Press, 1988).

Bradshaw, Paul F. *Daily Prayer in the Early Church: A Study of the Origin and Early Development of the Divine Office.* (London: Alcuin Club/SPCK, 1981).
———. "The Search for the Origins of Christian Liturgy: Some Methodological Reflections." *Studia Liturgica* 17 (1987) 26-34.
———. *The Search for the Origins of Christian Worship.* (New York: Oxford University Press, 1992).

Brettler, Marc. "Interpretation and Prayer: Remarks on the Composition of 1 Kings 8: 15-53." *Minhah le-Nahum: Biblical and Other Studies Presented to Nahum M. Sarna in Honour of His 70th Birthday.* M. Brettler and M. Fishbane, eds. (Sheffield: JSOT Press, 1993).

Brooke, George J. "Shared Intertextual Interpretations in the Dead Sea Scrolls and the New Testament." *Biblical Perspectives: Early Use and Interpretation of the Bible in Light of the Dead Sea Scrolls..* Michael E. Stone and Esther G. Chazon, eds. (STDJ 28; Leiden: Brill, 1998) 35-57.

Brown, Raymond E. *The Birth of the Messiah.* (Garden City, NY: Doubleday, 1977).

Brueggemann, Walter. *Theology of the Old Testament: Testimony, Dispute, Advocacy.* (Philadelphia: Fortress, 1997).

Campbell, Jonathan G. *The Use of Scripture in the Damascus Document 1-8, 19-20.* (BZAW 228; New York: de Gruyter, 1995).

Carmignac, Jean. "Les citations de l'Ancien Testament, et spécialement des Poèmes du Serviteur, dans les *Hymnes* de Qumrân" *Revue de Qumrân* 2 (1959-1960) 357-394.

Charlesworth, James H. "A Prolegomenon to a New Study of the Jewish Background of the Hymns and Prayers in the New Testament." *JJS* 33 (1982) 265-285.

Chazon, Esther G. "4Q DibHam: Liturgy or Literature?" *Revue de Qumran* 15 (1991) 447-456.
———. "Is *Divrei ha-me'orot* a Sectarian Prayer?" *The Dead Sea Scrolls: Forty Years of Research*. (D. Dimant and U. Rappaport, eds.; STDJ 10; Jerusalem: Magnes and Yad Izhak Ben Zvi, Leiden: Brill, 1992) 3-17.
———. "On the Special Character of Sabbath Prayer: New Data from Qumran" *Journal of Jewish Liturgy and Music* 15 (1993) 1-21.
———. "Prayers from Qumran and Their Historical Implications." *Dead Sea Discoveries* 1 (1994) 265-284.

Chester, Andrew. "Citing the Old Testament." *It is Written: Scripture Citing Scripture: Essays in Honour of Barnabas Lindars*. (D.A. Carson and H.G.M. Williamson, eds; New York: Cambridge University Press, 1988).

Childs, Brevard S. *The Book of Exodus*. (OTL; Philadelphia: Westminster, 1974).
———. "Psalm Titles and Midrashic Exegesis." *JSS* 16 (1971) 137-150.

Clements, Ronald. *In Spirit and In Truth*. (Atlanta: John Knox, 1985).

Cohen, Shaye J.D. *From the Maccabees to the Mishnah*. (LEC 7; Philadelphia: Westminster, 1987).

Collins, John J. "Before the Canon: Scriptures in Second Temple Judaism." *Past, Present and Future: Essays in Honor of Gene M. Tucker*. (Nashville: Abingdon, 1995) 225-41.
———. *Daniel*. (Minneapolis: Fortress, 1993).
———. *Jewish Wisdom in the Hellenistic Age*. (Louisville, KY: Westminster/John Knox, 1997).

The Community of the Renewed Covenant. Eugene Ulrich and James VanderKam, eds. (Notre Dame: University of Notre Dame Press, 1994).

Contributions to the Scientific Study of Jewish Liturgy. Jakob Petuchowski, ed. (New York: Ktav, 1970).

Corvin, J. *A Stylistic and Functional Study of the Prose Prayers in the Historical Narratives of the Old Testament* (Ph.D. Diss., Emory, 1972).

Craven, Toni. *Artistry and Faith in the Book of Judith* (SBLDS 70; Missoula, MT: Scholars Press 1983).

Cross, Frank Moore. *Canaanite Myth and Hebrew Epic*. (Cambridge: Harvard University Press, 1973).
———. "The Council of Yahweh in Second Isaiah." *JNES* 12 (1953) 274-277.

Crown, Alan. *Samaritans*. (Tübingen: Mohr, 1989).

Cullmann, Oscar. *Prayer in the New Testament*. (OBT; John Bowden, trans.; Minneapolis: Fortress, 1995). Orig. published as *Gebet im Neuen Testament*. (Tübingen: J.C.B. Mohr, 1994).

Daniélou, Jean. *The Bible and the Liturgy*. (Notre Dame, IN: University of Notre Dame Press, 1956).

Davies, Philip R. *In Search of Ancient Israel*. (JSOT Sup 148; Sheffield: Sheffield Academic Press, 1992).

The Dead Sea Scrolls: Forty Years of Research. D. Dimant and U. Rappaport, eds. (Studies on the Texts of the Desert of Judah; Leiden: Brill, 1992).

Dentan, Robert C. "The Literary Affinities of Exodus XXXIV 6f." *VT* 13 (1963) 34-51.

Dimant, Devorah. "Use and Interpretation of Mikra in the Apocrypha and Pseudepigrapha." *Mikra: Text, Translation, Reading and Interpretation of the Hebrew Bible in Ancient Judaism and Early Christianity*. (Compendia Rerum Iudaicarum ad Novum Testamentum, M.J. Mulder, ed.; Assen: Van Gorcum/Philadelphia: Fortress, 1990) 379-419.

Dix, Gregory. *The Shape of the Liturgy*. (Philadelphia: Westminster, 1945).

Döller, Johannes. *Das Gebet im Alten Testament in religionsgeschichtlicher Beleuchtung*. (Theologische Studien der Österreichischen Leo-Gesellschaft; Hildesheim: H.A. Gerstenberg, 1974).

Douglas, Mary. *Purity and Danger: An Analysis of the Concepts of Pollution and Taboo*. (New York: Ark/Routledge, 1984/1966).

Dozeman, Thomas B. "Inner-Biblical Interpretation of Yahweh's Gracious and Compassionate Character." *JBL* 108 (1989) 207-223.

Dugmore, C.W. *The Influence of the Synagogue on the Divine Office*. (London: Oxford University Press, 1944).

Dumoulin, Pierre. *Entre la manne et l'eucharistie: Etude de Sg 16,15-17,1a: La manne dans le livre de la Sagesse, synthèse de traditions et préparation au mystère eucharistique*. (AnBib 132; Rome: Pontifical Biblical Institute Press, 1994).

Ehrlich, Ernst L. *Kultsymbolik im Alten Testament und im nachbiblischen Judentum*. (Stuttgart: A. Hiersemann, 1959).

Elbogen, Ismar. *Gottesdienst und synagogale poesie*. (Frankfurt-Am-Main: J. Kauffmann, 1914).
——. *Jewish Liturgy: A Comprehensive History*. (Raymond P. Scheindlin, trans., Philadelphia: Jewish Publication Society, 1993); orig. pub.:

Judische Gottesdienst in seiner geschichtlichen entwicklung. (Grundriss der Gesamtwissenschaft des Judentums; Frankfurt am Main: J. Kauffmann, 1934; 3d ed.).
———. *Studien zur Geschichte der jüdischen Gottesdienstes.* (Schriften der Lehranstalt des Judenthums; Berlin: Meyer & Müller, 1907).

Endres, John C. *Biblical Interpretation in the Book of Jubilees.* (CBQMS 18; Washington, D.C.: Catholic Biblical Association Press, 1987).

Enermalm-Ogawa, Agneta. *Un langage de prière juif en grec: le témoignage des deux livres des Maccabees.* (Stockholm: Almqvist & Wiksell, 1987).

Ephrem the Syrian: Hymns. Trans. by Kathleen E. McVey. (Classics of Western Spirituality; New York: Paulist Press, 1989).

Eppel, Robert. *Le piétisme juif dans les Testaments des douze Patriarches.* (Paris: F. Alcan, 1930).

Eshel, E., H. Eshel, and A. Yardeni. "A Qumran Composition Containing Part of Ps. 154 and a Prayer for the Welfare of King Jonathan and his Kingdom." *IEJ* 42 (1992) 199-229.

Fensham, F.C. "Nehemiah 9 and Pss. 105, 106, 135 and 136. Post-Exilic Historical Traditions in Poetic Form." *JNSL* 9 (1981) 35-51.

Fiensy, David A. "The Hellenistic Synagogal Prayers: One Hundred Years of Discussion." *JSP* 5 (1989) 17-27.
———. *Prayers Alleged to Be Jewish: An Examination of the Constitutiones Apostolorum.* (Brown Judaic Studies 65; Chico, CA: Scholars Press, 1985).

Finkelstein, Louis. "The Birkat Ha-Mazon." *JQR* 19 (1929) 211-262.
———. "The Development of the Amidah." *JQR* 16 (1925-1926) 1-43, 127-170.

Fishbane, Michael. *Biblical Interpretation in Ancient Israel.* (New York: Oxford Unversity Press, 1985).
———. "Form and Reformulation of the Biblical Priestly Blessing." *JAOS* 103 (1983) 115-121.

Fitzmyer, J.A. "The Use of Explicit Old Testament Quotations in Qumran Literature and in the New Testament." *NTS* 7 (1960-61) 297-333.

Fleischer, Ezra. "The Diffusion of the *Qedushot* of the *'Amida* and the *Yoser* in the Palestinian Jewish Ritual." *Tarbiz* 39 (1978) 272-274 (Hebrew).
———. "On the Beginnings of Obligatory Jewish Prayer."*Tarbiz* 59 (1990) 397-441 (Hebrew).

Flusser, David. "Psalms, Hymns, & Prayers." *Jewish Writings of the Second Temple Period.* (Michael E. Stone, ed.; Compendia Rerum Iudaicarum ad Novum Testamentum: Section Two, Volume Two; Assen: Van Gorcum, 1984) 551–578.

————. "Sanktus und Gloria." *Abraham Unser Vater: Juden und Christen im Gespräch über die Bible.* (O. Betz, M. Hengel, P. Schmidt, eds.; Otto Michel Festschrift; Leiden: Brill, 1963) 129–52.

————. "Qumran and 'Apotropaic' Prayers." *IEJ* 16 (1966) 194–205.

Fossum, Jarl E. *The Name of God and the Angel of the Lord.* (Tübingen: J.C.B. Mohr, 1985).

Fraade, Steven. *Enosh and His Generation: Pre-Israelite Hero and HIstory in Postbiblical Interpretation.* (SBLMS 30; Chico, CA: Scholars PRess, 1985) 229–230.

Fretheim, Terence. "Prayer in the Old Testament: Creating Space in the World for God." *A Primer on Prayer.* (P. Sponheim, ed.; Philadelphia: Fortress, 1988) 51–62.

Frizzell, Lawrence. "The Hymn of Creation in Daniel." *Standing Before God: Studies on Prayer in Scriptures and in Tradition with Essays in Honor of John M. Oesterreicher.* Asher Finkel and Lawrence Frizzell, eds. (New York: KTAV, 1981) 41–52.

The Function of Scripture in Early Jewish and Christian Tradition. (Craig A. Evans and James A. Sanders, eds; JSNTSup 154; SSEJC 6; Sheffield: Sheffield Academic Press, 1998).

Garcia Martinez, Florentino. *Qumran and Apocalyptic: Studies on the Aramaic Texts from Qumran.* (Leiden: Brill, 1992).

Geller, Stephen A. "Fiery Wisdom: Logos and Lexis in Deuteronomy 4." *Prooftexts* 14 (1994) 103-139.

Gerstenberger, Erhard S. *Der bittende Mensch: Bittritual und Klagelied des Einzelnen im Alten Testament.* (WMANT 51; Neukirchen-Vluyn: Neukirchener Verlag, 1980).

Gieschen, Charles A. "The Seven Pillars of the World: Ideal Figure Lists in the Christology of the Pseudo-Clementines." *JSP* 12 (1994) 47–82.

Gilbert, Maurice. "La place de la loi dans la prière de Néhémie 9." M. Carrez et al. (eds.) *De la Tôrah au Messie.* (Paris: Gabalda, 1981) 307-316.

Gill, Sam D. "Prayer." *Encyclopedia of Religion.* Vol. 11 (Mircea Eliade, et al., eds.; New York: MacMillan & Free Press, 1987) 489–494.

Ginzberg, Louis. *The Legends of the Jews.* (Philadelphia: Jewish Publication Society, 1968)

Goppelt, Leonhard. *Typos: The Typological Interpretation of the Old Testament in the New.* (Grand Rapids, MI: Eerdmans, 1982).

Gray, John. *I and II Kings*. (OTL; 2d ed.; Philadelphia: Westminster, 1970).

Greenberg, Moshe. *Biblical Prose Prayer*. (Berkeley: University of California Press, 1983).
——. "On the Refinement of the Conception of Prayer in Hebrew Scriptures." *Association for Jewish Studies Review*. 1 (1976) 57-92.

Greiff, Anton. *Das Gebet im Alten Testament*. (Münster: Aschendorffsche, 1915).

Grimm, Carl L. W. *Kurzgefasstes exegetisches Handbuch zu den Apokryphen des Alten Testamentes: Vierte Lieferung. Das zweite, dritte, und vierte Buch der Maccabäer*. (Leipzig: S. Hirzel, 1857).

Grözinger, Karl, *Musik und Gesang in die Theologie der fruhen Judenheit*. (Tübingen: Mohr-Siebeck, 1982).

Gunkel, Hermann and J. Begrich. *Einleitung in die Psalmen*. (3d ed.; Göttingen: Vandenhoeck und Ruprecht, 1966).

Gunneweg, A.H.J. "'AM HA'AREṢ—A Semantic Revolution," *ZAW* 95 (1983) 437–440.

Haag, Ernst. *Studien zum Buche Judith*. (Trierer Theoligische Studien 16; Trier: Paulinus, 1963).

Hadas, Moses. *The Third and Fourth Books of Maccabees*. (New York: Ktav, 1976; reprint of New York: Harper & Brothers, 1953).

Hallo, William W. "Individual Prayer in Sumerian: The Continuity of a Tradition." *JAOS* 88 (1968-69) 71-89.
——. "The Royal Correspondence of Larsa: A Sumerian Prototype for the Prayer of Hezekiah?" *Kramer Anniversary Volume: Cuneiform Studies in Honor of Samuel Noah Kramer* (AOAT 25; ed. B.L. Eichler, et al.; Kevelaer: Butzon & Bercher, 1976) 209-24.

Halpern, Baruch. *The First Historians: The Hebrew Bible and History*. (New York: Harper & Row, 1988).

Hanson, Paul D. *The Dawn of Apocalyptic: The Historical and Sociological Roots of Jewish Apocalyptic Eschatology*. (2nd ed.; Philadelphia: Fortress, 1979).
——. *Isaiah 40-66* (Louisville, KY: John Knox, 1995).
——. "Rebellion in Heaven, Azazel, and Euhemeristic Heroes in 1 Enoch 6-11" *JBL* 96 (1977) 195-233.

Haran, Menachem. "Temple and Community in Ancient Israel." in *Temple in Society* (M.V. Fox, ed; Winona Lake, IN: Eisenbrauns, 1988) 17-25.

Hatchett, Marion J. *Commentary on the American Prayer Book*. (New York: HarperCollins, 1980).

Hays, Richard B. *Echoes of Scripture in the Letters of Paul.* (New Haven: Yale University Press, 1989).

Heiler, Friedrich. *Prayer: A Study in the History and Psychology of Religion.* (orig. published in German as *Das Gebet* 1918; most recently in English, New York: Oxford University Press, 1958).

Heinemann, Joseph. "Birkath ha-Zimmun and Havurah Meals." *Journal of Jewish Studies* 13 (1962) 23-29.
———. *Prayer in the Talmud: Forms and Patterns.* Richard Sarason, transl. (Studia Judaica, Bd. 9; New York: de Gruyter, 1977) Originally published in Hebrew as *Prayer in the Period of the Tannaim and Amoraim.* 1964.

Hempel, Johannes. *Gebet und Frömmigkeit im Alten Testament* (Göttingen: Vandenhoeck und Ruprecht, 1922).

Hengel, Martin. *Judaism and Hellenism.* (John Bowden trans.; Philadelphia: Fortress, 1974).
———. *Die Zeloten: Untersuchungen zur jüdischen Freiheitsbewegung in der Zeit von Herodes I bis 70 n. Chr.* (Leiden: Brill, 1961; second edition 1976)

Hirsch, Emil G. "Shemoneh Esreh." *Jewish Encyclopedia* (New York: Funk & Wagnall's, 1901–1906) 11.270–282.

Hoffman, Lawrence A. *Beyond the Text: A Holistic Approach to Liturgy.* (Notre Dame, IN: University of Notre Dame Press, 1987).
———. *The Canonization of the Synagogue Service.* (Notre Dame, IN: University of Notre Dame Press, 1979).

Holm-Nielsen, Svend. *Hodayot: Psalms from Qumran.* (Aarhus: Universitets-forlaget, 1960).

Horbury, William. "Old Testament Interpretation in the Writings of the Church Fathers." *Mikra: Text, Translation, Reading and Interpretation of the Hebrew Bible in Ancient Judaism and Early Christianity.* (Compendia Rerum Iudaicarum ad Novum Testamentum, M.J. Mulder, ed.; Assen: Van Gorcum/Philadelphia: Fortress, 1990) 727-787.

Horgan, Maurya P. *Pesharim: Qumran Interpretations of Biblical Books.* (CBQMS 8; Washington, D.C.: Catholic Biblical Association, 1979).

van der Horst, Pieter, and Gregory Sterling. *Prayers of Antiquity: Greco-Roman, Jewish and Christian Prayers.* (John W. Medendorp, transl; CJS 11; Notre Dame: University of Notre Dame Press, 1997).

Ideal Figures in Ancient Judaism: Profiles and Paradigms. (J.J. Collins and G.W.E. Nickelsburg, eds.; Chico, CA: Scholars, 1980).

Idelsohn, Abraham Zebi. *Jewish Liturgy and Its Development.* (New York: Holt & Co., 1932).

It is Written: Scripture Citing Scripture: Essays in Honour of Barnabas Lindars. (D.A. Carson and H.G.M. Williamson, eds; New York: Cambridge University Press, 1988).

Jacobsen, Thorkild. "Primitive Democracy in Ancient Mesopotamia." *JNES* 2 (1943) 159-172.

Jacobson, Howard. *A Commentary on Pseudo-Philo's Liber Antiquitatum Biblicarum With Latin Text and English Translation.* 2 Volumes. (Leiden: Brill, 1996).
———. *The Exagoge of Ezekiel* (Cambridge: Cambridge University Press, 1983).

Japhet, Sara. *The Ideology of the Book of Chronicles and its Place in Biblical Thought.* (Frankfurt: Peter Lang, 1989).

James, William. *The Varieties of Religious Experience: A Study in Human Nature.* (New York: Vintage Book, 1990). Orig. published in 1902.

Jepsen, Alfred. *Die Quellen des Königsbuches.* (Halle: Max Niemeyer, 1953).

Johnson, Aubrey. *The Cultic Prophet in Ancient Israel.* (2d ed.; Cardiff: University of Wales, 1962).

Johnson, Norman B. *Prayer in the Apocrypha and Pseudepigrapha: A Study of the Jewish Concept of God.* (SBLMS 2: Philadelphia: Society of Biblical Literature and Exegesis, 1948).

Jones, B.W. "The Prayer in Daniel ix" *VT* 18 (1968) 488-93.

Kaufmann, Yehezkel. *The Religion of Israel.* (M. Greenberg, transl.; Chicago: University of Chicago Press, 1960).

Kelber, Werner H. *The Oral and the Written Gospel: The Hermeneutics of Speaking and Writing in the Synoptic Tradition, Mark, Paul, and Q.* (Bloomington, IN: Indiana University Press, 1997; first published by Philadelphia: Fortress, 1983).

Kister, Menahem. "Biblical Phrases and Hidden Biblical Interpretations and *Pesharim.*" *The Dead Sea Scrolls: Forty Years of Research.* Devorah Dimant and Uriel Rappaport, eds. (Leiden: Brill, 1992) 27–39.

Kittel, Bonnie. *The Hymns of Qumran.* (Chico, CA: Scholar's Press, 1981).

Klein, Ralph. "Ezra and Nehemiah in Recent Studies." *Magnalia Dei: the Mighty Acts of God.* (Garden City, NY: Doubleday, 1976) 361–376.

Knohl, Israel. "Between Voice and Silence: The Relationship between Prayer and Temple Cult." *JBL* 115 (1996) 17-30.

——. *The Sanctuary of Silence: The Priestly Torah and the Holiness School.* (Minneapolis: Fortress, 1995).

Knoppers, Gary N. "Prayer and Propaganda: Solomon's Dedication of the Temple and the Deuteronomist's Program." *CBQ* 57 (1995) 229-254.

Koch, Klaus. *The Growth of the Biblical Tradition: The Form-Critical Method.* (NY: Charles Scribner's Sons, 1969).

Koenig, John. *Rediscovering New Testament Prayer: Boldness and Blessing in the Name of Jesus.* (Harrisburg, PA: Morehouse, 1998; orig. pub., San Francisco: HarperSanFrancisco, 1992).

Kovalevsky, Jean. *La liturgie céleste.* (Paris: Éditions Friant, 1982).

Kraeling, E.G. "The Significance and Origin of Gen. 6:1–4." *JNES* 6 (1947) 192-213.

Krintezki, L., *Israels Gebet im Alten Testament* (Aschaffenburg: Paul Pattlock, 1965).

Kronholm, Tryggve. *Motifs from Genesis 1-11 in the Genuine Hymns of Ephrem the Syrian.* (Coniectanea Biblica; Lund: CWK Gleerup, 1978).

Kugel, James L., and Rowan A. Greer. *Early Biblical Interpretation.* (Philadelphia: Westminster, 1986).
——. *In Potiphar's House: The Interpretive Life of Biblical Texts.* (San Francisco: HarperCollins, 1990).
——. "The Jubilees Apocalypse." *DSD* 1 (1994) 322-337.
——. "The Story of Dinah in the *Testament of Levi.*" *HTR* 85 (1992) 1-34.
——. "Topics in the History of the Spirituality of the Psalms." *Jewish Spirituality I.* A. Green, ed. (New York: Crossroad, 1986) 113-144.

Kugler, Robert A. *From Patriarch to Priest: The Levi-Priestly Tradition from Aramaic Levi to Testament of Levi.* (EJL 9; Atlanta: Scholars, 1996).

Lambert, W.G. "Three Literary Prayers of the Babylonians." *AfO* 19 (1959/60) 47-66.

Lauha, Aarre. *Die Geschichtsmotive in den alttestamentlichen Psalmen.* (Helsinki: Finnischen Akademie der Wissenschaften, 1945).

Lee, Thomas R. *Studies in the Form of Sirach 44-50.* (SBLDS 75; Atlanta: Scholars, 1986).

Lehmann, Manfred R. "A Re-Interpretation of 4Q Dibrei Ham-Me'oroth" *Revue de Qumran* 5 (1964) 106-110.

Levenson, Jon D. *The Death and Resurrection of the Beloved Son.* (New Haven: Yale University Press, 1993).

———. "From Temple to Synagogue: 1 Kings 8." *Traditions in Transformation: Turning Points in Biblical Faith.* B. Halpern, J. Levenson, eds. (Winona Lake, IN: Eisenbrauns, 1981) 142–66.

———. "The Jerusalem Temple in Devotional and Visionary Experience." *Jewish Spirituality I.* A. Green, ed. (New York: Crossroad, 1986) 32-61.

———. "The Paranomasia of Solomon's Seventh Petition." *Hebrew Annual Review* 6 (1982) 135-138.

———. *Sinai and Zion.* (New York: Harper & Row, 1985).

Levine, Lee I. "The Second Temple Synagogue: The Formative Years." *The Synagogue in Late Antiquity.* Lee I. Levine, ed. (New York: American Schools of Oriental Research, 1987) 7–31.

Liebreich, Leon J. "The Impact of Nehemiah 9:5–37 on the Liturgy of the Synagogue." *HUCA* 32 (1961) 227-237.

———. "The Songs of Ascents and the Priestly Blessing." *JBL* 74 (1955) 33–36.

Loader, J.A. *A Tale Of Two Cities: Sodom and Gomorrah in the Old Testament, Early Jewish and Early Christian Traditions.* (CBET 1; Kampen, the Netherlands: Kok, 1990).

The Lord's Prayer and Jewish Liturgy. J. Petuchowski and M. Brocke, eds. (London: Burns & Oates, 1978).

The Lord's Prayer and Other Prayer Texts from the Greco-Roman Era. J.H. Charlesworth, M. Harding, and M. Kiley, eds. (Valley Forge, PA: Trinity Press International, 1994).

Lumpe, Adolf. "Exemplum" *Reallexikon für Antike und Christentum.* (Stuttgart: Anton Hiersemann, 1966) 6.1229–1257

Mack, Burton. *Wisdom and the Hebrew Epic: Ben Sira's Hymn in Praise of the Fathers.* (Chicago: Chicago Studies in the History of Judaism, 1985).

The Making of Jewish and Christian Worship. Paul Bradshaw and Lawrence Hoffman, eds. (Notre Dame: University of Notre Dame Press, 1991).

Mathys, Hans-Peter: *Dichter und Beter. Theologen aus spätalttestamentlicher Zeit.* (Orbis Biblicus Orientalis 132; Göttingen: Vandenhoeck & Ruprecht, 1994).

Mayer, Günter. "Die Funktion der Gebete in den alttestamentliche Apokryphen." *Theokratia. Jahrbuch des Institutum Judaicum Delitzschianum II 1970–1972* (Leiden: Brill, 1973) 16–25.

Mayer, Werner. *Untersuchungen zur Formensprache der babylonischen Gebetsbeschwörungen.* (Studia Pohl, Series Maior 5; Rome: Pontifical Biblical Institute, 1976).

McCarter, P. Kyle, Jr. *II Samuel.* (AB 9; Garden City, NY: Doubleday, 1984).

McFayden, John Edgar. *The Prayers of the Bible*. (New York: A.C. Armstrong & Son, 1906).

Meade, David G. *Pseudonymity and Canon: An Investigation into the Relationship of Authorship and Authority in Jewish and Earliest Christian Tradition*. (WUNT 39; Tübingen: Mohr/Siebeck, 1986).

Mettinger, Tryggve N.D. *The Dethronement of Sabaoth: Studies in the Shem and Kabod Theologies*. (ConBOT 18; Lund: CWK Gleerup, 1982).

Milgrom, Jacob. *Studies in Cultic Theology and Terminology*. (Leiden: Brill, 1983).
———. *Studies in Levitical Terminology*. (Berkeley: University of California Press, 1970).

Milik, J.T. *The Books of Enoch: Aramaic Fragments of Qumran Cave 4*. (New York: Oxford University Press, 1975).

Miller, Patrick D. *The Divine Warrior in Early Israel*. (Cambridge, MA: Harvard University Press, 1973).
———. "'Enthroned on the Praises of Israel': The Praise of God in Old Testament Theology." *Interpretation* 39 (1985) 5–19.
———. *They Cried to the Lord: The Form and Theology of Biblical Prayer*. (Minneapolis: Fortress, 1994).
———. "Trouble and Woe: Interpreting the Biblical Laments." *Interpretation* 37 (1983) 32-45.

Mirsky, Aharon. *Ha-Piyyut: The Development of Post Biblical Poetry in Eretz Israel and the Diaspora*. (Jerusalem: Magnes, 1990) 31. (Hebrew)

Montgomery, J. *I Kings*. (Edinburgh: T&T Clark, 1951).

Moore, Carey A. *Judith*. (AB 40; Garden City, NY: Doubleday, 1985).
———. *Tobit* (AB 40A; Garden City, NY: Doubleday, 1996).

Mowinckel, Sigmund. *The Psalms in Israel's Worship*. (New York, 1962).
———. *Religion und Kultus*. (Göttingen: 1953).

Muffs, Y. "Reflections on Prophetic Prayer in the Bible" *Eretz-Israel* 14 [H.L. Ginsberg Festschrift] (Jerusalem, 1978) 48-54.

Mullen, E. Theodore Jr. "Divine Assembly." *ABD* II, 214-217.
———. *The Divine Council in Canaanite and Early Hebrew Literature*. (HSM 24; Chico, CA: Scholars Press, 1980).

Myers, J.M. *Ezra-Nehemiah*. (AB 14; Garden City, NY: Doubleday, 1965).

Myth, Ritual, and Kingship. S.H. Hooke, ed. (New York: Oxford University Press/Clarendon, 1958).

Najman, Hindy. *Reading, Writing, and Interpretation: A Study in the Pre-History of the Bible*. (Ph.D. dissertation, Harvard University, 1998).

Nelson, Richard D. *The Double Redaction of the Deuteronomistic History*. (Sheffield: JSOT Press, 1981).

Newman, Judith H. "Lot in Sodom: The Post-Mortem of a City and the Afterlife of a Biblical Text." *The Function of Scripture in Early Judaism and Christianity*. (Craig A. Evans and James A. Sanders, eds; JSNT Sup. 154; SSEJC 6; Sheffield: Sheffield Academic Press, 1998) 34-44.
———. "Nehemiah 9 and the Scripturalization of Prayer in the Second Temple Period." *The Function of Scripture in Early Judaism and Christianity*. 112-123.

Newman, Murray L. *The People of the Covenant : A Study of Israel from Moses to the Monarchy*. (New York: Abingdon, 1962).

Newsom, Carol A. "The 'Psalms of Joshua' from Qumran Cave 4." *Journal of Jewish Studies* 39 (1988) 56-73.
———. "'Sectually Explicit' Literature from Qumran." *The Hebrew Bible and its Interpreters*. (W.H. Propp, B. Halpern, and D.N. Freedman, eds.; Winona Lake, IN: Eisenbrauns, 1990) 167-87.
———. *Songs of the Sabbath Sacrifice: A Critical Edition*. (Harvard Semitic Studies 27; Cambridge, MA: Harvard University Press, 1985).

Nickelsburg, G.W.E. "The Epistle of Enoch and the Qumran Literature." *JJS* 33 (1982) 333–48.

Nitzan, Bilhah. *Qumran Prayer and Religious Poetry*. (Jonathan Chipman, trans.; Studies on the Texts of the Desert of Judah 22; Leiden: Brill, 1994).

O'Connor, Michael. *Hebrew Verse Structure*. (Winona Lake, IN: Eisenbrauns, 1980).

van Oorschot, Jürgen. "Nachkultische Psalmen und spätbiblische Rollendichtung." *ZAW* 106 (1994) 69-86.

Oppenheim, A. Leo. *Ancient Mesopotamia: Portrait of a Dead Civilization*. (Chicago: University of Chicago Press, 1977).

Otto, Rudolph. *The Idea of the Holy*. (New York: Oxford University Press, 1950).

Patte, Daniel. *Early Jewish Hermeneutic in Palestine*. (SBLDS 22; Missoula, MT: Scholars Press, 1975).

Perelman, Ch. and L. Olbrechts-Tyteca. *La nouvelle rhétorique: Traité de L'argumentation*. (Paris: Presses Universitaires de France, 1958).

Perlitt, Lothar. "Sinai und Horeb." *Beiträge zur alttestamentlichen Theologie.* (Göttingen: Vandenhoeck & Ruprecht, 1977) 302-322.

Peterson, Erik. *The Angels and the Liturgy.* (New York: Herder and Herder, 1964).

Petuchowski, Jakob J. "The Liturgy of the Synagogue: History, Structure, and Contents." *Approaches to Ancient Judaism.* Vol. 4. (W.S. Green, ed.; Chico, CA: Scholars, 1983) 1–64.

Plöger, Otto. "Reden und Gebete im deuteronomistischen und chronistischen Geschichtswerk." *Festschrift für Günther Dehn.* (W. Schneemelcher, ed.; Neukirchen: Kreis Moers, 1957).

Pratt, Richard L. *Royal Prayer and the Chronicler's Program.* (Cambridge, MA: Harvard Th.D. thesis, 1987).

Prayer from Alexander to Constantine: A Critical Anthology. Mark Kiley et al., eds. (London: Routledge, 1997).

von Rad, Gerhard. *Old Testament Theology* Vol. 1-2. (New York: Harper & Row, 1962, 1965).

Reif, Stefan C. "Jewish Liturgical Research: Past, Present and Future."*Journal of Jewish Studies* 34 (1983) 161-70.
———. *Judaism and Hebrew Prayer: New Perspectives on Jewish Liturgical History.* (New York: Cambridge University Press, 1993).

Reventlow, Henning Graf. *Gebet im Alten Testament.* (Stuttgart: W. Kohlhammer, 1986).

Rhoads, David. "Zealots," *ABD* VI 1045

Robinson, H. Wheeler. "The Council of Yahweh." *JTS* 45 (1944) 151–157.

Robinson, James M. "Die Hodayot-Formel in Gebet und Hymnus des Frühchristentums." *Apophoreta: Festschrift für Ernst Haenchen.* (Berlin: Töpelmann, 1964) 194-235.

Rordorf, Willy. "The Bible in the Teaching and the Liturgy of Early Christian Communities." *The Bible in Greek Christian Antiquity.* (Paul M. Blowers, ed. and transl.; Notre Dame, IN: University of Notre Dame Press, 1997) 69–102.

Sacred History and Sacred Texts in Early Judaism. J.N. Bremmer and F. García Martínez, eds. (Kampen: Kok Pharos, 1993).

Salmonsen, Børge. "Some Remarks on the Zealots with Special Regard to the Term 'Qannaim' in Rabbinic Literature." *NTS* 13 (1966) 164-176.

Sanders, James A. *From Sacred Story to Sacred Text*. (Philadelphia: Fortress, 1987).
———. *The Psalms Scroll of Qumran Cave 11*. (DJD 4; Oxford: Oxford University Press, 1965).

Sarason, Richard S. "On the Use of Method in the Modern Study of Jewish Liturgy." *Approaches to Ancient Judaism: Theory and Practice*. (W.S. Green, ed., Brown Judaic Studies 1; Missoula, MT: Scholars, 1978, 97-172; reprinted in J. Neusner, ed., *The Study of Ancient Judaism 1*. (New York: Ktav, 1982) 107–79.

Sarna, Nahum. *Genesis*. (Philadelphia: Jewish Publication Society, 1989).

Sasson, Jack M. *Jonah*. (AB 24B; New York: Doubleday, 1990).

Schäfer, Peter. "Der synagogale Gottesdienst." *Literatur und Religion des Frühjudentums*. (Würzburg: Echter Verlag, 1973), 391-413.

Scharbert, J. "Formgeschichte und Exegese von Ex 34, 6f und seiner Parallelism." *Biblica* 38 (1957) 130–150.

Schiffman, Lawrence H. "The Dead Sea Scrolls and the Early History of Jewish Liturgy." *The Synagogue in Late Antiquity*. Lee I. Levine, ed. (New York: Jewish Theological Seminary, 1987) 33–48.
———. *From Text to Tradition: A History of Second Temple and Rabbinic Judaism*. (Hoboken, NJ: Ktav, 1991).
———. *Reclaiming the Dead Sea Scrolls*. (Philadelphia: JPS, 1994).

Schirmann, Jefim. "Hebrew Liturgical Poetry and Christian Hymnology." *JQR* NS 44 (1953) 123-161.

Schmid, H. H. *Der sogennante Jahwist: Beobachtungen und Fragen zur Pentateuchforschung*. (Zurich: Theologischer Verlag, 1975).

Schmidt, Heinrich. "Gebet II. Gebet und Gebetssitten in Israel und in nachexilischen Judentum," *Die Religion in Geschichte und Gegenwart*. (2d ed., 1928) 2.875-79.

Schmitt, Armin. "Struktur, Herkunft und Bedeutung der Beispielreihe in Weish 10." *BZ* 21 (1977) 1-22.

Schniedewind, William. "The Problem with Kings: Recent Study of the Deuteronomistic History." *RelStR* ev22 (1996) 24–25.

Schuller, Eileen M. "4Q372; 1: A Text about Joseph." *Revue de Qumran* 14 (1990) 349-376.
———. *Non-Canonical Psalms from Qumran*. (HSS 28; Atlanta: Scholars Press, 1986).

———. "Prayer, Hymnic and Liturgical Texts from Qumran." *The Community of the Renewed Covenant: The Notre Dame Symposium on the Dead Sea Scrolls*. (Notre Dame: University of Notre Dame Press, 1994) 153–171.
———. "The Psalm of 4Q372 1 Within the Context of Second Temple Prayer" *CBQ* 54 (1992) 67-79.
———. "The Use of Biblical Terms as Designations for Non-Biblical Hymnic and Prayer Compositions." *Biblical Perspectives: Early Use and Interpretation of the Bible in Light of the Dead Sea Scrolls*. Michael E. Stone and Esther G. Chazon, eds. (STDJ 28; Leiden: Brill, 1998) 207–222.

Schürer, Emil. *The History of the Jewish People in the Age of Jesus Christ*. (Edinburgh: T & T Clark, 1973/1987).

Senn, Frank C. *Christian Liturgy: Catholic and Evangelical*. (Minneapolis: Fortress, 1997).

Simon, Marcel. "Les saints d'Israël dans la dévotion de l'église ancienne." *RHPR* 34 (1954) 98-127.

Simon, Uriel. *Four Approaches to the Book of Psalms: From Saadiah Gaon to Abraham Ibn Ezra*. (Albany: SUNY Press, 1991).

Skehan, Patrick. "The Hand of Judith." *CBQ* 25 (1963) 94-110.

Smith, Jonathan Z. "Jerusalem: The City as Place." in *Civitas: Religious Interpretation of the City*. (P.S. Hawkins, ed.; Atlanta: Scholars, 1986) 25-38.

Speiser, E.A. *Genesis*. (AB1; Garden City, NY: Doubleday, 1964).

Srawley, J.H. *The Early History of the Liturgy*. (Cambridge: Cambridge University Press, 1913).

Standing Before God: Studies on Prayer in Scriptures and in Tradition with Essays in Honor of John M. Oesterreicher. Asher Finkel and Lawrence Frizzell, eds. (New York: KTAV, 1981).

Staudt, Edwin E. *Prayer and the People in the Deuteronomist* (Unpub. dissertation, Vanderbilt, 1980).

Sternberg, Meir. *The Poetics of Biblical Narrative* (Bloomington, IN: Indiana University Press, 1985).

Stone, Michael E. *4 Ezra*. (Hermeneia; Minneapolis: Fortress, 1990).
——— and Jonas C. Greenfield. "The Prayer of Levi." *JBL* 112 (1993) 247-66.

Strugnell, John. "The Angelic Liturgy at Qumran. 4QSerek Shirot 'Olat hashshabbat." *Congress Volume, Oxford 1959* (SVT 7; Leiden: Brill, 1960) 318–345.

Talmon, Shemaryahu. "The Emergence of Institutionalized Prayer in Israel in the Light of the Qumran Literature." *Qumrân: Sa piété, sa théologie et son milieu*. M. Delcor, ed. (Bibliotheca Ephemeridum Theologicarum Lovaniensium, 49; Paris: Duculot, 1978) 265–82.
———. "The Manual of Benedictions of the Sect of the Judean Desert." *Revue de Qumran* 2 (1960) 475-500.

Talstra, Eep. *Solomon's Prayer*. (Kampen: Kok Pharos, 1993).

Thiselton, Anthony. *Language, Liturgy and Meaning*. (Bramcote Nottingham, England: Grove Books, 1975).

Thompson, Thomas L. *The History of the Patriarchal Narratives*. (BZAW 133; Berlin: de Gruyter, 1974).
———. *The Origin Tradition of Ancient Israel: The Literary Formation of Genesis and Exodus 1-23*. (JSOTSup 55; Sheffield: JSOT Press, 1987).

Throntveit, Mark A. *When Kings Speak: Royal Speech and Royal Prayer in Chronicles*. (SBLDS 93; Atlanta: Scholars, 1987).

Tigay, Jeffrey. "On Some Aspects of Prayer in the Bible." *Association for Jewish Studies Review* 1 (1976) 363-378.

The Triumph of Elohim: From Yahwisms to Judaisms. Diane V. Edelman, ed. (Kampen: Kok Pharos, 1995).

Urbach, E.E. *The Sages: Their Concepts and Beliefs*. (Jerusalem: Magnes, 1975).

VanderKam, James C. *Enoch and the Growth of an Apocalyptic Tradition*. (CBQMS 16; Washington, D.C.: Catholic Biblical Association Press, 1984).

Van Seters, John. *Abraham in History and Tradition*. (New Haven: Yale University Press, 1975).

de Vaux, Roland. *Ancient Israel. Volume 2: Religious Institutions*. (New York: McGraw Hill, 1961).

Vermes, Geza. *Scripture and Tradition in Judaism*. (Leiden: Brill, 1961).

Wallenstein, Meir. *Some Unpublished Piyyutim from the Cairo Genizah*. (Manchester, England: Manchester University Press, 1956).

Waltke, Bruce K. and Michael O'Connor. *An Introduction to Biblical Hebrew Syntax*. (Winona Lake, Ind: Eisenbrauns, 1990).

Weber, Max. *Ancient Judaism*. (New York: Free Press, 1952).

Weinfeld, Moshe. "The Day of the Lord: Aspirations for the Kingdom of God in the Bible and Jewish Liturgy." *Scripta Hierosolymitana: Studies in Bible* Vol. 21. (Jerusalem: Magnes, 1986) 341-372.

———. *Deuteronomy and the Deuteronomic School*; (New York: Oxford University Press, 1972).

———. "Prayer and Liturgical Practice in the Qumran Sect." *The Dead Sea Scrolls: Forty Years of Research.* Devorah Dimant and Uriel Rappaport, eds. (Leiden: Brill, 1992) 241–58.

———. "The Prayers for Knowledge, Repentance and Forgiveness in the 'Eighteeen Benedictions'--Qumran Parallels, Biblical Antecedents, and Basic Characteristics." *Tarbiz* 98 (1979) 188-200 (Hebrew).

Weitzman, Steven. *Song and Story in Biblical Narrative: The History of a Literary Convention in Ancient Israel.* (Bloomington: Indiana University Press, 1997).

Wendel, A. *Das freie Laiengebet im vorexilischen Israel.* (Leipzig: Eduard Pfeiffer, 1931).

Werner, Ernst. *The Sacred Bridge.* (New York: Schocken, 1959).

Westermann, Claus. *Elements of Old Testament Theology.* (Atlanta: John Knox, 1982; orig. pub. Göttingen: Vandenhoeck & Ruprecht, 1978).

———. *Praise and Lament in the Psalms.* Keith R. Crim and Richard N. Soulen, trans. (Atlanta: John Knox, 1981).

Williamson, H.G.M. *Ezra, Nehemiah.* (Waco, TX: Word, 1985).

———. "Isaiah 63:7-64:11: Exilic Lament or Post-Exilic Protest?" *ZAW* 102 (1990) 48-58.

———. "Structure and Historiography in Nehemiah 9." *Proceedings of the Ninth Congress of Jewish Studies.* (Jerusalem: Magnes, 1988) 117-131.

Winter, Paul. "Magnificat and Benedictus." *BJRL* 37 (1954) 328–43.

Wolff, Hans Walter. "The Kerygma of the Deuteronomic Historical Work." *The Vitality of Old Testament Traditions*, (W. Brueggemann and H.W. Wolff, eds.; Atlanta: John Knox, 1975) 83-100, originally published as, "Das Kerygma des deuteronomischen Geschichtswerk." *ZAW* 73 (1961) 171-186.

Wright, George E. *Shechem.* (London: Duckworth, 1965).

Zahavy, Tzvee. "A New Approach to Early Jewish Prayer." *History of Judaism: The Next Ten Years.* (B. Bokser, ed; Chico, CA: 1980) 45–60.

———. *Studies in Jewish Prayer.* (Lanham, MD: Scholars Press, 1990).

———. "Three Stages in the Development of Early Rabbinic Prayer." *From Ancient Israel to Modern Judaism: Intellect in Quest of Understanding. Essays in Honor of Marvin Fox.* Jacob Neusner, E.S. Frerichs, and Nahum M. Sarna, eds. Vol. 1 (Atlanta: Scholars Press, 1989).

Zakovitch, Yair. *"And You Shall Tell Your Son. . .": The Concept of the Exodus in the Bible.* (Jerusalem: Magnes, 1991).

Zeitlin, Solomon. *Studies in the Early History of Judaism.* (Vol. 1; New York: Ktav, 1973).